Designing Integrated Industrial Policies Volume I

This comprehensive reference work gives an overview of the industrial development and current state of industrialization and deindustrialization in Asia, specifically Southeast Asia and China. It introduces typologies of industrial policies and discusses the manufacturing sector and its evolving role in the region. *Designing Integrated Industrial Policies* examines the integration of SMEs in global value chains and provides macro-econometric and firm-based micro-econometric analyses of (de)industrialization.

This book will be a very useful reference, particularly as a how-to guide on industrial promotion and designing integrated industrial policies not only for economic growth and job creation but also for "inclusive" development. It presents country cases and illustrates useful tools for industrial policy simulation and for evidence-based policy-making through these concrete examples.

Shigeru Thomas Otsubo is Professor of Development Economics/International Development and the Director of the Economic Development Policy & Management Program at the Graduate School of International Development (GSID), Nagoya University, Japan.

Christian Samen Otchia is Associate Professor of Development Economics at the Graduate School of International Development (GSID), Nagoya University, Japan. He is also an affiliate member at the African Growth and Development Policy modeling consortium.

Routledge Studies in the Modern World Economy

For more information about this series, please visit: www.routledge.com/
Routledge-Studies-in-the-Modern-World-Economy/book-series/SE0432

Designing Integrated Industrial Policies Volume I

For Inclusive Development in Asia

Edited by Shigeru Thomas Otsubo and Christian Samen Otchia

Routledge
Taylor & Francis Group

LONDON AND NEW YORK

First published 2021
by Routledge
2 Park Square, Milton Park, Abingdon, Oxon OX14 4RN

and by Routledge
52 Vanderbilt Avenue, New York, NY 10017

Routledge is an imprint of the Taylor & Francis Group, an informa business

British Library Cataloguing-in-Publication Data
A catalogue record for this book is available from the British Library

Library of Congress Cataloging-in-Publication Data
Names: Otsubo, Shigeru, editor. | Otchia, Christian Samen, editor.
Title: Designing integrated industrial policies / edited by
Shigeru Thomas Otsubo and Christian Samen Otchia.
Description: Abingdon, Oxon ; New York, NY : Routledge, 2021. |
Series: Routledge studies in the modern world economy |
Includes bibliographical references and index. |
Contents: Volume I. For inclusive development in Asia
Volume II. For inclusive development in Africa and Asia.
Identifiers: LCCN 2020023099 (print) | LCCN 2020023100 (ebook) |
ISBN 9780367896355 (hardback : vol. 1) | ISBN 9780367896379 (hardback : vol. 2) |
ISBN 9781003020233 (ebook) | ISBN 9781003020240 (ebook)
Subjects: LCSH: Industrial policy–Developing countries. |
Industrial promotion–Developing countries. |
Economic development–Developing countries.
Classification: LCC HD3616.D443 D47 2021 (print) |
LCC HD3616.D443 (ebook) | DDC 338.9009172/4–dc23
LC record available at https://lccn.loc.gov/2020023099
LC ebook record available at https://lccn.loc.gov/2020023100

ISBN: 978-0-367-89635-5 (hbk)
ISBN: 978-1-003-02023-3 (ebk)

Typeset in Galliard
by Newgen Publishing UK

Contents

Contents in Volume II

Figures

Tables

Contributors

Kucuk Ali Akkemik, Professor, Faculty of Economics, Yamaguchi University, Japan.

Juergen Amann, PhD Fellow, School of Economics, University of Nottingham, the United Kingdom.

Chalaiporn Amonvatana, Associate Professor, Faculty of Economics, Chulalongkorn University, Thailand.

Teguh Dartanto, Vice Dean of Academic Affairs, Faculty of Economics and Business, University of Indonesia, Indonesia.

Anang Gunawan, Regional Development Planner, Ministry of National Development Planning (BAPPENAS), Republic of Indonesia, Indonesia.

Kana Haraguchi, PhD student, Graduate School of International Cooperation Studies (GSICS), Kobe University, Japan.

Nobuya Haraguchi, Chief, Research and Industrial Policy Advice Division, Department of Policy Research and Statistics, United Nations Industrial Development Organization (UNIDO), Austria.

Ken Itakura, Professor, Graduate School of Economics, Nagoya City University, Japan.

Utumporn Jitsutthiphakorn, Senior Economist, Central Bank of Thailand, Thailand.

Jean-Claude Maswana, Professor, School of Economics, Ritsumeikan University, Japan.

Nobuaki Matsunaga, Professor, Graduate School of International Cooperation Studies (GSICS), Kobe University, Japan.

Carlos Mendez, Associate Professor, Economic Development Policy and Management Program, Graduate School of International Development (GSID), Nagoya University, Japan.

Hawa Munisi, Lecturer, Institute of Finance Management (IFM), Dar es Salaam, Tanzania.

Izumi Ohno, Professor, National Graduate Institute for Policy Studies (GRIPS), Japan.

Eric Osei-Assibey, Associate Professor, Department of Economics, University of Ghana, Ghana.

Christian Samen Otchia, Associate Professor, Economic Development Policy and Management Program, Graduate School of International Development (GSID), Nagoya University, Japan.

Shigeru Thomas Otsubo, Professor, Economic Development Policy and Management Program, Graduate School of International Development (GSID), Nagoya University, Japan.

Alay Phonvisay, Assistant Professor, Faculty of Economics and Business Management, National University of Laos, Laos.

Rulyusa Pratikto, Head of Graduate School of Social Science, Parahyangan Catholic University, Indonesia.

Phanida Roidoung, Economist, Public Debt Management Office, Ministry of Finance, Kingdom of Thailand, Thailand.

Nalitra Thaiprasert, Assistant Professor, Faculty of Economics, Chiang Mai University, Thailand.

Sayoko Uesu, Research Associate, National Graduate Institute for Policy Studies (GRIPS), Japan.

Tetsuo Umemura, Professor, Economic Development Policy and Management Program, Graduate School of International Development (GSID), Nagoya University, Japan.

Chanhphasouk Vidavong, Deputy Director, Trade Policy Research Division, Economic Research Institute for Industry and Trade, Ministry of Industry and Commerce, Lao People's Democratic Republic, Laos.

Souksavanh Vixathep, Associate Professor, School of Economics and Management, University of Hyogo, Japan.

Murat Yülek, Professor and President, OSTIM Technical University, Ankara, Turkey.

Preface

Rationale for this book

Promotion of sustained development of domestic industry is essential to boost economic growth and employment creation that will bring about poverty reduction in developing countries. Under a system of international economic institutions that allowed a relatively broad policy space, Japan and the other East Asian countries that have achieved rapid economic growth have succeeded in developing their infant and key industries under a diverse set of industrial policies. They have also achieved higher productivity, advanced their industries, and promoted exports by making use of foreign capital and imported technology; thus, all these countries have realized "catch-up" industrialization through the traditional follower-country strategy. However, developing countries in the 1980s and onward have had to promote their industries under economic globalization and international economic systems that were oriented toward free trade and overseas investment. They also had to face competitive pressure from China and India, and were forced to develop their own industries within a limited policy space, attributed to the expanded global production network of multinational corporations (MNCs), while under stricter international economic governance. In addition, global manufacturing activities have considerably shifted into higher value-added products that embody innovations in the forms of product upgrading and branding, leaving little room for most manufacturers in developing countries unless they are content with lower value-added activities. However, this share of lower value-added manufacturing has been declining on top of the declining share of manufacturing itself in the global economy. As a result, the world has come to witness the process of deindustrialization, often at a premature stage of economic development, in many developing countries.

Taking into consideration that those economies of developing countries have been caught in low-income and middle-income traps, and that today the term "industrial policy" is considered in a rather broader sense as a collective development policy which is being applied more widely, this book, which is an outcome of international joint research projects financed by the Japan Society for the Promotion of Science (JSPS), intends to focus on the design of an "integrated industrial policy." The central aim of this book is to promote inclusive and sustainable industrialization (Sustainable Development Goal [SDG] 9) and to promote sustained, inclusive, and sustainable economic growth, as well as full and productive employment (SDG 8) in order to end poverty (SDG 1).

This book will do the following: (1) present the history and current state of industrialization and deindustrialization in developing countries; (2) introduce typologies of industrial policies and surrounding arguments; (3) discuss the importance of the manufacturing sector and the reasons for deindustrialization; (4) account for the roles of SMEs and global value chains (GVCs); (5) use both macro-econometric and firm-based micro-econometric analyses of (de)industrialization; (6) present country cases as concrete examples; (7) discuss and analyze topical issues such as the role of China in Africa's industrialization; (8) present tools for industrial policy simulation for evidence-based policymaking; and (9) address the roles of public-private partnership (PPP) and international development cooperation in promoting industrial development in developing countries. All in all, this book intends to serve as an integrated and balanced reference work which offers policymakers, researchers, and students in the international development cooperation community guidance in designing integrated industrial policies for inclusive development in today's globalized world.

Uniqueness of this book

The salient features of this book are the following:

1. It is compiled as the result of a well-coordinated four-year international joint research project participated in by 16 academic and research institutions with researchers from 11 countries (Austria, Bolivia, the Democratic Republic of Congo, Ghana, Indonesia, Japan, Laos, Tanzania, Thailand, Turkey, and the UK), with support from the Japan Society for Promotion of Science (JSPS).
2. It contains conceptual/typological discussions, rigorous empirical studies both at the macro- and micro-economic (firm) levels, with an interesting set of country case studies, and a collection of cross-cutting thematic issues and analyses.
3. It does not rehash the success stories of Japan and the Asian Tigers (Hong Kong, Singapore, South Korea, and Taiwan) as they have already been well documented and the global economic environment today is very different from when the "East Asian miracle" was created.
4. Instead, it focuses on ordinary developing countries in Asia and Africa, including countries such as Indonesia and Thailand, where governments have tended not to subscribe to industrial promotion by so-called industrial policies.
5. It includes analyses of "China in Africa" and an analysis on the future of China's industrial development "Made in China 2025" and its impact on developing countries.
6. It is produced as a joint venture between academic researchers and policymakers.

7. The contributors include those with working experiences in trend-setting international organizations, such as the UN, UNIDO, and the World Bank, as well as those working for national institutions in developing countries which deal with policymaking and its execution in industrial promotion, such as the National Developing Planning Agency of Indonesia (BAPPENAS), the Ministry of Industry and Commerce of the Laotian government, and the Ministry of Finance, and the Central Bank of Thailand.

8. It is also a contribution to the worldwide discussion of SDGs, as this book intends to present discussions/analyses of industrial promotion and industrial policies not only for the sake of economic growth and job creation but also for "inclusive" development. To this end, the book addresses impacts on income and spatial (geographical) inequalities, thereby capturing industrial promotion in the context of the poverty-growth-inequality (PGI) triangle.

At present, there is no single reference book that intends to serve as a well-balanced guide for those in the international development community on the subjects of inclusive industrial promotion in the PGI context in order to provide integrated policy packages that bridge interrelated Sustainable Development Goals (including SDGs 1, 8, and 9).

Readership of this book

The book's intended readership includes the following:

1. Policymakers (including their bureaucratic brains) and practitioners in the international development community, such as the governments (and aid-related agencies) of developed and developing countries, international organizations, NGOs, and so forth.

2. Academics, students, and other researchers seeking well-balanced and rather comprehensive references regarding the role of industrialization in development, the impacts of globalization on industrialization and deindustrialization, and the integrated strategies for industrial promotion of inclusive development.

3. International and local business leaders who wish to understand key trends in the ongoing process of (de)industrialization and the surrounding policy frameworks, including new public-private partnerships (PPPs).

Structure of this book

Having reconfirmed the importance of proactive industrial promotion policies for sustained economic growth and poverty reduction in developing countries, recent discussions focus more on design, implementation, and evaluation for evidence-based policymaking. It is also widely recognized today that policy coordination and integration are highly desired for industrial policies to take on the challenges of producing "inclusive" development under the SDGs framework. In order for us to deal with these issues and challenges in industrial promotion, this book consists of the following four parts in two volumes (Volume I and Volume II).

Part I Industrial Promotion in Retrospect and Prospect
Part II Designing Integrated Industrial Policies in Asia and the Pacific
Part III Designing Integrated Industrial Policies in Africa
Part IV Designing Integrated Industrial Policies in Sub- and Super-National Regions

Part I consists of three introductory chapters. Chapter 1 presents industrial promotion and industrial policies in retrospect and prospect. It provides concepts, definitions, and issues to be discussed in this volume while stressing the need for modern and integrated strategies. It also captures industrial promotion in the poverty-growth-inequality (PGI) triangle in order for us to discuss "inclusive" strategies. Chapter 2 presents data and descriptive statistics that constitute a common background. What do we really know about the changing state of global manufacturing? How and why has the trend of premature deindustrialization emerged in many parts of the developing world? Chapter 3 revisits the importance of manufacturing and the risks associated with premature deindustrialization in pursuing pro-poor growth and inclusive development. Chapters 2 and 3, together, present a holistic picture of the past and present state of industrialization, structural change, and their impact on increases in value-added and employment.

As most of the chapters in this book deal with issues/topics of industrial promotion not only by applying theories and conceptual frameworks but also in relation to existing problems and policies within a specific country context, the next two parts of the book present chapters by countries used as cases or targets of rigorous economic/econometric analyses. Part II (Chapters 4–12) is for countries in Asia and the Pacific region. Part III (Chapters 13–16) in Volume II presents chapters that take countries in Africa as their cases. However, this does not mean that any particular topic is only relevant to a particular set of countries or a region. Instead, it means that realistic industrial policy discussion needs cases and targets on the ground.

Part IV (Chapters 17 and 18) in Volume II contains two chapters that deal with regional issues/topics of industrial promotion. Chapter 17 discusses the impact of super-national regional economic cooperation such as the Regional Trading Agreement (RTA) and the Regional Comprehensive Economic Partnership (RCEP) for industrial promotion at the regional level. Chapter 18 discusses regional parity and regional "inclusiveness" in the context of sub-national regions as a country pursues industrial development in a balanced or unbalanced manner. Chapter 17 introduces policy simulations using Computable General Equilibrium (CGE) models. Chapter 18 introduces the analyses of regional convergence/divergence to investigate the interaction between industrial development and regional convergence.

Acknowledgments

Ms Lam Yong Ling, Commissioning Editor, Taylor & Francis Asia Pacific (Routledge, Singapore) and her assistants, Ms Phua Samantha and Mr Tan Sheng Bin, have been dedicated to this work in cooperating with us from planning, creating, and including up to publication of this book. On behalf of our team, we would like to express our deepest gratitude to them.

Our special thanks go to our Research Assistants for this phase of the project, Dr Sai Seng Sai, Dr Ibrahim Issifu, Dr Chanhphasouk Vidavong, Mr Anang Budi Gunawan, and Ms Utumporn Jitsutthiphakorn, who helped in processing data, conducting econometric analyses, and editing the work. Chanhphasouk, Anang, and Utumporn also contributed chapters to this book as development policymakers in the government ministries in their home countries. Our thanks also go to others who served as Research Assistants during the past phases of this research project, and who also participated as contributors to this book: Dr Nalitra Thaiprasert, Dr Eric Osei-Assibey, Dr Teguh Dartanto, Dr Phanida Roidoung, and Dr Carlos Mendez. They contributed chapters to this book as professors or development practitioners in their countries in Asia and Africa.

We would also like to express our sincere appreciation to Dr Adam Smith (yes, Adam Smith) for proofreading the English manuscripts. Last but not the least, we, the editors of this book, wish to extend our sincere gratitude to all the contributors/writers for their participation.

On a personal note, I, Shigeru Thomas Otsubo, wish to express my gratitude to my wife Mikako. Her devoted support keeps me hopeful, depite being a researcher in the process of losing the ability to see. Christian Samen Otchia also wishes to express his gratitude to his wife Hiroko for her inspiring assistance and constant understanding and patience.

Shigeru Thomas Otsubo
Christian Samen Otchia
March 2020

Abbreviations

2SLS	Two-stage Least Squares regression
3 Risers	India, Korea, and Indonesia
3SLS	Three-stage Least Squares regression
ADB	Asian Development Bank
ADLI	Agricultural Development Led Industrialization
AEC	ASEAN Economic Community
AFAS	ASEAN Framework Agreement on Services
AFC	Asian financial crisis
AFTA	ASEAN Free Trade Agreement
AGOA	African Growth and Opportunity Act
AI	Artificial Intelligence
AIA	ASEAN Investment Area
AKP	The Justice and Development Party (in Turkish: Adaletve Kalkınma Partisi)
AOTS	Association for Overseas Technical Cooperation for Sustainable Partnership, Japan
ARDL	autoregressive distributed lag
ASEAN	Association of Southeast Asian Nations
ATC	Agreement on Textiles and Clothing
ATT	assisted technology transfer
AU	African Union
B.E.	Buddhist Era
BAPPENAS	National Development Planning Agency of Indonesia
BB	Bureau of the Budget
BCtA	Business Call to Action
BGMEA	Bangladesh Garment Manufacturers and Exporters Association
Big Three	Japan, Korea, and Taiwan
BMZ	Federal Ministry for Economic Development and Cooperation, Germany
BOI	Board of Investment
BoP	balance of payment
BOP	base of the pyramid
BOT	Bank of Thailand

BRI	Belt and Road Initiative
BSS	business supporting survey
CAE	Chinese Academy of Engineering
CAIT	Climate Analysis Indicators Tool
CAMARTEC	Center for Agricultural Mechanization and Rural Technology
CARI	China-Africa Research Initiative
CC	Central Committee (China)
CCP	Chinese Communist Party
CCTV	closed-circuit television
CDE	constant difference of elasticities
CDM	Crepon, Duguet, and Mairesse
CEP	comprehensive economic partnership
CEPT	common effective preferential tariff
CES	constant elasticity of substitution
CGE	computable general equilibrium
CIP	competitive industrial performance
CLMV	Cambodia, Laos, Myanmar, and Vietnam
CO_2	carbon dioxide
COMECON	Council for Mutual Economic Assistance
COMESA	Common Market for Eastern and Southern Africa
COSTECH	Commission for Science and Technology, Tanzania
CSC	China State Council
CSOs	civil society organizations
CSR	corporate social responsibility
CTI	Confederation of Tanzanian Industries
DAC	Development Assistance Committee
DANIDA	Danish International Development Agency
DFAT	Department of Foreign Affairs and Trade, Australia
DFID	Department for International Development, UK
DIV	Development Innovation Ventures
DOSMEP	Department of Small and Medium-Sized Enterprise Promotion
DRC	Democratic Republic of the Congo
EAP	East Asia and Pacific
EBA	Everything-But-Arms
ECA	Europe and Central Asia
ECCSA	Ethiopian Chamber of Commerce and Sectoral Association (ECCSA)
EEC	Eastern Economic Corridor
EECO	Eastern Economic Corridor Office
EIC	Ethiopian Investment Commission
EKI	Ethiopia Kaizen Institute
EOI	Export-Oriented Industrialization
EPPCF	Ethiopia Public Private Consultative Forum
EPRDF	Ethiopian People's Revolutionary Democratic Front
EPZs	export processing zones

ERIA	Economic Research Institute for ASEAN and East Asia
ERMs	Extended Regression Models
ESCAP	Economic and Social Commission for Asia and the Pacific (in Thailand)
ETIDI	Ethiopian Textile Industry Development Institute
EU	European Union
FDI	foreign direct investment
FDRE	Federal Democratic Republic of Ethiopia
FOCAC	Forum on China-Africa Cooperation
FPO	Fiscal Policy Office
FSM	Federated States of Micronesia
FTAAP	free trade area of the Asia-Pacific
FYP	Five-Year Plan
G7	Group of Seven (Canada, France, Germany, Italy, Japan, the United Kingdom, and the United States)
GATS	General Agreement on Trade in Services
GATT	General Agreement on Tariffs and Trade
GCI	Global Competitiveness Index
GDA	Global Development Alliance
GDP	Gross Domestic Product
GGDC	Groningen Growth and Development Center
GIZ	Deutsche Gesellschaft für Internationale Zusammenarbeit
GMM	generalized method of moments
GNP	gross national product
GOI	Government of Indonesia
GOI-IMF	Government of Indonesia-International Monetary Fund
GOL	Government of Laos
GRIPS	National Graduate Institute for Policy Studies, Japan
GSID	Graduate School of International Development, Nagoya University, Japan
GSP	generalized system of preferences
GTAP	Global Trade Analysis Project
GTP	Growth and Transformation Plan, Ethiopia
GTZ	Deutsche Gesellschaft für Technische Zusammenarbeit
GVCs	global value chains
H&M	Hennes and Mauritz
HCI	Human Capital Index
HICs	high-income countries
HIP	Hawassa Industrial Park, Ethiopia
ICOR	incremental capital-output ratio
ICT	information and communication technology
IDE-JETRO	Institute of Developing Economies, Japan External Trade Organization
IDN	Indonesia
IDR	Industrial Development Report

IEA	International Energy Agency
IFC	International Financial Corporation
IFCT	Industrial Finance Corporation of Thailand
IFR	International Federation of Robotics
ILO	International Labour Organization
IMF	International Monetary Fund
INDSTAT	Industrial Statistics Database of the UNIDO
I-O	input-output
IoT	Internet of Things
IPD	Initiative for Policy Dialogue
IPDC	Industrial Park Development Corporation, Ethiopia
IPRs	Intellectual Property Rights
IPs	industrial parks
IR	Industrial Revolution
IR1	First Industrial Revolution
IR2	Second Industrial Revolution
IR3	Third Industrial Revolution
IR4	Fourth Industrial Revolution
ISI	import-substitution industrialization
ISIC	International Standard Industrial Classification
ISO	International Organization for Standardization
IT	information and technology
JETRO	Japan External Trade Organization
JICA	Japan International Cooperation Agency
KHM	Cambodia
KI	key indicators
LAC	Latin America and Caribbean
Lao PDR	Lao Peoples' Democratic Republic
LCR	local content requirement
LDCs	least developed countries
LICs	low-income countries
LIP	Law on Investment Promotion
LMICs	lower middle-income countries
LNCCI	Lao National Chamber of Commerce and Industry
LSB	Lao Statistic Bureau
LTA	Long-Term Arrangement on International Trade in Cotton Textiles
M&E	monitoring and evaluation
MDGs	Millennium Development Goals
MEDA	Mennonite Economic Development Associates
MENA	Middle East and North Africa
METI	Ministry of Economy, Trade and Industry, Japan
MFA	Multi-Fiber Arrangement
MFN	most-favored-nation
MHT	medium and high-tech

MIC 2025	Made in China 2025
MIDA	Malaysian Investment Development Authority
MIIT	Ministry of Industry and Information Technology, China
MIRAB	Migration (MI), Remittance (R), Foreign Aid (A), and Public Bureaucracy (B)
MITI	Ministry of International Trade and Industry, Japan
MJTD	Myanmar Japan Thilawa Development, Limited
MMR	Myanmar
MNC	multinational corporation
MOFA	Ministry of Foreign Affairs, Japan
MOFCOM	Ministry of Commerce of the People's Republic of China
MOI	Ministry of Industry
MOIC	Ministry of Industry and Commerce
MOU	memorandum of understanding
MP3EI	Master Plan for Acceleration and Expansion of Indonesia Economic Development
MPI	Ministry of Planning and Investment
MRIO	Multi-Regional Input-Output
MRTA	mega regional trade agreement
MVA	manufacturing value-added
MWP	Minimum Wage Province
MYS	Malaysia
NA	National Assembly
NAAMA	National Accounts – Analysis of Main Aggregates
NDRC	National Development and Reform Commission, China
NEDB	National Economic Development Board
NEDCO	National Estates & Designing Consultancy
NEM	New Economic Mechanism (*Chintanakan Mai*)
NEPAD	New Partnership for Africa's Development
NESDB	National Economic and Social Development Board
NGOs	non-governmental organizations
NIES	newly industrializing economies
NIFT	National Institute of Fashion Technology, India
NIGP	National Income Generation Program
NPC	National People's Congress, China
NPOs	non-profit organizations
NSEDP	National Socio-Economic Development Plan
ODA	Official Development Assistance
ODI	outward direct investment
OECD	Organization for Economic Co-operation and Development
OECF	Overseas Economic Cooperation Fund, Japan
OJT	on-the-job training
OOF	other official flows
OPM	Office of the Prime Minister

PASDEP	Plan for Accelerated and Sustained Development to End Poverty, Ethiopia
P-G-I	poverty-growth-inequality
PGI triangle	poverty-growth-inequality triangle
PHL	the Philippines
PISU	Private Investment in State Undertaking Act
PM	Prime Minister
PMG	pooled mean group
PPP	public-private partnership
PPP	purchasing power parity
PPSU	Public-Private in State Undertaking Act
PVH	Phillips-Van Heusen Corporation
QCD	quality, cost, delivery
R&D	research and development
RCA	revealed comparative advantage
RCEP	regional comprehensive economic partnership
RCT	randomized controlled trial
REER	real effective exchange rate
RFI	resource for infrastructure
RIIP	regionally inclusive industrial policy
RMG	ready-made garment
RoO	rules of origin
ROW	rest of the world
RTA	Regional Trade Agreement
(r)VA	(real, i.e. deflated) value-added
S&T	science and technology
SAM	social accounting matrix
SC	smiling curve
SCMs	subsidies and countervailing measures
SDGs	Sustainable Development Goals
SDPRP	Sustainable Development and Poverty Reduction Program, Ethiopia
SEC	State Economic Commission, China
SEI	strategic emerging industries
SEPO	State Enterprise Policy Office
SETC	State Economic and Trade Commission, China
SEZ	Special Economic Zone
SIDA	Swedish International Development Cooperation Agency
SIDO	Small Industries Development Organization
SIDS	Small Islands Developing States
SITES	small island tourists economies
SMEPDC	Small and Medium-Sized Enterprise Promotion and Development Committee
SMEs	small and medium-sized enterprises

SMRJ	Organization for Small and Medium Enterprises and Regional Innovation, Japan
SOE	state-owned enterprise
SPC	State Planning Commission, China
SRC	Structural Reform Commission, China
SSA	Sub-Saharan Africa
STA	Short-Term Arrangement Regarding International Trade in Cotton Textiles
STI	science, technology and innovation
TAFSIO	Tanzanian Federation of Small Industries Organizations
TEMDO	Tanzania Engineering and Manufacturing Design Organization
THA	Thailand
TICAD	Tokyo International Conference on African Development
TIKA	Turkish International Cooperation and Development Agency
TIRDO	Tanzania Industrial Research Development Organization
TMB	Thai Military Bank
TOURAB	Tourism (TOU), Remittance (R), Foreign Aid (A), and the Public Bureaucracy (B)
TPI	tourism penetration ratio
TPP	Trans-Pacific Partnership
TRIMS	trade-related investment measures
TRIPS	trade-related aspects of intellectual property rights
TTIP	Transatlantic Trade and Investment Partnership
TUSKON	Turkish Confederation of Businessmen and Industrialists
TVET	Technical and Vocational Education and Training
UK	United Kingdom
UMICs	upper middle-income countries
UN	United Nations
UN/CEFACT	United Nations Centre for Trade Facilitation and Electronic Business
UNCTAD	United Nations Conference on Trade and Development
UNDP	United Nations Development Programme
UNECA	United Nations Economic Commission for Africa
UNICEF	United Nations Children's Fund
UNIDO	United Nations Industrial Development Organization
UNSTAT	United Nations Statistics Division
UNU-MERIT	United Nations University – Maastricht Economic and Social Research Institute on Innovation and Technology
URT	United Republic of Tanzania
US	United States of America
USAID	United States Agency for International Development
USD	US dollar
VETA	Vocational Educational and Training Authority
VNM	Vietnam

WB	World Bank
WBES	World Bank Enterprise Survey
WDI	World Development Indicators
WEF	World Economic Forum
WGI	world governance indicators
WIOD	world input-output database
WIOT	world input-output tables
WTO	World Trade Organization
WWII	World War II

Part I

Industrial promotion in retrospect and prospect

1 Introduction

Leading issues in industrial promotion in today's globalized world

Shigeru Thomas Otsubo and
Christian Samen Otchia

1.1 Prologue

Following the UN Millennium Development Goals (MDGs) era that ended in 2015 with mixed results, the world development community has set about the new era with the UN Sustainable Development Goals (SDGs) as the post-2015 global goals.[1] In search of a sustainable society and a sustainable planet, the SDGs include 17 goals expanded from the 8 goals under the MDGs. Aside from the major changes made from the MDGs to the SDGs such as (1) an application of the goals not only to the developing world but also to the developed world (the global agenda); (2) diversifying areas where "sustainability" should apply; and (3) collaborative efforts to cope with factors that impede sustainability in each country (internal affairs), goals that explicitly deal with "growth engine(s)" and inequality are now included in this new set of global goals.

The number one goal of this global agenda continues to be poverty reduction. Under the MDGs, the following Goal 1 and Targets were set.

Goal 1: Eradicate extreme poverty and hunger.

> Target 1. Halve, between 1990 and 2015, the proportion of people whose income is less than $1 a day.
>
> Target 2. Achieve full and productive employment and decent work for all, including women and young people.
>
> Target 3. Halve, between 1990 and 2015, the proportion of people who suffer from hunger.

These are the only economic (growth-related) goal/targets in the MDGs. Inequality issues were not explicitly dealt with.

Table 1.1 summarizes the changing poverty profile under the MDGs. As the UN community declared in 2013, at an aggregate level, the poverty headcount ratio in the developing world was halved by 2010 as compared to the level that prevailed in the reference year of 1990.[2] However, a careful review of Table 1.1 reveals the following facts: (1) most of the poverty reduction was produced in China, the "factory of the world," up to 2005; (2) India, the "back office of the world," joined this successful club after 2005; and (3) Sub-Saharan Africa, due to its relatively high population growth, saw increasing numbers of poor, even though the poverty headcount ratio has been declining.

Table 1.1 Poverty reduction under the MDGs, 1990–2015

	(a) Changes in Regional Poverty HCR (%)						(b) Changes in Poor Population (million)					
Developing Regions	1990	1999	2005	2011	2013	2015	1990	1999	2005	2011	2013	2015
East Asia & Pacific	61.3	38.5	18.9	8.6	3.6	2.3	1117	781	403	191	81	53
China	66.2	40.2	18.5	7.9	1.9	0.7	751	504	241	106	26	10
Europe & Central Asia	5.2 (1993)	7.9	4.9	2.1	1.6	1.5	44 (1993)	68	43	19	14	14
Latin America & Caribbean	14.8	13.5	9.9	5.7	4.6	3.9	66	70	56	34	28	25
Middle East & North Africa	6.2	3.8	3.1	2.7	2.6	4.2	16	12	11	11	11	18
South Asia	47.3	.	33.7	19.8	16.1	.	536	.	510	327	274	.
India	45.9 (1993)	. 38.2 (2004)		21.2	.	.	. 424 (1993)	430 (2004)		264	.	.
Sub-Saharan Africa	54.7	58.3	50.8	45.0	42.4	41.0	280	381	389	.	.	.
Low & middle income	44.4	34.8	25.0	16.4	13.3	11.8	1887	1717	1342	953	793	722

Given these mixed accomplishments during the MDGs era and the resurgence of arguments for sustained economic growth as a necessary (but not sufficient) condition for employment generation, poverty reduction, and political stability in various corners of the world,[3] the post-2015 development agenda presented in Figure 1.1 as SDGs encompasses goals of inclusive economic growth, industrial development, and reduced inequalities.

> Goal 1: End poverty in all its forms everywhere.
> Goal 8: Promote inclusive and sustainable economic growth, employment, and decent work for all.
> Goal 9: Build resilient infrastructure, promote sustainable industrialization, and foster innovation.
> Goal 10: Reduce inequality within and among countries.

In the socioeconomic progress of a developing country, sustainable development of domestic industries is essential to boost economic growth and employment creation that brings about poverty reduction. Under a system of international economic institutions that allowed a relatively broad policy space, Japan and the Asian Tigers that achieved rapid economic growth succeeded in developing their infant and key industries under a diverse set of industrial policies.[4] They also achieved higher productivity, increased their industry, and promoted exports by making use of foreign capital and imported technology; thus, all these have realized the "catch-up" industrialization (through the traditional follower-country strategy). However, developing countries in the 1980s and later had to promote their industries under economic globalization and an international economic system that was oriented toward freer trade and overseas investment. They also had to face competitive pressure from China and India, and were forced to develop their own industries within a limited policy space, attributed to the expanded global production network of multinational corporations (global value chains; GVCs), and in a stricter international economic environment.

Taking into consideration that the economies of developing countries had been polarized, and that today the term "industrial policy" is considered in a rather broad sense as a collective development policy and is being applied more widely, this book (published in two volumes in order to disseminate the findings from an international joint research project) intends to focus on the design of an "integrated industrial policy" that tries to promote "inclusive" industrial development by using the various forces of globalization. It will (1) analyze

Figure 1.1 Sustainable Development Goals for 2015–2030
Source: Downloaded from www.un.org/sustainabledevelopment/news/communications-material/(2017.02.23)

comparatively the cases of industrial policies and institutions of selected countries in Asia and Africa: and (2) combine a wide range of empirical analyses such as macro (economy-wide) and micro (firm-level) econometric analyses, and indicative integrated industrial policy simulations with the use of Computable General Equilibrium models. The ultimate goal of this research is to advocate an integrated set of effective policies that will promote the survival of industries in developing countries, under global competition and integration, which includes domestic policies, policies that should be coordinated within a framework of regional economic cooperation, and present initiatives to be taken under the scheme of international development cooperation. This book pays extra attention to the potential of various public-private partnership (PPP) initiatives, and explicitly deals with business enterprises and entrepreneurs as key target actors of industrial policies.

Throughout these studies, the "poverty triangle" of economic growth, inequality, and poverty reduction under globalization presented in Figure 1.2 will be used as a common framework. In this context, the success in industrial promotion, corporate development, and employment generation are considered to be the keys to poverty reduction, while each country's development governance, institutions, and policies (and the levels of policy integration/coordination) will be dealt with as control factors.

1.2 Industrial policy debates in retrospect

Industrial policies were treated in a rather neutral manner (including discussions on their positive and negative sides) in the *East Asian Miracle: Economic Growth and Public Policy* (World Bank, 1993) under the propagated development strategy that stressed public-private partnership and "functionalism." Later on, with the expansion of neoliberalism, those industrial policies were considered in a negative light. Krueger (1997) and others pointed out the risk facing policymakers in selecting the right industries to be promoted. While the growth performance of the developing countries under globalization has become polarized, Chang (2003) argued that these developing nations should be given the same "policy space" in industrial policies as the industrialized countries had previously been. Rodrik (2008b) subscribed to the same view, even being joined by the OECD in the late 2000s. In the OECD, opinions such as "industrial policies are not dirty words" and "industrial policy is back" emerged. Following the policy recommendations made by Cimoli, Dosi, and Stiglitz (2009) in the Initiative for Policy Dialogue (IPD), based at Columbia University, Lin and Chang (2009), Lin and Monga (2010), and Lin (2012) and others discussed whether industrial policies ought to focus on industries with comparative advantage following the tradition, or whether new industries should be strategically created. These debates are often referred to now as new "competitive advantage" versus traditional "comparative advantage" of industries to be selected for promotion. Following this debate, industrial policies in a broader sense are argued, in the recent years, as being an integrated strategy for economic development. It is interesting to note that both Krueger and Lin served as chief economists at the World Bank, and during this time the policy stance of the Bretton Woods institutions was transformed into a more realistic one. It is now widely known that "integrated" industrial policies and supporting policy studies are essential for the proactive and dynamic promotion of surviving industries that can achieve international competitiveness in this globalized world.

Thus, industrial policy is once again at the top of the policy agenda. To a significant extent, economists demonstrate a broad consensus that "coordinated" measures to promote and facilitate industrial upgrading and diversification are determining factors to accelerate structural transformation, sustain growth, and create better jobs.[5] Unlike the success stories of Japan and the Asian Tigers in the past, the history of industrial policy in Africa and Latin America is filled with failure and cautionary tales. However, the new consensus is empirically supported by the wide variation of the pattern and process of structural transformation among countries; that is, it is growth-enhancing in countries that successfully implemented industrial policies and growth-reducing in countries that neglected investment in agriculture, infrastructure, and human skills. For instance, Salazar-Xirinachs et al. (2014) argued that East Asian countries used targeted measures to help them absorb know-how, technology, and knowledge from the rest of the world, assimilating these factors at a tremendous pace and diversifying into new and more sophisticated industrial powerhouses.

The reason for this intense use of industrial policies is that product diversification and sophistication are found to be the keys to translate high economic growth into good quality employment and poverty reduction (Felipe et al., 2012; Hausmann, Hwang, & Rodrik, 2007; Hausmann & Klinger, 2006; Mishra,

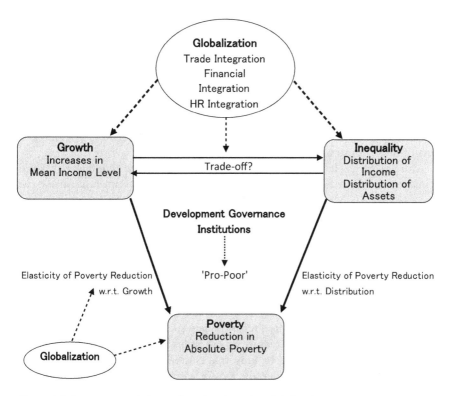

Figure 1.2 Poverty-growth-inequality triangle under globalization
Source: Adapted from Otsubo (2009, Figure 1.2) and Otsubo (2016, Figure 2.1).

Lundstrom, & Anand, 2011). According to Hausmann and Klinger (2006), countries that export goods associated with higher productivity levels grow more rapidly, even after controlling for initial income per head, human capital levels, and time-invariant country characteristics. Along the same lines, countries that export the greatest number of categories of products and those which have more products at different prices within those categories tend to have higher levels of gross domestic product (GDP) (ESCAP, 2011). Therefore, diversification toward higher-value products is crucial for developing countries to boost and sustain economic growth. To diversify, countries need to upgrade the technology in their production and upskill their existing labor (ACET, 2014).

It is, however, worth noting that industrial policies are country-specific, depending on the existing capabilities and institutional capacities (Chang, 2010; Crespi, Fernández-Arias, & Stein, 2014; Ferraz, Kupfer, & Marques, 2014; Hausmann & Hidalgo, 2011). Gabriele (2010), for example, pointed out that the role of the state in China, far from withering away, is massive, dominant, and crucial to China's industrial development. This role has been recently reflected by the position of China as the world's largest manufacturer and it is often called "the factory of the world." In China, the role of the state in economic development has taken the form of both creating the enabling environment and direct intervention, in terms of promoting structural change and thereby growth in productivity and employment (Lo & Wu, 2014). Felipe et al. (2013) further claimed that the key factor underlying China's rapid development during the last 50 years was its intrinsic ability to master and accumulate new and more complex capabilities, which was augmented in 1979 with the implementation of the Equity Joint Venture Law that paved the way for foreign direct investment (FDI) induction and the establishment of export processing zones (EPZs) as an integral part of their industrial policy.

More recently, Hallward-Driemeier and Nayyar published an influential World Bank report entitled *Trouble in the Making? The Future of Manufacturing-Led Development* (Hallward-Driemeier & Nayyar, 2018). This report issued a warning for today's developing countries about relying on the traditional manufacturing-led growth strategy where cross-border investments in low-skill labor-intensive manufacturing sectors were promoted for the sake of job creation in unskilled labor-abundant societies. While these lower-value-added manufacturing sectors have been under constant competitive pressure from producers in China and then India, this World Bank report pointed out that successful drivers for productivity and economic growth had already shifted to higher-value-added manufacturing, supported by newer and advanced technologies, such as robotics, design and factory automation, that in turn require a pool of highly skilled human capital and positive externalities produced by industrial clustering. Given this sea change in the global manufacturing system and GVCs, creation of locational advantages within developing countries, other than inexpensive labor, has become an even tougher challenge that calls for proper policy interventions and facilitations. In this context, this World Bank report suggested policy actions on competitiveness (higher productivity and a better business environment, improved institutions, and infrastructure), capabilities (new skills and better management), and connectedness (freer trade in goods and services) (Hallward-Driemeier & Nayyar, 2018). While the points and modalities of policy interventions are still debatable, the need for smart and coordinated industrial policies in a broader sense is clear and present.

1.3 Defining industrial policies

In general, the literature on industrial policy can be divided into three streams of research: (1) studies discussing the definition, the instruments, and the rationale/justification, and country experiences with industrial policy; (2) studies that discuss new and emerging issues related to industrial development/promotion, such as the changing role of "manufacturing" in the "industries" to be promoted and "policy space" for the developing world in their industrialization; and (3) studies that take on industrial policy evaluations, both in terms of methodologies and their applications. The literature on definition, instruments, and rationale of industrial policy has been the core in the past, joined by country case studies.

However, most of the recent discussions on industrial policy have gone beyond the issues of how to define industrial policies to how to design and implement them in today's context. With the heightened need for evidence-based policymaking (both design and implementation) in our development community, advances in industrial policy evaluation are called for. The issue has grown in importance also in the light of recent developments in evaluation methodologies and identification techniques in health, education, and labor market studies. Despite this, very few studies have discussed the quantitative methods for high quality evaluation of industrial policies.

Nonetheless, the first step is reviewing the discussions on the definitions and instruments of industrial policies since any analyses in this area of research can lead to significantly different conclusions if different definitions and instruments are presumed.

The definition of industrial policy has been the most controversial issue in the debate related to industrial policy. Because industrial policy is complex and holistic, its definition has implications in terms of the degree of government intervention, coverage of industry, choice of policy instruments, and the methods of evaluating the impact, and so forth. Therefore, most of the studies in the field start with a definition of industrial policy. Simply put, industrial policy means any policy that affects the evolution and advance of industry. However, there are several definitions of industrial policy.[6] We argue that, broadly, industrial policy is a large set of strategic and proactive government interventions to address market failures that prevail in the economy and to promote/develop new industrial capabilities and institutional capacities to accelerate the structural transformation necessary for growth and sustainable development. As a good example, Chapter 4 of this book introduces the discussion of international arrangements and public policies of developed countries potentially playing the role of *de facto* industrial policies for developing countries, using the case of the Multi-Fiber Arrangement (MFA) and the Generalized System of Preferences (GSP), which eventually promoted the garment industry in Bangladesh, one of the least developed countries.

Before going any further, we would like to present an indicative summary of definitions/types of industrial policies. Table 1.2 is constructed, partially drawing on the discussions presented in various studies including Di Maio (2014), in order to inform the readers of the kinds of traditional and new criteria that we normally use to classify industrial policies into categories.

Specific objectives of industrial policies may differ across countries, across time, and across stages of development. For most developing countries, the goal of industrial policy is to address market failures and create conditions for investment, productivity growth, and economic transformation, resulting in economic growth and job creation. In their efforts to replicate the success stories of the Asian Tigers and Asian newly industrializing economies (NIES), the latecomers to the Association of Southeast Asian Nations (ASEAN) (Cambodia, Myanmar, Laos, and Vietnam) and many African countries today align themselves in the general definition of industrial policy, where the goal is set to address market failures as a step toward economic transformation and productive job generation.

The United Nations Economic Commission for Africa (UNECA) and the African Union (AU), in championing the active mobilization of industrial policies in Africa, subscribe to a more holistic view. They focus on building strong and inclusive institutions, and on addressing gaps in infrastructure, energy supply, skills, and financing as identified by the industrial stakeholders (UNECA & AU, 2014). With the limitations caused by these identified gaps, African countries today are formulating and implementing new industrial policies centered on developing special economic zones (SEZs).[7]

With regard to the instruments of industrial policies, there is a wide range of policy tools/interventions used by governments to induce structural transformation from lower productive activities to more productive ones. In addition, readers will be exposed to different sets of narrowly or broadly defined industrial policy instruments both in the micro- and macro-economic dimensions, and in the geographical dimensions from domestic regional, national, and super-national regional to global economies. As a good example of categorizing industrial policy instruments, we would like to introduce one indicative 2x2 table created by Weiss (2016) for the classification of interventions (i.e., policy instruments) by adopting vertical vs. horizontal and public-input-based vs. market-based types/definitions shown in Table 1.2. It is replicated here, as Table 1.3, as one excellent example of how to summarize/categorize some of the key measures in industrial policymaking. By choosing and combining a particular set of types/definitions presented in Table 1.2, one can create a similar 2x2 table of policy instruments depending on the needs of policy design.

Table 1.2 Types/definitions of industrial policies

Selective/vertical/narrow vs. general/horizontal/broad (coverage)	Industrial policy is selective when it uses vertical measures that target specific industries, firms, sectors, or factors of production. Winners, key industries, and beneficiaries are picked. Industrial policies in a narrow sense.	On the other hand, general industrial policies are comprised of functional and horizontal measures that benefit all industries by producing investment-conducive environment. Industrial policies in a broader sense.
Small vs. large (scope)	Small scope refers to public inputs to improve productivity of existing activities.	Large scope refers to efforts to establish new industries.
Public-input-based vs. market-based (modality)	Public inputs refer to provisions of public goods/funds and organizational changes (legislation, accreditation, R&D, transport and other infrastructure specific to an industry) that private sector does not supply adequately.	Market-based incentives operate through price regulations and taxation.

Table 1.2 Cont.

Rising industries vs. sunset industries (facilitation)	Industrial policies that aim to promote dynamic/rising sectors of the economy or to create new industries.	Industrial policies that facilitate the "death" of sunset industries in order to free up resources for new activities. They may also provide social safety net for those who suffer in the transition. This facilitation should also minimize damage to accumulated capabilities that still may have relevance for the performance of new activities.
Competitiveness-GDP vs. beyond-GDP (goals)	Industrial policy has traditionally been targeted to increase productivity and competitiveness of a targeted sector or the economy as a whole.	Industrial policy could specifically target beyond-GDP goals such as environmental sustainability, subjective well-being, pro-poorness/inclusiveness, etc.
Piecewise vs. integrated (integration)	Industrial policies are designed and implemented in a piecewise manner without much coordination among policies, policymakers (ministries), or stakeholders such as businesses and communities.	Industrial policies are designed and implemented in an integrated manner with active coordination among policies, policymakers (ministries), and stakeholders such as businesses and communities.
National vs. sub-national vs. super-national (policy unit)	Industrial polices have been often discussed in the context of policy design and implementation at a national level. Central governments are the key players.	Industrial policies today should also be discussed at sub-national and super-national levels. At a sub-national level, regional/spatial distribution of industries is discussed in the context of equitable regional development. As a super-national level, new regional cooperation arrangements such as the AEC and the strengthened AU emerged as the key players in design and coordinated implementation of industrial strategies for the region as a whole.

(*continued*)

Table 1.2 Cont.

Old vs. modern (vintage)	In the old view, the term industrial policy referred to state intervention to reallocate resources in favor of the manufacturing sector and within manufacturing toward high productivity, dynamic sub-sectors (Weiss, 2016, p. 136). Industrial policy was solely in the hands of the state. Two key policies were particularly implemented, namely, infant industry protection and export promotion policies. Trade was used strategically to provide market opportunities for competitive sectors.	The modern industrial policy emphasizes the role of public-private partnership/ dialogue in the design and implementation of industrial policies. It involves active coordination among government agencies, between public and private entities, among entrepreneurs and local communities, etc. Dimensions of integration for integrated policy making and execution should be explored. It is a learning process, where the policy mix is continuously adjusted and adapted.

Source: Authors' construction.

Table 1.3 Classification of policy interventions

Policy intervention	Horizontal	Vertical
Public inputs	Broad-based skills training Infrastructure regulatory reform Banking sector regulatory reform Standard setting bodies	Sector-specific skills training Targeted infrastructure investment Business plans for selected sectors Public-private research consortia
Market-based provision	Corporation tax reform General labor subsidy Export promotion – credit availability, duty-drawbacks, tax treatment Export processing zones General venture capital funding General credit guarantees for SMEs Subsidized credit to all SMEs Tax incentives for R&D	Specific tax holidays Sector-specific labor subsidy Sector-specific export promotion Selective import protection Sector-specific venture capital funding Selective credit guarantees Directed credit Selective R&D incentives Price support schemes

Source: Weiss (2016, 138, Table 8.1). Reproduced by permission of Taylor and Francis, a division of Informa plc.

1.4 Arguments and theoretical underpinnings for industrial policies

In this section, we review typical arguments for and against industrial policies. The debate on the rationale of industrial policy has also evolved over time. There is a justification to use functional, horizontal, and general industrial policies as opposed to selective, vertical, and narrow industrial policies.[8] The need to combine horizontal industrial policy with sector-specific policy is advocated in Latin America (Alvarez, 2013). For Stiglitz and Monga (2013), the question is not whether any government should use industrial policy, but rather how best to apply it.

The common objection to industrial policies is built on two main arguments: asymmetric information and corruption. Having identified the active roles of government in pursuing industrial development in East Asia, it has often been argued that industrial policy might not work in Africa because of deficiencies in governance. Deficiencies in governance include corruption and rent-seeking activities. In contrast, Greenwald and Stiglitz (2013) argued that effective industrial policies can be implemented in countries with significant deficiencies in governance. An important reason for this is that industrial policies have succeeded in some instances in which they were designed to correct market failures or even have corrected government failures. The set of countries of South Korea, China, and Taiwan prioritized policies to address market imperfections before improving their respective institutions (Rodrik, 1995, 1996).

There is, in fact, a great deal of agreement on the theoretical and logical underpinnings for industrial policies. First of all, it is widely accepted that markets and economies are generally characterized by the existence of negative externalities, and under these circumstances, a competitive market system may not lead to a Pareto-efficient outcome (Greenwald & Stiglitz, 1986; Pack & Saggi, 2006).[9] According to Lall (2004), economic theory justifies selectivity where market failures affect some activities more than others, and restoring equilibrium calls for more intervention in specific activities. Therefore, industrial policy is called for in order to address market failure.[10] Theoretically speaking, there are two possible roles for industrial policies.[11] Industrial policies can be designed to address externalities and solve coordination problems (imperfect competition, pollution, coordination failure, capital market imperfection, and so on). They should also provide an enabling environment for innovation by promoting creation and dissemination of knowledge.

Government interventions to promote structural transformation were justified to variable degrees in countries such as Japan, the Asian Tigers, Indonesia, Malaysia, Thailand, China, Vietnam, and India, in order to protect infant industries (Lall, 2004) and foster industrial development. More recently, the case of infant industry protection is supported by the existence and persistence of information externality (Hausmann & Rodrik, 2003; Lin, 2012; Rodrik, 2004, 2008a). Tax incentives and subsidies can be used to build capabilities for industrial development, such as the capacity to acquire necessary imports (e.g., expensive machinery) and to provide workforce training.

Industrial policy is also important to fix market failures (Rodrik, 2004, 2008a). This argument has been supported both by those who view industrial policy as tools to shape sectoral allocation of economic activities and by those who advocate the general/horizontal type of industrial policies. Another justification stems from the fact that latecomer countries face more severe market failures than those faced by mature market economies. According to Altenburg (2013), industrial policy is needed to encourage entrepreneurship and an entrepreneurial class, promote skills development at all levels, and set up regulatory institutions and quality assurance. For instance, for a primary commodity producer/exporter to diversify into higher-value-added products, it takes numerous capabilities that can only be promoted with country-specific policies. The most often advocated generic policies in the literature (Felipe et al., 2010; Page, 2012) have highlighted policy interventions to address market failures by developing skills and an infrastructure as the basis to manufacture and export high-value products. For example, Felipe et al. (2010), in their study on how rich countries became rich, in which they categorized 779 products based on their sophistication and connectivity to other products, found that 75 out of 154 countries sampled belong to the "low product" trap as they mostly export unsophisticated and unconnected products.[12] They conclude that countries in the "low product" trap need to acquire skills, technology, and knowledge, and improve their organizational capabilities to escape from this trap. Similarly, Page (2012) discussed policies for African economies to reallocate resources to higher productivity activities in the agro-industry, manufacturing, or tradable services. He argued that Africa should focus on pushing exports, building capabilities, and supporting agglomeration in addition to investment climate reforms that aim to reduce the skill and infrastructure gaps. In the same vein, Lin and Treichel (2012) argued that technological innovation, industrial diversification, and industrial upgrading are typically accompanied by changes in capital and skills requirements for firms as well as by changes in their market scope and infrastructure needs due to the evolving nature of production that is embodied in the process of innovation. Put differently, diversification is typically accompanied by changes in hard and soft infrastructure requirements.

1.5 Structure of the book and the questions to be addressed

Having reconfirmed the importance of proactive industrial promotion policies for sustained economic growth and poverty reduction in developing countries, recent discussions focus more on design, implementation, and evaluation for evidence-based policymaking. It is also widely recognized today that policy coordination and integration are necessary requirements for industrial policies to take on the challenges of producing "inclusive" development under the SDGs' framework. In order for us to deal with these issues and challenges in industrial promotion, this book consists of the following four parts in two volumes:

Part I Industrial promotion in retrospect and prospect
Part II Designing integrated industrial policies in Asia and the Pacific
Part III Designing integrated industrial policies in Africa
Part IV Designing integrated industrial policies in sub- and super-national regions

Part I consists of three introductory chapters, contained in both Vol. I and Vol. II. Chapter 1 presents industrial promotion and industrial policies in retrospect and prospect. It provides concepts, definitions, and issues to be discussed in this book while stressing the need for modern and integrated strategies. It also captures industrial promotion in the Poverty-Growth-Inequality (PGI) triangle in order for us to discuss "inclusive" strategies. Chapter 2 presents data and descriptive statistics that constitute a common background. What do we really know about the changing state of global manufacturing? How and why has the trend of premature deindustrialization emerged in many parts of the developing world? Chapter 3 revisits the importance of manufacturing and the risks associated with premature deindustrialization in pursuing pro-poor growth and inclusive development. Chapters 2 and 3, together, present a holistic picture of the past and present state of industrialization, structural change, and their impact on increases in value-added and employment.

As most of the chapters in this book deal with issues/topics of industrial promotion not only in theories and conceptual frameworks but also in relation to existing problems and policies within a specific country context, the next two Parts of the book present chapters by countries used as cases or targets of rigorous economic/econometric analyses. Part II (Chapters 4–12) discusses countries in Asia and the Pacific region. Part III (Chapters 13–16) presents chapters that use countries in Africa as their cases. However, this does not mean that any particular topic is only relevant to a particular set of countries or a region. Instead, it means that realistic industrial policy discussion needs cases and targets on the ground.

Part IV contains two chapters that deal with regional issues/topics of industrial promotion. Chapter 17 discusses the impact of super-national regional economic cooperation such as the Regional Trading Agreement (RTA) and the Regional Comprehensive Economic Partnership (RCEP) for industrial promotion at the regional level. Chapter 18 discusses regional parity and regional "inclusiveness" in the context of sub-national regions as a country pursues industrial development in a balanced or unbalanced manner. Chapter 17 introduces policy simulations using computable general equilibrium (CGE) models. Chapter 18 introduces the analyses of regional convergence/divergence to investigate the interaction between industrial development and regional convergence.

This book does not rehash the success stories of Japan, South Korea, and Taiwan as they have already been well documented and the global economic environment today is very different from when the "East Asian miracle" was created. Instead, this book focuses on ordinary developing countries in Asia and Africa, including countries such as Indonesia and Thailand, where governments have tended not to subscribe to industrial promotion by so-called "industrial policies." The book includes analyses on "China in Africa" and an analysis on the future of China's industrial development initiative "Made in China 2025" and its impact on developing countries. This book also intends to contribute to the worldwide discussion of SDGs as discussions/analyses on industrial promotion and industrial policies not only for the sake of economic growth and job creation but also for "inclusive" development are presented. To this end, the book addresses impacts on income and spatial (geographical) inequalities, thereby capturing industrial promotion in the context of the Poverty-Growth-Inequality (PGI) triangle, as shown in Figure 1.2.

Another unique feature of this book comes from the fact that this book is produced as a joint venture between academic researchers and policymakers. Contributors include those with working experiences in trend-setting international organizations, such as the United Nations (UN), the United Nations Industrial Development Organization (UNIDO), and the World Bank, as well as those working for national institutions in the developing countries which deal with policymaking and the execution of industrial promotion, such as the National Development Planning Agency of Indonesia (BAPPENAS), the Ministry of Industry and Commerce of the Laotian government, and the Ministry of Finance and the Central Bank of Thailand.

The issues/questions and specific industrial policy options that each chapter tries to address are partly previewed in the next subsection in conjunction with the key questions, related to industrial promotion in today's globalized world economy, to be addressed in this book.

1.6 Leading issues in industrial promotion in today's globalized world

1.6.1 What is the present state of industrialization and deindustrialization?

Does manufacturing still matter?
Can manufacturing still be the engine of growth?

The classic and dominant view relates industry to the manufacturing sector for its role as the engine of economic growth (Chenery, Robinson, & Syrquin, 1986; Kaldor, 1966). Historically, rapid and sustained economic growth is highly correlated with an expansion of manufacturing and reallocation of resources to more productive activities (Hausmann, Hwang, & Rodrik, 2007; Hausmann & Klinger, 2006; Hausmann & Rodrik, 2003; McMillan & Rodrik, 2011; McMillan, Rodrik, & Verduzco-Gallo, 2014). Manufacturing has the fastest productivity growth, faster than services and agriculture, pays higher wages (ILO, 2014), and has strong spillover effects (backward and forward linkages) to other sectors (Hirschman, 1958). This means that a rapidly growing manufacturing sector enhances productivity growth in other sectors of the economy, and therefore, leads to higher economic growth.[13] For natural resource-based economies whose exports depend on a primary commodity, diversifying the export structure away from primary products to manufacturing has been a key policy in order to build resilience to external shocks (Amin Guitierrez de Pineres & Ferrantino, 2000) and sustain growth (McMillan & Harttgen, 2014). The other main argument in favor of diversifying into manufacturing lies in the fact that diversification is needed to sustain growth and significantly reduce poverty. This argument is supported by the fact that export diversification toward manufacturing is linked to increased employment, exports, and GDP growth (Agosin, 2007; Herzer & Nowak-Lehmann, 2006; Lederman & Maloney, 2007).

A more recent view argues that industrial policy should target all economic activities that have similar characteristics to manufacturing, such as tradable and high productive services and agro-processing. For example, Ohno (2013) includes manufacturing, agriculture, services, and logistics as a set of production sectors for industrial policy to focus on. The sector should be precisely targeted, for example, on non-traditional and high-yielding varieties of agricultural products or high-value service activities, such as software development and tourism (Altenburg, 2011; Rodrik, 2008a).

There are several reasons for this, the most important is that recent evidence shows that manufacturing is a necessary but not sufficient condition for eventual prosperity (Dadush, 2015; Felipe et al., 2014). For example, Felipe et al. (2014) related manufacturing employment and output shares to the GDP per capita of 52 economies to study whether it is currently possible to become rich without building large manufacturing sectors. The authors find that higher manufacturing employment shares are strongly related to a subsequent rise in income per capita. However, the findings also suggest that it is becoming more difficult for actual developing countries to achieve higher manufacturing shares and therefore this limits their potential to industrialize through manufacturing. Dadush (2015) conducted similar, but less robust, cross-country regression of GDP per capita growth for 107 countries over the period 2000–2012. The estimated effect of manufacturing share of value-added is significant and varies between 0.44 and 0.51 for developing countries. His findings corroborate those of Felipe et al. (2014) in that developing countries would have to achieve a very large increase in their manufacturing share to see an appreciable acceleration in their growth rate. Felipe et al. (2009) find that services had a larger effect than manufacturing on growth in developing Asia. The main reason for this finding is that, in recent decades, rapid productivity growth has occurred outside manufacturing, in large part due to the application of computer-based technologies. Another reason for targeting all economic sectors stems from the fact that the world has entered a post-industrial era where the service and other non-manufacturing sectors have come to dominate the economic structure of many economies, both in terms of output and employment.

The observed relationships between income levels and manufacturing (or industry) shares in total value-added and total employment in cross-country data for the three most recent decades (1994–1996, 2004–2006, and 2014–2016) are presented in Figures 1.3, 1.4, and 1.5.[14] In Figure 1.3, although the

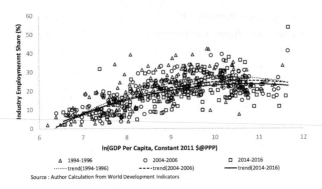

Figure 1.3 Share of employment in industry vs. GDP per capita
Source: Authors' compilation based on World Development Indicators, 2019.

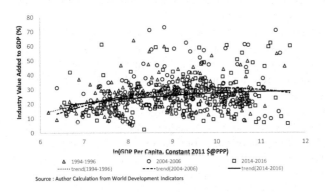

Figure 1.4 Share of value-added in industry vs. GDP per capita
Source: Authors' compilation based on World Development Indicators, 2019.

inverted U-shape relationship between the income levels and industry employment shares in a cross-country comparison have been preserved, throughout three decades, the curve has been shifting down, implicating a secular decline in the importance of industry in explaining/generating employment.[15] In terms of the relationships between income levels and value-added shares, Figure 1.4 (industry) and Figure 1.5 (manufacturing) again show that fitted curves have been shifting down, pointing to the declines in the peak shares at the middle range of per capita income. This pattern is more prominent when manufacturing is singled out of the industry group.[16]

Figure 1.6 (employment) and Figure 1.7 (value-added) present the relationships between income levels and service shares in total employment and total value-added in cross-country data for the same time points. Unlike the case for industry (or manufacturing), the shares of service continue to rise both in

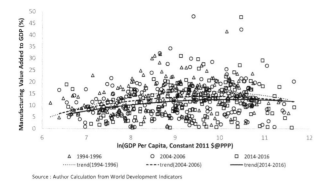

Figure 1.5 Share of value-added in manufacturing vs. GDP per capita
Source: Authors' compilation based on World Development Indicators, 2019.

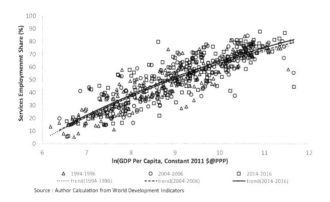

Figure 1.6 Share of employment in service sector vs. GDP per capita
Source: Authors' compilation based on World Development Indicators, 2019.

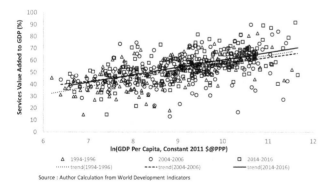

Figure 1.7 Share of value-added in service sector vs. GDP per capita
Source: Authors' compilation based on World Development Indicators, 2019.

employment and value-added as per capita income increases. Fitted curves have been shifting up over these three decades pointing to the increasing importance of the service sector in the global economy. Interestingly, the differences in the curvatures of fitted curves between employment and value-added shares seem to indicate higher productivity in the service sector in higher-income countries. The possibility of the service sector yielding higher productivities and real wages seem to have been supported by advances in technologies such as ICT and the Internet of Things (IoT).

Exports of commercial services, for example, have nearly tripled in the last decade and have surpassed agriculture and industry as the leading income-generating sector across Africa (UNECA & AU, 2014). This was made possible due to the revolution of ICT and transport technologies, and the growing importance of trade and value chains. Despite the fact that growth in the manufacturing sector has been partially responsible for the boom of high productive public utilities and construction, recent evidence also showed the contribution of coordinated measures to promote and accelerate growth in the non-manufacturing sectors, such as tourism and food production. For example Chang, Andreoni, and Kuan (2014) demonstrate how Brazil and Chile have successfully used policies to expand natural resource-processing industries and food production. In the context of African countries, even the relatively successful recent growth has been jobless. While services have surpassed agriculture and industry as the leading income-generating sectors across Africa, this has not created the quantity or quality of jobs normally expected from expanding manufacturing and labor-intensive production (UNECA, 2014).[17]

As a good case study from Asia, Chapter 5 discusses Indonesia's efforts towards pro-poor industrial policies. Indonesia, with its young and expanding population, and with a rising middle class, has observed a strong expansion of its service sector, but without shifting employment out of manufacturing. The government of Indonesia recently started its march toward manufacturing upgrading and promoting high-yielding manufacturing-related services with its Indonesian Industrial Revolution Version 4.0.

From a policy perspective, does this imply that industrial policy should target only high productive activities in service and agro-processing? As one of the key service sector-based industrialization trends, tourism development and international trade in tourism will be dealt with in Chapter 10 drawing on cases of development models from the Pacific Island Countries.

Chapter 2 looks further into these trends in industrialization and deindustrialization.

In Chapter 3, "The importance of manufacturing development and structural change for pro-poor growth," Haraguchi and Amann elaborate on the importance of industrial structural change by investigating development patterns within manufacturing. Their aim is to highlight the relevance of manufacturing and to promote pro-poor growth pathways of industrial development. The authors revisit the current debate on whether the importance of manufacturing for economic development has changed by reviewing the latest advances in the field linked to their own empirical analyses.

1.6.2 Have developing countries been marginalized to low value-added manufacturing?

Is there a space for the manufacturing industry in developing countries to grow?

Are there any opportunities for higher-value-added manufacturing and manufacturing-related services left for the majority of developing countries?

Related to the first set of questions, policymakers in developing countries and scholars have started to assess the existence of spaces that manufacturing industries in developing countries can grow into.

Discussed above, an influential World Bank report *Trouble in the Making? The Future of Manufacturing-Led Development* (Hallward-Driemeier & Nayyar, 2018) was introduced. This report issued a warning for today's developing countries about their continued reliance on the traditional manufacturing-led growth strategy where cross-border investments in low-skill labor-intensive manufacturing sectors were promoted for the sake of job creation in unskilled labor-abundant societies. Successful drivers for productivity and economic growth had already shifted to higher-value-added manufacturing supported by newer and advanced technologies, that in turn requires a pool of highly skilled human capital that is not readily available in most developing countries. The same report also pointed out that success in this higher-value-added manufacturing is limited to only a handful of economies. Some 55 percent of the world's manufactured goods were produced in developed/industrialized countries, and China, the world's largest manufacturing producer accounted for another 25 percent in 2015, leaving only one-fifth of the total pie for the other developing countries (Hallward-Driemeier & Nayyar, 2018).

Latecomers need specific and proactive industrial policy to accelerate the process of development and diversify into higher-value-added products. The reason often raised by economists is that the new initial conditions for Asia's latecomers and African economies to create manufacturing growth are different from those faced by the Asian Tigers. The difference stems from the fact that successful Asian economies followed highly unusual and distinctive paths of growth. In the initial stage of the (East) Asian industrial development, global trade was characterized by a rapidly growing manufacturing sector, whereas the nature of global trade today is characterized by highly-productive service (manufacturing-related service) sectors. In recent years, "Factory Asia" has become the new key player in global manufacturing and service trade, with China at the center due to its successful creation of "competitive" or "dynamic" comparative advantage, with India growing into a "back office of the world." The world economy is now driven by shifts in demand and innovations in products/services, processes/ operations, materials, and information technology. It contrasts with China's initial condition, which was characterized by the shifts in the cost and the availability of factor inputs (Manyika et al., 2012). That is, the initial conditions that China and other East Asian economies faced created an opportunity for them to industrialize with labor-intensive, export-oriented manufacturing. According to the projection by Anderson and Strutt (2014), China will become the world's top producing country not only of primary products but also of manufacturing products. In fact, China had already become the world's top manufacturing producer by 2015 (with 25 percent of the world's total manufacturing value-added in 2015). Global manufacturing is characterized by high specialization in small tasks due to the fragmentation of production processes and the extension of GVCs. This may not be beneficial for Asia's latecomers or African economies who contribute a small portion of low value-added labor-intensive activities to the global manufacturing value chains. The Asian Tigers benefitted from a rapidly expanding manufacturing sector. The Asian latecomers are trying to capitalize on the last extensions of the global production networks. The African Lions are benefitting from increases in productivity in selective service sectors, while the agricultural sector remains unproductive.[18] The food processing industry can be considered a groundbreaking sector for its path to manufacturing growth.

In recent years, China and Factory Asia started to move up the quality ladder by manufacturing more goods with high-skilled content. The production system has become very fragmented with an increasing role of trade in tasks (trade in intermediate goods) and efficient logistics (manufacturing-related services).[19] As a consequence, economies are becoming more and more integrated through supply/value chains. According to Manyika et al. (2012), high R&D and trade-intensive industries, such as automotives, the chemical sector, and pharmaceuticals, represent the largest share (34 percent) of global manufacturing value-added while labor-intensive goods represent only 7 percent. Regional processing of rubber, plastic, metal, and food products represents 28 percent of total manufacturing value-added and is labor- and trade-intensive. In 2012, China manufactured half of the industrialized countries' products (UNIDO, 2013). The projection by Anderson and Strutt (2014) indicates that China will remain the world's top manufacturer in 2030 with a share of 28.9 percent of global value-added.

Nonetheless, the new initial conditions for industrial development, with Factory Asia as the new player in the global manufacturing and service trade, offer exploitable possibilities for Africa and other developing regions to industrialize. For example, Page (2012) has argued that rising costs and demand in Asia can serve as an opportunity for Africa to industrialize. Similarly, UNIDO (2013) pointed out that Africa faces openings in low-tech labor-intensive industries such as agro-industry, textiles, and clothing and apparel. The same should be true for Asia's latecomers.

Many chapters in Part II (Asia) and Part III (Africa) of this book try to deal with this issue at least partially. In Chapter 5, "Toward pro-poor industrial policies in Indonesia: progress, challenges, and future directions," Gunawan, Pratikto, and Dartanto touch upon Indonesia's most recent industrial promotion strategy of Indonesia 4.0. In Chapter 9, "Thailand's industrial policy: its history and recent development," Thaiprasert and Roidoung introduce Thailand's most recent strategy of Thailand 4.0. Both of these master plans for industrial structural upgrading are aimed at responding to the new challenges presented in this section.

On the contrary, in Chapter 7, "Promoting local SMEs through GVCs: a framework and case study of Laotian SMEs," Vidavong and Otsubo introduce the difficulties that an Asian latecomer country, Laos, faces. They point out, by showing a so-called Smile Curve that portrays the value-added structure of typical GVCs, that latecomers like Laos are confined to the low-value-added product assembly-related segments of the value chains without much prospect for industry upgrading.

In Chapter 13, "Mechanisms and impacts of innovation on firm survival: evidence from Sub-Saharan Africa," Otchia explores the reasons for the observed differences in African firm survival in international markets. Using a unique dataset that matches firm-level panel data and intersectoral input-output linkages data, the research finds that product innovation and process innovation are strong determinants of firm survival in the international market, but the effect of process innovation is greater than that of product innovation. Chapter 13 establishes that the speed of propagation of technological innovation has a strong effect on firm survival, especially through backward linkages.

From the discussion presented in this section, it is obvious that the future direction of China's industrial development will certainly impact that of other developing economies. In Chapter 11, "'Made in China 2025' and the recent industrial policy in China," Akkemik and Yülek introduce China's Made in China 2025 master plan for industry upgrading and analyze its impact. After a long period of high economic growth and industrialization, the Chinese economy has recently entered a period of relatively low economic growth. Behind the past remarkable performance lies the government's ambitious and interventionist industrial policies. To ensure a swift transition and avoid falling into a middle-income trap, the Chinese government has recently devised a new industrial policy called "Made in China 2025." This strategy envisages that China will join the ranks of industrialized countries through a structural change toward high-tech industries and by nurturing domestic production and the adoption of "smart manufacturing" technologies. This new strategy favors domestic firms against foreign competitors and imposes strict domestic content requirements. In the past, these were essential characteristics of traditional industrial policies in East Asia (e.g., Japan, Korea, and Taiwan). But the scale of the Chinese economy ensures that such a policy will have a significant impact on the world economy. Chapter 11 overviews and evaluates contemporary industrial policies in China in conjunction with criticism from some advanced countries, which recently have led to trade frictions. Chapter 11 sets up a theoretical and analytical framework to analyze industrial policies in the context of the Chinese case.

1.6.3 Do we need modern/new industrial policies?

How can we design a new partnership between business and development?
How can we promote the role of public-private-partnership (PPP) for
inclusive industrial development?

The recent literature on industrial policy tends to contrast modern versus old
industrial policies. Modern industrial policy emphasizes the extent and nature
of the collaboration between government and the private sector as fundamental
to the effectiveness and success of industrial policy.[20] According to Devlin and
Moguillansky (2013), modern industrial policy stresses that the most successful
strategies and interventions emerge out of a social process of close alliance
between the public and private sectors. The new thinking promotes public-
private alliance as a way to design and implement industrial policy (Chang, 1994;
Devlin & Moguillansky, 2013; Evans, 1995; Rodrik, 2004; Wade, 2004). This
has changed the focus of the industrial policy debate from "what" to "how." As
part of the coordination of management of industrial policies, the private sector
contributes to the design, content, and implementation of industrial policies. The
coordination of management of industrial policies enables us to solve two major
weaknesses of the old industrial policy: coordination and monitoring within government (Devlin & Moguillansky, 2013), and market failure (Chang, 2015).
Industrial policies should serve the purpose of a clear vision for development and
structural change, based on consistent dialogue between the public and private
sectors. To this end, modern industrial policy calls for a more proactive intervention, rather than the traditional top-down approach, where the government
solely identified sectors to promote or protect. The concept of public-private
partnership (PPP) is given many definitions, some of them dating from as early
as the 1990s. More recently, Günther and Alcorta (2011) of UNIDO referred
to industrial policy as the public and private sectors jointly identifying and lifting
the constraints that impede the transformation of industry. To advance the discussion, it is important to create specific institutions that support PPP-related
developments.

There have been some successful cases of public-private dialogue for industrial policy in Sub-Saharan Africa. For example, the government of Ethiopia
and the private sector established the Ethiopia Public Private Consultative
Forum (EPPCF) in 2010 to serve as a platform for public-private dialogue for
industrial policy. The EPPCF also aimed to create an environment of mutual
understanding, increase the level of trust between the government and the private sector, and enhance the key actors' capacities in light of evidence-based
policy. It is decentralized at three levels (federal, state, and county). The dialogue is championed by the Ministry of Trade and Industry (on the government side) and the Ethiopian Chamber of Commerce and Sectoral Association
(ECCSA). As of March 2015, the EPPCF had conducted two high-level
national dialogues (chaired by the Prime Minister) and more than 15 dialogues
of other types (Mihretu & Eyob, 2015). The EPPCF claims positive results in

the areas of customs procedure, trade licensing, taxes, and trust among economic agents.

In Chapter 16, "A new partnership between business and development: a case study of Ethiopia's industrial development," Ohno and Uesu state that the interface between business and development cooperation activities is growing, and major donors have begun to introduce new instruments to promote PPPs for development. This is because, with accelerated globalization, private financial flows to developing countries have dramatically increased, superseding the volume of Official Development Assistance (ODA). Particularly after the 2008 financial crisis, multinational corporations (MNCs) actively expanded their business operations in emerging economies and developing countries. This chapter aims to review the recent trends of development partnerships with the private sector, analyze the practices of major donors (traditional donors such as Western donors and Japan, as well as non-traditional donors, such as China and Turkey) and MNCs, and draw implications for the industrialization of latecomer countries. In doing so, Chapter 16 consists of two main sections: (1) an overview of development partnerships with the private sector in recent years, and (2) a case study of Ethiopia, which is endeavoring to achieve inclusive and sustainable industrial development.

In Chapter 9, "Thailand's industrial policy: its history and recent development," Thaiprasert and Roidoung introduce the history and evolution of industrial development and *de facto* industrial policy for a country that has not officially recognized "industrial policy." The role of PPPs is explicitly discussed for this country where the relationships between business and government, and business and development have been closer, compared to those in the other ASEAN economies.

From the days of the East Asian miracle, industrial promotion in Thailand, like that in Indonesia, has been considered to be market-driven (private sector-driven) with minimal direct government intervention, as opposed to the widely known and well-studied models of Japan, South Korea, and Taiwan (World Bank, 1993). In reality, however, there exist conscious and unconscious efforts by the state to promote industrial growth and development. Chapter 9 introduces the history, issues, and initiatives of industrial promotion in the Kingdom of Thailand. It introduces: (1) the mix of direct and indirect interventions, modalities utilized, and the recent Thailand 4.0 initiative; (2) the roles of the US, Chinese immigrants, and Japan; and (3) the role of PPPs. Overall, Chapter 9 intends to provide the context for further discussion on whether industrial policies were/should be intentionally developed or occur spontaneously when opportunities arise in the constantly changing global economic environment.

1.6.4 Does today's developing world have industrial policy space under the WTO global rules?

Many economists argue that the current difficulties facing developing countries wishing to embark on the process of industrialization are related to the new rules of the game. There is still a debate on what should be the best "policy space" for developing countries to accelerate industrial development under the World Trade Organization (WTO) rules and the bilateral and regional trade and investment agreements.

Trade policies played a significant role in the East Asian miracle (Masuyama, Vandenbrink, & Yue, 1997). Governments of the countries involved used import protection to develop their infant industries, and then export promotion for their strategic industries to upgrade their productive structure and create new comparative and competitive advantages. Since the conclusion of the Uruguay Round trade negotiations in 1994 and the establishment of the WTO that followed in 1995, trade policy space for developing countries has been restricted, to the advantage of the neoliberal international economic order (Gallagher, 2005; Khan, 2007; Wade, 2003). Shadlen (2005) adds that the advanced countries have also used trade agreements to impose additional restrictions on developing countries. Under these circumstances, industrial policies in developing countries need to conform to commitments countries have made with their major trading partners and to the rules of the multilateral trade system. As a corollary, it has been argued that the WTO rules do not provide a greater policy space for industrial development, as they have reduced the ability of developing countries to achieve economic development.[21] The regulations that may reduce the range of policy options for developing countries include the General Agreement on Tariffs and Trade (GATT), the General Agreement on Trade and Services (GATS), the Agreement on Subsidies and Countervailing Measures (SCM), the Agreement on Trade Related Aspects of Intellectual Property Rights (TRIPS), and the Trade Related Investment Measures (TRIMS). For instance, policies such as import protection and export promotion, which were implemented by the East Asian economies to develop their infant industries and create comparative advantages, became illegal under the WTO rules (Chang, 2003; Di Maio, 2014). As far as import protection is concerned, the WTO regulations require that member countries limit their tariffs up to a ceiling. Despite the fact that developing countries were allowed to fix their ceiling at higher levels than their applied tariffs, authors such as Gibbs (2007) contend that it still reduces the ability of developing countries to adjust tariff protection with the improvement of technology, through a system of "cascading." Since the ceiling levels of tariffs are generally not allowed, developing countries have a limited amount of leeway to use tariff instruments when their economic structure changes or when they enter regional integration agreements.[22]

Similarly, WTO's SCM agreements are restricting the use of export subsidies and subsidies for domestic inputs (Di Maio, 2014; Rodrik, 2004; Shadlen, 2005), which had been the key interventions in the East Asian model of export-promotion-based growth. Rodrik (2004), in addressing the issue related to SCM agreements, contended that it renders export processing zones (EPZs) illegal. A clarification in this debate is provided by Shadlen (2005) and UNECA (2016), who state that developing countries can still use "actionable subsidies" as long as they do not create injury or cause adverse prejudice to the importing country's domestic industry or another country's export of the same product. UNECA (2016) adds that subsidies can still be used until they are challenged or countervailed, which can take 2 to 3 years.

Several other criticisms have been made of the introduction of TRIPS rules on copyrights, trademarks, industrial designs, trade secrecy, and patents. The criticisms stem from the fact that the TRIPS agreement has strengthened the patent rights and Intellectual Property Rights (IPRs) with regard to the developing countries whereas most of the developed economies—the USA, the European countries, Japan, Taiwan, and South Korea—had wide access to new technologies from other countries and could learn to imitate them to climb up the technological ladder and industrialize. Thus, TRIPS has been criticized for reducing the use of patents and is therefore responsible for a widening technology gap between developed and developing countries (Correa, 1999; UNDP, 2005). Other ambiguous effects of TRIM based on empirical studies include those found by Ahn, Hall, and Lee (2014) and Americo and Fredriksson (2007). For instance, Americo and Fredriksson (2007) find that the effects of TRIMs, using case studies in six countries, have been mixed or positive but small. We have to clarify what are the positive and negative effects. Static and dynamic impacts should also differ.

The WTO agreement of TRIMs which bans local content and performance requirements has mostly been criticized for restricting industrial policy toward foreign investment and reducing trade flows (Aggarwal & Evenett, 2014; Wade, 2003). The TRIMs agreement, however, does not limit the use of other regulatory investment measures, such as conditions for maintaining joint ventures with local firms, transfer of technology, and limitations on foreign equity ownership. These are important investment measures and can be used by developing countries to create a useful investment strategy.

In Table 1.4, we present a summary of indicative policy options for developing countries under the WTO global rules. We see that developing countries can still make use of industrial policies related to science and technology, regional development, the environment, infrastructure, human capital, and capacity building under the WTO regime. This corroborates the conclusion of UNECA (2016), which argues that the WTO rules restrict a few trade policy instruments and developing countries still have room for trade policy measures if they do not affect exports or imports. For instance, developing countries can fully apply the SCMs and TRIMS in services as the regulations cover only goods. The WTO rules and trade agreements give a restricted policy space for industrialization in manufacturing and agriculture. However, the service sector remains an interesting and promising frontier. Finally, the WTO rules might not be applied to certain industries in certain countries. For example, the TRIPs and GATS agreements have not been found to be of direct importance in the Malaysian and Thai automotive industries (Natsuda & Thoburn, 2014).

As WTO functions as the provider of negotiating tables and dispute settlement mechanisms, a proper understanding of the related rules and the cases of their applications including those handled under the Dispute Settlement mechanism

Table 1.4 Summary of policy options under the WTO

Import barriers	Tariffs and ODCs	Can be used for industrial policies, by virtue of "water." Countries can also renegotiate the bound tariffs for one or several products or apply the Government Assistance to Economic Development
	NTB (import quotas, import licensing, import prohibitions and local content requirements)	Local content requirements are not consistent with the Trade Related Investment Measures (TRIMs) agreement (and so are likely to be challenged). Alternative strategies that can spur domestic production and are allowed under WTO rules must be sought (for example, offset clauses).
	Quantitative restrictions on imports	Accepted under the WTO Agreement of Agriculture (AOA) or for balance of payments reasons
	National treatment	Accepted only for government procurement
	GATS-inconsistent measures	Allowed to promote the establishment of a particular industry
	Anti-dumping measures	Can be applied
	Countervailing duties	Can be applied to offset the effect of a subsidy
Exchange rate policies	Exchange rate policies	Can be applied as no WTO agreement explicitly deals with exchange rates
Aid to enterprises	Subsidies for goods (SCM)/domestic content subsidies	Prohibited since 31 December 2002
	Subsidies for goods (SCM)/production subsidies	Accepted if it meets the specificity requirement
	Subsidies for R&D	Accepted under WTO rules (up to 75 percent of research costs and 50 percent of pre-competitive development), but fiscally expensive
	Upgrading of disadvantaged regions and to develop environmentally friendly technology	Allowed but WTO members are simply required to notify any new R&D measure granted in favor of the agricultural sector
	Human capital development	
Export promotion	Export subsidies	Accepted for developing countries with a per capita income of less than $1,000
	Export finance; export insurance; export guarantee	Allowed
	Export quality management	Allowed

Table 1.4 Cont.

	Export taxes and duties	Export taxes are not regulated by the WTO agreements. However, the imposition of a prohibitive tax may be tantamount to a quantitative restriction according to the terms of GATT Article XI
Investment measures and incentives	FDI and TRIMS	Export performance requirements, joint ventures measures, technology transfer and equity repatriation (foreign equity ownership) are allowed by WTO but limited by some trade agreements
	SEZ	Accepted under WTO rules
	Technology-related requirements on domestic firms	Accepted but contents and implementation of requirement remain vague
	FDI policy on performance requirements	Generally forbidden
	Facilitating reverse engineering and imitation	TRIPS requires domestic IPR institutions and protection

Source: Authors' compilation from various sources including Guadagno (2015) and Rodrik (2008b).

seems to be imperative for policymakers and scholars to support their policy-making. Human capital development in developing countries, including sharing talent in regional cooperation frameworks, should be promoted. In 419 WTO disputes up to 2018, no single case was brought against low-income countries, suggesting that industrial policies undertaken by those countries might not result in legal actions by other members. However, after 2018, the world has started to observe cases brought against developing countries, such as China and India. Other developing countries, middle-income countries in particular, should be ready to discuss and defend their initiatives for "inclusive" industrial promotion. Continuous efforts should be made for the low-income countries to be supported by preferential arrangements. Various case chapters in this book will deal with some of the related issues.

In Chapter 4, "A *de facto* industrial policy and its effects on the least developed countries," Matsunaga and Haraguchi address issues related to this "policy space." It has been argued that an increasing number of international arrangements have limited the "policy space" in industrial policies for developing countries. Such WTO rules as the TRIPS, TRIMS, and SCM made poor countries face more difficulties in devising and implementing industrial policies to develop their economies. However, scrutiny of international arrangements could make some developing countries enjoy a *de facto* industrial policy, thereby widening the policy space. The authors demonstrate that the Multi-Fiber Arrangement (MFA) and the Generalized System of Preferences (GSP) functioned as a *de facto* industrial policy to foster the export-oriented garment industry in one of the least developed countries, Bangladesh. The industry has had latent comparative advantage but was totally different from the known comparative advantage industry (jute products). This case defied the theory of comparative advantage yet eventually succeeded. Likewise, the policy space can be widened by studying the possible effects of international arrangements on developing economies and using them as a *de facto* industrial policy. Even Brexit and the recent US-China trade frictions may have similar effects. Researchers should play a role in devising these policies.

1.6.5 Should industry policies cater for "pro-poorness" and "inclusiveness" in addition to promoting economic growth?

As shown above, in Figure 1.1, the SDGs encompass goals of inclusive economic growth, industrial development, and reduced inequalities:

> Goal 1: End poverty in all its forms everywhere.
> Goal 8: Promote inclusive and sustainable economic growth, employment and decent work for all.
> Goal 9: Build resilient infrastructure, promote sustainable industrialization and foster innovation.
> Goal 10: Reduce inequality within and among countries.

This focuses thoughtful and concurrent attention on the provision of decent employment for all, the promotion of sustainable industrialization with innovation, and the reduction of inequalities as imperative or at least desired elements of today's industrial policymaking. Furthermore, industrial policies, narrowly defined industrial policies in particular, tend to create/increase inequalities and disparities across industrial sectors, labor segments, and geographical regions of a country. This, in turn, should force policymakers to pay more attention to the "inclusiveness" of their policy initiatives.

In Chapter 1 and Chapter 2, Otsubo and Otchia introduce general views on the impact of industrialization, centering on the expansion of manufacturing on economic growth (enlargement of total value-added) and employment. With a concise but integrated literature survey and presentation of historical facts related to value-added and employment generation, Chapters 1 and 2 point to the importance of manufacturing development and more integrated and linked promotion of higher-yielding agriculture/agro-product processing and manufacturing-related services supported by technological innovation, such as ICT and IoT. This, in turn, should widen the beneficiaries of modern industrialization to various segments of sectors and workers for a more inclusive economic growth.

In Chapter 3, "The importance of manufacturing development and structural change for pro-poor growth," Haraguchi and Amann highlight the relevance of manufacturing in promoting pro-poor growth pathways of industrial development. This is done by means of carefully disaggregating and analyzing structural change patterns, taking into account various sources of heterogeneities and variations. Their analysis highlights the continued importance of manufacturing and the key role of industrial policies in the process of industrialization. Chapter 3 furthermore explores the dynamics of structural change within manufacturing and delineates a path of inclusive manufacturing development for pro-poor growth. With regard to the role of manufacturing for pro-poor growth, they offer a review of the stylized views, present long-term (1965–2017) statistics to support a positive relationship between manufacturing development and increased per capital income relative to the other countries in the world, and accumulated employment creation by key sectors in manufacturing industry. The chapter goes on to analyze the patterns of industrial structural changes for pro-poor growth by identifying key manufacturing industries which are particularly associated with pro-poor growth (higher levels of employment generation for the similar path of value-added), based on pooled cross-country data for 153 countries between 1963 and 2015. In doing so, they consistently control for differences in income levels and brackets, and thus are able to identify impacts on the lower-income groups in comparison to those in higher-income segments.

In Chapter 5, "Toward pro-poor industrial policies in Indonesia: progress, challenges, and future directions," Gunawan, Pratikto, and Dartanto address the question, "What explains the successful and unsuccessful impacts of Indonesia's industrial policies on poverty reduction?" Indonesia had accomplished three decades of remarkable industrial development since the mid-1960s that took off as trade and investment liberalization boosted foreign and domestic investments in manufacturing sectors. Indonesia's living standards had significantly improved, the incidence of poverty had significantly decreased and inequality had been maintained at a low level. However, in the aftermath of the Asian Financial Crisis that hit Indonesia's economy in 1997/1998, Indonesia began to face deindustrialization even before industrialization had matured, i.e., the issue of "premature deindustrialization." Focusing on trade orientation and protection, upstream-downstream linkages, minimum wage regulation, and transportation infrastructure, Chapter 5 aims to investigate which of Indonesia's industrial policies, or absence of particular policies, tend to be "pro-poor" or "anti-poor," and which particular set of industrial policies should be adopted and implemented by Indonesia's policymakers.

Given the fact that most of the labor force in a developing country is employed in small and medium-sized enterprises (SMEs), discussing and analyzing industrial development and industrial policies in the context of SMEs leads to the discussion of "inclusive" industrial promotion. In Chapter 7, "Promoting local SMEs through GVCs: a framework and case study of Laotian SMEs," Vidavong and Otsubo analyze the impact of local SMEs' participation in global value chains (GVCs) as the government of Laos intends to promote industry upgrading by promoting participation of their local firms in global production networks. While an extension of the GVC network would be conducive to job creation and income growth in developing countries, participation in GVCs should also bring about upgrading of supply capacity on the part of local firms. For the local SMEs that have only limited exposure to global business practices, GVC participation could provide access to new technologies, innovations, and new markets. This, in turn, should lead to improvements in productivity and competitiveness. In reality, however, the benefits for local firms are not automatically created, and proper facilitation by the state and conscious efforts by local firms to upgrade their capacities are called for. Vidavong and Otsubo's statistical analyses based on their firm-level data collected in the field surveys do not identify increases in wages supported by productivity improvements brought about by GVC participation. The results confirm, instead, the sad reality in latecomer economies in Asia where GVCs look for lower-cost labor-intensive production with a large pool of the supporting unemployed or underemployed, unskilled labor force. A traditional industrial promotion strategy that depends on the existence of abundant cheap labor and foreign investment that capitalizes on it is not only losing the room to grow, but also not offering the desired benefits to the host economies.

For readers to further understand the background of these sad realities observed in Asia's latecomer economy of Laos, Chapter 6, "Industrial policy and development in Laos: trade, industrial estates, and enterprise development" by Vixathep and Phonvisay introduces the history of industrial promotion in Lao where industrial policy has been embedded in the National Socio-Economic Development Plans (NSEDPs), which can be viewed as *de facto* industrial policy. Their chapter evaluates the contribution of industrial policy to economic development in three areas: trade liberalization, special economic zone development, and SME promotion. It also agrees that more efforts are necessary to improve capacity building for government officials and thereby enhance effective policy implementation.

In Chapter 12, "Promoting exports by the ASEAN SMEs: impediments, drivers, and conducive policies," Jitsutthiphakorn and Otsubo look at impediments, drivers, and conducive policies in internationalizing SMEs in developing countries. Access to export markets often signifies higher productivity and competitiveness, leading to firms' ability to survive. Using the World Bank Enterprise Surveys of eight countries in ASEAN, the authors introduce export experiences of these eight ASEAN countries in comparison to those of the East Asian economies, focusing on SMEs' shares in total employment, exports, and GDP. The need for higher export performance by the ASEAN SMEs is discussed. This chapter analyzes the dynamic changes in the problems faced by ASEAN firms, separately by country, by firm size, and by sector. The issue is discussed in the context of internal factors (firm characteristics, access to finance, ICT) and external factors (trade facilitation, real effective exchange rate, policies conducive to SME promotion) that may influence the export activities of SMEs. The chapter then introduces key results obtained from econometric analyses on the drivers of SMEs' export activities.

For most developing countries where resources are limited to support more balanced industrial development in either the sectoral dimension or geographical dimension, industrial policies naturally create disparities and inequalities that, in turn, can undermine the attempts at "inclusive" industrial development.

In Chapter 18, "Promoting both industrial development and regional convergence: toward a regionally inclusive industrial policy," Mendez deals with this conflict between industrial promotion and regional disparities. Industrial policy boosts economic growth through targeted interventions that affect the allocation of skilled labor, output composition, and industrial productivity growth. A commonly omitted consequence of these changes is that, depending on the initial cross-regional distribution of income, policies aiming to foster industrial development may change regional inequality in unintended ways. In this context, this chapter aims to explore the interaction between industrial development and regional divergence/convergence. The ultimate goal of this exploration is to identify possible lessons that could guide the design and implementation of "regionally inclusive" industrial policies (RIIPs). The first part of Chapter 18 revisits some key facts about industrial development and regional divergence/convergence. Next, industrial and regional interactions are evaluated through the lens of an industry-based model of regional convergence. Chapter 18 concludes by outlining some lessons that may prove helpful to the design and implementation of "regionally inclusive" industrial policies.

1.6.6 What are the dimensions of integration in designing "integrated" industrial policies?

Regarding the dimensions and levels of "integration" that we have to take into consideration when designing "integrated," not piecewise, industrial promotion policies/initiatives for multiple goals of industrial promotion, discussions so far in Chapter 1 have already presented the most important factors. First of all, we discussed the multiple/combined goals of industrial promotion under the SDGs. Industrial policy should now target not only economic growth, but also employment generation (provision of decent work for all segments in society) and human capital development (making people more productive) in an inclusive and pro-poor manner. How can a "pro-poor" impact be secured/promoted in packaging policies? How should "sustainability" be treated in line with the SDG goal of promoting sustainable industrialization and fostering innovation (Goal 9)? Multiple goals, in principle, require a combination of multiple policies/initiatives.

Second, the types of industrial policies presented in Table 1.2 can/should be combined or integrated. When types/definitions of industrial policies are combined, we can categorize tools of policy interventions to be selected or combined as Weiss's classification (Table 1.3) nicely portrayed. The efficacy of the narrow and targeted industrial policies depends on the performance of broader and general policies such as preserving a stable and investment-conducive macro-economic environment.

As the integration of old and new models of industrial policies, above we discussed the importance of the public-private partnership (PPP) in industrial promotion both in national policies and in international development cooperation. How should we view the "new PPP" as a coordination model of innovation, productivity, and international cooperation? How should "integrated" policies deal with coordination failure, market failure, and government (governance) failure?

Questions addressed in Section 1.6.1 and Section 1.6.2 point to the need to integrate certain segments of service (such as manufacturing-related services, transportation/logistics) and agriculture (such as agro-production and processing) into "industry" when we discuss industrial promotion. Advances in ICT and IoT that are highly desired for the future of manufacturing require strong support from the service sectors.

As we try to promote industries in developing countries in today's globalized world with the active extension of production and service networks of MNCs and GVCs, border policies (such as trade, investment, exchange rate policies) and domestic policies should be integrated. On the domestic front, goods/service market policies and policies that work on factor (capital and labor) markets should also be integrated.

Although the list of dimensions of integration seems endless, this book, in addition to the aforementioned elements of integration, also tries to shed some light on the following new dimensions.

1.6.6.1 Regional Comprehensive Economic Partnerships (RCEPs)

One new dimension of integration in designing industrial policy is related to the recent surge in super-national regional arrangements, such as the ASEAN Economic Community (AEC) in Asia and the reinforced Africa Union (AU) in Africa. Particularly when they take a form of Regional Comprehensive Economic Partnerships (RCEPs), industrial policies may well be coordinated together with coordination in trade and investment policies. In this sense, integrated designs of national and super-national regional industrial promotion policies are called for.

In Chapter 8, "The role of Thailand's industrial promotion in ASEAN," Amonvatana asserts that, as the ASEAN Economic Community (AEC) is now fully effective, the Thai government is obliged to help increase the region's competitiveness. Although the AEC Blueprint has attracted attention from researchers and policymakers, much attention has been placed on the impact on individual countries of this AEC Blueprint. For Thailand, economic growth is one clear positive result from the region's economic integration. Empirical studies also suggest a positive impact of poverty reduction in relation to this accelerated economic growth. However, what has been questionable is the relationship between economic growth and income disparity, especially between Bangkok and other regions. More importantly, what has been understudied is the impact of the industrial policy of particular countries on the growth and development of ASEAN as a whole. Taking into account the existing literature, this chapter looks at two levels of Thailand's industrial policies. First, it aims to analyze whether the policies that the Thai government adopted have helped to close the poverty gap or have instead created a wider gap and worsened Thailand's regional disparities. Second, it aims at examining whether the policies initiated by the Thai government have promoted regional growth and development for the AEC.

In Chapter 17, "Taking part in RCEP: CGE analysis focusing on industrial impact," Itakura conducts policy simulations in order to analyze the impacts of RCEPs and GVCs on the member economies' industrial development, using computable general equilibrium (CGE) models. CGE models are based on inter-industry input-output data, and therefore, are considered to be useful tools for industrial policy simulations. After all, most of the industrial policies aim to create industrial structural changes, often in favor of targeted sectors, by impacting the inter-industry (productive) resource flows. Multi-sector and multi-country models can also ensure macro-economic consistency, such as balancing investment and savings in a national and/or world/regional context. They are also suitable to evaluate the impacts of industrial promotion with international initiatives under the globalizing world economy. This chapter considers taking part in a mega-regional trade agreement (MRTA) as an industrial policy one country can adopt for industrial development. It takes the Regional Comprehensive Economic Partnership (RCEP) as a policy scenario for a CGE simulation. While some industries expand in the RCEP, other industries contract because of resource constraints. Three features in simulating RCEP are: (1) accommodation of GVCs; (2) liberalization of trade in goods and services; and (3) investment measures.

1.6.6.2 The service-tourism "industry"

Another dimension of integration is to include the designs of industrial promotion for the economies where manufacturing industries may not have many chances to grow into a key engine of development. In Chapter 10, "The process of change in the economic development model of the Pacific Island Countries under the influence of globalization," Umemura introduces a development model of the Service-Tourism "industry" for Small Island Developing States (SIDS) in the Pacific region. This is a good example of promoting non-manufacturing industry as industry to make it an engine of growth and inclusive development.

Although the Pacific SIDS achieved independence after WWII, economic development was initiated by the production of commodities under colonization and a subsistence economy. The main feature of the Pacific SIDS is the so-called "MIRAB" (Migration (MI), Remittance (R), Foreign Aid (A), and Public Bureaucracy (B)). These countries were affected by their small domestic markets and populations, and their remoteness from continents or developed countries. The MIRAB model has been developed into the "TOURAB" (Tourism (TOU), Remittance (R), Foreign Aid (A), and the Public Bureaucracy (B)) model and the "SITES" (Small Island Tourists Economies) model. In this chapter, economic development models of the Pacific SIDS are examined in three periods: (1) postwar independence; (2) the first wave of globalization in the 1990s when international trade had grown at a much faster pace than before; and (3) the second stage of globalization during the 2000s onward when international tourism had expanded. These changes in the international economic environment have affected the development policies and management of industrial promotion in the Pacific SIDS.

1.6.6.3 The presence of China

In the context of today's developing countries in Africa, and the same is true of Asia's latecomer economies, integrating the ever-increasing presence of China in their economies into their designs of industrial policies has become one crucial part of policymaking. In Chapter 15, "Is China's growing interest in Africa a blessing or curse for the continent's industrialization drive?," Osei-Assibey addresses this issue from the macro-economic viewpoint. He investigates the effect of increasing Chinese engagements in Africa on value-added manufacturing and industrial growth in Africa. More specifically, Chapter 15 investigates, first, the effects of China's investments, trade, loans, and financing of infrastructure in Africa on the manufacturing and on overall industrial sector growth in Africa. Second, it examines the potency or effectiveness of Chinese activities on industries within a differing enabling policy and institutional context (such as political stability, government effectiveness, control of corruption, or rule of law). Using data from 40 African countries that spans from 2003 to 2016 and applying an Autoregressive Distributed Lag model and a Pooled Mean Group estimator, the study reveals a range of interesting findings. The study finds generally that Chinese activities such as exports, FDI, and infrastructure contracts in Africa have had a positive impact on industry growth but only in the short run. In the long run, however, Chinese activities have a negative influence on manufacturing and industry GDP growth. Further, the negative impact becomes more pronounced in the context of weak institutions, such as government effectiveness and corruption. These findings suggest that without a stronger institutional and governance framework, Africa cannot benefit from China's growing influence on the continent.

In Chapter 14, "Local and Chinese-invested SMEs' contribution to industrial development through knowledge spillovers in Africa: the case of Tanzania," Maswana and Munisi address this issue from the micro-economic viewpoint. While spillover effects generated by the presence of large foreign firms have been well documented in the literature, little is known of the case of spillovers associated with small foreign-owned or returnee-migrant-owned enterprises in developing countries. Focusing on these two unaddressed aspects and based on a case-study approach, the authors outlined interviews of SMEs in Tanzania and examined their technology spillover mechanisms from the perspective of industrial development. Major findings indicate that, for the most part, entrepreneurs have little or no knowledge of how to upgrade the technical capabilities of their firms, and many of them end up with failed businesses that could have been profitable. Moreover, the lack of interactions with their counterparts owned by Tanzanian returnee migrants and Chinese-invested enterprises seems to have been hindering their opportunities for technology absorption and upgrading. For this reason, the presence of foreign- and returnee-owned firms might not be helping in the technology upgrading of SMEs. Therefore, policy priority should focus on overcoming some of the identified limitations of SMEs, such as through identification of their technological needs and strengthening their exchange of information through networking. There is a need for a platform of knowledge-sharing for entrepreneurs so that they can better manage the accumulation of technical knowledge. Therefore, similar to the macro-analyses in Chapter 15, firm-level micro-analyses in Chapter 14 also point to the need for capacity building on the part of the state to act as coordinators/facilitators of desired exchanges between local firms and foreign-invested (Chinese-invested) firms.

1.6.7 How can we properly assess the efficacy of industrial policies for evidence-based policymaking?

Evaluation of the causal effects of industrial policy on a selected outcome variable consists of assessing the difference between the value of the outcome variable after the policy has been implemented (or simulated) and the value of the outcome variable in the absence of the policy. Another possible method is to relate changes in the value of the industrial policy instrument with those of the outcome variables. However, the practice in the field has been to pick a successful case (or failure), demonstrate that a deliberate government policy existed, and make the case for (or against) the use of industrial policy (Haggard, 2015). Gathering sufficient empirical evidence on the causal effect of the industrial policy has been a key impediment in the debate on industrial policies. According to Rodrik (2008a), pro-industrial policies tend to select case studies where industrial policies worked to back up their argument whereas anti-industrial policies tend to make use of cross-industry econometrics. But at the end of the day, the empirical analyses leave us no better informed than when we started.

Leaving this discussion aside, the empirical assessment of industrial policy faces several unique challenges. The main challenge so far has been the difficulty in finding a credible counterfactual and the timing for the effect of the policy to materialize. Finding a credible counterfactual consists of finding a situation that we would observe, had the policy not been implemented. For instance, an ideal counterfactual to evaluate the impact of a government policy on infrastructure upgrading would be to compare what happened to firms who benefited from the infrastructure against what would have happened to them in the absence of the infrastructure. The results from such exercises will most likely depend on the nature of the data and the outcome variable(s), as well as the timing for the effect to materialize. For example, infrastructure development is likely to produce sizable effects many years after the completion of the project when income is used as the outcome variable. The effect can also vary when we compare the benefits for direct beneficiaries versus benefits for the region as a whole.

Even though the effects of industrial policy are likely to vary, three techniques have been widely used in the empirical evaluation or assessment of industrial policy, either ex-ante or ex-post. The most popular methods include control case studies, cross-firm regressions (cross-firm, cross-sector, cross-country, and their panel studies), and structural models (including input-output, econometric, and computable general equilibrium models). In this book, we offer piecewise and combined applications of those methods of assessment. The recent Nobel Economics Prize awarded to Professor Abijit Banerjee, Professor Esther Duflo, and Professor Michael Kremer jointly for their use of randomized controlled trials (RCTs) in the analyses of micro-policies/initiatives on micro-poverty outcomes heightened our expectation of a leapfrog advance in the assessment of industrial policies. However, even if we succeed in proving a causational relationship between a certain piece of industrial policy and a certain outcome variable such as increased profits or survivability of local firms, we still have to keep in mind that the multifaceted targets of industrial policies that we discussed here would still require tools to assess the superiority of designing and implementing more combined and integrated policies to work on multiple goals, such as growth and inclusiveness at the same time. How can/should we assess the efficacy of integrated (or coordinated) industrial policies in various dimensions against piecewise (uncoordinated) ones in order for us to avoid the "fallacy of composition" in designing integrated industrial policies for inclusive growth in today's globalized world?

Notes

1 Refer to the United Nations Resolution A/RES/70/1 of 25 September 2015, *Transforming Our World: The 2030 Agenda for Sustainable Development*. Official SDGs website available at: www.un.org/sustainabledevelopment/.

2 The MDGs period was from 2000 to 2015, but used 1990 as the reference year for goal settings. For the official account of the MDG results, visit the official MDGs website at: www.un.org/millenniumgoals/bkgd.shtml.

3 One can recall the Arab Spring of 2010–2012 that stormed North Africa and the Middle East regions. The lack of job creation that introduces young entrants to job markets was (and still is) considered to be a key trigger.

4 Asian Tigers, or the four Asian Tigers, refers to Hong Kong, Singapore, South Korea, and Taiwan.

5 OECD countries renewed industrial policies mainly as a direct response to 2008 economic and financial crisis (OECD, 2013). However, there is a growing discussion on industrial policy for industrialized countries, which can be understood as a strategy to promote "high-road competitiveness." In this context, industrial policy is expected to combine strategic policy in the field of advanced skills, innovations, supporting institutions, ecological ambition, and an active social policy to achieve "Beyond-GDP" Goals (Aiginger, 2015).

6 See, for example, Chang (1994), Peres and Primi (2009), and Di Maio (2014).

7 See, for example, Newman and Page (2017) for a recent discussion on industrial clusters in Africa.

8 Lall (2004) notes that the distinction between functional and selective industrial policy is not easy in practice.

9 Pareto efficiency refers to a state where resources cannot be further reallocated to improve one party's welfare without causing damage to the other party. It is a

notion of market efficiency. However, it does not guarantee equitable allocation of resources.

10 Studies on market imperfection include Acemoglu and Verdier (2000), Dustmann and Schönberg (2012), Krueger (1990), and Wasmer and Weil (2004).

11 For detailed theoretical arguments in favor of industrial policy, see Pack and Saggi (2006), Rodrik (2008a), and Lall (2004).

12 This group of 75 countries includes developed economies such as Australia and Iceland. In their study, 154 sample countries are divided into 34 high-core countries with exportation of "good products," another 28 high-core countries in the "middle products" trap, 17 low-core countries in the "middle products" trap, and the aforementioned 75 low-core countries in the "low products" trap.

13 Haraguchi and Amann (the UNIDO team) discuss the importance of manufacturing development and structural change for pro-poor growth in Chapter 3. For further reading on the role of manufacturing, see Amable (2000), Peneder (2003), Rodrik (2013), Szirmai (2012), and UNIDO and UNU-MERIT (2012).

14 Unfortunately, reliable cross-country data on manufacturing employment is not yet available. Observation years are chosen encompassing three recent decades and avoiding years affected by financial crises such as the Asian Financial Crisis and the Global Financial Crisis. Three-year averages are used.

15 Earlier, Ghani and O'Connell (2014) also found a similar changing pattern for three decades (the late 1980s, the late 1990s, and the late 2000s).

16 GDP value-added sectors have traditionally been trisected into Agriculture, Industry, and Service sectors. Industry is further split into Manufacturing and Non-Manufacturing industries. Non-Manufacturing industry normally includes Mining and Quarrying, and Public Utilities (electricity, gas, water supply). Although some earlier studies also included Construction in the Non-Manufacturing industry, it is included in the Service sector in this book. The coverage of economic activities of each subsector follows that of the United Nations International Standard Industrial Classification of All Economic Activities (ISIC), Rev. 4.

17 Conversely, the service sector has contributed to growth and employment in India, and has been playing an important role in Brazil and South Africa.

18 Analogous to the Asian Tigers, the term, "African Lions" has been used in the Africa Rising narrative, but unlike the Asian Tigers, African Lions do not refer to a specific group of countries.

19 The report by IDE-JETRO and World Trade Organization (2011) provides a clear picture of the trade patterns and GVCs in the East Asia region.

20 See Alvarez (2013), Herzberg and Sisombat (2016), and Devlin (2014) for a discussion of public-private collaboration. In Chapter 16, Ohno and Uesu discuss the new partnership between business and development in a PPP context, taking a case study from Ethiopia's industrial development.

21 For a recent detailed discussion, see UNECA (2016). Also, the issue of "policy space" for developing countries in their fight against poverty and inequality was actively discussed at the World Economic Forum 2016 in Davos, Switzerland.

22 Initially, this book planned to include a chapter by a WTO team in the subject area of policy space and the proper understanding of the global trading rules for developing countries. Heightened political tension due to the US-China trade disputes during 2018–2020, however, made it difficult for us to obtain a completed manuscript. WTO, however, offers online information sources and training courses for policymakers to aid proper understanding of their rules.

References

Acemoglu, D., & Verdier, T. (2000). The choice between market failures and corruption. *American Economic Review*, 90(1), 194–211.

ACET. (2014). *2004 African transformation report: Growth with depth*. Accra, Ghana: The African Center for Economic Transformation.

Aggarwal, V. K., & Evenett, S. J. (2014). Do WTO rules preclude industrial policy? Evidence from the global economic crisis. *Business and Politics*, 16(4), 481–509.

Agosin, M. R. (2007). Export diversification and growth in emerging economies. Working Paper No. 233. Department of Economics, University of Chile.

Ahn, S., Hall, B. H., & Lee, K. (2014). *Intellectual property for economic development*. Cheltenham: Edward Elgar Publishing.

Aiginger, K. (2015). Industrial policy for a sustainable growth path. In D. Bailey, K. Cowling, & P. Tomlinson (Eds.), *New perspectives on industrial policy for a modern Britain*. Oxford Scholarship, Online.

Altenburg, T. (2011). Industrial policy in developing countries: Overview and lessons from seven country cases. Discussion paper no. 4/2011. Bonn: German Development Institute.

Altenburg, T. (2013). Can industrial policy work under neopatrimonial rule? In A. Szirmai, W. Naudé, & L. Alcorta (Eds.), *Pathways to industrialization in the twenty-first century: New challenges and emerging paradigms*. Oxford: Oxford University Press.

Alvarez, C. V. (2013). Comments on "What's New in the New Industrial Policy in Latin America?" by Robert Devlin and Graciela Moguillansky. In J. E. Stiglitz & J. Y. Lin (Eds.), *The industrial policy revolution I: The role of government beyond ideology* (pp. 318–323). London: Palgrave Macmillan.

Amable, B. (2000). International specialisation and growth. *Structural Change and Economic Dynamics*, 11, 413–431.

Americo, B. Z., & Fredriksson, T. (2007). *Elimination of TRIMs: The experience of selected developing countries*. Geneva: United Nations.

Amin Guitierrez de Pineres, S., & Ferrantino, M. J. (2000). *Export dynamics and economic growth in Latin America*. Burlington, VT: Ashgate Publishing Ltd.

Anderson, K., & Strutt, A. (2014). Emerging economies, productivity growth and trade with resource-rich economies by 2030. *Australian Journal of Agricultural and Resource Economics*, 58(4), 590–606.

Chang, H.-J. (1994). *The political economy of industrial policy*. New York: St. Martin's Press.

Chang, H.-J. (2003). *Kicking away the ladder: Development strategy in historical perspective*. London: Anthem Press.

Chang, H.-J. (2010). Hamlet without the Prince of Denmark: How development has disappeared from today's 'development' discourse. In S. R. Khan & J. Christiansen (Eds.), *Towards new developmentalism: Markets as means rather than master*. Abingdon: Routledge.

Chang, H.-J., Andreoni, A., & Kuan, M. L. (2014). Productive capabilities transformation: Institutions, linkages and policies for manufacturing growth and employment. Background paper for World of Work Report, 2014— Developing with Jobs. Geneva: ILO.

Chang, J.-M. (2015). The Republic of Korea's financial support for small and medium-sized enterprises and venture businesses. In J. Felipe (Ed.), *Development and modern industrial policy in practice: Issues and country experiences* (pp. 247–278). Cheltenham: Edward Elgar Publishing.

Chenery, H., Robinson, S., & Syrquin, M. (1986). Structural transformation. In H. Chenery, S. Robinson, & M. Syrquin (Eds.), *Industrialization and growth: A comparative study*. New York: Oxford University Press.

Cimoli, M., Dosi, G., & Stiglitz, J. E. (2009). *Industrial policy and development: The political economy of capabilities accumulation*. Oxford: Oxford University Press.

Correa, C. M. (1999). Review of the Trips Agreement. *The Journal of World Intellectual Property*, 2(6), 939–960.

Crespi, G., Fernández-Arias, E., & Stein, E. (2014). *Rethinking productive development: Sound policies and institutions for economic transformation*. Washington, DC: Inter-American Development Bank.

Dadush, U. (2015). Is manufacturing still a key to growth? OCP Policy Paper No. 15/07. OCP Policy Center.

Devlin, R. (2014). Towards good governance of public-private alliance councils supporting industrial policies in Latin America. IDB Technical Note No. 615. Washington, DC.: Inter-American Development Bank.

Devlin, R., & Moguillansky, G. (2013). What's new in the new industrial policy in Latin America? In J. E. Stiglitz & J. Y. Lin (Eds.), *The industrial policy revolution I: The role of government beyond ideology* (pp. 276–317). London: Palgrave Macmillan.

Di Maio, M. (2014). Industrial policy. In B. Currie-Alder, R. Kanbur, D. M. Malone, & R. Medhora (Eds.), *International development: Ideas, experience, and prospects*. Oxford Scholarship Online.

Dustmann, C., & Schönberg, U. (2012). What makes firm-based vocational training schemes successful? The role of commitment. *American Economic Journal: Applied Economics*, 4(2), 36–61.

ESCAP. (2011). Sustaining recovery and dynamism for inclusive development: Connectivity in the region and productive capacity in least developed countries. Economic and Social Survey of Asia and the Pacific Bangkok: United Nations Economic and Social Commission for Asia and the Pacific.

Evans, P. (1995). *Embedded autonomy: States and industrial transformation*. Princeton, NJ: Princeton University Press.

Felipe, J., Kumar, U., & Abdon, A. (2010). How rich countries became rich and why poor countries remain poor: It's the economic structure … Duh! Working Paper No. 644. The Levy Economics Institute.

Felipe, J., Kumar, U., Abdon, A., & Bacate, M. (2012). Product complexity and economic development. *Structural Change and Economic Dynamics*, 23(1), 36–68.

Felipe, J., Kumar, U., Usui, N., & Abdon, A. (2013). Why has China succeeded? And why it will continue to do so. *Cambridge Journal of Economics*, 37, 791–818.

Felipe, J., León-Ledesma, M., Lanzafame, M., & Estrada, G. (2009). Sectoral engines of growth in developing Asia: Stylized facts and implications. *Malaysian Journal of Economic Studies*, 46(2), 107–133.

Felipe, J., Mehta, A., & Rhee, C. (2014). Manufacturing matters … but it's the jobs that count. ADB Economics Working Paper Series No. 420. Manila: Asian Development Bank.

Ferraz, J. C., Kupfer, D., & Marques, F. S. (2014). Industrial policy as an effective development tool: Lessons from Brazil. In J. M. Salazar-Xirinachs, I. Nübler, & R. Kozul-Wright (Eds.), *Transforming economies: Making industrial policy work for growth, jobs and development*. Geneva: International Labour Office.

Gabriele, A. (2010). The role of the state in China's industrial development: A reassessment. *Comparative Economic Studies*, 52(3), 325–350.

Gallagher, K. P. (2005). *Putting development first: The importance of policy space in the WTO and international financial institutions*. London: Zed Books.

Ghani, E., & O'Connell, S. D. (2014). Can service be a growth escalator in low income countries? Policy Research Working Paper, No. 6971. Washington, DC: The World Bank.

Gibbs, M. (2007). *Trade policy national development strategies: Policy notes*. New York: United Nations Department of Economic and Social Affairs

Greenwald, B. C., & Stiglitz, J. E. (1986). Externalities in economies with imperfect information and incomplete markets. *The Quarterly Journal of Economics*, 101(2), 229–264.

Greenwald, B. C., & Stiglitz, J. E. (2013). Learning and industrial policy: Implications for Africa. In J. Esteban, J. E. Stiglitz, & J. Y. Lin (Eds.), *The industrial policy revolution II: Africa in the 21st century* (pp. 25–49). Houndmills: Palgrave Macmillan.

Guadagno, F. (2015). Industrial policies in lower-middle-income countries. The E15 Expert Group on Reinvigorating Manufacturing. Geneva: International Centre for Trade and Sustainable Development (ICTSD).

Günther, T., & Alcorta, L. (2011). Industrial policy for prosperity: Reasoning and approach. Development Policy, Statistics and Research Branch Working Paper 02/2011. Vienna: UNIDO.

Haggard, S. (2015). The developmental state is dead: Long live the developmental state! In J. Mahoney & K. Thelen (Eds.), *Advances in comparative-historical Analysis*. Cambridge: Cambridge University Press.

Hallward-Driemeier, M., & Nayyar, G. (2018). *Trouble in the making? The future of manufacturing-led development*. Washington, DC: World Bank Group.

Hausmann, R., & Hidalgo, C. A. (2011). *The atlas of economic complexity: Mapping paths to prosperity*. Cambridge, MA: MIT Press.

Hausmann, R., Hwang, J., & Rodrik, D. (2007). What you export matters. *Journal of Economic Growth*, 12(1). 1–25.

Hausmann, R., & Klinger, B. (2006). Structural transformation and patterns of comparative advantage in the product space. Working Paper No. 128. Center for International Development, Harvard University.

Hausmann, R., & Rodrik, D. (2003). Economic development as self discovery. *Journal of Development Economics*, 72(2), 603–633.

Herzberg, B., & Sisombat, L. (2016). *State of play: Public-private dialogue*. Washington, DC: World Bank Group.

Herzer, D., & Nowak-Lehmann, F. D. (2006). What does export diversification do for growth? An econometric analysis. *Applied Economics*, 38, 1825–1838.

Hirschman, A. O. (1958). *The strategy of economic development*. New Haven, CT: Yale University Press.

IDE-JETRO, & World Trade Organization. (2011). *Trade patterns and global value chains in East Asia: From trade in goods to trade in tasks*. Geneva: World Trade Organization.

ILO. (2014). *Global employment trends 2014: Risk of a jobless recovery?* Geneva: ILO.

Kaldor, N. (1966). *Causes of the slow rate of growth of the United Kingdom: An inaugural lecture*. Cambridge: Cambridge University Press.

Khan, S. R. (2007). WTO, IMF and the closing of development policy space for low-income countries: A call for neo-developmentalism. *Third World Quarterly*, 28(6), 1073–1090.

Krueger, A. O. (1990). Government failures in development. *Journal of Economic Perspectives*, 4(3), 9–23.

Krueger, A. O. (1997). Trade policy and economic development: How we lean? *American Economic Review*, 87(1), 1–22.

Lall, S. (2004). Selective industrial and trade policies in developing countries: Theoretical and empirical issues. In C. Soludo, O. Ogbu, & H.-J. Chang (Eds.), *The politics of trade and industrial policy in Africa: Forced consensus?* New Jersey: Africa World Press & IDRC.

Lederman, D., & Maloney, W. F. (2007). *Natural resources: Neither curse nor destiny.* Washington, DC: The World Bank.

Lin, J. Y. (2012). *New structural economics: A framework for rethinking development and policy.* Washington, DC: The World Bank.

Lin, J., & Chang, H.-J. (2009). Should industrial policy in developing countries conform to comparative advantage or defy it? *Development Policy Review*, 27(5), 483–502.

Lin, J. Y., & Monga, C. (2010). Growth identification and facilitation: The role of the state in the dynamics of structural change. Policy Research Working Paper, No. 5313. Washington, DC: The World Bank.

Lin, J. Y., & Treichel, V. (2012). Learning from China's rise to escape the middle-income trap: A new structural economics approach to Latin America. Policy Research Working Paper No. 6165. Washington, DC: The World Bank.

Lo, D., & Wu, M. (2014). The state and industrial policy in Chinese economic development. In J. M. Salazar-Xirinachs, I. Nübler, & R. Kozul-Wright (Eds.), *Transforming economies: Making industrial policy work for growth, jobs and development.* Geneva: International Labour Office.

Manyika, J., Sinclair, J., Dobbs, R., Strube, G., Rassey, L., Mischke, J., ... Ramaswamy, S. (2012). *Manufacturing the future: The next era of global growth and innovation.* New York: The McKinsey Global Institute.

Masuyama, S., Vandenbrink, D., & Yue, C. S. (1997). *Industrial policies in East Asia.* Tokyo: Nomura Research Institute.

McMillan, M. S., & Harttgen, K. (2014). What is driving the 'African Growth Miracle'? Working Paper No. 20077. Cambridge, MA: National Bureau of Economic Research.

McMillan, M. S., & Rodrik, D. (2011). Globalization, structural change and productivity growth. Working Paper No. 17143. Cambridge, MA: National Bureau of Economic Research.

McMillan, M. S., Rodrik, D., & Verduzco-Gallo, Í. (2014). Globalization, structural change, and productivity growth, with an update on Africa. *World Development*, 63(0), 11–32.

Mihretu, M., & Eyob, T. T. (2015). ETHIOPIA: Ethiopian Public Private Consultative Forum (EPPCF). In Public-Private Dialogue 2015 Workshop, Copenhagen, Denmark.

Mishra, S., Lundstrom, S., & Anand, R. (2011). Service export sophistication and economic growth. Policy Research Working Paper No. 5606. Washington, DC: The World Bank.

Natsuda, K., & Thoburn, J. (2014). How much policy space still exists under the WTO? A comparative study of the automotive industry in Thailand and Malaysia. *Review of International Political Economy*, 21(6), 1346–1377.

Newman, C., & Page, J. (2017). Industrial clusters: The case for Special Economic Zones in Africa. WIDER Working Paper No. 2017/15. Helsinki: UNU-WIDER.

OECD. (2013). *Perspectives on global development 2013: Industrial policies in a changing world.* Paris: OECD Publishing.

Ohno, K. (2013). *Learning to industrialize: From given growth to policy-aided value creation.* London: Routledge-GRIPS Development Forum Studies.

Otsubo, S. (2009). *Globalization to Kaihatsu.* Tokyo: Keisoshobo.

Otsubo, S. (2016). *Globalization and development,* vol. I: *Leading issues in development with globalization.* London: Routledge.

Pack, H., & Saggi, K. (2006). Is there a case for industrial policy? A critical survey. *World Bank Research Observer,* 21(2), 267–297.

Page, J. (2012). Can Africa industrialise? *Journal of African Economies,* 21(suppl. 2), 86–124.

Peneder, M. (2003). Industrial structure and aggregate growth. *Structural Change and Economic Dynamics,* 14, 427–448.

Peres, W., & Primi, A. (2009). Theory and practice of industrial policy: Evidence from the Latin American experience. Productive Development Series 187 (LC/L.3013-P). Santiago, Chile: Economic Commission for Latin America and the Caribbean,.

Rodrik, D. (1995). Getting interventions right: How South Korea and Taiwan grew rich. *Economic Policy,* 10(20), 53–107.

Rodrik, D. (1996). Coordination failures and government policy: A model with applications to East Asia and Eastern Europe. *Journal of International Economics,* 40(1–2), 1–22.

Rodrik, D. (2004). Industrial policy for the twenty-first century. Paper prepared for UNIDO. Boston, MA: Harvard University.

Rodrik, D. (2008a). Normalizing industrial policy. Commission on Growth and Development. Working Paper No. 3. Washington, DC: World Bank.

Rodrik, D. (2008b). *One economics, many recipes: Globalization, institutions, and economic growth.* Princeton, NJ: Princeton University Press.

Rodrik, D. (2013). Unconditional convergence in manufacturing. *Quarterly Journal of Economics,* 128, 165–204).

Salazar-Xirinachs, J. M., Nübler, I., & Kozul-Wright, R. (2014). Transforming economies: Making industrial policy work for growth, jobs and development. Geneva: International Labour Office.

Shadlen, K. (2005). Policy space for development in the WTO and beyond: The case of intellectual property rights. Working Paper No. 05-06. Global Development and Environment Institute.

Stiglitz, J. E., & Monga, C. (2013). Introduction: The rejuvenation of industrial policy. In J. E. Stiglitz & J. Y. Lin (Eds.), *The industrial policy revolution. I. The role of government beyond ideology.* London: Palgrave Macmillan.

Szirmai, A. (2012). Industrialisation as an engine of growth in developing countries, 1950–2005. *Structural Change and Economic Dynamics,* 23(4), 406–420.

UNDP. (2005). *Human development report 2005.* New York: United Nations Development Programme.

UNECA (United Nations Economic Commission for Africa). (2014). Dynamic industrial policy in Africa: Innovative institutions effective processes and flexible mechanisms. ECA Policy Brief No. 011. Available at: http://repository.uneca.org/handle/10855/22765

UNECA. (2016). *Transformative industrial policy for Africa.* Addis Ababa, Ethiopia: Economic Commission for Africa.

UNECA, & AU. (2014). Dynamic industrial policy in Africa: Economic report on Africa. Addis Ababa, Ethiopia: UNECA. Available at: www.uneca.org/publications/economic-report-africa-2014

UNIDO. (2013). Sustaining employment growth: The role of manufacturing and structural change. Industrial Development Report 2013. Vienna: UNIDO.

UNIDO, & UNU-MERIT. (2012). *Structural change, poverty reduction and industrial policy in the BRICS*. Vienna: UNIDO.

Wade, R. H. (2003). What strategies are viable for developing countries today? The World Trade Organization and the shrinking of 'development space'. *Review of International Political Economy*, 10(4), 621–644.

Wade, R. H (2004). *Governing the market: Economic theory and the role of government in East Asian industrialization* (2nd ed.). Princeton, NJ: Princeton University Press.

Wasmer, E., & Weil, P. (2004). The macroeconomics of labor and credit market imperfections. *American Economic Review*, 94(4), 944–963.

Weiss, J. (2016). Industrial policy: Back on the agenda In J. Weiss & M. Tribe (Eds.), *Routledge handbook of industry and development* (pp. 135–150). New York: Routledge.

World Bank. (1993). *East Asian miracle*. Washington, DC: The World Bank.

2 The state of global manufacturing and risks of deindustrialization in the developing world

Christian Samen Otchia and Shigeru Thomas Otsubo

2.1 Introduction

Two of the most important developments in the global economy in recent decades have been the rapid integration of many poorer countries into global value chains (GVCs) and the rapid growth of automation. These unprecedented changes are forcefully pointed out by Baldwin (2019), who refers to the combined phenomena as "globotics." Alongside these developments are three striking and unprecedented global trends: (1) the emergence of new manufacturers in the highly concentrated group of manufacturing production; (2) significant deindustrialization, with developing countries losing industrialization opportunities at much lower levels of income, against large and persistent increases in high-value-added manufacturing production and export in developed countries; and (3) the growing importance of "industries without smokestacks."

For a variety of reasons, including the perception that industrial policy plays an important role in enhancing structural change and economic development, these global patterns have stirred up intense discussion among both policymakers and academics. This debate can broadly be summarized as a dispute between leapfrogging manufacturing and promoting industries without smokestacks as deindustrialization has occurred in many countries. In principle, and as discussed in Chapter 1, manufacturing has been the key to economic development. Nevertheless, the data seems to point to the changing role of manufacturing, especially in recent decades. As illustrated in panel (a) of Figure 2.1, global manufacturing employment generally followed an upward trend but remained below non-manufacturing employment until 2008 when non-manufacturing employment began to decelerate. Panel (b) furthermore shows that both global manufacturing value-added and non-manufacturing value-added have moved upward at a similar rate, but the growth rate of manufacturing value-added decelerated after 2008. The recent changes in the pace of manufacturing employment and value-added are even more dramatic when contrasted with the level of economic development. Using this metric, value-added and employment in manufacturing in many developing countries started to decrease prematurely at a lower level of GDP per capita before reaching the peak that is character-istic of early industrializers.[1] How has the trend of premature deindustrialization

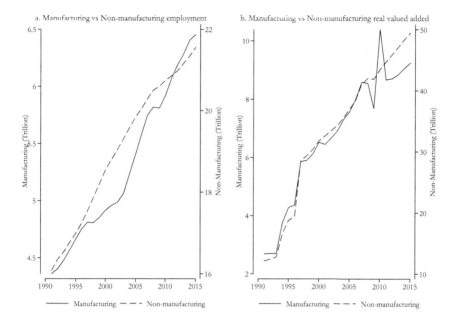

Figure 2.1 World manufacturing employment and real value-added

emerged in many parts of the developing world? How have the changing shares of manufacturing in total value-added, total employment, and international trade been associated with international income convergence/divergence? With the rapid technological upgrading and extension of GVCs for manufacturing, are there any spaces where developing countries can find a niche for manufacturing activities?

In this chapter, we provide an overview of the changing state of global manufacturing and manufacturing-related services as a first step toward answering these questions. We then present new empirical evidence on patterns in industrialization and structural change. In order to document these patterns, we exploit a variety of datasets on value-added and employment by income groups and geographical regions.[2] The choice of the database is dictated by the level of geographical coverage and the time dimension necessary for the analysis. Particularly useful data is provided by the World Development Indicators (WDI) from the World Bank, the UNSTAT National Accounts—Analysis of Main Aggregates (NAAMA),[3] the Groningen Growth and Development Center (GGDC) 10-Sector Database (Timmer, de Vries, & de Vries, 2015), the UNIDO Competitive Industrial Performance Database,[4] and the ILOSTAT Database.[5] For historical analyses, we use data from Mitchell (2007). This is a well-known international historical database that has been widely used for comparisons across both time and geography. We include data starting in 1780 extending through 2005.

The rest of this chapter is organized as follows. In Section 2.2, we present the changing state of global manufacturing, discuss the unconditional convergence in manufacturing and how focusing on medium and high-tech manufacturing can spur reindustrialization. In Section 2.3, we present evidence from a time series test of the patterns of industrialization, and document new findings on deindustrialization. Section 2.4 examines structural transformation and its potential effect on premature deindustrialization. Section 2.5 presents new evidence on servicification. Concluding remarks follow.

2.2 State of global manufacturing

The main aim of this section is to document changes in manufacturing by income groups and geographical regions. We mainly use per capita manufacturing value-added (MVA), that is, the total manufacturing value-added adjusted by the country's population, as our indicator for measuring progress in industrialization. The advantage of using this indicator is that it focuses on production, essentially the addition of value by manufacturing firms on their primary inputs.[6]

2.2.1 Heterogeneity in manufacturing growth

Traditionally, the manufacturing sector has been the engine of the economy in many countries. As discussed in Chapter 1, rapid and sustained economic growth has been strongly correlated with the expansion of manufacturing and the reallo-cation of resources to more productive activities. The key feature is that activ-ities in this sector have a high capacity for productivity growth, externalities, and increasing returns to scale. Indeed, manufacturing has faster productivity growth than services and agriculture, pays the highest wages, and has strong spillovers (backward and forward linkages) to other sectors. This means that rapid growth in the manufacturing sector promotes productivity growth in other sectors of the economy and, as a result, leads to stronger economic growth. For resource-based economies whose exports depend on commodities, diversification of the export structure from primary commodities to manufacturing has been a key policy to strengthen resilience to external shocks and sustain growth. Table 2.1 illustrates this strong correlation between the expansion of world MVA and rapid economic growth, particularly evident before the 2010s. The per capita MVA growth in the last three decades is virtually identical to average per capita growth.

There is less consensus, however, on what the reasons for these correlations are. Many authors, including the editors of this book, put forward the argu-ment that coordinated measures to promote and facilitate industrial upgrading and diversification have led countries to attain higher levels of development. Nonetheless, it is agreed that there are varying patterns of manufacturing growth across countries and across different periods. This is again illustrated in Table 2.1, but perhaps better visualized in Figure 2.2. Focusing on the geographical regions, East Asia and Pacific (EAP) and Europe and Central Asia (ECA) show remarkable improvements in per capita MVA while North America fell behind. In particular,

Table 2.1 Recent trends in global manufacturing output

	GDP per capita growth (annual %)			Per capita manufacturing valued added growth			Manufacturing, value-added (% of GDP)			Industrialization intensity index		
	1990s	2000s	2010s	1990s	2000s	2010s	1990s	2000s	2010s	1990s	2000s	2010s
Geographical region												
East Asia & the Pacific	2.2	3.0	2.6	3.7	4.0	2.9	14.2	12.9	12.3	0.37	0.41	0.41
Europe & Central Asia	1.2	3.3	2.2	0.0	2.8	2.7	17.7	13.7	12.6	0.38	0.38	0.40
Latin America & the Caribbean	1.7	1.7	1.3	0.8	1.3	-0.2	13.6	11.9	11.0	0.31	0.31	0.29
Middle East & North Africa	2.7	1.5	0.5	4.8	3.3	-2.5	16.9	18.4	14.5	0.28	0.30	0.30
North America	1.9	0.9	0.5	2.7	-1.9	-1.4	16.3	9.3	9.0	0.36	0.33	0.33
South Asia	3.2	4.2	3.5	3.3	3.7	3.4	12.5	12.4	11.4	0.26	0.28	0.26
Sub-Saharan Africa	1.0	2.4	1.5	0.2	1.9	2.2	11.1	10.4	10.1	0.22	0.21	0.21
Income group												
Low-income	-0.1	1.9	1.4	0.4	2.3	0.7	10.3	9.3	8.7	0.21	0.20	0.19
Lower middle-income	0.9	3.6	2.7	0.9	4.3	3.6	14.3	12.5	12.0	0.28	0.30	0.30
Upper middle -income	2.4	3.5	1.9	1.1	3.0	0.9	14.2	13.3	12.6	0.31	0.31	0.30
High-income	2.3	1.5	1.3	2.5	1.2	1.0	16.4	14.0	12.2	0.38	0.40	0.42
World	1.6	2.6	1.8	1.5	2.5	1.5	14.2	12.8	11.8	0.32	0.32	0.33

Notes: The industrialization intensity index was developed by UNIDO to capture the level of technological deepening and upgrading. It is computed as the average of the share of MVA in GDP and the share of medium and high-technology activities in MVA. The last year for the decade of the 2010s is 2017.

Source: Compiled by author using World Bank World Development Indicators and UNIDO Competitive Industrial Performance Database.

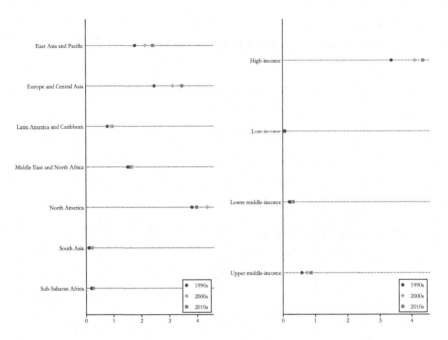

Figure 2.2 Log of per capita manufacturing value-added

EAP is the fastest industrializing region, with an average annual manufacturing growth of 3.7 percent in the 1990s, 4 percent in the 2000s, and 2.9 percent in the 2010s. Industrialization in East Asia was achieved by intensive use of industrial policy. This can be seen from the variations in the industrialization intensity index, which measures the technological complexity of production structures, technological capabilities, and knowledge intensity of production systems. In fact, the industrialization intensity rose from 0.37 in the 1990s to 0.41 in the 2000s. The experience of East Asia in designing and implementing industrial policies has been largely documented (Akkemik, 2009; Chang, 2006). In particular, Otchia (2015) pointed out that East Asian countries have diversified their exports into labor-intensive, export-oriented manufacturing due to the widespread availability of cheap labor, before starting to climb up the quality ladder. In recent years, these countries have been focusing on high-skill-dependent goods such as electronics, automotive products, heavy equipment, and consumer durable goods. China, as the leader of manufacturing exports, has been moving away from labor-intensive goods and specializing in automobiles, industrial equipment, and heavy machinery.

South Asia has followed a similar pattern of manufacturing growth to East Asia; per capita MVA grew almost constantly by a factor of about 3.3–3.7 percent. However, South Asia achieved this growth with lower industrialization intensity. The Middle East and North Africa (MENA) started with an average per capita manufacturing value added of 4.8 percent in the 1990s but eventually fell behind, with growth falling into negative territory. The industrialization intensity of the region, however, has increased from 0.28 to 0.30. Per capita manufacturing value-added in Sub-Saharan Africa (SSA) has experienced a significant increase since the 2000s. However, the industrialization intensity has been almost unchanged.

The manufacturing performance of African countries raises both enthusiasm and concern, depending on the circumstances of the specific country. African countries have low manufacturing value-added per capita and annual growth in manufacturing value-added has been stagnant or almost negative for many of them between 1990 and 2014. While China, Vietnam, and Cambodia have been very dynamic over the last two decades, some African countries have not given up the race to industrialization either. However, the process of structural transformation remains particularly difficult for African countries. Africa's efforts to industrialize and diversify are taking place in an interdependent global economy where industrialized countries have already accumulated both enabling and core productive capacities that give their firms considerable cost and productivity advantages and enable them to push the technological frontier through research and innovation.

We next turn our attention to the income groups. We use the World Bank classification of countries into high-income (HICs), upper middle-income (UMICs), lower middle-income (LMICs), and low-income countries (LICs). HICs stand out as the only income group where there is a clear decline in per capita manufacturing valued added growth (Figure 2.2). The bottom panel of Table 2.1 indicates that HICs experienced a significant per capita manufacturing value-added growth of about 2.5 percent in the 1990s but growth was reduced to 1.2 percent in the 2000s and 1 percent in the 2010s. The industrialization intensity index increased to 0.42 in the 2010s from 0.38 in the 1990s. One other feature is that LMICs started with low per capital manufacturing value-added growth (0.9 in the 1990s), but have been achieving high growth since the 2000s, at rates that are much higher than economic growth. Interestingly, Table 2.1 also illustrates that the 2000–2009 decade stands out as a notable industrialization period for UMICs and LICs, as the average per capita manufactured value-added rose to 3 percent and 2.3 percent, respectively, but the change was meaningful for UMICs, given the higher initial manufacturing valued added per capita (Figure 2.2).

To provide further insight on the heterogeneity in global manufacturing performance, it is useful to focus on exports. The main reason for this being that trade policy was a key driver of industrialization and economic development. Figure 2.3 plots the manufacturing exports index calculated from the UNIDO statistics as the ratio of the manufacturing exports to the manufacturing value-added and normalized to the year 1990. Starting with panel (a), which reports results by geographical regions, it is obvious that each geographical region has followed a different pattern, particularly after 2001. South Asia shows a very flat trend in the manufacturing exports index. There is little change over the period in the manufacturing exports index of SSA. What is striking is the significant change that occurred in Latin America and the Caribbean (LAC), which started expanding in 2002, but had been badly hit by the 2007–2008 global financial crisis, before experiencing a recovery in 2010. We expect exports to have played a role in EAP because of the reason mentioned earlier. The region experienced the second largest increase in the manufacturing exports index, following LAC. EAP experienced an increase in manufacturing exports of about 5 percent between 1990 and 2000, increasing its world share from 12.6 percent to 13.3 percent.

The bottom panel of Figure 2.3 shows some similarities in the evolution of the manufacturing exports index by income groups. In contrast to the geographical region, which depicted a flat trend between 1990 and 2000, the manufacturing exports index picked up quickly for all income groups, with the largest growth in UMICs and LMICs. Again, a sharp decline is observed in 2008 during the financial crisis and after 2014 due to the falling oil prices. The drop is much larger for HICs. Second, there is a perception that export-led growth strategies in developing countries face more constraints than in the past, in particular due to the slower growth of global demand, especially from industrialized countries (UNCTAD, 2016). Finally, Figure 2.3 shows that it has been difficult for LICs to maintain a positive trend by producing manufacturing products that are marketable in the global economy (as the declining indicator shows).

2.2.2 Global concentration of manufacturing production

Since the end of the global financial crisis in 2008, there has been strong growth in manufacturing value-added. According to the UNIDO (2017), global manufacturing value-added reached US$12.3 trillion (at constant 2010 prices) in 2016, thanks to strong growth in emerging and developing countries, whose MVA doubled between 2010 and 2016, rising from 21.7 percent to 44.6 percent. With this strong growth, the growth in MVA in emerging and developing countries continues to outpace that of developed countries. As a result, the share of developing countries in world MVA has been steadily increasing and is expected to reach 44.6 percent in 2016 compared to its share of only 26.5 percent in 2000. By far the most important changes are the increase in the share of the least developed countries in Asia and the Pacific and the sharp declines in Africa (6.5 percent to 4.4 percent) and Latin America (29.3 percent to 13 percent). China has been remarkably dynamic, increasing its manufacturing world share from 3 percent in 1990 to 25 percent in 2018 (UNIDO, 2019).

Figure 2.4 illustrates the way China is positioning itself as a global manufacturer due to a significant increase in its share of world MVA. For comparison purposes, we also include the G7, three other fast industrializers (India, Indonesia, and Korea), and the rest of the world. Between 2005 and 2017, China increased its share of value-added. In particular, its share moved from 20 percent in 2009 to reach 25 percent in 2015. Other emerging economies registered an increase in their shares in the world MVA but at a slower pace than China. This group,

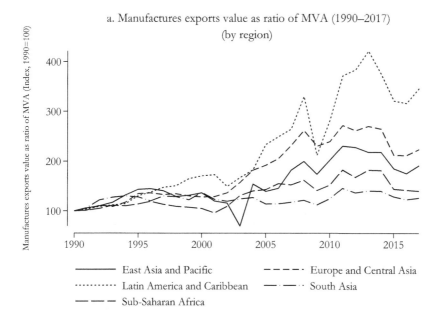

a. Manufactures exports value as ratio of MVA (1990–2017)
(by region)

East Asia and Pacific ——————

Europe and Central Asia – – – – –

Latin America and Caribbean ·············

South Asia — · — · ·

Sub-Saharan Africa — — —

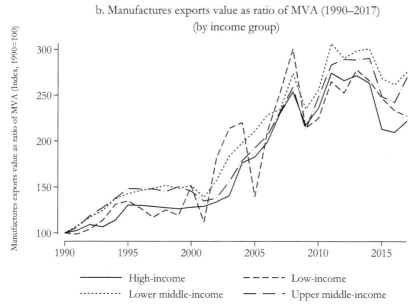

b. Manufactures exports value as ratio of MVA (1990–2017)
(by income group)

High-income ——————

Low-income – – – – –

Lower middle-income ·············

Upper middle-income — · — · ·

Figure 2.3 Manufactures exports

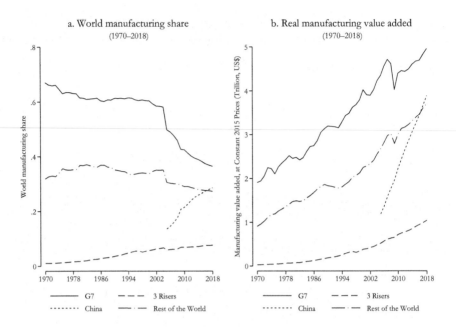

Figure 2.4 G7, China, and 3 Risers' share of world manufacturing and real value-added

which we label the "3 Risers," is India, Korea, and Indonesia. What is striking about Figure 2.4 is the dramatic decline in the G7's share of world MVA, especially since 2005. We thus see that manufacturing production became increasingly concentrated with the G7 losing their strong position.

In addition, we show a similar trend in Figure 2.4 panel (b), where we plot the per capita MVA using 2015 constant prices. It is important to note the G7 is losing its share but the per capita MVA has been rising. As will be discussed later, this is because the G7 is moving to higher value-added yielding manufacturing activities. What can be clearly seen in Figure 2.4 is that the convergence between G7 countries, China, and the 3 Risers is due to the fact that fast catching-up economies are industrializing faster than the former. For instance, there has been a sharp increase in the MVA of China from 2005 to 2017.

The case of China, India, Indonesia, and Korea demonstrates good catching-up validity. This raises interesting questions: Is the global industrial landscape changing? Can convergence occur between the most industrialized countries and the latecomers? Figure 2.5 presents an attempt to answer these questions, by plotting the MVA growth rate over 1990–2018 against the 1990 level of real per capita MVA and fitting a regression line within each income group. For presentation purposes, we group LMICs and UMICs together as middle-income countries. Consistent with Figure 2.3, late industrializers exhibit higher MVA growth compared to early industrializers. As one would expect, most

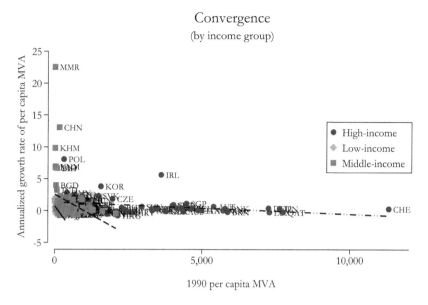

Figure 2.5 Convergence by income group

of them are Asian countries such as Vietnam and Cambodia. Poland has been listed by Baldwin, Ito, and Sato (2014) as part of the 6 Risers together with Korea, India, Indonesia, Thailand, and Turkey. The most interesting aspect of Figure 2.5 concerns, however, the catching-up behavior across income group. Despite variability in MVA growth rates, it is obvious that there is a negative relationship with MVA in the starting year and subsequent industrialization, implying that there is a catching-up behavior within income growth. A closer inspection evinces that there is strong catching-up behavior among LICs and MICs.

To better understand the patterns of catching-up, Figure 2.6 plots the relationship between growth rate of per capita MVA and per capita MVA for two time periods: 1990–2017 and 2000–2017. In both panels, the lines show a local polynomial regression without weights. Figure 2.6 is quite revealing in several ways. First, late industrializers were initially catching up because they were industrializing faster than industrialized countries. Second, convergence in the post-2000 period occurred because of rapid industrialization of late industrializers but also slow growth in industrialized countries. Third, the local polynomial fit shows that three groups of industrialization emerged in the post-2000 period. In addition to the group of industrialized countries such as Japan and the United States, where the local polynomial fit is decreasing, the second group, which is stagnant, includes India, Russia, and Brazil, while the fast-growing group includes Indonesia, Nigeria, and China.

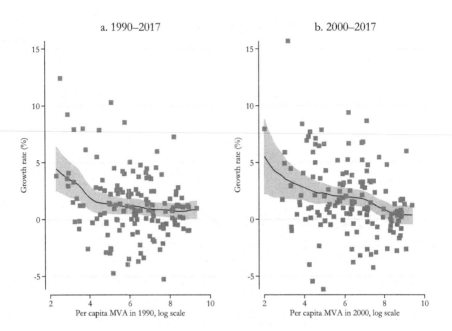

Figure 2.6 Convergence by time period

2.2.3 Relocation of manufacturing employment

The slowdown of MVA growth among early industrializers is particularly due to the fact that these countries are moving toward capital-intensive and technologically sophisticated industries. While manufacturing is generally a labor-intensive industry, the movement toward sophisticated industries will increase the demand for high-skilled workers and manufacturing-related services, thus decreasing manufacturing jobs. Figure 2.7 illustrates that as HICs are shifting to sophisticated industries, manufacturing jobs are being relocated to developing countries. In fact, as can be seen in panel (a) of Figure 2.7, HICs accounted for 21.4 percent of global manufacturing jobs in 1991, but this share decreased to 15.6 percent in 2005 and 13.4 percent in 2017. Panel (b) of Figure 2.7 shows that the reduction of manufacturing jobs was faster between 2000 and 2008 and then slowed down. The greatest beneficiary of the relocation of manufacturing jobs are UMICs such as China, where manufacturing employment's share of total employment increased slightly from 21.9 percent in 2007 to 22.7 percent in 2017. Furthermore, there seems to be a relocation to LMICs, especially since 2012. Panel (a) shows that LMICs are the only income group that exhibits a strong upward trend in manufacturing employment growth since 2010.

What remains to be understood is the extent to which the concentration in manufacturing production and relocation of manufacturing employment relate to labor productivity growth in the manufacturing sector. According to ILO (2019), the shift in employment toward sophisticated industries in HICs and

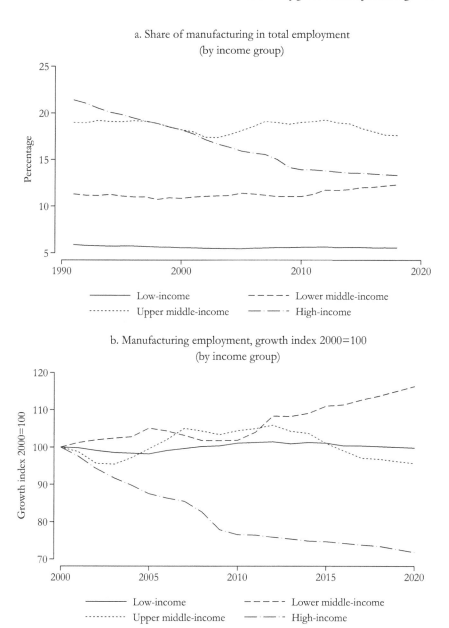

Figure 2.7 Manufacturing employment, growth index, and shares

the relocation of labor-intensive manufacturing to developing countries require an improvement in productivity. They further note that industrial policies that foster technology upgrading, skills development, and institutional capabilities are required to accelerate productivity growth. The evidence for the importance of industrial policy in accelerating industrialization for early industrializers and East Asia is well documented. An interesting recent study has taken advantage of the rapid growth in China to identify the impact of specific industrial policy that favored place-based policy. Lu, Wang, and Zhu (2019) looked at the incidence and effectiveness of Special Economic Zones (SEZs) in China. They found that establishing SEZs increased the number of firms in the designated areas and had an overall positive effect on capital investment, employment, output, and productivity. They found that these positive effects were driven by new firms.

One aspect that we wish to highlight is the unconditional convergence in manufacturing industries. There is substantial work in the growth literature on unconditional convergence in total output. Only recently has there been an interest in the convergence in manufacturing industries. Using a sample of 118 countries and 23 manufacturing (ISIC two-digit level) industries, Rodrik (2013), for instance, found that manufacturing exhibits strong unconditional labor productivity convergence, unlike the rest of the economy. The estimated beta-coefficient in these industries is close to 2–3 percent. However, Rodrik's findings are viewed as applying to formal parts of manufacturing because of data coverage. We contribute to this new strand of literature by documenting unconditional convergence using aggregated manufacturing data that goes back to 1960. In Figure 2.8, we plot the beta-coefficients from the unconditional convergence regression relating average growth of manufacturing labor productivity to its initial level. We see a clear pattern of unconditional convergence depicted by the statistically significant negative betas for both

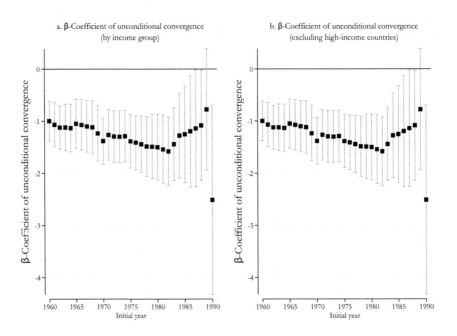

Figure 2.8 Unconditional convergence in manufacturing labor productivity

the sample of all income groups and the sample that excludes HICs. The point estimates are qualitatively consistent among the two panels. While the period of analysis may be short, it is interesting the note that the unconditional convergence in labor productivity became weaker in the 1980s.

2.2.4 Manufacturing upgrading

Despite its role in accelerating structural transformation, manufacturing upgrading has also been praised for its role in sustaining growth. The empirical literature on industrialization and structural transformation has largely documented the structural transformation from agriculture to industry or from industry to service. An important but less highlighted regularity that recent research on patterns of economic growth has not shown is the process of diversification and expansion of the range of activities within manufacturing. The 2018 UNIDO report noted a significant change in the world's major manufacturing industries, the most important being food and beverages, chemicals and chemical products, base metals, computer, electronic and optical products, and motor vehicles, trailers and semi-trailers. The growing share of these manufacturing industries mainly reflects technological advances that are accelerating the specialization of industrialized and emerging countries in technology-intensive industries, leaving low-technology activities behind. This shift has also led to strong growth in manufacturing employment (UNIDO, 2018).

Figure 2.9 compares patterns of structural change within manufacturing. Panel (a) depicts the value-added share of medium and high-tech manufacturing against the per capita GDP in constant 2000 US$, while we plot the medium and high-tech manufactured exports share in panel (b). First note that panel (a) exhibits a positive and increasing relationship between medium and high-tech manufacturing value-added share and the log GDP per capita. These regularities underscore the importance of industrial development as an engine of economic growth. Panel (b) shows that the importance of manufacturing is even stronger when countries diversify into medium and high-tech manufactured exports. The unconditional *lowess* shows a strong correlation between high income and high MVA share. The relation is stronger for log per capita GDP of 6 and above because many developing countries have a low share of high MVA.

This finding supports existing research that points to the fact that economic diversification is needed to sustain growth and reduce poverty significantly. This argument is supported by the fact that export diversification toward manufacturing is linked to increased employment, exports, and GDP growth (Agosin, 2007; Herzer & Nowak-Lehmann, 2006; Lederman & Maloney, 2007). Moreover, recent theories on structural change suggest that producing high value-added products is a condition for sustained growth (Hausmann, Hwang, & Rodrik, 2006; Hausmann & Klinger, 2006; Hausmann & Rodrik, 2003). This is because development has been associated with the movement of resources from lower productivity sectors to higher productivity sectors (McMillan, Rodrik, & Verduzco-Gallo, 2014; McMillan & Rodrik, 2011).

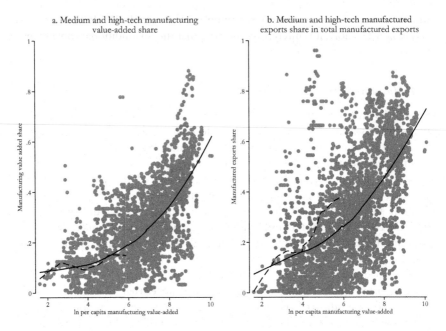

Figure 2.9 Medium and high-tech manufacturing value-added and exports

The good news for developing countries is that they can realize rapid economic development by increasing their share of high MVA in their exports. Figure 2.10 confirms that exports of medium and high technology goods as a share of total manufacturing exports tend to increase with the level of countries' industrialization. The gap between HICs and UMICs is large but has remained almost constant during the period of analysis. LMICs and LICs have increased their exports shares since 2011, closing the gap with UMICs. However, the single most striking observation to emerge from these charts is the spectacular catching-up of China, which has doubled its share within 10 years.

2.2.5 Volatility

Diversification toward higher value-added products is crucial for developing countries to reduce the volatility of their production and exports. While the experience of East Asia has validated the role of diversification into higher value-added products in sustaining economic growth, economic diversification has received plenty of attention in policy discussions and empirical research in recent decades, especially with regard to African economies. The argument in support of this is that the concentration of exports into few commodities exports has increased the volatility of export revenue, reducing the productivity and employment in these countries (Bleaney & Greenaway, 2001; Ghosh & Ostry, 1994).

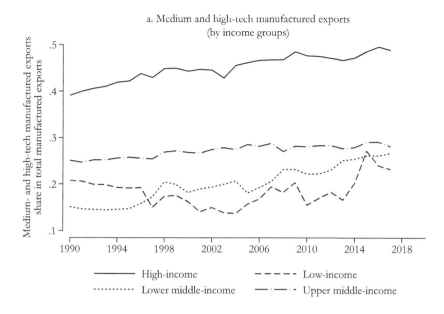

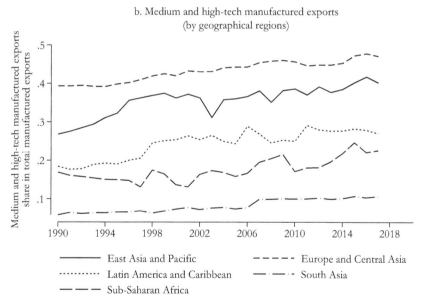

Figure 2.10 Medium and high-tech manufacturing value-added and exports by income groups and regions

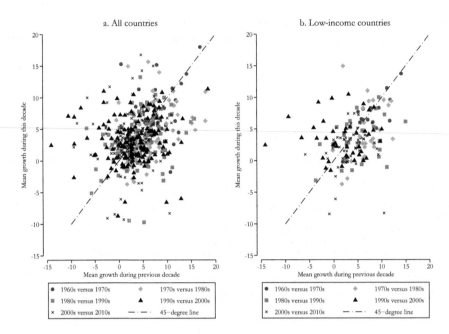

Figure 2.11 Correlation of per capita manufacturing value-added growth in consecutive decades

Recent evidence suggests that MVA is more volatile than GDP. UNIDO (2019), for instance, demonstrates that when the GDP growth rates were rising, MVA growth rates were rising even higher, and when GDP growth rates were declining, MVA growth rates were declining even lower. We analyze the volatility of manufacturing in detail through the lens of contrasting the growth rate for each decade with that from the previous decade from 1960. Figure 2.11 illustrates the volatility in the manufacturing growth rate for all countries (developed and developing) in the WDI and LICs. Comparison with the 45-degree line reveals the instability of manufacturing growth from one decade to another, especially since the 1990s. In order to assess the importance of volatility for developing countries, we also perform the same analysis for LICs. There is even more instability for LICs as Figure 2.11 shows the existence of a lesser density of points around the 45-degree line. The timing of instability seems also to start in the 1980s with many negative points. This is largely due to the advent of the debt crisis. Another shock for the decade of the 1990s was the 1989 fall of the Berlin Wall and the birth of transitional economies after the collapse of the former Soviet Union. The 1980s were also the decade of currency realignment (after the Plaza Accord of 1985) that triggered foreign direct investments (FDIs) to developing countries, starting with FDIs to Asian developing countries. The volatility of MVA growth results from the difficulties many countries face in sustaining long periods of industrial expansion. In Section 2.3, we will analyze the timing of deindustrialization in detail for selected countries.

2.3 Time series test of industrialization and deindustrialization

Given the facts so far presented in this chapter, the natural questions are why and when is deindustrialization happening? This section reports a time series test of the patterns of industrial growth. The time series test focuses on the differences in the rate of changes in the industrial structure between successive time periods. Put differently, this analysis compares time effects with a reference period to gauge the effects of common shocks felt by manufacturing in each of the time periods (Rodrik, 2016). Such calculations enable us to understand the speed of industrialization over time. A seminal work by Temin (1967) tested these patterns using 20-year intervals from 1870 to 1950 for nine countries. The findings indicate that the share of manufacturing has been rising over time, but no systematic evidence in the rate of change of the share of this sector between time periods was found. In the agriculture sector, on the other hand, the share of agriculture was falling over time, and importantly, it fell faster in the periods 1870–1890 and 1910–1930 than 1890–1910 and 1930–1950. In recent empirical studies, the main evidence typically cited for time series patterns of industrial growth is perhaps the premature deindustrialization documented by Dasgupta and Singh (2006). In their paper, Dasgupta and Singh document that the share of employment in manufacturing in developing countries is peaking at lower levels of GDP per capita than it does in present-day industrialized countries. In the same vein, Rodrik (2016) recently showed that the share of manufacturing has been decreasing faster in recent decades and at much lower levels of income for most countries in the analysis. This section revisits the classical analysis that was initiated by Dasgupta and Singh (2006). We provide new evidence using recent data with more coverage of countries.

2.3.1 Which indicator to use?

For a quantitative analysis of deindustrialization, it is useful to highlight some aspects of the measurement used, as a debate is taking place with respect to which indicator is the best proxy for industrialization. The three most common measures of economic activity at the sectoral level are labor force (Clark, 1940), consumption patterns, and value-added shares. Due to the availability of data for time series and cross-country analyses, labor force and value-added shares have been intensively used in the literature. While these two measures often coincide in their conclusion of industrialization patterns, there are cases in which they differ. For example, Felipe, Mehta, and Rhee (2019) draw on correlations between countries' average income per capita and their peak in manufacturing to conclude that manufacturing employment is a better predictor of eventual prosperity than is manufacturing output. While Felipe et al. (2019) use a large database of countries' manufacturing employment and output shares, their study does not consider the country fixed effect that affects the variability in manufacturing value-added shares. Other researchers such as Diao, McMillan, and Wangwe (2017) have preferred to use employment share as a measure of industrialization because of their interest in drawing lessons for employment creation, which is a policy priority in Africa.

Value-added share and employment share are both related to production. However, they can yield different results because they can contain different information. Surprisingly, there has been comparatively little research examining the issue of measurement in developing countries. It is clear that the roles of the informal sector and service-related manufacturing activities are underreported. Based on this discussion, several authors have been using both measures simultaneously or as a robustness analysis. For instance, Rodrik (2016) finds that advanced economies have lost considerable employment (especially of the low-skilled kind), but they have done surprisingly well in terms of keeping manufacturing output shares. Rodrik (2016) adds that the differential patterns may be due to globalization and labor-saving technological progress in manufacturing. These findings suggest that the decline in share of employment due to labor-saving technology implies that the manufacturing sector itself is not shrinking. Second, the loss of employment due to the shrinkage of manufacturing under globalization is a sign of deindustrialization. Third, the decreasing share of employment in the manufacturing sector is related to the worsening performance in aggregate productivity within the economy.

An important question for policy and practice is whether changes in value-added shares are correlated with changes in employment shares. Figure 2.12 plots the changes in manufacturing employment and value-added between 1990 and 2010. Four groups are clear. The first group of countries have experienced an increase in the share of manufacturing value-added and an increase in the share of manufacturing employment. This group of countries represents 15 percent of our sample

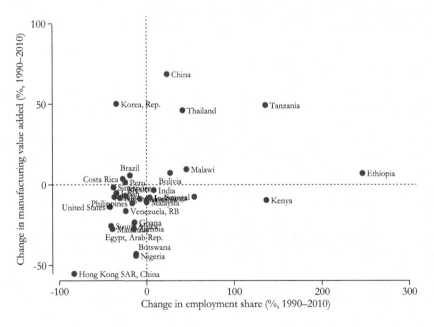

Figure 2.12 Correlation of employment share and manufacturing value-added share

and includes fast-growing economies, such as China, Thailand, Ethiopia, Kenya, Malawi, and Bolivia. A similar number of countries (13 percent) have experienced an increase in the share of manufacturing value-added alongside a decline in manufacturing employment. This pattern may signal a positive deindustrialization where improvements in labor efficiency are accompanied with increasing output of manufacturing. More importantly, 44 percent of countries have experienced a decline in both the share of manufacturing value-added and employment. Finally, the last group includes countries (28 percent) experiencing a decline in the share of manufacturing output but an increase in employment, a signal of a rise in inefficiency in the manufacturing sector. Taken together, these findings show that by utilizing both readily available measurements, value-added and employment, we not only can improve the robustness of the analyses but also can extract additional information on the patterns of structural changes surrounding manufacturing.

2.3.2 Time series test of patterns of industrialization

To put into context the discussion of deindustrialization, we take a small detour to revise early evidence (Temin, 1967) on the time of the pattern of industrial growth. We use data from Mitchell (2007), which provide historical statistics on 20-year intervals from 1870 to 2010 for nine countries (Australia, Canada, France, Germany, Italy, Sweden, the United Kingdom, Japan, and the United States). We extend the seminal work by Temin (1967) in two important ways. First, we extend the sample to include more recent years as Temin was only able to cover data until 1950. Second, we use a more robust econometric specification that includes a quadratic function of log GDP whereas Temin used a linear specification. His findings show that the industry sector was rising over time but there were no systematic differences in the rate of change of the share of industry between time periods.

We present our time trends in Figure 2.13, together with 95 percent confidence intervals around them. The increase in the industry value-added share is evident until the 1950s but we also find that the rate of change during this period is not statistically significant. As can be seen, this finding corroborates that of Temin (1967). Interestingly, however, we document a statistically significant negative time trend in the post-1950s period. Figure 2.13 shows a steady decline in the industry value-added share, but with large variations between countries. In Section 2.3.3, we extend this analysis for the period post-1960s and we cover developing countries.

2.3.3 Time series test of deindustrialization

Much research has documented time trend patterns of deindustrialization (Dasgupta & Singh, 2006; Rodrik, 2016) over recent decades. Using data up to the 2000s, Rodrik (2016) points to a steady decrease over time in manufacturing value-added and employment shares. Using a similar specification that controls for income trends and recent data, we show in Figure 2.14 that this general

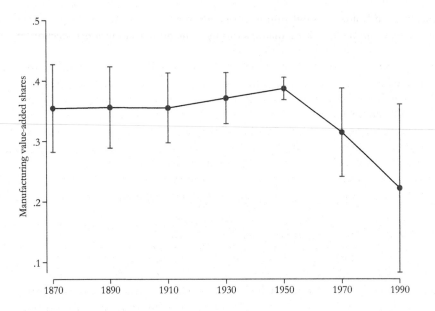

Figure 2.13 Industrialization: estimated period share in early industrialized countries

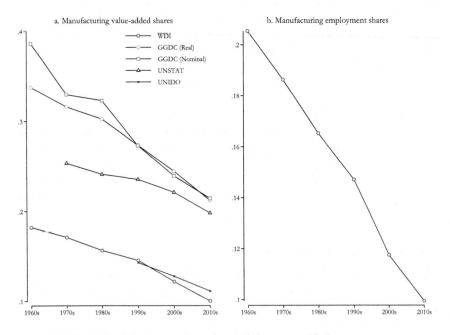

Figure 2.14 Deindustrialization: estimated period share, post-1960

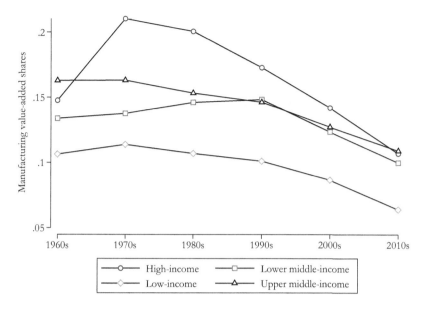

Figure 2.15 Deindustrialization: estimated period share by income group

decline in manufacturing value-added shares was more severe in the 2010s. While most of the data set shows that deindustrialization is particularly evident since the 1980s, the WDI has shown that the shares of MVA have exhibited a significant downward trend since 1960s, and this pattern does not appear to be random. One of the reasons for this difference may be the coverage in terms of countries. Similar to Rodrik (2016), Figure 2.14 panel (b) shows a systematic difference in the rate of manufacturing employment shares between periods, but the trend might have slowed since the 2010s.

Figure 2.15 presents the manufacturing value-added trends over time by income group. Here again, countries are divided into HICS, UMICS, LMICS, and LICS. The shares of manufacturing value-added increased in the 1970s for HICS, and then decreased. However, the decrease is not statistically significant. HIMCS and LMICS exhibit similar time trends, particularly since the 1990s. The striking observation is the manifest failure to industrialize among poor countries and the existence of deindustrialization at very low levels of manufacturing value-added share. After a stagnant period in the 1970s, LICs embarked on the processes of deindustrialization which accelerated after the 1980s.

In Figures 2.16 and 2.17 we present the deindustrialization patterns by geographical regions using value-added share.[7] The results point to different regional patterns. The first striking observation is that South Asia is the only region where the share of MVA has been increasing over time. The trend was to accelerate in the 1980s but decelerate in the 2000s. The share of MVA in ECA has been falling

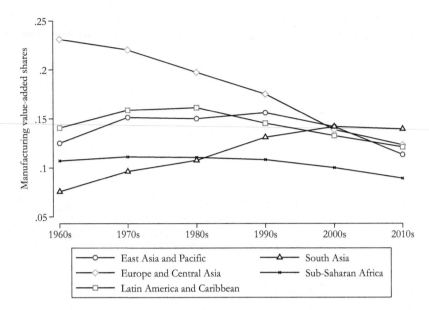

Figure 2.16 Deindustrialization: estimated period share by geographical region

over time and the trend is highly influenced by Northern Europe and Western Europe. In Central Asia, the share of MVA exhibited a rising trend from the 1960s to 1980s, then stagnated in the 1990s before steadily dropping. In LAC, even if the time trend increased slightly, it has declined steadily since 1980s. Within the region, it appears that the share of MVA in South America has been falling over time, particularly since the 1980s. The fall in the manufacturing sector in Central America started earlier in the 1970s but the speed of deindustrialization has been slower than in Central America. Finally, it is interesting to note that the Caribbean exhibits a time trend in deindustrialization.

We find no evidence of the existence of a time trend for deindustrialization in EAP, but the region exhibits a positive increase in the share of manufacturing value-added until the 1990s. In the sub-region, it is only Eastern Asia that exhibits a negative time trend in the manufacturing since the 1980s whereas there is no evidence for the time trend in Micronesia, Melanesia, and Polynesia. Interestingly, South-eastern Asia exhibits a significant positive time trend in all the period of analysis. The effect is higher for ASEAN but the speed does not significantly change. We also find no evidence of a time trend in SSA. On the contrary, Southern Africa exhibits a strong and positive time trend until the 2000s, but the effect is highly influenced by Botswana. Excluding Botswana shows that Southern Africa exhibits no time trend, expect in the 2000s when manufacturing falls.

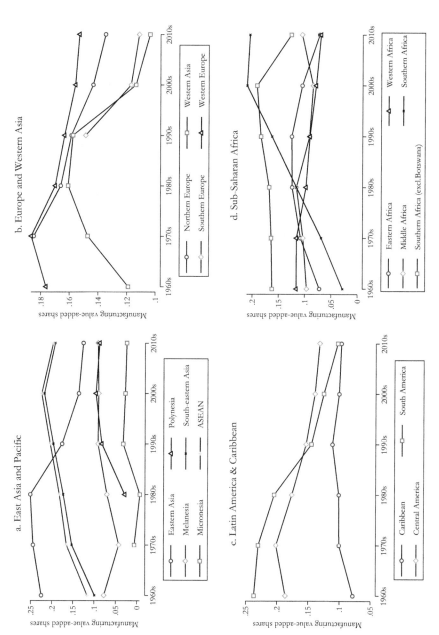

Figure 2.17 Deindustrialization: estimated period share by geographical sub-regions

2.4 Structural change and premature deindustrialization

The reallocation of resources and output away from agriculture toward industry and services is now a well-established fact in the growth literature (Chenery, 1960; Clark, 1957; Kuznets, 1966; Syrquin, 1988). Also documented as one of the most important facts about structural change; this theory generally states that the economic development of nations begins with a rise in industrial production and a relative decline of agriculture, followed by a decrease in the industrial sector and a sustained increase of services. The early research literature observed these patterns of structural change for the early industrializers and predicted that other regions would follow the same development pattern. Recent studies such as Herrendorf, Rogerson, and Valentinyi (2014) and Bah (2011) have also documented these development processes for the late industrializers. Together, these studies indicate substantial heterogeneities across countries. The previous section has clearly demonstrated that there has been a major change in the structure of manufacturing value-added for many developing countries, and that the speed of deindustrialization has been faster in recent decades. It is also clear that there has been an improvement in the quality and coverage of data so that it is worthwhile reexamining the stylized facts of structural transformation. This is what we do in this section.

2.4.1 Structural change and premature deindustrialization

As is standard in the growth literature, we start by presenting stylized facts about structural change for developed countries. Since we are interested in historical patterns, we use value-added shares as they are available in longer spans than employment shares. Specifically, we use a long time series of nine developed countries for the period 1870–2018 from Mitchell (2007) and the WDI to show a panel data with unequally-spaced intervals. Following Bah (2011), we regress the sectoral value-added shares of GDP against a quadratic log of GDP per capita and country fixed effects and we estimate corrected value-added shares by filtering out country fixed effects. In Figure 2.18, we plot the log of GDP per capita (solid line) together with the corrected share of each country during each time period and the confidence interval around the estimates (two dotted lines). We observe the well-known fact that as countries develop, agriculture value-added share monotonically declines, the share of services increases, and the share of industry follows a clear hump-shape pattern, that is to say, the share of industry increases for lower levels of GDP per capita, reaches a peak, and subsequently decreases.

Some other interesting aspects of Figure 2.18 are worth noting. First, a closer look shows that the corrected shares for all the countries lie within the two standard deviations' confidence interval, indicating that developed countries followed a similar process of structural transformation, as described by Kuznets (1973). Second, focusing on the hump shape, we see that the average peak share of manufacturing is 0.4 (40 percent) and occurs at log GDP per capita of 9 (about $8,100). Third, the speed of transformation differs across countries but

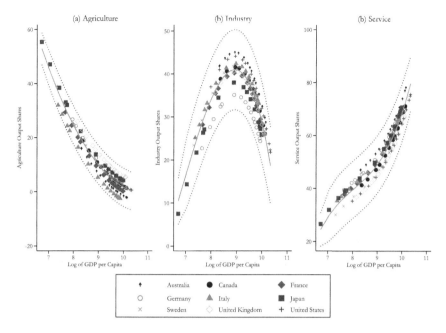

Figure 2.18 Structural change for developed countries

all countries exhibit a late acceleration after log GDP per capita of 9. For instance, Japan started low in the increasing part of the share of industry but converged faster to the levels of other developed countries. Using recent time series data, we are able to document that the speed of transformation for all developed countries is very fast at the decreasing part of the share of industry. This feature is consistent with our previous finding on the change in the speed of deindustrialization in recent years. Fourth, we document that the share of manufacturing expands more quickly than does the service sector at low levels of GDP per capita. Similar to Herrendorf et al. (2014), we document that the share for manufacturing peaks around the same log GDP per capita at which the share of the service sector accelerates, meaning that the acceleration of services goes hand in hand with the decline of manufacturing.

Moving on now to consider the case of developing countries, Figures 2.19, 2.20, and 2.21 compare the pattern of developed countries with developing countries of Asia, Latin America, and Africa, and for comparison, we plot the fitted curve of developed countries.[8] Figure 2.19 shows that Asia, with few exceptions, has been following similar patterns as the developed countries, but structural transformation has been happening at lower levels of log GDP per capita. For manufacturing, the pattern of Southeast Asia is very close to the one for developed countries, but deindustrialization seems to occur at a slower pace and acceleration occurs faster. South Asia followed a different pattern but started

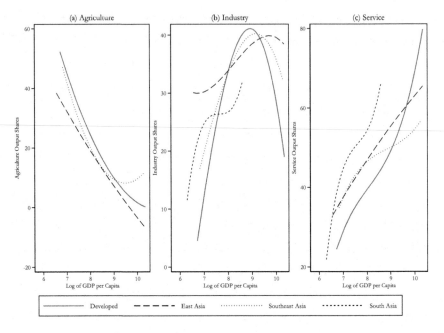

Figure 2.19 Structural change: within Asia comparisons

deindustrialization a little below 0.4 peak share. However, there are a lot of heterogeneities within East Asia, with Korea reaching the peak with a share of manufacturing larger than 0.4 and China still growing. Interestingly, South Asia is still in the first phase of industrialization driven by India and Sri Lanka.

Figure 2.20 presents the patterns for Latin America divided into Central America and South America. The region follows a similar path of developed countries in agriculture and industry. We observe a monotonic decline in agriculture while the share of manufacture shows a hump-shape. Both Central and South America started to deindustrialize at lower levels of GDP per capita and share of manufacturing. There is also large heterogeneity in Central America due to Mexico and Panama. Countries like Nicaragua and Honduras are at the first stage of industrialization. There is also large heterogeneity in South America, but they have done well in agriculture as their pattern converges with developed countries, especially after log per capita GDP of 9. Another important feature we observe is that deindustrialization is also taking place during periods of economic stagnation and even decline.

Finally, Figure 2.21 shows the results for Africa. We document a monotonic decline in the share of agriculture in Eastern Africa and Southern Africa, whereas Central Africa and West Africa are slow at starting agricultural transformation. We also observe a hump-shaped pattern of the share of industry in Southern Africa and less clearly in West Africa, but at very low levels of log GDP per capita.

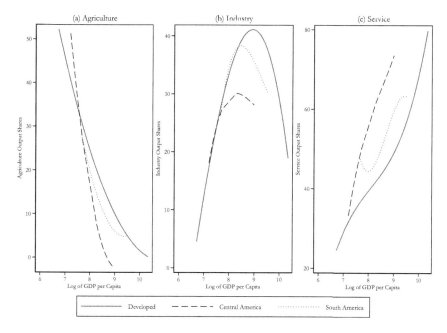

Figure 2.20 Structural change: within Latin America comparisons

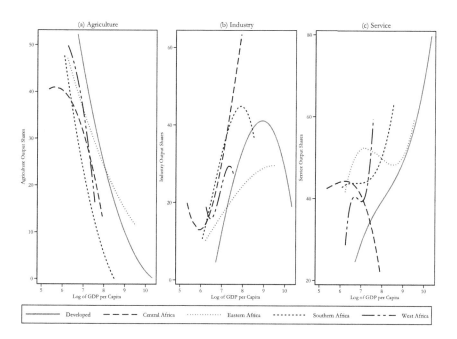

Figure 2.21 Structural change: within Sub-Saharan Africa comparisons

Compared to developed countries, Africa has started with a high share of service value-added at very low levels of GDP per capita. The qualitative pattern of the share of service is, however, very different across sub-regions. Here again, Southern Africa and Eastern Africa are following a close pattern but at the second phase of service growth. The plots also show that the qualitative patterns of structural change are very different to within Africa.

2.4.2 Flying geese and industrialization in Asia

There is a tradition among development economists that lessons from certain successful models should be applied to less successful countries. A popular academic finding suggests that Asian countries followed a different pattern for development that is closer to Japan, based on the "flying geese" patterns of development. According to this theory, the catching-up process of industrialization of latecomers can be explained by the subsequent relocation process of industries from advanced to developing countries during the latter's catching-up process. Arguably, this theory has been useful to explain growth and the pattern of FDI flows from Japan to East Asia and South Asia, but data limitations have constrained its validation. We test whether the East Asian model and the flying geese theory hold with the data for the Asia region, and whether convergence among the sub-regions (late industrializers) is possible. Our strategy is as follows. First, we refer to the Big Three (Japan, Korea, and Taiwan) as the East Asian model, following Chang (2006). Then, we simulate the industrialization path of the Big Three and test whether the latecomers are following a similar path by plotting the prediction bounds for the Big Three.

Figure 2.22 presents the patterns of structural change followed by the Big Three. The vertical axis is the share of value-added in agriculture, industry, and the services sectors. The horizontal axis is the log of GDP per capita in 1990 international dollars. The solid line represents the fitted curves while the dashed lines plot the upper and lower bounds at two standard deviations of the forecast values. These graphs in Figure 2.22 clearly show that the Big Three followed a more homogeneous pattern of structural transformation, whereby increases in GDP per capita were associated with a rapid decrease in the share of agriculture, a humped-shape pattern of the share of manufacturing, and an increase in the share of service. We also find that the decrease in the share of manufacturing is simultaneous with an acceleration in the increase in the share of service.

In Figure 2.23, we verify whether East Asia is following a similar pattern of structural transformation as that of the Big Three. Panels (a), (b), and (c) plot the corrected sectoral shares against the log of GDP per capita. Since our interest is to compare these patterns with the Big Three, we therefore also plot the fitted upper and lower bounds at two standard deviations of the forecasted values from the Big Three. Figure 2.23 shows that the basic qualitative patterns of structural transformation of the Big Three do not hold in East Asia. Specifically, the pattern of Hong Kong is outside of the prediction bounds for the Big Three. The first phase of the structural transformation of China shares the basic regularities of

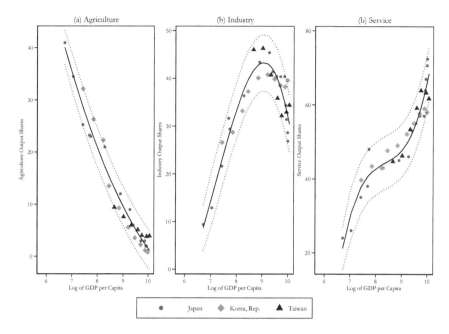

Figure 2.22 Structural change of the Big Three

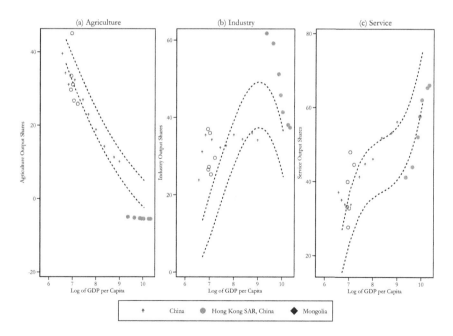

Figure 2.23 Structural change: comparing the Big Three and East Asia

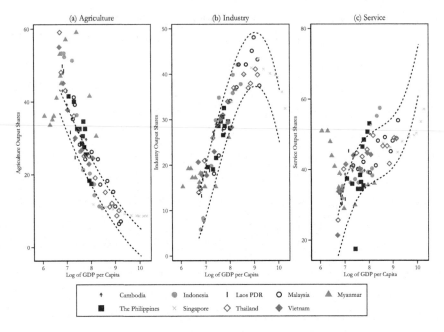

Figure 2.24 Structural change: comparing the Big Three and Southeast Asia

structural transformation as the share of agriculture converged to the bounds for the Big Three. We can also see a similar convergence in the service sector whereas these regularities do not hold in manufacture. China's value-added share of manufacture is flattening out but this started to happen at faster and at lower levels of manufacturing valued added and GDP than the Big Three. Interestingly, Mongolia seems to be following a similar pattern to China, with the difference being that Mongolia shows some signs of premature deindustrialization.

Figure 2.24 tests whether Southeast Asia is following a similar transformation as the Big Three. We can see that the plots reveal some qualitative regularities that we found for the Big Three. However, it is interesting to note that there are some outlier countries, such as Myanmar and Singapore. Agriculture and service value-added of Singapore have similar patterns to Hong Kong while its manufacturing is almost the same as the Big Three. However, Singapore has reached the roof of manufacturing value-added and has started to move to the second phase of structural transformation. Myanmar follows an irregular pattern that we have not observed before. In an analysis not reported here, we removed Myanmar and Singapore and found that most of the Southeast Asian countries are following the Big Three's patterns of structural change. Two patterns are observed: the agriculture value-added is decreasing (faster) with the level of development while the service value-added is increasing (slowly) with development. The manufacturing value-added is increasing but has not reached the maximum. Compared to Vietnam and the Philippines, Malaysia, Thailand, and Indonesia are closer

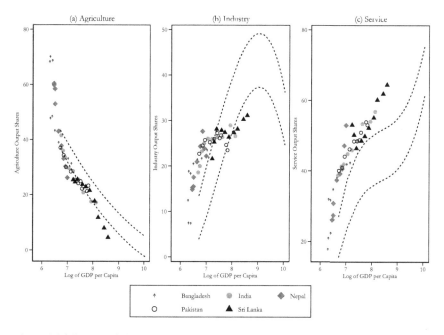

Figure 2.25 Structural change: comparing the Big Three and South Asia

to the maximum of manufacture value-added for the Big Three. However, the Philippines and Indonesia tend to show acceleration in service value-added, which can be a sign of exhausted manufacturing growth. As we need to further monitor structural changes in these countries, Chapter 5 analyses the Indonesian case in detail.

Figure 2.25 compares South Asia with the Big Three. The plots show that South Asia on average does not follow the same regularities as the Big Three. Nevertheless, some patterns of structural change are observed, specifically in the first phase. We see that agriculture value-added shares are decreasing with development while service value-added shares are increasing with development. It is important to highlight that Sri Lanka decreased the agriculture value-added shares very quickly because the initial values were also low. In this group, India, Sri Lanka, and Pakistan tend to follow the same patterns but Pakistan has started deindustrializing. We see that India seems to follow a similar pattern as China. We will come back to that later. Before that, we focus on Bangladesh and Nepal. Isolating Bangladesh and Nepal show some interesting features. While their level of development is still low, Bangladesh and Nepal are going through the first phase of structural change. The value-added shares of manufacturing are still increasing. Their patterns are parallel to the bounds for the Big Three. Our assumption is that they are more likely to follow the same pattern as India, Pakistan, and Sri Lanka. Sri Lanka might have experienced decreasing value-added shares in service when GDP was increasing. Figure 2.25 also shows high growth of the

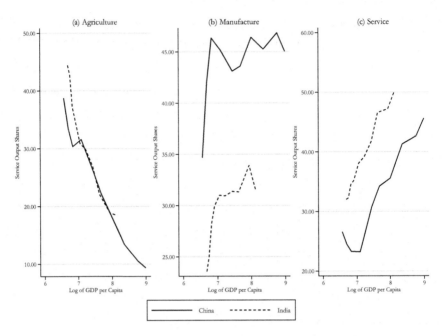

Figure 2.26 Structural change: comparing the Big Three and India and China

service sector due to a rapid decrease in the agriculture value-added shares. This pattern is also unusual.

2.4.3 Structural change in China and India

Finally, we compare whether China and India follow a unique pattern. In Figure 2.26, we simply plot the shares of value-added instead of corrected share. As discussed earlier, China and India seem not to follow closely the Big Three's patterns. However, they seem to move closer to the bounds for the Big Three when they reach higher levels of development. Their manufacture value-added shares point to the fact that China and India might have reached their maximum value-added share because it has flattened out. On a final note, India is following China's path but at lower levels of value-added shares, especially in manufacture. India, with its reputation as the "back office of the world" and traditionally high share of service value-added, may follow a new path to a high-yielding service (including medical services) and service-related manufacturing.

2.4.4 Premature deindustrialization and manufacturing employment

So far, we have used value-added shares in Sections 2.4.1–2.4.3 to present stylized facts on structural change and premature deindustrialization. In this approach, comparing the patterns of developed countries versus developing countries provides a direct test of premature deindustrialization. In contrast to early industrializers, latecomers have experienced falling manufacturing value-added shares at lower level of GDP per capita, without reaching the peak share of 0.4. As a result, the manufacturing sector in many developing countries has remained very small and not enough to generate productive jobs. Similarly, deindustrialization has reduced the potential of overall economic growth to generate employment and reduce poverty. According to UNCTAD (2013), countries with faster GDP growth achieved this with relatively less employment creation. In addition, employment elasticity declined to about half of the Least Developing Countries (LDCs) in the period 2000–2008, and that elasticity tended to fall more frequently in precisely those LDCs that were growing faster.

To determine the extent to which countries have been losing manufacturing employment after reaching the peak share of manufacturing value-added, we measure the timing of the deindustrialization in the year in which manufacturing employment begins to decline. Then, for each country, we calculate the growth rate of employment between the year of the peak in manufacturing shares and the last year of the data, which is 2018. Of the 182 countries with available data in the WDI, we found that 71 countries have already reached the employment peak and started to deindustrialize, while the share of manufacturing employment has been shrinking in 63 countries before 1960 and increasing in 48 countries. Figure 2.27 shows the average percentage reduction in the share of manufacturing employment between the peak year and the last year of data available. We can see that deindustrialization seems to be severe as many countries are losing more than 10 percent of manufacturing jobs.

2.5 Servicification

Changes in labor allocation across sectors are naturally dictated by the changes in demand for various goods and services that, in turn, are brought about by two factors: changes in income (income effect), and changes in relative prices of goods resulting from different speeds of productivity growth across sectors (Duarte & Restuccia, 2010; Ngai & Pissarides, 2007; Rogerson, 2008). Traditionally, a key feature of rapid economic growth is the movement of labor out of agriculture and into other sectors of the economy. Given the substantial impact of manufacturing job losses due to deindustrialization, a key question remains as to whether manufacturing can still be the engine of growth. While part of the answer to this question has already been given in Chapter 1 of this book, it merits its own consideration.

2.5.1 Servicification and manufacturing productivity differences

The premature decline of manufacturing and the subsequent growing importance of the service sector in both developed and developing countries provide ample evidence arguing that structural transformation has occurred in

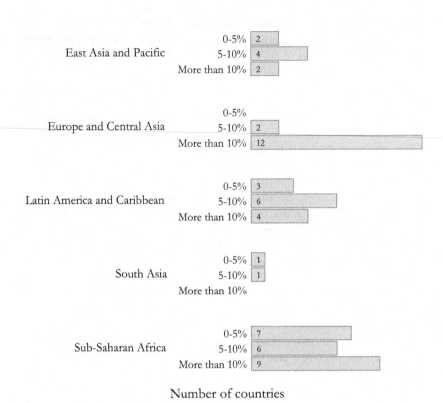

Figure 2.27 Reduction in the share of manufacturing employment since the peak year of manufacturing employment

the boundaries of manufacturing where the service sector has expanded due to technological innovation. The previous discussion has provided evidence of the increasingly important role played by the service sector in the international economy. It is also clear that this transition to the service economy has benefited less developed countries more. For instance, Newfarmer, Page, and Tarp (2018) argue that the future of Africa lies in the service sector because of the emergence of industries without smokestacks, such as agro-industrial and horticultural value chains; tourism; and business and trade services (including ICT- based services, and transport and logistics). Newfarmer et al. note that these sectors are growing in importance in the global economy and also in Africa. Figure 2.28 illustrates the growing importance of services, especially in the last decade. Historically, the service sector increased slowly in the early stages of development, and then accelerated when manufacturing sector reached the hump shape. Figure 2.28 shows that the share of service sector is moving to the left, meaning that the sector is becoming increasingly important for developing countries.

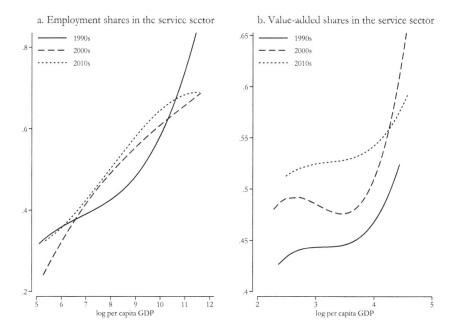

Figure 2.28 Changing landscape of the service sector

Perhaps the most dramatic structural change toward the service sector in developing countries is the growth-reducing structural change, as documented by McMillan et al. (2014). Using sector data on productivity and employment between 1990 and 2005, they identified the movement of labor from high-productive tradable sectors in agriculture and manufacturing to low (negative-productive non-tradable sectors in service. This movement was apparent in Africa and LAC while Asian countries exhibited a growth-enhancing structural change. The advances in technology and the current nature of global trade characterized by high productive service (manufacturing-related service) sectors create new conditions for developing countries to industrialize. While the shift began in tradable services, such as some industries without smokestacks, it appears that productivity in the service sector is still lagging.

Figure 2.29 provides a visual comparison of productivity growth across countries and sectors by plotting the annualized growth rate of labor productivity against the sectoral productivity growth rate. We see large differences in productivity growth between countries and over periods. Over the long run, agriculture and manufacturing productivity growth have been almost three times higher than productivity growth in the service sector. Our results are qualitatively similar to those found by Duarte and Restuccia (2010) using a sample of 29 countries for the period 1956–2004. Not surprisingly, China has made substantial progress in both manufacturing and non-manufacturing productivity growth and its performance has been sustained over time.

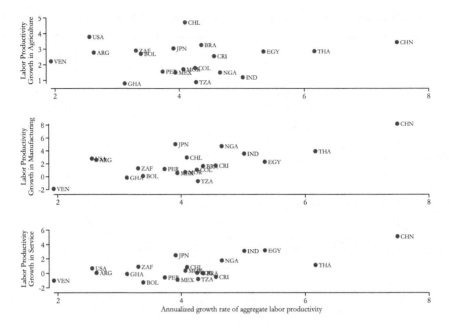

Figure 2.29 Sectoral growth rates of labor productivity

Stiglitz (2018) highlights that deindustrialization may occur when manufacturing is a victim of its own success, meaning when productivity exceeds the rate of increase in demand. Since labor flows from higher-productive sectors to lower-productive sectors, we can test whether differentials in productivity can explain the structural change observed. To do so, we explore the relationship between manufacturing labor productivity and employment in the service sector in Figure 2.30 and see clear correlations between labor productivity in manufacturing and share of employment in the service sector. This shows that the service sector can become an important tool for employment when a country industrializes. This confirms our previous findings on the structural change occurring between manufacturing and the service sector. Newfarmer et al. (2018) likewise use firm-level data for 580,000 firms in over 100 countries to show the considerable effects of services on manufacturing productivity. They find that, at an average level of services use, a 10 percent improvement in services productivity is associated with an increase in manufacturing productivity of between 0.3–0.6 percent, depending on country-specific fixed effect and institutional variables. However, it should be highlighted that manufacturing labor productivity exhibits strong unconditional convergence. According to Rodrik (2013), manufacturing labor productivity in poorer countries is on average catching up with manufacturing labor productivity in HICs, independent of the policies, qualities of institutions, education, or other growth determinants of low- and middle-income

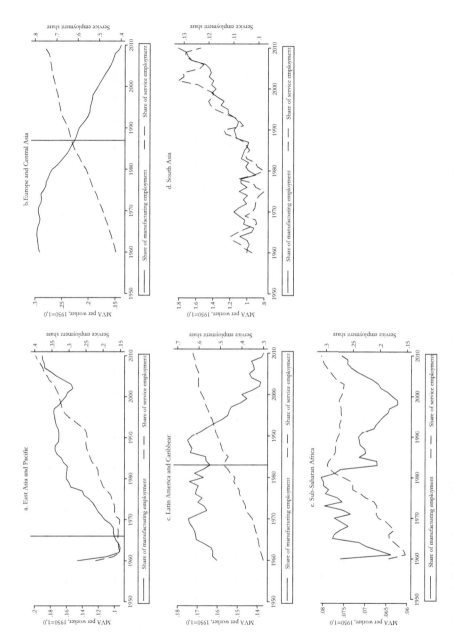

Figure 2.30 Manufacturing labor productivity versus manufacturing employment shares over time

countries. Describing these strongly correlated trends in manufacturing product-ivity and service employment in a different way, we reconfirm the ever declining share of labor in manufacturing value-added pointed out in Chapter 1.

2.5.2 GVCs, deindustrialization, and reindustrialization

The empirical economic literature has provided substantial evidence that the growing of servicification has been highly related to the development of value chains. According to Baldwin et al. (2014), the emergence of GVCs has contributed to the reduction in the role of manufacturing relative to the service sector through outsourcing certain tasks such as R&D, marketing, and design work. Similarly, joining value chains can help developing countries industrialize through offshoring of production. Baldwin et al., however, are concerned with the fact that innovations in ICT make it easy to distribute labor-intensive stages of the production process in low-wage countries and skill-intensive stages in skill-abundant countries. This issue is discussed and analyzed further in Chapter 7 of this book, taking GVCs in Laos as a case. This creates new patterns of production and specialization where countries can focus on stages or tasks that fit their com-parative advantage, instead of focusing on the entire production process. Linking into these international production and distribution networks could, therefore, help developing countries initiate their industrialization with labor-intensive tasks and further upgrade to medium and high-tech manufacturing.

Guided by this assumption, a wide range of formal econometric tests using macro-, micro-, and firm-level data led to the conclusion that GVC participation has contributed to inclusive growth, reducing poverty, and increasing gender participation and equity in the workplace (UNIDO, 2018; World Bank, 2020). A key question for our purpose is whether there are any spaces where developing countries can find manufacturing activities with the rapid technological upgrading and extension of GVCs for manufacturing. To answer this question, we make use of the recent GVC linkages indicators proposed by the World Bank (2020). They proposed a measure of GVCs linkages based on the type of product the country exports and their participation in GVCs. These measures are classified into four types, namely, commodities, limited manufacturing, advanced manufacturing and services, and innovative activities.

Figure 2.31 presents four GVC linkages measures by income groups, in panel (a), and geographical regions, in panel (b). It is clear from panel (a) that the levels of GVC linkages are correlated with income groups. LICs are mainly engaged in commodities and to a lesser extent in limited manufacturing. Panel (b) clearly shows that this group is located in Africa, Central Asia, and Latin America. LMICs and UMICs are engaged in limited manufacturing and advanced manufacturing and services while HICs are also engaged in innovative activities. With regards to region, it appears that East Asia and Pacific, Europe, and North America are engaged in advanced manufacturing and services GVCs and innovative GVC activities.

Figure 2.32 panel (a) shows that countries that join limited manufacturing from commodities GVCs exhibit a positive and strong growth in the per capita

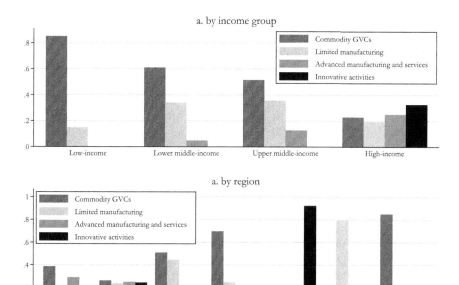

Figure 2.31 Global value chains linkages by income group and region

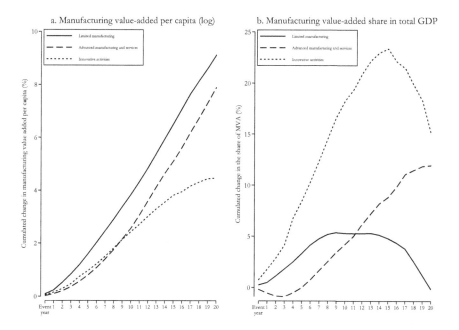

Figure 2.32 Impact of global value chains on manufacturing

MVA. Figure 2.32 suggests that such performance can be expected to continue over 20 years but at varying speeds. Panel (b) shows that the share of manufacturing increases after entering limited manufacturing GVCs but the effects tend to become smaller and even negative if countries do not upgrade. To achieve sustained industrialization, countries should upgrade from limited manufacturing to advanced manufacturing and services, and then into innovative tasks. This evidence suggests several promising ways to accelerate industrialization in developing countries, particularly in Sub-Saharan Africa. These regions have the lowest share of medium and high technology goods (as share of total manufacturing exports) but they have been closing the gap with other regions since 2011. This is a bit surprising given that the period coincides with a significant increase in commodity prices for oil, petroleum, and basic metals. Africa's industrial performance is weak but has strong growth potential. Agriculture, service sectors, and natural resources also remain at the heart of Africa's industrial development. Indeed, investment in the manufacturing and mining sectors has not crowded out investment in the agricultural sector, which means that Africa is attracting investment in the agricultural and non-agricultural sectors at the same time. Since these sectors differ in terms of resource endowment, Africa can develop by promoting labor-intensive industries and capital- or technology-intensive sectors simultaneously, as there is no competition and reallocation of resources between these industries. However, the economic difficulties and poor performance of industrial sectors and sub-sectors in developing countries are due to low productivity and lack of capacity at the firm level.

2.5.3 Are SEZs the solution?

In recent years, the rapid rise of SEZs has jump-started a multitude of countries as a strategy for industrialization: virtually every country or region wants to establish SEZs or other place-based policies such as industrial parks (IPs), export processing zones, eco-industrial parks (EIPs), technology parks (TPs), and innovation district (IDs), to achieve economies of agglomeration, attract (foreign) investment, alleviate unemployment, and implement special policy experiments. UNCTAD's inventory for its 2019 World Investment Report (UNCTAD, 2019) states that the rate of establishment of new SEZs is accelerating as governments increasingly compete for internationally mobile industrial activity. The report identified about 5,400 SEZs in 147 economies, and at least 500 more are in the pipeline. This number expanded from 500 in 73 countries in 1995 to 3,500 SEZs in 130 countries in 2006, before reaching 4,300 in about 140 countries in 2014. Impressively, the world has established more than 1,000 SEZs since 2014.

Has this dramatic expansion of SEZs helped build an industrial base? While research is at the embryonic stage in evaluating the impact of SEZs, we can obtain some insights about their potential using simple correlations. We do this in Figures 2.33 and 2.34 for MVA shares and employment, respectively. In each figure, we plot the growth rate over 1990–2018 against the accumulated number of SEZs up to 2018. The solid line is a linear regression fit line. Some

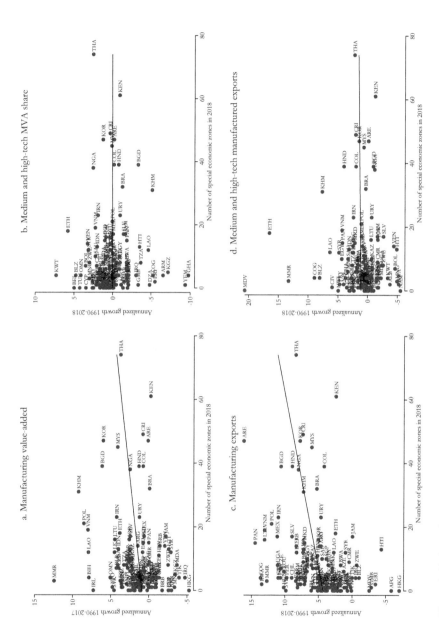

Figure 2.33 Special Economic Zones and manufacturing value-added

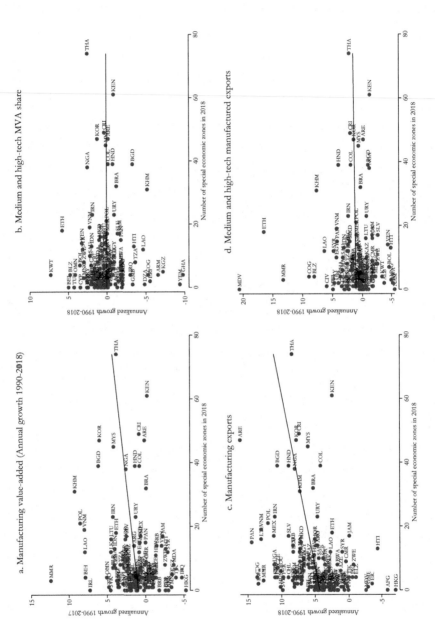

Figure 2.34 Special Economic Zones and manufacturing employment

interesting observations are immediately apparent. First, there is a positive cor-relation between the number of SEZs and MVA growth. This is rather expected because of the basic nature of SEZs. The results are highly driven by Asian coun-tries like Thailand, Cambodia, Vietnam, and South Korea. Contrasting Thailand with Kenya, or Cambodia with Brazil, *ceteris paribus*, highlights the importance of other factors like the design and implementation of SEZs.

The results with respect to Asia and the contribution that manufacturing exports make to the process of industrialization suggest strongly that SEZs have been promoting industrialization through exports, and in particular, regardless of geographic location. Figure 2.33 panel (c) points to a stronger correlation between SEZs and manufacturing exports. The effect is more pronounced for certain countries such as Vietnam, Uganda, Mexico, Poland, and Panama, to name but a few. The case of Vietnam is worth noting, as it is based on a unique dual non-overlapping system governed by the central government and the provin-cial government. The central government establishes industrial zones providing generous corporate tax incentives while local governments promote industrial clusters with land rent incentives. The industrial clusters are designed to promote local business activities but they play a key role in supporting the export-oriented industrial zones through linkages and spillovers. This can be seen in Figure 2.33 as SEZs tends to be highly correlated with both MVA and manufacturing exports in Vietnam.

Like Vietnam, there is evidence that the development of SEZs in Ethiopia has generated industrial-based and manufacturing exports. Figure 2.34 shows that Ethiopia is one of the few African countries to have achieved high growth of MVA between 1990 and 2018, and the MVA is highly correlated with manu-facturing exports. Similar to Vietnam, SEZs in Ethiopia have been piloted by the prime minister.

Even if Figure 2.34 shows little evidence of the relationship with medium and high-tech MVA to draw general conclusions, some notable patterns are revealing. SEZs can be a tool for resource-rich countries to industrialize. Figure 2.34 shows that Iran, Indonesia, Nigeria, Saudi Arabia, Venezuela, and Kuwait have both high growth in medium and high-tech MVA and the number of SEZs. Among them, Nigeria stands out. Second, some countries, like Ethiopia, have been leapfrogging from agriculture to medium and high-tech MVA using labor-intensive SEZs. Figure 2.33 panel (b) confirms the findings from the MVA that the industrialization of Ethiopia in both MVA and medium and high-tech MVA is happening through SEZ-led exports. Laos, Myanmar, and Cambodia also stand out.

Figure 2.34 presents the correlations between employment in manufacturing and the accumulated number of SEZs in a short-run spell (2000–2010) and long-run spell (1990–2010) using GGDC data. Figure 2.34 confirms that SEZs are correlated with manufacturing employment growth, and, in particular, that these correlations are even larger in the long run. In addition, all African economies plotted in Figure 2.34 lie above the linear regression fit line, suggesting larger SEZ-led employment for Africa. These calculations are only suggestive as we do not claim any causality with this simple analysis for Africa. But the implication is clear for policymakers who are striving to promote employment and welfare. Furthermore, this finding is consistent with existing evidence that finds strong and positive effects of SEZs on employment and industrialization.

2.5 Conclusion

Following the presentation of the leading issues in industrial promotion in today's globalized world in Chapter 1, this chapter introduced a variety of facts and trends pertaining to industrial structural changes. As our UNIDO team looks into the manufacturing industries in detail in Chapter 3, we tried to present a more holistic picture of structural change surrounding manufacturing.

In Section 2.2, we portrayed the state of global manufacturing with the use of substantial and diverse empirical evidence. There is a great degree of heterogeneity in manufacturing growth across time and across regions. In its diversity in the patterns of structural changes, we found ongoing concentration and convergence in manufacturing activities and the roles of manufacturing. The early industrializers are losing their share in global manufacturing with China and a small number of emerging economies taking over. Late industrializers are growing at a faster pace relative to that of early industrializers. However, most of them focus on labor-intensive manufacturing. Production of medium and high-tech manufacture products is concentrated in HICs. As we have shown here, the core of global manufacturing value-added has shifted away from traditional labor-intensive manufacturing into products that embody higher technology. Industrial promotion today, thus, calls for facilitations for industrial (manufacturing) upgrading, rather than a mere expansion of low tech labor-intensive manufacturing activities.

In Section 2.3, we used historical data combined with recent panel datasets to examine how the trend of premature deindustrialization emerged in many parts of the developing regions. We took advantage of our data coverage in examining heterogeneity in the timing of deindustrialization among regions. Furthermore, we provided new evidence on the timing of (de)industrialization by examining historical data of early industrializers. The patterns that we found are rather robust to a variety of measures (i.e., value-added, employment, exports) and across the different datasets we used. The peaks of industrialization, measured in manufacturing value-added (MVA) shares in total value-added, are much lower for the income groups of developing countries as compared to the peaks experienced by the early industrializers (over 40 percent in today's HICs). And these peaks tend to come at earlier stages of development (at lower levels of per capita income).

We extended this method of analyzing structural changes to characterize the patterns of (de)industrialization in Asian countries that followed the so-called "flying geese" pattern where Asia's later industrializers follow the Big Three (Japan, Korea, and Taiwan) in their industrial structural transformation as the leading industries of the Big Three move out to East and South-East Asian economies in sequences as newer and higher technology manufacturing (new leading industries) develops in the economies of the Big Three. The structural changes in China and India were also analyzed in the same manner, as both of these economies have been following a similar pattern with an element of uniqueness identified for India. India, with its reputation as the "back office of the world" and with its traditionally high share of service value-added, may follow a new path to a high-yielding service (including medical services) and manufacturing-related service (including call centers for manufacturing/service enterprises). This is related to the servicification and the growing share of service trade in global transactions. Africa and other regions are similarly analyzed for their patterns of (de)industrialization.

In Section 2.4, we looked at the process of servicification, both within manufacturing and outside manufacturing, with a consideration of how GVCs and SEZs could provide spaces where developing countries can find manufacturing activities. Here we portrayed a seemingly strong correlation between trends in manufacturing productivity and service employment. This reconfirms the ever-declining share of labor in manufacturing value-added pointed out in Chapter 1.

Regarding the roles of GVCs that could provide spaces for manufacturing in developing countries can grow into, we analyzed the time frameworks of increases and decreases of value-added shares of manufacturing activities after GVC participation, categorized by technology intensity (low-tech to innovative manufacturing activities) of participating manufacturing activities. The results suggest that premature deindustrialization tends to emerge when countries are confined to low-tech manufacturing even when they can participate in GVCs.

For the use of SEZs in promoting manufacturing value-added, employment, and exports, our analyses indicate a great potential, particularly if the promotion of SEZs is coupled with facilitation of technology/product/activity upgrading on the part of the participating local firms.

We hope that readers keep these identified facts and trends in mind as the context for the following chapters of this book.

Notes

1 This is illustrated in Figures 1.4 and 1.5 of Chapter 1.
2 Available at https://unstats.un.org/unsd/snaama/Index.
3 Available at https://stat.unido.org/database/CIP%202019.
4 Available at https://ilostat.ilo.org/data/.
5 Andreoni, Chang, Konzelmann, and Shipman (2018) provide a useful discussion on why economists should re-focus on production.
6 Figure 2.17 in particular follows the UN Department of Economic and Social Affairs' classification of sub-regions, see (https://esa.un.org/MigFlows/Definition%20of%20regions.pdf).
7 We followed the World Bank's classification of income groups and geographical regions. For income groups, the 2020 fiscal year uses the 2018 Gross National Income per capita, calculated based on the Atlas method, to define countries as low-income economies (US$1,025 or less), lower middle-income economies (between US$1,026 and US$3,995), upper middle-income economies (between US$3,996 and US$12,375),

and high-income economies (US$12,376 or more). The regions are divided into East Asia and the Pacific, Europe and Central Asia, Latin America and the Caribbean, Middle East and North Africa, South Asia, and Sub-Saharan Africa.

8 Results on the heterogeneity within each group are available up on request.

References

Agosin, M. R. (2007). Export diversification and growth in emerging economies. Working Paper No. 233. University of Chile, Department of Economics.

Akkemik, K. A. (2009). *Industrial development in East Asia: A comparative look at Japan, Korea, Taiwan, and Singapore.* Singapore: World Scientific Publishing.

Andreoni, A., Chang, H.-J., Konzelmann, S., & Shipman, A. (2018). Introduction to the Special Issue: Towards a production-centred agenda. *Cambridge Journal of Economics*, 42(6), 1495–1504.

Bah, E.-h. M. (2011). Structural transformation paths across countries. *Emerging Markets Finance and Trade*, 47(suppl. 2), 5–19.

Baldwin, R. (2019). *The globotics upheaval: Globalisation, robotics, and the future of work.* London: Weidenfeld & Nicolson.

Baldwin, R., Ito, T., & Sato, H. (2014). *Portrait of a factory: Production network in Asia and its implication for growth—the "smile curve."* Joint Research Program Series No. 159. Chiba: Institute of Developing Economies, Japan External Trade Organization (IDE-JETRO).

Bleaney, M., & Greenaway, D. (2001). The impact of terms of trade and real exchange rate volatility on investment and growth in Sub-Saharan Africa. *Journal of Development Economics*, 65(2), 491–500.

Chang, H.-J. (2006). *The East Asian development experience: The miracle, the crisis and the future.* London: Zed Books.

Chenery, H. B. (1960). Patterns of industrial growth. *The American Economic Review*, 50(4), 624–654.

Clark, C. (1940). *The conditions of economic progress.* London: Macmillan.

Clark, C. (1957). *The conditions of economic progress* (3rd ed.). London: Macmillan.

Dasgupta, S., & Singh, A. (2006). Manufacturing, services and premature deindustrialization in developing countries: A Kaldorian analysis. United Nations University Research Paper, No. 2006/49. UNU-WIDER.

Diao, X., McMillan, M., & Wangwe, S. (2017). Agricultural labour productivity and industrialisation: Lessons for Africa. *Journal of African Economies*, 27(1), 28–65.

Duarte, M., & Restuccia, D. (2010). The role of the structural transformation in aggregate productivity. *The Quarterly Journal of Economics*, 125(1), 129–173.

Felipe, J., Mehta, A., & Rhee, C. (2019). Manufacturing matters… but it's the jobs that count. *Cambridge Journal of Economics*, 43(1), 139–168.

Ghosh, A. R., & Ostry, J. (1994). Export instability and the external balance in developing countries. *IMF Staff Papers*, 41, 214–235.

Hausmann, R., Hwang, J., & Rodrik, D. (2006). What you export matters. NBER Working Paper.

Hausmann, R., & Klinger, B. (2006). Structural transformation and patterns of comparative advantage in the product space. Working Paper No. 128. Center for International Development, Harvard University.

Hausmann, R., & Rodrik, D. (2003). Economic development as self-discovery. *Journal of Development Economics*, 72(2), 603–633.

Herrendorf, B., Rogerson, R., & Valentinyi, Á. (2014). Growth and structural transformation. In P. Aghion & S. N. Durlauf (Eds.), *Handbook of economic growth* (2, pp. 855–941). Oxford: Elsevier,

Herzer, D., & Nowak-Lehmann, F. D. (2006). What does export diversification do for growth? An econometric analysis. *Applied Economics*, 38, 1825–1838.

ILO. (2019). *World employment and social outlook: Trends 2019.* Geneva: ILO.

Kuznets, S. (1966). *Modern economic growth.* New Haven, CT: Yale University Press.

Kuznets, S. (1973). Modern economic growth: Findings and reflections. *The American Economic Review*, 63(3), 247–258.

Lederman, D., & Maloney, W. F. (2007), *Natural resources: Neither curse nor destiny.* Washington, DC: The World Bank.

Lu, Y., Wang, J., & Zhu, L. (2019). Place-based policies, creation, and agglomeration economies: Evidence from China's economic zone program. *American Economic Journal: Economic Policy*, 11(3), 325–360.

McMillan, M., & Rodrik, D. (2011). Globalization, structural change and productivity growth. NBER Working Paper No. 17143.

McMillan, M., Rodrik, D., & Verduzco-Gallo, Í. (2014). Globalization, structural change, and productivity growth, with an update on Africa. *World Development*, 63, 11–32.

Mitchell, B. (2007). *International historical statistics 1750–2005: Europe.* Basingstoke: Palgrave Macmillan.

Newfarmer, R. S., Page, J., & Tarp, F. (2018). Industries without smokestacks: Industrialization in Africa reconsidered. In *UNU-WIDER studies in development economics.* Oxford: Oxford University Press.

Ngai, R., & Pissarides, C. (2007). Structural change in a multi-sector model of growth. *American Economic Review*, 97.

Otchia, C. S. (2015). Mining-based growth and productive transformation in the Democratic Republic of Congo: What can an African Lion learn from an Asian Tiger? *Resources Policy*, 45, 227–238.

Rodrik, D. (2013). Unconditional convergence in manufacturing. *Quarterly Journal of Economics*, 128, 165–204.

Rodrik, D. (2016). Premature deindustrialization. *Journal of Economic Growth*, 21(1), 1–33.

Rogerson, R. (2008). Structural transformation and the deterioration of European labor market outcomes. *Journal of Political Economy*, 116(2), 235–259.

Stiglitz, J. E. (2018). From manufacturing-led export growth to a twenty-first-century inclusive growth strategy: Explaining the demise of a successful growth model and what to do about it. WIDER Working Paper 2018/176.

Syrquin, M. (1988). Patterns of structural change. In H. Chenery & T. N. Srinavasan (Eds.), *Handbook of economic development.* Amsterdam: Elsevier Science Publishers.

Temin, P. (1967). A time-series test of patterns of industrial growth. *Economic Development and Cultural Change*, 15(2), 174–182.

Timmer, M. P., de Vries, G. J., & de Vries, K. (2015). Patterns of structural change in developing countries. In J. Weiss & M. Tribe (Eds.), *Routledge handbook of industry and development* (pp. 65–83). London: Routledge.

UNCTAD. (2013). *Least developed countries report 2013: Growth with employment for inclusive and sustainable development.* New York: United Nations Publications.

UNCTAD. (2016). *Trade and development report.* Geneva: UNCTAD.

UNCTAD. (2019). *World investment report 2019: Special economic zones.* New York: United Nations Publications.

UNIDO. (2017). *Industrial development report 2018: Demand for manufacturing: driving inclusive and sustainable industrial development.* Vienna: UNIDO.

UNIDO. (2018). *Global value chains and industrial development.* Vienna: UNIDO.

UNIDO. (2019). *Industrial development report 2020: Industrializing in the digital age.* Vienna: UNIDO.

World Bank. (2020). *The world development report 2020: Trade for development in the age of global value chains.* Washington, DC: World Bank.

3 The importance of manufacturing development and structural change for pro-poor growth

Nobuya Haraguchi and Juergen Amann

3.1 Introduction

The analysis presented in this chapter highlights the dynamic and heterogeneous nature of structural change within manufacturing and delineates a path of inclusive manufacturing development for pro-poor growth. In doing so it illustrates the continuous importance of manufacturing development and the key role of industrial policy design.

In the first part of the chapter we revisit the current debate on whether the importance of manufacturing for economic development has changed or not, and discuss both past contributions as well as more recent advances in the related literature to emphasize the continued importance of manufacturing and the key role of industrial policies.

The second part of this chapter elaborates on the importance of industrial structural change by highlighting the relevance of manufacturing development and emphasize pro-poor growth pathways of industrial development. Our analysis is informed by a careful dis-aggregation of structural change patterns, and provides a detailed account of generally industry-level heterogeneities, their intertemporal dynamics, as well as employment linkages to other industries and sectors of the economy before touching on the question of manufacturing sustainability. The fourth and final section offers a conclusion.

3.2 The importance of manufacturing development

3.2.1 *Manufacturing as the engine of growth: An empirical regularity*

It is universally acknowledged in both the theoretical and empirical economic literature that manufacturing is widely regarded as a shaping and growth-promoting factor at early stages of a country's economic development and that it undergoes notable structural change as economies grow richer, see, among others, Kuznets (1953), Lewis (1954), Kaldor (1967), and Matsuyama (1992) as well as Bluestone and Harrison (1982), and Brady and Denniston (2006). This observation of

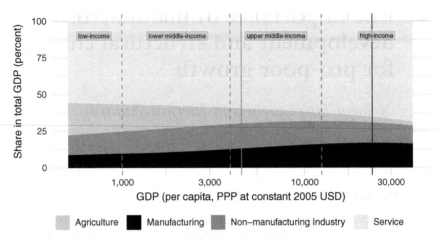

Figure 3.1 GDP composition by income and sector
Note: Constructed using pooled data for 153 countries, 1950–2017. Vertical lines in grey (black) identify the highest contributing share of non-manufacturing industries (manufacturing) and the equivalent GDP per capita level of USD 4,500 (USD 23,000), respectively. X-axis in logs. Income group cut-offs identified by the dashed vertical lines at USD 995, USD 3,896 and USD 12,375 as defined by World Bank Country and Lending Groups (World Bank 2019a).
Source: Calculations based on World Development Indicators (World Bank 2019b) and Penn World Tables 9.1 (Feenstra, Inklaar, and Timmer, 2015) following IDR (2013).

the "classical" (de-)industrialization pattern is illustrated in Figure 3.1. There, a first noteworthy increase in both the share of manufacturing as well as non-manufacturing-related industries at lower-income levels, followed by a steady decline of both sector shares at higher-income levels is shown. The turning point at which the sectoral contribution of both industry-related aggregates reduces can be identified by the two vertical lines at a GDP per capita of around US$4,500 for the non-manufacturing industries and at roughly US$23,000 for manufacturing respectively. This means that, by and large, developing countries have typically experienced a steady increase in the share of manufacturing at around 20 percent, after which deindustrialization patterns can historically be observed for higher-income economies.

Similar to the works on the sectoral composition of the economy, the history of research on sectoral structural change in manufacturing is long and influential.[1] One of the first attempts to identify regularities of growth differentials across industries within the manufacturing sector was undertaken by Chenery (1960). In this seminal contribution and through further works with Taylor and Syrquin,[2] the authors attempted to identify the underlying forces in the transformation processes of developing countries and to quantify how structural change manifests itself through compositional changes of the manufacturing sector. For example, Chenery and Syrquin (1975) investigate development patterns in a cross-country setting and identify country size in particular as having a significant impact on the development pattern of countries: Large countries are found to transform their economic structure at earlier points of their development process than small countries, which implies that small countries "catch up" to bigger economies at higher-income levels.[3] Unfortunately, attempts to understand the development patterns of manufacturing at the level of its industries have received somewhat less attention after the works of Chenery and Syrquin. In the years after their study, most structural change analyses were based on broad economic sectors with little systematic investigation of the development patterns of manufacturing industries. Most recently, Haraguchi and Amann (2020b) reconnect to this earlier strand of the literature through a synthesis of revisiting some key findings of the founding works of this field and by expanding on the empirical analysis with more comprehensive data.

3.2.2 *Manufacturing as the engine of growth: Running out of steam?*

As already noted in Syrquin and Chenery (1989a), advances in the field of industrial development have shown that the dynamics of the industry sector in general, and of manufacturing in particular, are not only subject to changes in the income level but seem to have an intertemporal dimension as well. In more recent history, these trends have been found to be more pronounced. For example, Haraguchi (2015) observes that the contribution of manufacturing to GDP along the income trajectory was more dynamic between the 1960s and the 1980s than during more recent periods. Similar observations were made by Rodrik (2016) and Palma (2014). Both authors note that the hump-shaped relationship between manufacturing-related employment and the value-added shares has moved to a lower tipping point at lower-income levels for more recent periods. This corresponds to a projected decline of employment and value-added shares at earlier stages of economic development than experienced by earlier industrializers. Palma (2014) also notes that the hump-shaped relationship for employment seems to collapse in more recent periods.

In this vein, visual evidence presented in Figure 3.2 lends support to this notion: While the pre-2000s follow a similar industrialization with deindustrialization tendencies at higher-income levels, the post-2000s see a notable reduction in the structural change dynamics (through a flattening of the regression line in Figure 3.2) for both middle-income country aggregates as well as the group of high-income countries. What is more, the positive relationship between manufacturing and income seems to break down completely for low-income economies in the post-2000s. Against this backdrop, doubts have been cast on the continuing importance of manufacturing as a shaping factor of economic prosperity for future development: It is the identification of these time-related patterns of premature deindustrialization that has led researchers to argue that manufacturing-led growth has become a more difficult path for currently developing countries to follow as they "are running out of industrialization opportunities sooner and at much lower levels of income compared to the experiences of earlier industrializers" (Rodrik, 2016, p. 1).

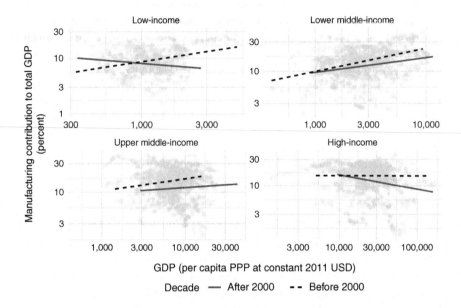

Figure 3.2 Manufacturing value-added contribution to GDP, 1950–2017
Note: Constructed using pooled data for 153 countries. Country classification following
World Bank (2019a). X- and y-axis in log scale.

Source: Calculations based on World Development Indicators (World Bank 2019b) and
Penn World Tables 9.1 (Feenstra, Inklaar, and Timmer 2015).

3.2.3 Manufacturing as the engine of growth: A more complex future ahead

While aggregated inter-temporal dynamics may paint a rather bleak picture for
manufacturing's capacities for promoting growth for the road ahead, recent
research also shows that these stylized findings are far from universal and to a
notable degree the result of heterogeneities and fragmentation both across countries and industries alike.

3.2.3.1 Fragmentation across countries

Findings in Rodrik (2016) seem to suggest that there is indeed (regional)
heterogeneity among developing countries.[4] Rodrik explains the variation in
manufacturing-related growth outcomes as being the consequence of comparative advantages. He finds that countries with a strong comparative advantage,
i.e., extensive manufacturer exporters, have experienced much less pronounced
reduction in manufacturing value-added shares and employment figures than
their less competitive, i.e., non-exporting counterparts. In the same vein,
Dasgupta and Singh (2006) describe the three pillars of premature industrialization as: (1) lower-income level turning points as well as (2) "jobless growth"
in manufacturing combined with comparatively faster-growing services for

low(er)-income countries. Noting significant regional discrepancies in their analysis, the authors argue that this development may be due to "nonconforming structures unable to satisfy changes in consumer demand" (Dasgupta & Singh, 2006, p. 1) and that departures from historic trajectories could suggest that the service industry in some countries might be gaining more importance in earlier stages of economic development.

Discussing evidence of hampered industrial development in the more recent past, Ghani and O'Connell (2014) reason that the low pick-up rate of industrial development in less developed countries may be due to productivity gains by means of better technology and demand side effects. The same argument is also made in Rodrik (2016), who identifies both changes in preferences as well as technology, as the driving forces behind deindustrialization. Ghani and O'Connell (2014) also stress that the "third industrial revolution" has been much more about a well-thought integration of industry, services, and trade and that the globalization of services may provide a different experience for currently developing countries compared to other past experiences. This is an important observation. It goes without saying that the last decades have brought about many changes in the political and economic environment, which have been fuelled by technological progress and globalization. Through the emergence of the fourth industrial revolution with smart technology and fully integrated and automated production processes, i.e., the *smart factory* in the domain of *industry 4.0,* these tendencies will only accelerate and bring new challenges for developing economies (UNIDO, 2020). Yet, given the observation that "the dividing line between manufacturing and services is becoming increasingly blurred" (Ghani & O'Connell, 2014, p. 4), doubts may be raised about the definite statement that premature deindustrialization, as observed in the aggregate, leads to both a decline in manufacturing's importance as an engine of growth or the argued redundancy of political ramifications of policy-led industrial development.

Emphasizing the challenges of the changing global environment, researchers have indicated the more complex, multi-dimensional nature of industrial development of the more recent past. For example, Szirmai and Verspagen (2015) stress the importance of industrial development and manufacturing with regards to productivity, capital accumulation, and economies of scale as well as linkages, spillovers, and demand-side effects, and state that manufacturing is an important contributor to inclusive labor-force mobilization. The latter argument is very important as strong linkages between manufacturing and services are found for advanced economies and, in some cases, dependence structures have been identified where manufacturing provides a necessary foundation for service activities (Guerrieri & Meliciani, 2005). What is more, the composition of linkages is also strongly connected to the degree of development of an economy. Consequently, not accounting for inter-sectoral linkages in employment, output will not fully represent the employment impact of the manufacturing industry in its full context (UNIDO, 2013).

Lin and Monga (2010) discuss industrial development in the context of government-led industrial policy interventions and argue that exploiting comparative advantages should be an important objective in well-targeted industrial development. The authors show that attempts at copying too advanced economies (measured by the percentage difference of GDP) may do the economy of the industrializing country more harm than good. Consequently, they stress the importance of a policy-led framework for growth identification and facilitation of potential industries based on comparative advantage. In other words, the authors make a strong case that successful industrialization is the result of careful and far-sighted policy interventions to "identify industries that are appropriate for a given country's endowment structure and level of development" (Lin & Monga, 2010, p. 4).

3.2.3.2 *Heterogeneity within manufacturing*

Finally, in order to fully understand the nature of patterns of industrialization as well as (premature) de-industrialization alike, it is imperative to unravel the dynamics in manufacturing itself. This is because an aggregated analysis alone is not sufficient to assess whether deindustrialization tendencies can be attributable to country-specific policy-related factors, or if they are the consequence of a long-term shift in the global economic structure. Haraguchi, Cheng, and Smeets (2017) argue that opportunities for manufacturing development have not changed as the global contributions of employment as well as value-added have not decreased for developing countries over the last four decades. They explain that industrial development remains strong for developing countries with certain characteristics. Rather than losing its development potential, the authors identify a shift of manufacturing activities to a relatively small number of populous countries, which leads to a concentration of manufacturing-related industries for a distinct group of developing countries. In other words, when not aggregating manufacturing and employment figures on a country level, but globally, they find no evidence of a reduction of either employment or value-added to the global aggregate over the last four decades. Since those populous successful countries, China, in particular, are now mostly at the upper middle-income levels and likely to follow a normal pattern of deindustrialization in the future, hitherto less successful developing countries could experience faster manufacturing development if they implemented the right policies.

Haraguchi and Amann (2020b) discuss sectoral differences in patterns of innovation. The authors connect Pavitt-type classifications with structural change, thus linking technology classes with manufacturing industries. Their analysis reveals a substantial degree of heterogeneity in manufacturing as far as development patterns are concerned. The authors make the important argument that the aggregate figures on deindustrialization in advanced economies can be misleading. Some high-technology sectors continue to grow at high levels of income, while others do not. They also document that the effect of premature deindustrialization and productivity growth varies significantly across manufacturing industries and that notable heterogeneities can also be associated with exogenous factors such as resource endowment and country size.

To summarize, the importance of manufacturing as an engine of growth is of a quite dynamic nature. Not only is it subject to changes with regards to the income level of an economy, it is also found to vary considerably over time. There is little doubt that the growth dynamics of manufacturing as a contributory factor to economic development have become more stagnant on an aggregated level. The reasons for this can be found in the "classical argument"—at higher-income levels, industrially developed countries become more and more service-oriented—with its unarguable effect on aggregated statistics. Additionally, further empirical evidence seems suggestive of the fact that deindustrialization also appears to occur at lower-income levels and is accompanied by decreasing employment opportunities; however, it is subject to striking regional differences. All of this seems to suggest that more recent industrial development is more complex than how it was experienced by the early industrializing nations in the past, and the reasons for this may be the same ones that are argued to be among the driving patterns behind industrial change itself: technological progress, global trade, and specialization as well as demand-side effects. What remains unchanged is that finding the right policy mix and targeting the right industry present industrializing countries with a complex challenge which some will cope with more successfully than others.

3.2.3.3 *The role of manufacturing for pro-poor growth: A stylized view*

While the previous discussion has added a bit of nuance to the debate on manufacturing development by stressing the complex nature of manufacturing development, little has been said about the connection between a strong manufacturing base and pro-poor growth in particular. In order to get a more contextualized understanding of the two, Figure 3.3 compares the evolution of per capita GDP levels of two selected groups of countries against the quintile distribution of global per capita GDP from 1965 to 2017. Consequently, the lowest dashed line indicates the GDP per capita level of the poorest country at any given time, the next dashed line indicates the same GDP per capita measure where 20 percent fall below (and 80 percent remain above). Given this representation, we can easily assess the growth performances of the group of selected countries vis-à-vis the overall performance of all world economies as a whole, thereby indicating which countries have "climbed the income ladder" relative to others.[5]

As the upper panel in Figure 3.3 reveals, the two country aggregates start off at a very similar and relatively low-income level, putting both countries into the lowest per capita income quintile in 1966. However, while the set of (climbing) countries move to around the 40th percentile in per capita GDP by the mid-2010s, the other (non-climbing) group remains within the lowest quintile. See Figure 3.4 for the individual country series. The lower panel of Figure 3.3 contrasts this with the average sectoral shares for both sets of aggregates over the same time period. Most interestingly, both aggregates are found to start with a rather similar share of services and agriculture with a much lower contribution for manufacturing and (non-manufacturing) industry. However, while both see a robust share of roughly 20 percent for the climbing aggregate, these sectors remain largely undeveloped for the group of non-climbing economies. What is more, the non-climbing aggregate shows a moderate shift from agriculture into services for the post-2000s with both the (non-manufacturing) industry and manufacturing sector remaining stagnant over the same time window. This is

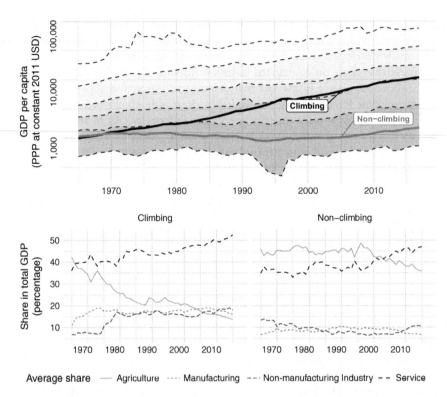

Figure 3.3 Pro-poor growth over time
Upper panel: Quintile Distribution of per Capita GDP, 1965–2017. Lower panel: Sectoral GDP Composition by Sectors over Time for Selected Countries, 1965–2015.
Note: Upper panel based on pooled data for 182 countries for quintile distribution. Selected countries by group are highlighted by solid lines. Y-axis in log scale. Lower panel shows sectoral composition of selected countries by group. Selected countries included: Botswana, Bosnia and Herzegovina, China, Egypt, Thailand Republic of Korea, Indonesia, Bhutan, Cabo Verde, Lao People's DR, Viet Nam, Myanmar, India, Cambodia Lesotho (*climbing*) and Nepal, Uganda, Rwanda, Burkina Faso, Mali, Togo, Ethiopia, Guinea-Bissau, Madagascar, Malawi, Niger, Liberia, Burundi, Central African Republic (*non-climbing*). See Figure 3.4 for individual country series.

Source: Own calculations based on World Development Indicators (World Bank 2019b) and Penn World Tables 9.1 (Feenstra, Inklaar, and Timmer 2015).

in line with the point made by Dasgupta and Singh (2006) regarding the service industry potentially gaining more importance in earlier stages of economic development than in the past. Yet with the shift from agriculture into services, it does not appear as if these dynamics translate well into increases in income as the overwhelming majority of surveyed non-climbing economies seem to have lost in relative income compared to the global trend, as can be seen in Figure 3.4. The bigger relative reduction in agriculture reflects the argument made by Szirmai and Verspagen (2015) that manufacturing is an important contributor to inclusive

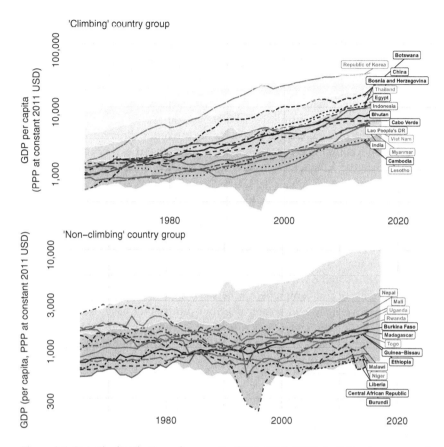

Figure 3.4 Quintile distribution of per capita GDP, 1965–2017; individual country series by group

Note: Quintile distribution based on pooled data for 182 countries for quintile distribution. Y-axis in log scale.

Source: Own calculations based on World Development Indicators (World Bank 2019b) and Penn World Tables 9.1 (Feenstra, Inklaar, and Timmer 2015).

labor-force mobilization with strong backward linkages to the primary sector for developing countries which we illustrate in Section 3.4. Before this, however, Section 3.3 will expand on designated structural change patterns for pro-poor growth in manufacturing.

3.3 Designated patterns of structural change for pro-poor growth

Ideally, rapid economic growth will lead to a broad and stable generation of employment as well as value-added in all industries, thereby creating quantitatively high and qualitatively diverse jobs across all industries. This goes hand-in-hand with an increase in the demand for jobs that require different skill sets and will both reduce unemployment rates as well as enable people to transition from subsistence into the labor force. As the previous discussion has shown, structural change dynamics depend on multiple different and often counteracting sources, making it a highly complex topic. What is more, while robust growth patterns have been found not to be the general rule of growth patterns (Pritchett, 2000), it is worthwhile investigating ways in which manufacturing development could be made more inclusive by putting special emphasis on exploring pro-poor growth patterns. Since structural change dynamics are strikingly different for low and middle-income countries versus high(er-)income countries, we illustrate the structural change dynamics by concentrating on the low end of the income range. For a more general discussion, see Haraguchi and Amann (2020b).

To this end, in this section we identify key manufacturing industries which are particularly associated with pro-poor growth. The analysis benefits from an up-to-date data set on global manufacturing at the industry level which is used to provide a detailed account of structural change dynamics in manufacturing. The novelty of our analysis comes from the uniquely compiled manufacturing industry data set which is based on INDSTAT (2017) and improves upon other data sets by its level of detail and comprehensiveness (Haraguchi & Amann, 2020a). The nine industries we analyze in greater depth in this chapter have been chosen to be reflective of the representative performance of the numerous components of the manufacturing sector.[6] A detailed discussion on the methodology used in this part of the chapter is provided in Appendix B.

3.3.1 A pro-poor path of manufacturing development: An overview

Figure 3.5 visualizes the relationship between the value-added and employment share contribution of selected manufacturing industries in total manufacturing at different income levels and illustrates the compositional changes of the manufacturing sector as countries grow richer. The projections start at a per capita income level of US$500 and, in increments of US$1,000, move up to US$15,000. The final projection point of US$15,000 is identified by the connecting label. Using Figure 3.5, one can also infer the speed of structural change: For each sector aggregate, the connecting lines indicate the projected trajectory of employment or value-added as the income level of the economy rises by US$1,000. Consequently, the greater the distance between two connecting points, the bigger the structural change of the sector with respect to either value-added (by a strict horizontal movement), employment (by a strict vertical movement) or both (a combination of both).

For low-income countries, low-technology industries are of particularly high importance relative to medium and high-technology industries in terms of their value-added and employment generation, as they offer a noteworthy accelerator in both domains. Arguably, this is because of low unit labor costs and comparative advantages. While *food and beverages* are found to be remarkably robust with regards to changes in income per capita, both *wearing apparel* and *textiles* are highly affected by structural change along both dimensions. However, at least for durable consumer products, this advantage is short-lived. While, at low-income levels, *wearing apparel* is found to increase its relative employment share in manufacturing, this sector experiences a decline in both value-added and employment generation at moderate incomes. The industry-level pattern of deindustrialization is even more pronounced for *textiles*. While this is the second most important sector for low-income countries right after *food and beverages*, a steady decrease in its relative importance can be observed for increasing income levels. This transformation is also quite fast, as can be seen in Figure 3.5. The rationale behind this is simple from an economic point of view: If comparative advantages are the driving mechanism for these sorts of goods, durability implies that countries compete more internationally and small differences in a country's cost structure can have a considerable impact on its sectoral performance. Non-durable and domestic-oriented industries like food and beverages, on the other hand, are less substitutable and hence more demand-inelastic. Particularly for *food and beverages*, consumption may be innately informed by consumer taste which can be more heterogeneous and country-specific and, consequently, might

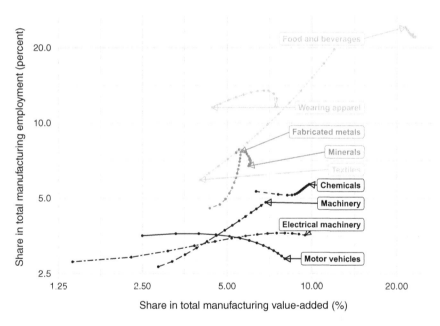

Figure 3.5 Value-added and employment share by income for selected manufacturing industry

Note: Based on pooled cross-country data for up to 153 countries between 1963 and 2015. Projections from per capita GDP USD 500 up to USD 15,000 in increments of USD 1,000. Final projection point at USD 15,000 is highlighted by the connecting label.

Source: Calculations based on INDSTAT (2017) and Penn World Tables 9.1 (Feenstra, Inklaar, and Timmer 2015) following Haraguchi and Amann (2020a).

be less affected by changes in income structure. In general terms, however, while being of the utmost importance at low-income levels, the importance of low-technology industries producing durable products decreases dramatically in terms of its contribution to value-added and employment of the manufacturing sector. In Figure 3.5, this is illustrated by a downward-sloping trajectory from the upper-right to the lower-left corner.

At the same time, while being the most underdeveloped industries at low-income levels, high-technology industries see a continuous growth in value-added contribution as well as in employment (for *chemicals, machinery,* and *electrical machinery*). At the upper middle-income levels, these industries have surpassed their low-technology counterparts in terms of value-added contribution while they remain below in terms of employment, thereby displaying their immense scalability potential. As far as medium-technology industries are concerned, these are typically identified as the least dynamic technology aggregate. However, it has to be noted that particularly these industries are subject to significant country-specific variation due to the difference in resource endowment (Chenery & Syrquin, 1975) which naturally is not fully exploited by an aggregate analysis similar to the one presented here.

3.3.2 Development patterns in manufacturing

Based on the discussion so far, two observations seem worthy of being pointed out. On the one hand, evidence based on a disaggregated analysis of the nine individual manufacturing industries shows a notable difference in development patterns across industries: Some aggregates seem to be subject to deindustrialization tendencies at much lower income levels than others. On the other hand, evidence presented so far does not make any inference regarding the contribution of any manufacturing industry in absolute terms, as a rising share of one industry could simply be the result of a lower negative growth rate of this particular industry relative to the manufacturing sector as a whole. To address this issue, the analysis in this section differs from the one in Section 3.3.1 as it looks at the actual contribution of each industry to value-added per capita, as well as the employment-to-population ratio. This approach is preferred for an in-depth analysis as it is not influenced by any volatility of other industries and hence is better suited to shed light on actual industry characteristics.

3.3.2.1 The baseline case

Figure 3.6 and Figure 3.7 highlight the trajectory of selected manufacturing industries as countries' per capita income levels increase. At very early stages of development, the low technology industries are of central importance in order to promote both employment and value-added growth. Particularly from the lowest levels of income, *food and beverages* as well as *textiles* and *wearing apparel* are found to have by far the highest contribution to value-added and employment generation. Among other industries that develop substantial employment

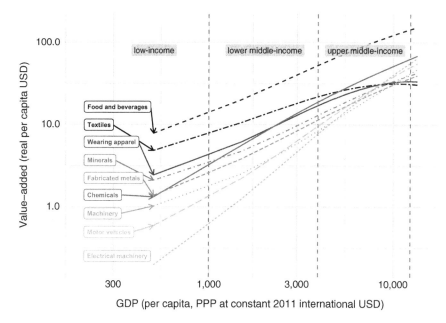

Figure 3.6 Value-added by income for selected manufacturing industry
Note: Based on pooled cross-country data for up to 153 countries between 1963 and 2015. Income group cut-offs identified by the dashed vertical lines at USD 995, USD 3,896 and USD 12,375 as defined by World Bank Country and Lending Groups (World Bank 2019a).
Source: Calculations based on INDSTAT (2017) and Penn World Tables 9.1 (Feenstra, Inklaar, and Timmer 2015) following Haraguchi and Amann (2020a).

dynamics at the lowest income margins are chemicals—which is identified as the most dynamic industry at low income levels in value-added generation—as well as *(non-metallic) minerals.* This is because they produce important input factors such as fertilizers, dyes, or soap as well as building materials such as glass, cement, and bricks—all of which, together with *food and beverages* as well as *textiles* and *wearing apparel,* are of the utmost importance at low development levels as they all accommodate the basic needs of the country's citizens. These goods can be seen as necessary requisites for stable, long-run development and poverty reduction: Only if these input factors are both abundant and cheap, can more advanced industries develop free of constraints or limitations. What is more, particularly *food and beverages* as well as chemicals have been identified as retaining their growth potential even at high-income levels and over time, thereby indicating their critical role as cornerstones of well-balanced and successful industrial development. The low technology group is also the most labor-intensive in its production processes. This fact is illustrated in Figure 3.7 which shows the striking impact of the low technology group in the creation

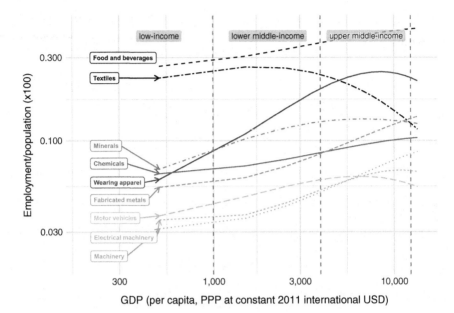

Figure 3.7 Employment-to-population by income for selected manufacturing industry
Note: Based on pooled cross-country data for up to 153 countries between 1963 and 2015. Income group cut-offs identified by the dashed vertical lines at USD 995, USD 3,896 and USD 12,375 as defined by World Bank Country and Lending Groups (World Bank 2019a).

Source: Calculations based on INDSTAT (2017) and Penn World Tables 9.1 (Feenstra, Inklaar, and Timmer 2015) following Haraguchi and Amann (2020a).

of formal manufacturing employment for often agrarian economies. Among these labor-intensive, low-technology industries, it is particularly the *food and beverages* industries that can sustain long-run growth in employment whereas both *textiles* and *wearing apparel* experience significant employment reductions at lower-middle as well as upper middle-income levels, respectively. In other words, labor-intensive industries seem to be crucial for the development of employment opportunities at low incomes and early stages of industrial development. As the population moves from agriculture into formal, paid employment, labor-intensive industries offer a pivotal option to facilitate big movements in the labor force and accommodate the productive absorption of job-seekers. Particularly at the early development stage of an economy, there is also ample opportunity for capital accumulation which, however, as economies transition to and beyond the group of upper middle-income countries, becomes restricted to *food and beverages*. In Haraguchi (2012), the previously mentioned industries were classified as "original," as they both exist in almost all countries and meet citizens' basic needs even before industrialization. Consequently, the production processes of these industries are very likely to be notably different in low-income versus high-income countries. It is thus necessary for developing countries to carefully modernize these "original" industries while continuously developing and promoting new industries in order to sustain the growth trajectories in value-added as well as employment generation. In this context, Figure 3.6 and Figure 3.7 also illustrate an interesting point regarding the dynamics within the low technology aggregate. Already at low-income levels, *textiles* experience a reduction in employability which, together with the observation that their value-added growth potential remains strong in the lower-income ranges, become more capital-intensive at very early stages of economic development. What is more, *wearing apparel* is the first industry that develops its employment base relative to other industries: This industry displays a moderate employment potential at lowest incomes but experiences significant employment growth with increases in a country's income level. It can be argued that modernization and success in this industry may represent a first experience of how industrialization can make a difference to a country's development.

High technology industries, on the other hand, consistently develop at medium to late stages of development while they are typically the most fast-growing industries in terms of their value-added generation across all manufacturing industries, even at low-income levels. Medium technology industries share common elements of both the low-technology as well as the high-technology group. They are particularly robust for countries within the range of upper middle-income countries while we also acknowledge their pivotal position as an integral building block of an evolving economy: Producing bricks, cement, and glass, the *minerals* industries are largely driven by domestic demand. Similar to low-technology industries, they are further typical early developers in both employment and value-added. Different from the set of low-technology industries, however, and apart from *food and beverages*, *minerals* retain their value-added growth at much higher income levels while also experiencing only a slight reduction in employment. In general, medium-technology industries offer investment potential for middle-income as well as upper middle-income countries and may potentially remain significant at high-income levels. Even though they do not develop employment opportunities as early along the income trajectory as low-technology industries, they do offer more robust and stable development opportunities at higher-income levels. On top of that, they are typically high-productivity industries and provide ample investment opportunities (UNIDO, 2013).

3.3.2.2 Development classification

Based on the previous discussion, this section summarizes the industry dynamics based on the relative importance in generating both employment and value-added at early stages of development.[7] Rearranged in this way we can see that the major contributors to both value-added (Figure 3.8) and employment (Figure 3.9) are the two low-technology industries *textiles* as well as *wearing apparel*. They remain the strongest players in the generation of value-added up to a per capita income of US$4,000 and about US$10,000 for employment. At their peaks, *textiles* and

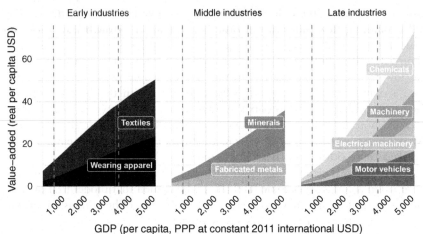

Figure 3.8 Accumulated value-added by income for selected manufacturing industry
Note: Based on pooled cross-country data for up to 153 countries between 1963 and 2015. Income group cut-offs identified by the dashed vertical lines at USD 995 and USD 3,896 as defined by World Bank Country and Lending Groups (World Bank 2019a).

Source: Calculations based on INDSTAT (2017) and Penn World Tables 9.1 (Feenstra, Inklaar, and Timmer 2015) following Haraguchi and Amann (2020a).

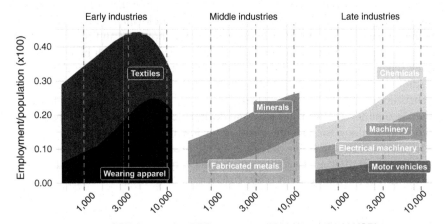

Figure 3.9 Accumulated employment by income for selected manufacturing industry
Note: Based on pooled cross-country data for up to 153 countries between 1963 and 2015. Income group cut-offs identified by the dashed vertical lines at USD 995, USD 3,896 and USD 12,375 as defined by World Bank Country and Lending Groups (World Bank 2019a).

Source: Calculations based on INDSTAT (2017) and Penn World Tables 9.1 (Feenstra, Inklaar, and Timmer 2015) following Haraguchi and Amann (2020a).

wearing apparel alone employ more people than all other manufacturing industries (except for *food and beverages*) combined. In light of this, it is argued that for low-income countries, successful development of the *wearing apparel* industry could provide an incredibly important boost to both value-added generation and labor force mobilization with the positive side effects of promoting personal income growth, firm growth, and increases in firm profits, as well as government revenue for investment in better education and infrastructure, which as a whole could make an important contribution to poverty reduction. In other words, successfully developing the *wearing apparel* industry will also have a significantly positive effect in the context of institutional development as well as policy and managerial learning as these early experiences of industrial development will thereafter provide a fruitful foundation for continuous and future industrial development efforts.

Since there are no middle or late industries that are comparable to the early, low-technology group in terms of their labor force absorption capacity, Figure 3.9 emphasizes that a country needs to develop middle and late industries more broadly in order to compensate for the decline of the major employment sources provided by the low-technology group at earlier income stages. Particularly the extent and direction of substitutability of capital and labor in the context of comparative advantages should serve as a warning sign for developing countries not to wait too long before diversifying their industrial portfolio when approaching the US$10,000 mark. Consequently, middle and late industries need to play an increasingly important role in the context of industrial development to ensure that the country remains on a prosperous growth trajectory by creating new employment opportunities and increasing growth potential and also to counterbalance reductions in employment experienced by the low technology/early industries. In other words, with increasing income levels, manufacturing development paths become more complex and diverse: In order to retain the initial boost in employment and value-added generation, developing economies have to develop several middle and late industries simultaneously.

3.3.2.3 Substitutability of input factors

It is one of the characteristics of the manufacturing sector that production processes become more capital-intensive as income rises and production becomes more elaborate. This substitutability between the input factors of labor and capital is one of the driving factors that explains the extensive scalability of manufacturing production. Given the very strong heterogeneity of manufacturing industries, it should not be surprising that notable differences can also be observed in that respect.

Figure 3.10 illustrates the income elasticities of value-added and the employment-to-population ratio of *electrical machinery* and *wearing apparel*. These elasticities reflect the change in each of these variables expressed in changes of per capita GDP. One of the unique characteristics of the *wearing apparel* industry is its limited potential to substitute production factors. This means, even

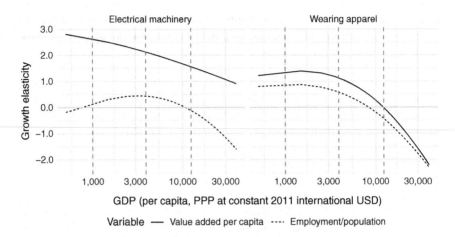

Figure 3.10 Growth elasticities of value-added and employment/population by income for
   selected manufacturing industry

Note: Based on pooled cross-country data for up to 153 countries between 1963 and
2015. Income group cut-offs identified by the dashed vertical lines at USD 995, USD
3,896 and USD 12,375 as defined by World Bank Country and Lending Groups (World
Bank 2019a).

Source: Calculations based on INDSTAT (2017) and Penn World Tables 9.1 (Feenstra,
Inklaar, and Timmer 2015) following Haraguchi and Amann (2020a).

at high(er) income levels, *wearing apparel* will always remain relatively labor-
intensive compared to other industries with fewer opportunities to substitute
labor for capital. Put differently, as this industry loses its comparative advantages
due to increasing labor costs, value-added-led growth patterns brought about by
a more rigorous utilization of capital—which can be witnessed in more capital-
intensive industries such as late and high technology industries—are not feasible
for this industry. Therefore, once a country reaches an upper middle-income
level, it tends to lose competitiveness in the industry and reduces both value-
added and employment relatively quickly. With low-wage labor being the key
input factor, *wearing apparel* has little scope for productivity increase. The
almost parallel decline of value-added and employment-to-population changes
indicates only limited room for this industry to substitute capital for labor. This
stands in sharp contrast to the *electrical machinery* industry where the estimated
patterns show significant potential for such a substitution. Even though labor
input declines, the increase in labor productivity helps to sustain the value-added
growth of the industry.

3.3.3 Premature deindustrialization across manufacturing industries

The previous sections established the heterogeneous development of manufacturing industries and highlighted the importance of a set of key industries in the

early stages of economic development. We now shift to the question of whether these general dynamics have remained unchanged over time or if the most recent decades have seen a transformation in the development patterns of manufacturing industries. We do this by revisiting the topic of premature deindustrialization and identify emerging characteristics within manufacturing by estimating Equation (3.1) in Appendix A separately for the 1970s, the 1980s and the 1990s as well as the period from 2000 onwards; see Appendix B. We will also refer to these four distinct periods as decades for the remainder of this section. As before, we limit the discussion to the same sub-sample of representative industries and the low-income to upper middle-income range.

In Figure 3.11 we can identify some time-dependent dynamics for value-added in the low-technology group and in particular for *textiles*. As a matter of fact, this industry seems to be most affected by a decrease in average value-added contribution in the last 20-odd years. However, Figure 3.11 also indicates that this trend seems far from general. Particularly for high technology industries, development potentials appear very robust in the post-2000s compared to earlier

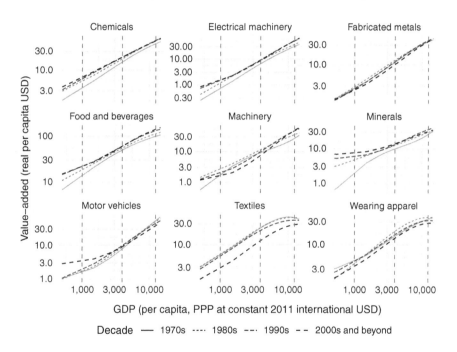

Figure 3.11 Changes in value-added over time by income for selected manufacturing industry

Note: Based on pooled cross-country data for up to 153 countries between 1970 and 2015. Income group cut-offs identified by the dashed vertical lines at USD 995, USD 3,896 and USD 12,375 as defined by World Bank Country and Lending Groups (World Bank 2019a).

Source: Calculations based on INDSTAT (2017) and Penn World Tables 9.1 (Feenstra, Inklaar, and Timmer 2015) following Haraguchi and Amann (2020a).

decades. When looking at employment patterns in Figure 3.12, we see a less uniform picture. Among low-technology industries, employment in *textiles* as well as *wearing apparel* has been markedly lower in more recent decades. For both industries, we can see a reduction in the hump-shaped relationship as well as a shift of the tipping point of maximum employment generation to earlier industries. Particularly for the *textile* industry, the employment trajectory has become much more stagnant compared to earlier periods. Another observation is that across most industries, the employment potential appears less dynamic at lower-income levels. In other words, at lower-income levels, employment generation across most industries in the post-2000s is not at the level of earlier periods. The effect is particularly strong for low-skilled manual labor industries. While these findings are in line with the results of Haraguchi, Cheng, and Smeets (2017) and could hint at the centralization of certain industries in a handful of large, populous countries, an alternative explanation could be that improvements in production technologies simply have resulted in a much more capital-intensive initial industrialization kick-off than observed in earlier decades.

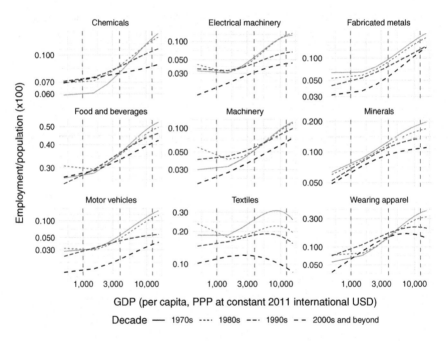

Figure 3.12 Changes in employment over time by income for selected manufacturing industry

Note: Based on pooled cross-country data for up to 153 countries between 1970 and 2015. Income group cut-offs identified by the dashed vertical lines at USD 995, USD 3,896 and USD 12,375 as defined by World Bank Country and Lending Groups (World Bank 2019a).

Source: Calculations based on INDSTAT (2017) and Penn World Tables 9.1 (Feenstra, Inklaar, and Timmer 2015) following Haraguchi and Amann (2020a).

Based on these observations, a natural question is whether the overall contribution of manufacturing in the value-added and employment generation has increased as an aggregate from the 1970s to the 2000s and onwards. We present the aggregated figures in Figure 3.13 and Figure 3.14, respectively. Overall, a notable change in the composition of the industries can be seen by a bump-up and increase in particularly high-technology/late industries in the later decades. What is more, *textiles* seems to have lost in relative importance based on its contribution to value-added and also very notably in employment generation; see Figure 3.14. As a whole, manufacturing structural change over time has strongly been subject to increase in capital intensity. What is interesting is the observation that this trend seems to mainly have happened between the 1970s to 1990s, as the last 25 years have seen very little change in the levels of the employment-to-population ratio across industries with overall peak employment being roughly the same from the early 1990s onwards. What is more, we see the industry-level

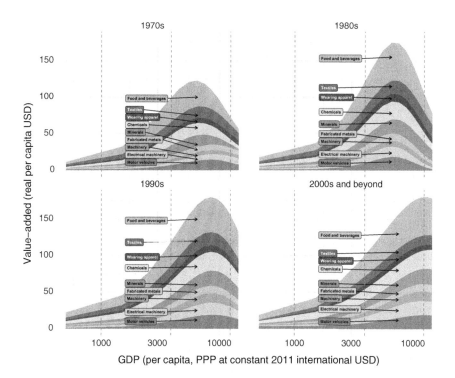

Figure 3.13 Changes in accumulated value-added by income for selected manufacturing industry

Note: Based on pooled cross-country data for up to 153 countries between 1970 and 2015. Income group cut-offs identified by the dashed vertical lines at USD 995, USD 3,896 and USD 12,375 as defined by World Bank Country and Lending Groups (World Bank 2019a).

Source: Calculations based on INDSTAT (2017) and Penn World Tables 9.1 (Feenstra, Inklaar, and Timmer 2015) following Haraguchi and Amann (2020a).

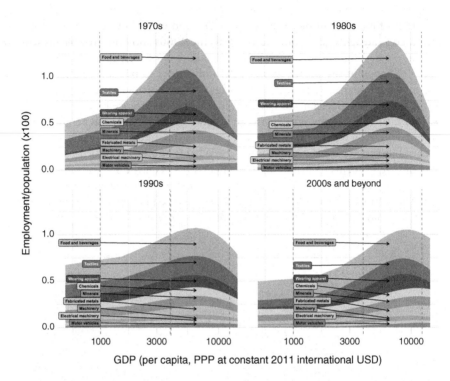

Figure 3.14 Changes in accumulated employment by income for selected manufacturing industry

Note: Based on pooled cross-country data for up to 153 countries between 1970 and 2015. Income group cut-offs identified by the dashed vertical lines at USD 995, USD 3,896 and USD 12,375 as defined by World Bank Country and Lending Groups (World Bank 2019a).

Source: Calculations based on INDSTAT (2017) and Penn World Tables 9.1 (Feenstra, Inklaar, and Timmer 2015) following Haraguchi and Amann (2020a).

contribution has changed significantly over time as well and most notably for the low-technology group. Whereas *food and beverages* have remained a strong and stable developer over time, particularly the *textile* industry appears to be hit the hardest by inter-temporal structural change. Even though it still remains a significant industry, particularly in the early stages of development, its relative share in total employment generation has experienced a steady decline. Another very interesting observation can be made with regards to *wearing apparel* which, because of its unique characteristics, has shown little signs of capital intensification. This emphasizes the important position this industry has in the context of sector-level, manufacturing development of low-income countries.

The above analysis suggests a significant shift and reduction in the importance of the *textile* industry mainly brought about by technological advances and higher capital intensity over the last decades. Among the other low-technology industries, *food and beverages* as well as *wearing apparel* increase their fundamental importance for successful industrial development in relative terms. Whereas the former serves as one of the biggest promoters of employment and value-added for all income levels, the latter retains its predominant position as the first industry that should specifically be targeted by policymakers to improve industrial growth dynamics from early levels of economic development onwards, due to its impact on both growth and poverty reduction. In addition to these two main pillars, chemicals play an additional integral role in the development of an economy and have to be highlighted for their unprecedented growth potential for value-added across all income ranges of development.

3.3.4 Employment mobilization beyond manufacturing

It goes without saying that the development impact of manufacturing is not restricted to value-added and employment in manufacturing alone but is well integrated in the grand scheme of the economy (Szirmai & Verspagen, 2015). With this in mind, it may be reasonable that a particular manufacturing industry may see a reduction in industry-level (direct) employment while total industry-induced employment is actually on the rise, due to particularly strong employment links to other parts of the economy. In this section we examine the extent and nature of such manufacturing industry-related employment links on the sector level in Figure 3.15. For more information on data and methodology, see Appendix C.

Manufacturing industries are very different in terms of their employment links (Figure 3.15). Particularly, low technology industries like food, beverages, and tobacco or *textiles, wearing apparel*, and *leather* have very strong links to the primary sector. Not surprisingly, food, beverages, and tobacco are found to have the strongest employment-inducing effect toward the primary sector underscoring their importance in contributing to inclusive labor-force mobilization. The medium-technology industries (such as *minerals* or *fabricated metals*) only show very moderate links to other sectors of the economy. This is an important result as these industries, despite their robust growth and important position in the creation of raw material necessary to further economic development (such as glass or concrete), are less connected to other parts of the economy through the employment process but remain so through their production output. While low technology industries have particularly pronounced links to the primary sector, high technology industries are much more connected to services. These results appear particularly noteworthy in the context of the more difficult separation of manufacturing- and service-related production (Ghani & O'Connell, 2014).[8]

Another important insight is that the linkage structure of manufacturing industries dramatically changes depending on the development stage of the economy. This is stressed in Figure 3.17 which contrasts the share of employment backward-linkages across sectors for advanced and emerging economies. A particular feature of manufacturing industries is that their employment linkages typically move from more primary-related to more service-related business at higher-income levels: Irrespective of the industry, manufacturing induces notable employment in the primary sector for emerging industries while notable business

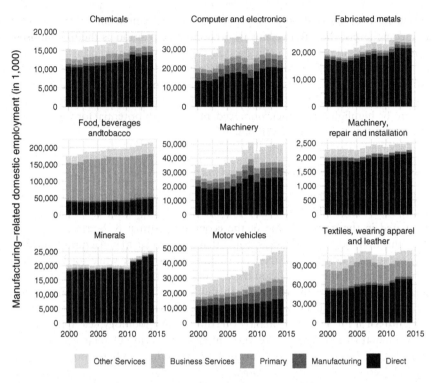

Figure 3.15 Domestic employment linkages over time by selected manufacturing industry
Note: World Input-Output Table based on 28 EU countries and 15 other major countries
in the world for the period from 2000 to 2014. Domestic employment linkages within the
same industry is referred to as direct employment. The remaining four categories in this
figure sum up domestic linkages of the corresponding sectors, respectively. See Appendix
C for more information on data and methodology.
Source: Calculations based on World Input-Output Database (WIOD) Release 2016
(Timmer et al., 2015).

upgrading and a stronger connection with the service sectors can be observed
across the vast majority of industries at higher incomes.

This insight is particularly useful and important when analyzing the growth
trajectory for industrializing countries, as this aggregated analysis shows
that thoughtful industrialization plays an integral role in the development of
manufacturing-related employment opportunities for developing and developed
countries alike. In other words, industrial development not only helps an economy
to fully integrate its employment potential at lower incomes but it also generates
more employment opportunities within as well as outside of manufacturing. This
positive acceleration effect of manufacturing, where medium- and high-technology
industries, particularly those sustaining high value-added growth at high(er)
incomes, do not only make up for the overall decline of manufacturing jobs as
illustrated above, but also compensate by generating modern jobs in services and

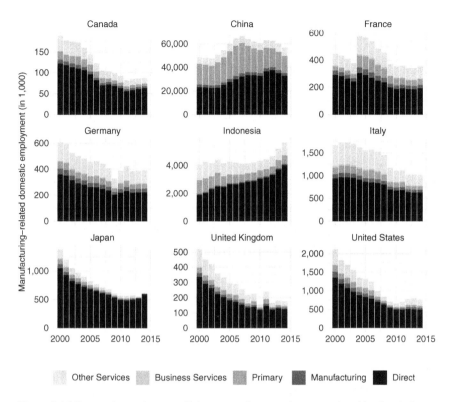

Figure 3.16 Domestic employment linkages: textiles, wearing apparel and leather industry over time for selected countries

Note: World Input-Output Table based on 28 EU countries and 15 other major countries in the world for the period from 2000 to 2014. Domestic employment linkages within the same industry is refereed to as direct employment. The remaining four categories in this figure sum up domestic linkages of the corresponding sectors, respectively. See Appendix C for more information on data and methodology.

Source: Calculations based on World Input-Output Database (WIOD) Release 2016 (Timmer et al., 2015).

other manufacturing-related industries. Therefore, careful and targeted manufacturing development is not only necessary in order to unleash manufacturing's full employment potential across all its industries, but it also plays a crucial role in using and promoting innovative service activities which, in turn, are by themselves of increasing importance as an economy moves along its income trajectory.

3.3.5 Sustainability and manufacturing development: An inevitable trade-off?

Discussing industrial growth policies in the twenty-first century is incomplete without discussing its implications with regards to sustainability in general and climate change in particular. For developing economies, there are meaningful

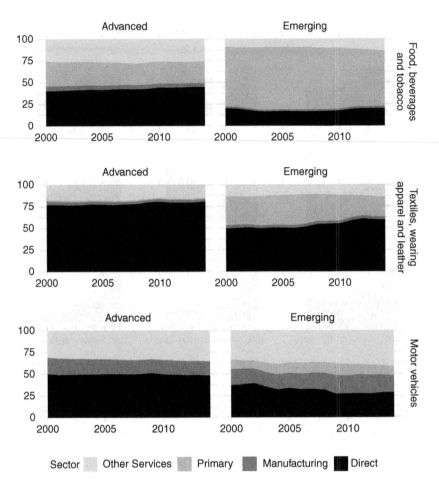

Figure 3.17 Domestic employment linkages: shares over time by economic development and selected manufacturing industry

Note: World Input-Output Table based on 28 EU countries and 15 other major countries in the world for the period from 2000 to 2014. Domestic employment linkages within the same industry is refereed to as direct employment. The remaining four categories in this figure sum up domestic linkages of the corresponding sectors, respectively. See Appendix C for more information on data and methodology. Country classification following World Bank (2019a).

Source: Calculations based on World Input-Output Database (WIOD) Release 2016 (Timmer et al., 2015).

trade-offs to consider. On the one hand, environmental stress tends to have disproportionately negative impacts on less developed economies as a strong association between (climate change) adaptation and economic development has been reported in the literature; see among others, Klien, Schipper, and Dessai (2005); Schipper and Pelling (2006). Jerneck and Olsson (2008); Pouliotte, Smit, and Westerhoff (2009). On the other hand, climate change mitigation in emerging and developing countries might pose a challenge from a development perspective if it requires more costly, low-carbon energy sources (Jakob & Steckel, 2014).

We expand the conceptual approach proposed in UNIDO (2016) as we express the environmental sustainability of manufacturing industries by measuring their industry-level value-added per unit of carbon dioxide emission. Even though this measure does not fully capture all the necessary characteristics of environmentally friendly development, it is argued that it may serve as an important proxy as it has taken the centerstage in much of the policy debate in the most recent past, such as at the 2019 Sustainable Development Impact Summit in New York or the Climate Summit in Madrid in the same year. General trends on an aggregated level of manufacturing as in Figure 3.18 seem to suggest a non-linear relationship between environmental sustainability and economic growth, following the concept of the environmental Kuznets (1955) curve where environmental indicators are typically found to deteriorate first with economic development before improving again at higher incomes (Grossman & Krueger 1995).

Rather than on the aggregate, the interest of this section is to illustrate the industry-level dynamics of CO_2 emissions. This is done in Figure 3.19. In Figure 3.19, an industry is considered environmentally sustainable the lower the emission per unit of real value-added is and steep, downward-sloping lines indicate improvements in emission patterns as economies move up the income trajectory.

It should not go unnoticed that many manufacturing industries generally improve their emission performance as countries move up to higher incomes.

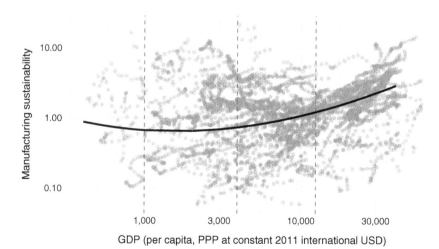

Figure 3.18 Manufacturing environmental sustainability
Note: Based on 5-year averages for 98 countries between 1970 and 2014. Manufacturing sustainability is calculated as the log of constant manufacturing value-added per tonne of emitted carbon dioxide.

Source: Calculations based on INDSTAT (2017) and Penn World Tables 9.1 (Feenstra, Inklaar, and Timmer 2015) and CAIT Climate Data (WRI 2015) following IDR (2016).

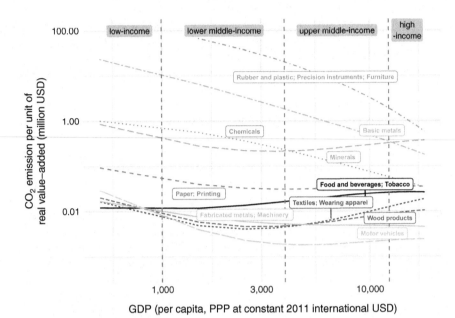

Figure 3.19 Manufacturing industry-level CO₂ emission per unit of real value-added
Note: Real value-added series calculated following Haraguchi and Amann (2020a).
Source: Calculations based on INDSTAT (2017) and Penn World Tables 9.1 (Feenstra, Inklaar, and Timmer 2015) and IEA (2015).

The decrease in emissions is particularly strong for the heavier emitters at early development stages such as the aggregate rubber and plastic; precision instruments; furniture as well as basic metals and *chemicals*. Second, there is also a notable dispersion in the degree of CO₂ emissions across industries. In particular, the earlier industries stand out. While they have by and large moderate emission rates at lower-income levels, their carbon intensity increases at upper middle-income levels again, which can be attributed both to the higher energy demand and, more extensively for *food and beverages and tobacco*, changes in the direction of a more meat-heavy diet (Carlsson-Kanyama & González, 2009). At the same time initial industrialization for low-income countries can be achieved through environmentally sustainable, industrial growth. This holds particularly true when recognizing the heavy emitters at low incomes such as *chemicals* that also play a crucial role in the development of an economy and therefore should be given special attention. Our analysis indicates that initial industrialization for low-income countries can be achieved through environmentally sustainable industrial development without compromising growth objectives under the right policy environment. It goes without saying that even if low-technology, labor-intensive industries may not be among the heavy emitters, this does not imply that emissions for the economy as a whole may not be subject to an increase as it transitions from an agriculturally-dominated state to a more industrially developed stage.

3.4 Conclusion

In this chapter we set out to elaborate on the importance of manufacturing development by discussing the dynamics of structural change within manufacturing itself. In doing so, we have first tried to shed light on the aggregated dynamics of structural change by paying close attention to the recent literature on premature deindustrialization and linking them to more as well as less successful stories of economic development in the recent past.

Section 3.2 carefully breaks down structural change patterns to the industry level in manufacturing. We do so by describing paths of sustainable manufacturing development for pro-poor countries by carefully addressing industrial development dynamics at the low(er)-income spectrum. We illustrate that manufacturing is a highly complex and dynamic sector with an important mandate to promote and retain economic success at different stages of economic development. It is stressed in this chapter that not accounting for these growth potentials by not capturing the underlying dynamics in manufacturing adequately may result in a suboptimal allocation of resources which, in turn, may adversely affect development opportunities for countries. This is particularly true in the context of manufacturing-induced employment *outside* of manufacturing. Having said this, it is of even more importance to understand the dynamics and inter-connectivity of industrial development within manufacturing. Whereas it might appear as if, in aggregated terms, manufacturing might have lost parts of its reputation as the engine of growth over the past decades, a more in-depth analysis proposed in this chapter has attempted to shed light on the complex growth dynamics in manufacturing and across different aggregates and periods. In doing so, it has tried to touch on some of the fundamental principles of industrial development by reflecting on the ideas of structural change and (premature) deindustrialization in the most important dimensions identified in the literature. This has resulted in an outline of a possible road map for inclusive and sustainable industrial growth for the twenty-first century and a clear mandate for the importance of manufacturing as an important contributor to sustainable and long-term economic growth for decades to come.

Notes

1 To this end we refer to the economic aggregates that correspond to sub-sectors of manufacturing as "industries." For more information on the classification of these respective industries, see Appendix A.
2 See, among others, Chenery and Taylor (1968); Chenery and Syrquin (1975); Chenery (1982); Syrquin and Chenery (1989a); and Syrquin and Chenery (1989b).
3 Additionally, Chenery and Syrquin (1975) observe that development processes in smaller countries are typically (more) affected by trade factors, such as capital inflows and external markets. More importantly, small countries with a primary export orientation stemming from their rich endowment in resources experience a notable delay in their average transformation of their export structure and fail to close this gap for manufacturing exports compared to more industry-oriented, non-oil-exporting small economies.
4 As the author reports, even though developed countries have kept a relatively constant share in real manufacturing value-added, its nominal counterpart as well as

manufacturing employment have experienced big losses in the past. There are sharp contrasts between Asia and Latin America as well as Sub-Saharan Africa (excluding Mauritius). Whereas the former group has managed to perform well in manufacturing production and employment, both Latin American and Sub-Saharan African countries have seen prolonged and significantly negative trends in the evolution of employment and manufacturing value-added generation.

5   We do not include countries which have experienced strong income growth brought about by the extraction of fossil fuel or gas in this analysis.

6   These are *food and beverages* (ISIC Rev. 3 code 15); *textiles* (17); *wearing apparel* (18+19); *chemicals* (24), *(non-metallic) minerals* (26); *machinery and equipment* (29+30); *electrical machinery and apparatus* (31+32); and *motor vehicles* (34+35). More information on the industry aggregates is provided in Appendix A.

7   To this end, we define them as early, middle, and late industries based on their highest, moderate, and low contribution to employment and value-added generation at early income stages. Coincidentally, but not very surprisingly, this classification almost perfectly overlaps with the technology classification introduced in the earlier sections of this chapter. In some arguable cases, e.g., chemicals, we retain the technology classification approach for the sake of keeping the analysis concise and the fact that the industries in question retain their relative importance even at later stages of development. Furthermore, recognizing the unprecedented role of the food and beverage industry as one of the most important industry throughout all the development stages of an economy, we exclude this particular industry from the subsequent analysis as this allows us to better look at the dynamics within and across the aggregates. It goes without saying that we will, of course, include the food and beverages industry when talking about policy implications and recommendations.

8   It is important to note that Figure 3.15 shows aggregate figures of total employment across the set of available countries through the WIOTS database. This makes the patterns only partly comparable with the regression analysis of the previous section, which are based on average patterns. The differences in findings (for example, by the robust performance of the *textiles* and *wearing apparel* industry since the 1990s) can, to a noteworthy extent, be attributed to a concentration of some industries in a handful of large, populous economies (Haraguchi, Cheng, & Smeets, 2017) such as China or Indonesia, which are also included in this analysis; see Figure 3.16.

References

Bluestone, B., & Harrison, B. (1982). *The deindustrialization of America: Plant closings, community abandonment, and the dismantling of basic industry.* New York: Basic Books.

Brady, D., & Denniston, R. (2006). Economic globalization, industrialization and deindustrialization in affluent democracie. *Social Forces.* https://doi.org/10.2307/ 3844417.

Carlsson-Kanyama, A., & González, A. J. (2009). Potential contributions of food consumption patterns to climate change. *The American Journal of Clinical Nutrition,* 89(5), 1704S–1709S.

Chenery, H. (1960). Patterns of industrial growth. *The American Economic Review,* 50(4), 624–654.

Chenery, H. (1982). Industrialization and growth: The experience of large countries. World Bank Staff Working Paper No. 539.

Chenery, H., & Syrquin, M. (1975). Accumulation and allocation processes. In H. Chenery & M. Syrquin (Eds.), *Patterns of development, 1950–1970.* New York: Oxford University Press.

Chenery, H., & Taylor, L. (1968). Development patterns: Among countries and over time. *The Review of Economics and Statistics*, 50(4), 391–416.

Dasgupta, S., & Singh, A. (2006). Manufacturing, services and premature deindustrialization in developing countries. *UNU-Wider*. 7.

Feenstra, R., Inklaar, R., & Timmer, M. (2015). The next generation of the Penn World Table. *American Economic Review*, 105(10), 3150–3182. https://doi.org/10.1257/aer.20130954.

Ghani, E., & O'Connell, S. D. (2014). Can service be a growth escalator in low-income countries? http://papers.ssrn.com/sol3/papers.cfm?abstract/_id=2470231.

Grossman, G. M., & Krueger, A. B. (1995). Economic growth and the environment. *The Quarterly Journal of Economics*, 110(2), 353–377.

Guerrieri, P., & Meliciani, V. (2005). Technology and international competitiveness: The interdependence between manufacturing and producer services. *Structural Change and Economic Dynamics*, 16(4), 489–502.

Haraguchi, N. (2012). Pro-employment manufacturing development in large countries. UNIDO Working Paper, Development Policy, Statistics and Research Branch.

Haraguchi, N. (2015). Patterns of structural change and manufacturing development. In J. Weiss & M. Tribe (Eds.), *Routledge handbook of industry and development* (pp. 36–64). London: Routledge,

Haraguchi, N., & Amann, J. (2020a). Measuring structural change for developing countries: A new approach to analysing manufacturing value added with application. UNIDO Working Paper, forthcoming.

Haraguchi, N., & Amann, J. (2020b). Sectoral dynamics. In *New perspectives on structural change*. Forthcoming.

Haraguchi, N., Cheng, C. F. C., & Smeets, E. (2017). The importance of manufacturing in economic development: Has this changed? *World Development*, 93, 293–315. https://doi.org/10.1016/j.worlddev.2016.12.013.

IEA (International Energy Agency). (2015). Energy flow charts. Available at: www.iea.org/ data-and-statistics.

INDSTAT. (2017). INDSTAT 2 based on International Standard Industrial Classification (ISIC), Revision 3. *UNIDO Statistics*. Available at: https://unstats.un.org/unsd/cr/registry/regcst.asp?Cl=2.

Jakob, M., & Steckel, J. C. (2014). How climate change mitigation could harm development in poor countries. *WIREs Climate Change*, 5(2), 161–168. https:// doi.org/10.1002/wcc.260.

Jerneck, A., & Olsson, L. (2008). Adaptation and the poor: Development, resilience and transition. *Climate Policy*, 8(2), 170–182.

Kaldor, N. (1967). *Strategic factors in economic development*. Ithaca, NY: Cornell University Press.

Klien, R. J. T., Schipper, E., & Dessai, S. (2005). Integration mitigation and adaptation into climate and development policy: Three research questions. *Environmental Science and Policy*, 8, 579–588.

Kuznets, S. (1953). International differences in income levels: Reflections on their causes. *Economic Development and Cultural Change*, 2(1), 3–26.

Kuznets, S. (1955). Economic growth and income inequality. *The American Economic Review*, 45(1), 1–28.

Lewis, W. A. (1954). Economic development with unlimited supplies of labour. *The Manchester School*, 22(2), 139–91. https://doi.org/10.1111/j.1467-9957.1954.tb00021.x.

Lin, J. Y., & Monga, C. (2010). Growth identification and facilitation: The role of the state in the dynamics of structural change. *World*, May.

Matsuyama, K. (1992). Agricultural productivity, comparative advantage, and economic growth. *Journal of Economic Theory*. https://doi.org/10.1016/0022-0531(92)90057-O.

OECD. (2011). ISIC Rev. 3 Technology Intensity Definition. OECD Directorate for Science, Technology and Industry; Economic Analysis and Statistics Division. Available at: www.oecd.org/ sti/ind/48350231.pdf.

Palma, J. G. (2014). De-industrialisation, 'premature' de-industrialisation and the Dutch disease. Available at: http://stat.ijie.incubadora.ufsc.br/index.php/necat/article/view/3118.

Pouliotte, J., Smit, B., & Westerhoff, L. (2009). Adaptation and development: Livelihoods and climate change in Subarnabad, Bangladesh. *Climate and Development*, 1(1), 31–46.

Pritchett, L. (2000). Understanding patterns of economic growth: Searching for hills among plateaus, mountains, and plains. *The World Bank Economic Review*, 14(2), 221–250.

Rodrik, D. (2016). Premature deindustrialization. *Journal of Economic Growth*, 21(1), 1–33. https://doi.org/10.1007/s10887-015-9122-3.

Schipper, L., & Pelling, M. (2006). Disaster risk, climate change and international development: Scope for, and challenges to, integration. *Disasters*, 30(1), 19–38.

Syrquin, M., & Chenery, H. (1989a). *Patterns of development, 1950 to 1983*. Washington, DC: World Bank.

Syrquin, M., & Chenery, H. (1989b). Three decades of industrialization. *The World Bank Economic Review*, 3(2), 145–181. https://doi.org/10.1093/wber/3.2.145.

Szirmai, A., & Verspagen, B. (2015). Manufacturing and economic growth in developing countries, 1950–2005. *Structural Change and Economic Dynamics*, 34, 46–59. https:// doi.org/10.1016/j.strueco.2015.06.002.

Timmer, M., Dietzenbacher, E., Los, B., Stehrer, R., & Gaaitzen, J. (2015). An illustrated user guide to the world input-output database: The case of global automotive production. *Review of International Economics*, 23(3), 575–605. https:// doi.org/10.1111/roie.12178.

UN. (2014). National account statistics: Analysis of main aggregates. Available at: http:// unstats.un .org/unsd/snaama/Introduction.asp.

UNIDO. (2013). Sustaining employment growth: The role of manufacturing and structural change. Industrial Development Report (IDR), United Nations Industrial Development Organization (UNIDO).

UNIDO. (2016). The role of technology and innovation in inclusive and sustainable industrial development. Industrial Development Report (IDR), United Nations Industrial Development Organization (UNIDO).

UNIDO. (2020). Industrializing in the digital age. Industrial Development Report (IDR), United Nations Industrial Development Organization (UNIDO).

World Bank. (2019a). World Bank country and lending groups. Available at: https:// datahelpdesk.worldbank.org/knowledgebase/articles/906519-world-bank-country-and-lending-groups.

World Bank. (2019b). *World development indicators 2019*. Washington, DC: World Bank. https://datacatalog.worldbank.org/dataset/world-development-indicators.

WRI. (2015). World Resource Institute. Climate analysis indicators tool: WRI's climate data explorer. Available at: http://cait2.wri.org.

Appendix A: Manufacturing industry classification

The data used for the industry analysis within manufacturing builds on the International Standard Industrial Classification (ISIC), Revision 3 data base by the United Nations Statistics Division (INDSTAT, 2017). Out of the 18 manufacturing industries that are representative of manufacturing, nine industries are analyzed in greater detail, and have been chosen to be reflective of the representative performance of the numerous components of the manufacturing sector. These are *food and beverages* (ISIC Rev. 3 code 15); *textiles* (17); *wearing apparel* (18+19); *chemicals* (24), *computer and electronics, (non-metallic) minerals* (26); *machinery and equipment* (29+30); *electrical machinery and apparatus* (31+32);

Table 3.1 Manufacturing industry classification based on ISIC Revision 3

ISIC Rev.3 Code	ISIC Rev.3 Industry Description	Abbreviation	Technology group
15	*Manufacture of food products and beverages*	*Food and beverages*	*Low*
16	Manufacture of tobacco products		Low
17	*Manufacture of textiles*	*Textiles*	*Low*
18+19	*Manufacture of wearing apparel and leather*	*Wearing apparel*	*Low*
20	Manufacture of wood and of products of wood and cork		Low
21	Manufacture of paper and paper products		Low
22	Publishing, printing and reproduction of recorded media		Low
23	Manufacture of coke, refined petroleum products and nuclear fuel		Medium
24	*Manufacture of chemicals and chemical products*	*Chemicals*	*High*
25	Manufacture of rubber and plastics products		Medium
26	*Manufacture of other non-metallic mineral products*	*Minerals*	*Medium*
27	Manufacture of basic metals		Medium
28	*Manufacture of fabricated metal products*	*Fabricated metals*	*Medium*
29+30	*Manufacture of machinery and equipment (incl. office, accounting and computing machinery)*	*Machinery*	*High*
31+32	*Manufacture of electrical machinery and apparatus and radio television and communication equipment*	*Electrical*	*High*
33	Manufacture of medical, precision and optical instruments		High
34+35	*Manufacture of motor vehicles, trailers, semi-trailers and of other transport equipment*	*Motor vehicles*	*High*
36	Manufacture of furniture; manufacturing n.e.c.		Low

and *motor vehicles* (34+35) and account for around 75 percent of manufacturing value-added and employment within manufacturing.

With regards to the technology classification of the industries, all manufacturing industries are further classified by their technology intensity following the technology classification of the Organisation for Economic Co-operation and Development (OECD), which is based on research and development (R&D) intensity relative to value-added and gross production statistics (OECD, 2011). The OECD classifies manufacturing industries into four categories of high-technology, medium high-technology, medium low-technology, and low-technology industries. For the purpose of this analysis, high-technology and medium high-technology industries are combined and referred to as "high-technology" sub-sectors, while low-technology and medium-low technology sub-sectors are categorized as "medium-technology" sub-sectors respectively; see Table 3.1 for a detailed description.

Appendix B: Data and methodology regression analysis

Data

For the industry-level analysis, we combine manufacturing-level data from INDSTAT (2017) with Penn World data 9.1 (Feenstra, Inklaar, & Timmer, 2015). The construction of the real value-added series follows Haraguchi and Amann (2020a). Country-level classification is based on the World Development Indicators (World Bank, 2019a).

The sustainability analysis in Section 3.4 is based on National Account statistics (UN, 2014) as well as CAIT climate data (WRI, 2015) and from the International Energy Agency (IEA 2015), respectively. The industry definitions in Figure 3.4 are based on IEA (2015) data and follow a slightly different industry-level aggregation.

Regression model

The basic empirical set-up for the industry-level analysis of this chapter expands on Haraguchi's (2015) study. More specifically, we estimate a panel fixed effects model in order to analyze the development patterns for 18 industries of manufacturing of which the group of nine industries (see Table 3.1) is discussed in greater depth. For each industry i we estimate

$$y_{cit} = \alpha_{ci} + \beta_i X_{cit} + \tau_{it} + \varepsilon_{cit} \tag{3.1}$$

where y_{cit}, is either the log of real value-added per capita or the log of the employment-to-population ratio of country c's industry i in period t. Note that this model is estimated separately for all i individual industries and we retain subscript i to highlight this feature of our model. Furthermore, the employment-to-population ratio is defined as the ratio of country c's employment head count in

Table 3.2 Input-output table structure of n-sector economy

	$Sector_1$	...	$Sector_i$	...	$Sector_n$	$Foreign_1$	...	$Foreign_i$	...	$Foreign_n$	Final demand	Output
$Sector_1$	z_{11}	...	z_{1i}	...	z_{1n}	x_{11}	...	x_{1i}	...	x_{1n}	f_{d1}	y_1
...	...	...	...	...	...	...	...	...	...	...	...	...
$Sector_i$	z_{i1}	...	z_{ii}	...	z_{in}	x_{i1}	...	x_{ii}	...	x_{in}	f_{di}	y_i
...	...	...	...	...	...	...	...	...	...	...	...	...
$Sector_n$	z_{n1}	...	z_{ni}	...	z_{nn}	x_{n1}	...	x_{ni}	...	x_{nn}	f_{dn}	y_n
$Foreign_1$	imp_{11}	...	imp_{1i}	...	imp_{1n}	...	...	...	...	...	...	...
...	...	...	...	...	...	...	...	...	...	...	...	...
$Foreign_i$	imp_{i1}	...	imp_{ii}	...	imp_{in}	...	...	...	...	...	...	out_i
...	...	...	...	...	...	...	...	...	...	...	...	...
$Foreign_n$	imp_{n1}	...	imp_{ni}	...	imp_{nn}	...	...	...	...	...	...	out_n
Value-added	v_{a1}	...	v_{ai}	...	v_{an}							
Output	y_1	...	y_i	...	y_n							

industry i at time t relative to its population, that is (employment$_{cit}$ / population$_{ct}$). The explanatory variables in **X** contain the logs of real GDP per capita (in constant PPP 2011 international US dollars) and are added in their linear, quadratic, and cubic representation. Furthermore, α_{ci} and τ_{it} denote country and time effects. We retain this rather simple specification in our attempts to identify different forms of heterogeneities by means of sub-sample analyses throughout this chapter. Finally, we use the predictions obtained through the above model to analyze the compositional changes in terms of their absolute contribution to per capita GDP and employment over a grid of a GDP per capita level of US$500 to US$15,000.

In order to investigate the time dynamics of the manufacturing sector in Section 3.3, we interact the right-hand side of Equation (3.1) with a dummy identifier for each decade $TD_d, d = \{1970s, 1980s, 1990s, 2000 \, and \, beyond\}$ where we eliminate the 1960s for the sake of robustness from the data.

Sustainability analysis

In order to analyze the impact of industrial production and CO_2 emissions, we modify the basic regression set-up in Equation (3.1) by defining manufacturing sustainability in y_{cit} as the log of manufacturing value added per tonnes of emitted carbon dioxide (CO_2). For Figure 3.19, industry-level CO_2 emission per unit of real value-added is utilized as the dependent variable.

Appendix C: Data and methodology input-output analysis

Data

The input-output analysis is based on World Input-Output Tables (WIOT, Release 2016) by Timmer et al. (2015). There, we represent the evolution of reported, domestic employment for each industry over time as direct employment. The remaining four categories in this figure sum up domestic linkages of the corresponding sectors respectively, e.g., manufacturing is comprised of domestic linkages to other domestic manufacturing industries across all countries considered for this analysis.

Methodology

Table 3.2 shows the structure of the input-output table of an n-sector economy. For convenience, Table 3.2 can be written as

$$Z + FD = X$$

Table 3.3 Employment contribution table structure of n-sector economy

	$Sector_{j,1}$	...	$Sector_{j,I}$	...	$Sector_{j,n}$	$Sector_{k,1}$	...	$Sector_{k,i}$	...	$Sector_{k,n}$
$Sector_{j,1}$	$n_{j,1}$	...	$n_{j,1} \times a_{j,1i}$	...	$n_{j,1} \times a_{j,1n}$	$n_{j,1} \times b_{j,11}$	...	$n_{j,1} \times b_{j,1i}$	...	$n_{j,1} \times b_{j,1n}$
...	...	...	...	...	...	...	...	...	...	...
$Sector_{j,i}$	$n_{j,i} \times a_{j,i1}$	...	$n_{j,i}$	...	$n_{j,i} \times a_{j,in}$	$n_{j,i} \times b_{j,i1}$	...	$n_{j,i} \times b_{j,ii}$	...	$n_{j,i} \times b_{j,in}$
...	...	...	...	...	...	...	...	...	...	...
$Sector_{j,n}$	$n_{j,n} \times a_{j,n1}$	...	$n_{j,n} \times a_{j,ni}$	...	$n_{j,n}$	$n_{j,n} \times b_{j,n1}$	...	$n_{j,n} \times b_{j,ni}$	...	$n_{j,n} \times b_{j,nn}$
$Sector_{k,1}$	$n_{k,1} \times b_{k,11}$	...	$n_{k,1} \times b_{k,1i}$	...	$n_{k,1} \times b_{k,1n}$	$n_{k,1}$	...	$n_{k,1} \times a_{k,1i}$	...	$n_{k,1} \times a_{k,1n}$
...	...	...	...	...	...	...	...	...	...	...
$Sector_{k,i}$	$n_{k,i} \times b_{k,i1}$	...	$n_{k,i} \times b_{k,ii}$	...	$n_{k,i} \times b_{k,in}$	$n_{k,i} \times a_{k,i1}$	...	$n_{k,i}$	...	$n_{k,in} a_{k,in}$
...	...	...	...	...	...	...	...	...	...	...
$Sector_{k,n}$	$n_{k,n} \times b_{k,n1}$	...	$n_{k,n} \times_{k,ni}$	...	$n_{k,n} \times b_{k,nn}$	$n_{k,n} \times a_{k,n1}$	...	$n_{k,n} \times a_{k,ni}$	...	$n_{k,i}$

where Z denotes the (international) transaction matrix and FD and X denotes the final demand and output, respectively. The above expression can also be rewritten as

$$AX + FD = X$$

with $A_{ij} = \dfrac{Z_{ij}}{Xj}$ to arrive at

$$X = (I - A)^{-1} FD \tag{3.2}$$

Using Equation (3.2) and the employment multiplication $EM = Employment/Output$, manufacturing-related employment can be recovered as

$$Employment = EM \times X$$

$$= EM \times (I - A)^{-1} F \ (3) \tag{3.3}$$

where the row sums of each line correspond to total employment of the respective sector and the column sums correspond to the backward linkages in terms of employment.

In order to differentiate between domestic and foreign effects, the latter are obtained by summing up all backward linkages from abroad. For domestic effects, direct linkages are replaced with reported employment. The resulting structure is presented in Table 3.3 for an n-sector economy and two countries $\{j, k\}$.

Part II

Designing integrated industrial policies in Asia and the Pacific

4 A *de facto* industrial policy and its effects on the least developed countries

Nobuaki Matsunaga and Kana Haraguchi

4.1 Introduction

According to Stiglitz and Greenwald (2014, p. 371), "[a]ll the rules and regulations, the legal frameworks and how they are enforced, affect the structure of the economy. Therefore, unwittingly, government is always engaged in industrial policy." This also applies to the global economy, with international arrangements and public policies of developed countries potentially playing the role of *de facto* industrial policies for developing countries. The aim of this chapter is to demonstrate this by considering the case of the Multi-Fiber Arrangement (MFA) and the Generalized System of Preferences (GSP), which eventually promoted the garment industry in one of the least developed countries, Bangladesh.

It is generally admitted that, in the presence of *negative* externalities such as pollution, the government should intervene in the market. This is true also for *positive* externalities. However, if the government is incapable of correcting such market distortions, alternative solutions need to be found.

As Stiglitz and Greenwald (2014, p. 15) emphasized, *learning* is "the most important determinant of increases in standards of living," and it is one of the most important positive externalities. We will examine how the MFA and the GSP, not the government, played a key role in promoting learning in the garment industry in Bangladesh.

The remainder of this chapter is organized as follows. In Section 4.2, we briefly outline the history of the MFA and its predecessors (the STA and the LTA). Then, the GSP and the Rules of Origin are explained in Section 4.3. In Section 4.4, we describe how the MFA and the GSP affected the garment industry in Bangladesh. In Section 4.5, we summarize the findings and suggest the use of international arrangements to promote the industrialization of developing countries as *de facto* industrial policies.

4.2 A brief history of the MFA

In the 1950s and early 1960s, a massive amount of cotton textiles poured into the US market from East Asian exporters, including Japan. The US textile industry strongly appealed for the restriction of such imports. Hence, the US government successfully proposed this to the General Agreement on Tariffs and Trade (GATT), which in 1961 created the Short-Term Arrangement on the International Trade in Cotton Textiles (STA). This was an international arrangement allowing a one-year restriction of cotton textiles imports. This arrangement apparently violated the GATT fundamental principles (free, non-discriminatory, and multilateral), which explains why it was limited to only one year.

In October 1961, the US government proposed the renewal of the Arrangement. Consequently, the STA was replaced by a Long-Term Arrangement on International Trade in Cotton Textiles (LTA), which came into force in 1962. The LTA was renewed twice and remained effective until 1973. According to Article 3 of the LTA:

> [i]f imports from a participating country ... of certain cotton textile products[1] ... should cause or threaten to cause disruption in the market of the importing country, that country may request ... to consult with a view to removing or avoiding such disruption.
>
> (GATT, 1962, paragraph 1)

In addition, it stipulates that, in the absence of an agreement, the importing country may *unilaterally* decline to accept the imports of cotton textile products.[2]

After the enactment of the LTA, the US government concluded bilateral agreements with countries such as Mexico, Jamaica, Nicaragua, Colombia, Italy, Poland, Spain, Greece, Yugoslavia, Czechoslovakia, Malta, Israel, Turkey, India, Pakistan, Singapore, Japan, South Korea, China, and Hong Kong. The LTA also allowed the importing country to conclude equivalent bilateral agreements with non-participant countries. However, since the import restrictions for the non-participants were not confined to the LTA rules,[3] the strong exporters of cotton textiles found it more convenient to participate. Thus, most of the above-mentioned countries were LTA participants.

The LTA strengthened the position of the participating importing country and also enhanced the possibility of restricting the imports of textile products other than cotton. In the 1960s, 82 countries participated in the LTA, but the import restriction was still limited to cotton textiles. In this period, the exports of wool and man-made fibers textile products expanded rapidly. The US government perceived this as a problem and began to negotiate to restrict such textile imports from Japan in 1969 and 1971. After the successful negotiation with Japan, similar bilateral trade agreements were negotiated and concluded with South Korea, Taiwan, and Singapore.

Initially, European countries were against such agreements since they themselves exported man-made fibers textile products. However, as the imports of such products from Asian countries to their own markets rapidly increased, they modified their trade strategy to protect the domestic industries by collaborating with the US. This eventually paved the way to the Multi-Fiber Arrangement (MFA).

The MFA was established among 50 countries and came into effect in 1974. With the aim of controlling the textile trade through bilateral trade agreements, it basically took over the LTA. Nonetheless, it should be noted that, at least at the beginning, the MFA emphasized the importance of the production and trade of textile products for developing countries. This point will be fully explained later.

Just as in the LTA, the MFA stipulated that the importing country could restrict the imports of a certain textile product through bilateral trade agreements if such imports disrupted the domestic market (GATT, 1973, Article 3.3). Moreover, if "there has been no agreement either on the request for export restraint or on any alternative solution, the requesting participating country may decline to accept imports for retention from the participating country" (GATT, 1973, Article 3.5).[4]

Thus, the position of importing countries was strengthened by the new arrangement. Nonetheless, the MFA also stipulated that

> it shall be considered appropriate ... for those importing countries ... to provide more favourable terms ... In the case of developing countries whose exports are already subject to restrictions ... provisions should be made for higher quotas and liberal growth rates.
>
> (GATT, 1973, Article 6.1)

The Article highlights several important points for the least developed countries: once they start to export textile products under the MFA, they are favorably treated. Specifically, the second paragraph of Article 6 stipulates that "the criterion of past performance shall not be applied in the establishment of quotas for their exports ... and a higher growth rate shall be accorded to such exports ...," while the third paragraph stresses that "[r]estraints on exports from participating countries whose total volume of textile exports is small in comparison with the total volume of exports of other countries should normally be avoided ..." (GATT, 1973, Articles 6.2 and 6.3). These two paragraphs ensure the possibility for developing countries of entering the world textile products market.

The consignment manufacturing trade (or the international subcontracting system) is the key to shift the production of textiles and clothing from the newly industrializing economies (NIEs: Taiwan, South Korea, Hong Kong, Singapore, etc.) to the least developed countries (LDCs), and it is only possible if re-exports after processing and re-imports are allowed within the MFA.[5]

As in the LTA, the MFA treated the participating exporting country more favorably than non-participant ones. Specifically,

> the participating importing country ... shall take steps to ensure that the participating country's exports against which such measures are taken shall not be restrained more severely than the exports of similar goods of any country not party to this Arrangement ...
>
> (GATT, 1973, Article 8.3)

After it entered into force in 1974, the MFA was renewed six times (in 1977, 1981, 1986, 1991, 1992, and 1993). During this period, the textile industries in the US and the European countries had increasingly declined. Every time the MFA was renewed, unfavorable conditions for the participant exporting countries were added. In 1981, for example,

> in exceptional cases where there is a recurrence or exacerbation of a situation of market disruption ..., a lower positive growth rate for a particular product from a particular source may be agreed upon between the parties to a bilateral agreement ...

> (GATT, 1981, paragraph 9)

With this rule, it was finally possible to conclude a bilateral agreement for a "particular" product from a "particular" source. This possibility had been banned in the GATT rules until then.

Another example is the import restriction based on the regulation on the country of origin. The 1986 Protocol Extending the Arrangement on International Trade in Textiles points out that "[i]t was further agreed that the appropriate administrative action ... should in principle, ... include adjustment of charges to existing quotas to reflect the country of true origin ..." (GATT, 1986, paragraph 16). At the same time, however, due consideration was given to the least developed countries. It states that "[t]he participating countries ... agreed that: (a) Restraints shall not normally be imposed on exports from small suppliers, new entrants and least developed countries" (GATT, 1986, paragraph 13).

To take an example, Bangladesh, one of the least developed countries, exported garment products under the MFA system. In 1985, the US, Canada, France, and the UK decided to impose quotas on the Bangladeshi exports of garment products. After extensive negotiations in Washington, DC, and Brussels, France and the UK agreed to withdraw their quotas in 1986 (Quddus & Rashid, 2000, pp. 49, 67, 78), but the US and Canada kept them until recently (United Nations, 2001, p. 17). The European Union had been more generous to adopt the "non-quota system" from 1995, when the import quotas terminated. These advanced countries showed a preference in protecting their own industries.

It should be noted that the restraints within the MFA system attempted to guarantee positive rates of imports' growth, even though the rates were lower than those achievable by strong exporters. The restrictive quantities must be higher than those in the previous year (by 6 or 7 percent or more), and the growth rates were decided through negotiations (consultations) between the participating countries.[6]

From 1961 to 1994, the international trade of textile products was treated as an exception to the general rules of GATT (free, non-discriminatory, and multilateral). Specifically, for 34 years, the trade of textile products was restricted through country-discriminatory treatment and bilateral agreements, and both the MFN (most-favored-nation) and the national treatments were denied. However, the LDCs somewhat received a preferential treatment.

In 1995, the World Trade Organization (WTO) replaced the GATT. At the same time, the Agreement on Textile and Clothing (ATC) came into effect, which implied the phasing out of the quantitative restrictions on textile and clothing imports with a ten-year grace period (GATT, 1994, Articles 6 and 8). Nonetheless, the termination was not smooth, as "[t]he looming end of quota restrictions in line with the ATC caused much debate internationally among stakeholders ... One such initiative, known more formally as the 'Istanbul Declaration', proposed an extension of quotas for a further three years ..." (Naumann, 2006, p. 20).

On January 1, 2005, however, the MFA terminated as scheduled, after strong pressure by China, which had been a fully-fledged WTO member since 2001. As soon as quotas on textiles and clothing trade were lifted, clothing flooded into the US market: "over the first half of 2005, ... [b]oth HS61 (knitwear) and HS62 (wovens) imports from China recorded year-on-year growth of close to 100%, with selected categories far exceeding this average" (Naumann, 2006, p. 25). The EU market experienced a similar situation.

In May 2005, after negotiations with China, the US government implemented a "transitional safeguard" under China's WTO Accession Protocol.[7] The EU also negotiated with China, and the result was an agreement aimed at containing the increase in the main garment exports by China at a rate of around 10 percent for the subsequent three years. The United States concluded a similar agreement holding until the end of 2008 (Fukunishi & Yamagata, 2014, p. 32).

Thanks to these safeguard agreements, some least developed countries such as Bangladesh and Cambodia could take a breath between 2005 and 2008, to which could be added a non-temporary relief provided by China. More specifically, around 2005, the Chinese economy reached a "turning point," as there was no longer a labor surplus, and the wage rates started to rise so rapidly and steadily that China lost its comparative advantage in the low value-added textiles and clothing industry, thus favoring some least developed countries that already had or had gained a competitive edge.

4.3 GSP and Rules of Origin

Along with the development of international trade arrangements for textiles and clothing, the 1960s saw the start of a big movement of developing countries in the United Nations, which led to the creation of the United Nations Conference on Trade and Development (UNCTAD) in 1964 and the GSP in 1971.

In January 1961, the United Nations resolved in the General Assembly that the 1960s would be the "Decade of Development" and sought as a specific economic target for developing countries the attainment by 1970 of a minimum annual growth rate of 5 percent for the aggregate national income, as well as a target of international assistance and capital flows to developing countries amounting to 1 percent of the total GNP of developed countries (Jolly, Emmerij, Ghai, & Lapeyre, 2004, p. 87).

In July 1962, a conference on the "Problems of Economic Development" was held in Cairo, where the 31 participating developing countries made the so-called "Cairo Declaration." This declaration emphasized that "despite universal acknowledgement of the necessity to accelerate the pace of development in less developed countries, adequate means … have not been adopted to enable the developing countries to attain a reasonable rate of growth" and that "[t]he Conference invites the industrial countries to adopt … a programme of measures for the abolition of tariff and non-tariff … barriers adversely affecting the exports of developing countries" (United Nations, 1962, Articles 2 and 31).

In 1964, the UNCTAD was held in Geneva, becoming one of the permanent organizations of the United Nations since then. Mr. U Thant, UN Secretary-General at the time, wrote in the Foreword of the Proceedings that "[t]he Conference has taken the first steps towards the establishment of a new trade policy for development" (United Nations, 1964, Foreword).

At the Conference, 15 General Principles were recommended to govern international trade relations and related policies conducive to development. Among others, the Conference suggested that "developed countries should grant concessions to all developing countries and … all concessions they grant … should not … require any concessions in return from developing countries" (United Nations, 1964, pp. 10–11).

Nonetheless, this General Principle of non-reciprocity concessions to developing countries was not adopted unanimously in the Conference, but by a roll-call vote of 78 to 11, with 23 abstentions. Major developed countries were against it (e.g., the US, Canada, and the UK) or opted for abstention (e.g., France, Germany, Italy, Spain, and Japan).[8] This seemed to pave the way to the GSP, but such a way was expected to be winding.

The second session of the UNCTAD was held in New Delhi, where Resolution 21 (II), "Preferential or free entry of exports of manufactures and semi-manufactures of developing countries to the developed countries," was adopted. (United Nations, 1968, p. 23).

Here, the UNCTAD agreed "that the objectives of the generalized non-reciprocal, non-discriminatory system of preferences in favour of the developing countries … should be: (a) To increase their export earnings; (b) To promote their industrialization; (c) To accelerate their rates of economic growth" (United Nations, 1968, p. 38). This led to the creation of the Generalized System of Preferences (GSP), a preferential tariff system that unilaterally provides reduced or zero tariff rates over the most-favored-nation (MFN) rates to developing countries. The LDCs receive special and preferential treatment for a wider coverage of products, as well as deeper tariff cuts.

Although the Conference adopted this resolution unanimously in 1968, it took more time for the GSP to enter into force. In 1971, the GATT Contracting Parties approved a 10-year waiver to Article I of the General Agreement in order to authorize the GSP scheme.[9] Most developed countries (including the EC and Japan) implemented it soon in 1971, but the US only did it in 1976.

In 1979, the GATT approved the GSP definitively. The Contracting Parties decided to adopt the Enabling Clause (Differential and More Favorable Treatment, Reciprocity and Fuller Participation of Developing Countries),[10] which created a permanent waiver to the MFN clause in order to allow preference-giving countries to grant preferential tariff treatment under their respective GSP schemes.

The GSP has served a useful purpose especially for LDCs, but it has been troublesome in practice. Its three principles (generality, non-reciprocity, and non-discrimination) have not been fully complied with. Generality requires a common scheme to be applied by all preference-giving countries to all developing countries. In practice, however, "there are wide differences among the various GSP schemes in terms of product coverage, depth of tariff cuts, safeguards and rules of origin." As for non-reciprocity, "certain preference-giving countries attach conditions to eligibility and some have withdrawn preferences indirectly," while for non-discrimination, "a 'positive' differentiation among beneficiaries allows for special measures for LDCs, which are justified by the particular economic and development situation of such countries" (UNCTAD, 2009, p. 4).

Moreover,

> The 1996 Singapore Ministerial Declaration refocused the attention of the trading community on the idea of unilateral preferences ... In response to the Singapore proposal, a number of initiatives were undertaken to provide more favorable market access conditions for LDCs.
>
> (UNCTAD, 2009, p. 1)

In this respect, the 2001 Doha Ministerial Declaration specifically states that "[w]e commit ourselves to the objective of duty-free, quota-free market access for products originating from LDCs" (WTO, 2001, paragraph 42).

The initiatives included are the following ones: the 2001 Everything-But-Arms (EBA) initiative by the EU; the improved GSP scheme in 1997 and the African Growth and Opportunity Act (AGOA) by the US in 2003; the revised GSP scheme of Japan in 2003; and the enlarged GSP scheme of Canada in 2003. As a result, these developed countries unilaterally provided the LDCs with duty-free and/or quota-free market access through the GSP or regional and bilateral agreements, despite being subject to the Rules of Origin (RoO) with different depths and coverages. Similar special trade preferences for LDCs were granted by Australia, Iceland, New Zealand, Norway, Switzerland, Turkey, Brazil, China, India, South Korea, Morocco, and Eurasian Customs Union around 2000 (UNCTAD, 2012, pp. 11–12).

UNCTAD stresses that

> All these initiatives ... may not be completely satisfactory ... LDCs argued that, in order to be meaningful and effective, duty-free and quota-free treatment should be covering all products and incorporate rules of origin requirements matched with the industrial capacity of LDCs.
>
> (2012, p. 5)

The 2005 Hong Kong Ministerial Decision relaunched the idea of providing the LDCs with duty- and quota-free market access:

> We agree that developed-country Members shall ... (a) (i) Provide duty-free and quota-free market access ... for all products originating from all LDCs

by 2008 ... (b) Ensure that preferential rules of origin ... are transparent and simple, and contribute to facilitating market access.

(WTO, 2005: Annex F, 36)

This decision has been almost fully accomplished by major developed countries. More specifically, as of 2015, looking at tariff lines and import values, according to the WTO (2017, p. 30), the duty-free coverages in favor of LDCs are, respectively:

- EU: 99.0 percent and 100 percent;
- US: 82.6 percent and 39.7 percent;
- Japan: 97.9 percent and 98.9 percent;
- Canada: 98.6 percent and 99.5 percent;
- Australia: 100 percent and 100 percent.

Except for the US,[11] major developed countries have granted nearly 100 percent duty-free market access for LDC exports, which thus boosted them significantly. The extent is confirmed by the assessment of the costs to LDCs of losing LDC-specific trade preferences, which in G20 markets are estimated as follows: 11 percent of exports for Cambodia, 8 percent for Ethiopia and Tanzania, 7 percent for Bangladesh and Myanmar (UNCTAD, 2017, p. 135).

These estimates suggest that, for instance, duty-free market access to G20 markets has the potential to increase exports from Cambodia by 11 percent, from Bangladesh by 7 percent, and from Myanmar by 7 percent. However, the real contributions of the GSP need to be examined together with the MFA in more detail. Actually, these international trade arrangements functioned as a *de facto* industrial policy to promote economic development in some LDCs.

Due to space limitations, we concentrate on the case of Bangladesh's garment industry in Section 4.4. Nonetheless, this case can illustrate how a combination of the MFA and the GSP could play the role of an industrial policy to "discover" and nurture an industry with a latent comparative advantage in this extremely poor and populous country.

4.4 A *de facto* industrial policy for the Bangladeshi garment industry

After British rule during 1757–1947, Bangladesh was part of Pakistan until its independence in 1971, which came after the bloody nine-month Liberation War. Bangladesh is one of the poorest countries in the world, with a per capita Gross Domestic Product (GDP) of only US$1,698 in 2018 at current prices, and is currently included in the list of LCDs by the United Nations (World Bank, 2019).

After independence, the Bangladeshi economy stagnated, and it took about two decades for the real per capita GDP to reach its pre-independence level (Figure 4.1). Although the annual growth rates of real GDP are not high, they

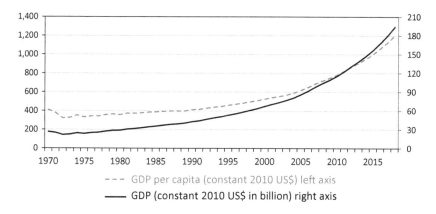

Figure 4.1 GDP and GDP per capita in Bangladesh
Source: World Bank, *World Development Indicators*

have been rising consistently over decades: 4.0 percent in the 1980s, 4.7 percent in the 1990s, 5.6 percent in the 2000s, and 6.7 percent from 2010 to 2018. The leading industry in the country is manufacturing, characterized by rising value-added growth rates that recently reached rather high levels: 4.9 percent, 7.2 percent, 7.5 percent, and 10.7 percent, respectively (World Bank, 2019).

In 1981, when the ready-made garment (RMG) industry started to export, Bangladesh's exports mainly consisted of raw jute (16.7 percent), jute products (51.5 percent), frozen fish and shrimp (5.6 percent), and tea (5.8 percent) (Quddus & Rashid, 2000, p. 230). At that time, the country had a comparative advantage in these primary goods and their simple related products. According to the conventional theory of international trade, Bangladesh should have promoted these industries to enjoy gains from trade. However, if Bangladesh had kept specializing in these industries, it would have still remained a poor agriculture-based economy without an RMG industry. Instead, the country defied such comparative advantage and moved to the RMG industry, which represented a prime mover of its manufacturing sector.

As Figure 4.2 shows, RMG exports were negligible until 1983 (US$19 million, 3.9 percent of total exports), but they surpassed US$1 billion in 1991, and have kept growing to US$2 billion in 1994, US$10 billion in 2007, and US$34 billion in 2018. The percentage of RMG exports in total exports rose rapidly from less than 4 percent in 1983 to 50 percent in 1990, 75 percent in 1998, more than 80 percent from 2013, and 84 percent in 2018. In 2018, around 4 million workers are directly employed in 4,621 factories in this industry alone (BGMEA, n.d.).

Why and how did the Bangladeshi RMG industry succeed in developing so rapidly? Many studies try to answer this question. For example, Fukunishi and Yamagata (2014, p. 100) conclude that

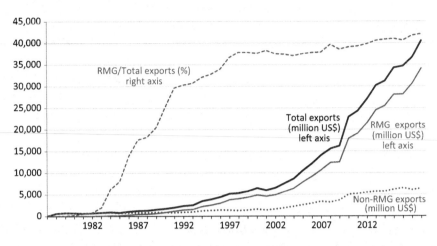

Figure 4.2 RMG exports of Bangladesh and its percentage in total exports
Source: Export Promotion Bureau Compiled by BGMEA

> the success of the garment industry in Bangladesh symbolizes the strength of the fundamental determinants of market competitiveness over government policies and trade control. Bangladesh ... has prospered in the export-oriented garment business by mobilizing its ample workers and entrepreneurial potential that supersede the stiff bureaucracy and controlled trade regime imposed by developed countries.

We agree with the authors that the industry's success is attributable to "its ample workers and entrepreneurial potential that supersede the stiff bureaucracy." However, we must contend that the "controlled trade regime imposed by developed countries" did not hinder the garment industry growth. On the contrary, it triggered the birth of this industry and fostered its impressive growth thereafter.

Quddus and Rashid (2000, pp. 20–21) investigated whether the growth of the garment sector in Bangladesh was enhanced or hindered by the quotas in the global clothing market. They found that "undoubtedly it was the quota system that propelled the industry on the fast track to export growth in the early stages of the industry." Specifically, the authors claimed that under the MFA "the buyers and the producers had a strong incentive to move production to newer locations in quota-free region ... where the industry would have comparative advantage."

As we have seen earlier, the MFA was effective between 1974 and the end of 2004. The newly industrializing economies (NIEs) (including South Korea, Taiwan, and Hong Kong) had the quotas imposed upon them, but the latecomer Bangladesh did not have the quotas imposed until 1985. The late 1970s and early 1980s represent a critical period for the country in building the RMG industry.

Quddus and Rashid emphasized that:

> The initiative that resulted in a breakthrough for the industry came in 1978 with the collaborative agreement between Desh Garment and Daewoo, a Korean multinational that at the time was a major producer and exporter of garments in the world.
>
> (2000, pp. 97–98)

In 1977, Reaz Garments exported 10,000 pieces of men's shirts to a Paris-based firm. However, in 1977/1978, the average daily employment in the wearing apparel, except footwear, was only 76 persons in Bangladesh.[12] On the other hand, Desh Garment started to produce shirts in April 1980 with 450 machines and 500 workers, and exported 43,200 pieces in just three months between 1979 and 1980. Its exports grew to 284,500 pieces in 1980/1981, 758,800 pieces in 1981/1982, and so forth (Rhee, 1990, p. 339).

Noorul Quader, the founder of Desh Garment, said in an interview that at the time, "Desh had the single largest factory in the subcontinent, and the biggest in Asia outside South Korea" (Quddus & Rashid, 2000, p. 196). While Reaz Garments had its roots in the domestic markets for made-to-order and ready-made garments, Desh Garment was a newly established firm producing RMGs for exports with state-of-the-art technology and equipment.

Although the introduction of state-of-the-art technologies and equipment in Bangladesh could have been easy, it was not so easy to adapt them so that they could function well in a totally different context from South Korea. It was all the more difficult to start a 100 percent export-oriented RMG industry with a mass-production system, which was an innovation for Bangladesh at the time. The following famous story explains how this was achieved:

> The breakthrough ... came in 1978. That year Mr. Noorul Quader ... was invited by Kim Woo Chong, Chairman of Daewoo, the South Korean conglomerate, to collaborate for five years in the production and export of apparel. In return, for an eight percent marketing commission on all exports by Desh during a five-year contract period, Daewoo gave free training to 130 Desh supervisors and managers at its ultra-modern Pusan garment plant, at the time the biggest in the world.
>
> (Quddus & Rashid, 2000, p. 62)

In seven months of intensive training from April till November 1979, Desh workers developed the skills to produce world-quality garment goods, exportable to the markets Daewoo so far operated in. They also learned "the whole system of production, marketing and management that Daewoo had developed ... to enter international market." After the workers returned to Bangladesh in December 1979, three Daewoo engineers were dispatched for three months to assist the machinery installation and the factory start up. In April 1980, Desh had the production started. From March 1980 to March 1981, Daewoo sent nine experts, each staying three to six months, for quality control, training of workers, and administration (i.e., export and import procedures and documents) (Rhee, 1990, pp. 337–339).

Incidentally, on October 26, 1979, President Park Chung Hee was assassinated in South Korea, and a coup d'état followed on December 12. On May 17, 1980, martial law was extended to the whole nation, which triggered nation-wide protests demanding democracy, resulting in political turmoil. After the coup d'état, Noorul Quader of Desh went to South Korea, where he found out that Kim Woo Chong of Daewoo had been forced to leave the country to go to America. He said in an interview, "I could not find anyone I could trust or do business with in Korea after the coup" (Quddus & Rashid, 2000, p. 196).

On June 30, 1981, Desh canceled the collaborative agreement with Daewoo. However, as it had fully mastered production, marketing, and management know-hows, Desh could keep on its business without Daewoo and reap big profits. Furthermore, the company could expand its capital facilities, labor force, production, and exports dramatically between 1979 and 1987: from 450 machines to 750, from 500 workers to 1,400, and from US$55,500 to around US$10 million, respectively. In addition, "Desh was handling all its own export marketing, and was getting all its raw materials from non-Daewoo sources" (Rhee, 1990, pp. 340–341).

The big profits reaped by Desh generated a boom of garment factories in Bangladesh: 115 workers out of the 130 trained by Daewoo left Desh after the second half of 1981 to set up their own factories or to assist others to do so. "In 1985, … there were more than 700 garment export manufacturing factories in Bangladesh. … Desh workers transmitted their production, marketing and management know-hows to hundreds of factories" (Rhee, 1990, p. 341).

This is how the 100 percent export-oriented garment industry "emerged" in Bangladesh, which allowed people to "learn" how to do business in this promising industry. Quddus and Rashid (2000, p. 134) clearly state that "[t]he quota system based on the MFA … actually was the most important immediate catalyst in the genesis of the garment industry in Bangladesh." The MFA played a critical role at a critical time, when the country was free from quotas.

Under the quota-free status before 1985, Bangladesh expanded the garment exports remarkably from US$1.32 million in 1980 to US$97.50 million in 1985. This rapid growth induced the UK, France, Canada, and the US to impose quota restrictions in 1985, which caused a massive closedown of around 500 garment factories out of 750 (Quddus & Rashid, 2000, pp. 51, 67, 100).

Nonetheless, this eventually strengthened the garment industry in several ways. First, in 1986, the Bangladesh Garment Manufacturers and Exporters Association (BGMEA, an industrial association) sent teams to negotiate with these countries and succeeded in having the quotas withdrawn by the UK and France. The negotiations with the US were tougher, but they managed to almost triple the quotas. Thus, the demand-side constraint was relaxed.

Second, the closure of many garment factories increased the resources available to the other factories. Factory buildings, machines, trained workers, supervisors, and so on were ready to be used by newcomers and bigger firms that had survived the shock (Quddus & Rashid, 2000, p. 101). The surviving firms increased their size and strength by absorbing these resources. According to BGMEA data, the number of workers per factory rose from 299 in 1984 to 450 in 1986. Thus, the supply-side constraint was also partially relaxed.

Third, the industry's entrepreneurs realized that market and product differentiation were essential to avoid a similar situation being repeated. Before the quota imposition, Bangladesh exported about 80 percent of garment products to the US, with the exported products concentrated in a small number of categories. With an increased capacity and more players in the industry, new markets could be developed, including Japan, Australia, and the Middle East, and a greater variety of garments could be produced and exported: 35 categories of garments made of cotton, wool and man-made fabrics for men, women, boys, girls, and infants. The industry's fragility feature was thus improved (Rhee, 1990, pp. 343–344).

Here, it is important to remember the argument for infant industry protection, whose essence "rests on 'dynamic learning effects' that will allow an industry that is not currently competitive to achieve comparative advantage after a temporary period of protection" (Meier, 1995, p. 475). The dynamic learning effects stem from the accumulated experience of workers and entrepreneurs (learning by doing), which raises the industry's productivity and thus competitiveness in the long run.

An infant industry is usually protected against imports by trade barriers, with the cost of such protection shouldered by domestic consumers in the form of higher prices. For the 100 percent export-oriented garment industry in Bangladesh, however, the higher price was not paid by the consumers in Bangladesh, but by those in the importing countries that imposed MFA quotas.[13] The garment industry in Bangladesh was thus "protected" against the more competitive exporters (like China) constrained by the MFA quotas at the expense of importing countries such as the US.

In addition to the MFA quotas, the GSP strengthened the competitiveness of the RMG industry in Bangladesh. As we have seen earlier, the GSP came into effect in 1971, and it was permanently approved by the GATT in 1979. As the GSP provided reduced or zero tariff rates to developing countries in general and LDCs in particular, the competitiveness of these countries was strengthened. The EC and Japan implemented the GSP in 1971: Japan granted duty-free market access for LDCs, including Bangladesh, in 1980, while the EU implemented EBA in 2001, which provided LDCs with duty-free access to the EU market.

For example, in 1996, the average import tariff rate applied to clothing was 12.4 percent in the EU.[14] The tariff preference for Bangladesh made the imports duty free; thus, the GSP strengthened the price competitiveness of the country's garment products by these same rates on average. Nonetheless, it should be noted that stringent Rules of Origin (RoO) limited the benefits of the GSP.

Even after the EBA implementation, Bangladesh could not fully enjoy duty-free access to the EU market. "The EU RoO for apparels used to require a 'two-stage conversion': from yarn to fabrics to apparels." The high number of

Bangladeshi import fabrics did not allow them to meet this requirement. As a result, in 2009, "[o]nly about 28 per cent of Bangladeshi woven exports [were] able to enter the EU market at zero duty" (Rahman, 2014, p. 14).

However, the situation was different for knitwear, in 2009:

> Bangladesh had been able to build strong backward linkages … in the production of yarn and knit fabrics. For knitwear, the utilisation rate (i.e., the proportion of the total value of Bangladesh's knitwear imports admitted duty-free) is about 92 per cent.
>
> (Rahman, 2014, p. 14)

Therefore, most Bangladeshi exporters could enjoy duty-free access to the EU market and get a competitive advantage over their competitors from China, India, Pakistan, Turkey, Vietnam, etc.

The difference in treatment between woven and knitwear exports arose from the different levels of capital investment necessary to produce the fabrics. Woven fabrics need approximately ten times more investment in plant and equipment than knitted fabrics. When the EU relaxed the "stages of production" requirement for EBA from three to two in 2004, Bangladeshi entrepreneurs (including knitwear manufacturers/exporters) were "encouraged to invest in backward linkages in textiles in order to receive duty-free market access in the EU" (Rahman, 2014, p. 14). Therefore, this little change in the EU RoO functioned as a *de facto* industrial policy to stimulate backward linkage industries in Bangladesh.

Figure 4.3 shows how Bangladesh's knitwear exports increased both in absolute and relative terms. Knitwear exports occupied only 14.2 percent in the total apparel exports in 1992 and less than 30 percent until 1999, but their growth rates were almost always higher than those of woven exports. In 2007, knitwear exports superseded woven exports.

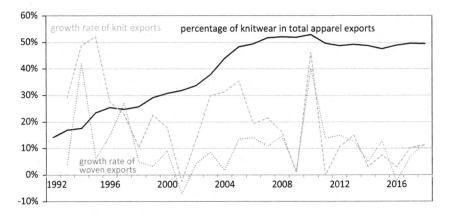

Figure 4.3 Percentage of knitwear in total apparel exports, growth rate of knit and woven exports

Source: Export Promotion Bureau Compiled by BGMEA

From 2003 to 2009, the knitwear exports increased by 201.8 percent, while woven exports increased by 70.0 percent at current US dollars (BGMEA, n.d.). This rapid expansion exerted a strong backward linkage effect on the textile industry. The quantum index of industrial production in textiles grew at almost the same pace as that in garments (83.5 percent and 84.5 percent, respectively, from 2003 to 2009) (Bangladesh Bureau of Statistics, 2011, 2013).

In 2010, the EU revised the RoO from two stages to one (from fabrics to apparels) for both woven and knitwear. This revision benefited woven exporters more than knitwear exporters, as the former still required imported fabrics for production. From 2009 to 2011, woven exports rose by 59.7 percent, while knitted exports rose by 46.3 percent (BGMEA, n.d.). Over the same period, the quantum index of industrial garments' production grew by 80.4 percent, although for textiles the same index grew by 0.6 percent only (Bangladesh Bureau of Statistics, 2013, p. 167). High numbers of fabrics were imported for garment production. Thus, it is important to note that even a small revision of the EU RoO influenced the industrial structure in Bangladesh.

4.5 Conclusion

In this chapter we have analyzed how Bangladesh's garment industry was affected by the MFA and the GSP with revised Rules of Origin. The MFA, which came into force in 1974, restricted garment exports from specific countries, including the NIEs and China until 2004. Bangladesh could enjoy the quota-free status before 1985, which triggered the development of the garment industry. If the Korean producer (Daewoo) had not been compelled to move its production to the quota-free region, there would be no story about Desh Garment, and thus no mushrooming of garment factories that followed in Bangladesh.

Cheap and abundant labor, as well as aggressive entrepreneurs, have given Bangladesh a latent comparative advantage in the garment industry. However, in the early 1980s, this country had an actual comparative advantage in such products as raw jute, jute products, and tea. The export-oriented garment industry had still to be "discovered" and nurtured before its latent advantage materialized through "dynamic learning effects." As we have seen, in Bangladesh this role was exactly played by the combination of the MFA and the GSP.

The MFA was originally launched to protect the domestic garment industry in developed countries from NIEs' imports. However, it became a *de facto* industrial policy, promoting the 100 percent export-oriented garment industry in Bangladesh, as it was more favorably treated under the MFA. It was the temporary protection of an infant "export" industry at the expense of the importing developed countries which imposed the MFA quotas on NIEs (by the amount of the "quota rent").

The GSP also played a role in protecting the garment industry in Bangladesh, since it granted zero or reduced tariff rates to the LDCs, including Bangladesh. In particular, the EU provided the country with quota-free and duty-free access to its market, which strengthened the competitiveness of Bangladeshi garment exports, despite the stringent Rules of Origin (RoO) limiting the benefits from the duty-free access.

However, even the revision of RoO was able to stimulate backward linkage effects in the Bangladeshi knitwear industry. When the EU relaxed the stages of production requirement from three to two in 2004, the backward linkage (textile manufacturing) was encouraged in the knitwear industry. When the RoO requirement was further relaxed (from two stages to one stage) in 2010, Bangladeshi garment exports (especially woven exports) expanded rapidly, despite the stagnation of textile manufacturing.

To sum up, the international arrangements on external trade (the MFA and the GSP) functioned as a *de facto* industrial policy to discover and foster the industry with latent comparative advantage (the export-oriented garment industry) in Bangladesh. Such an industry was totally different from the one with the known comparative advantage (e.g., jute products) at the time. A change in the RoO requirement could also function as a *de facto* industrial policy to stimulate the backward linkage industry (textile manufacturing) as well as garment exports. Then, was Bangladesh only simply lucky?

It should be noted that not only such external opportunities but also the internal capacity of learning and the related spillovers were essential for the industry's latent comparative advantage to materialize in the country. Desh workers and staff learned by training at Daewoo, and then they transmitted that know-how to other Desh workers. Also, some of them became entrepreneurs themselves and trained their workers, and others became trainers in some other factories to produce world-quality garments. Thanks to these spillovers, it was possible for an innovation (the export-oriented garment industry) to materialize in Bangladesh.

Nowadays, there are more international arrangements in the global economy, and some of them tend to limit the policy space for the economic growth of developing countries. Such arrangements include certain WTO rules such as the Agreement on Trade-Related Aspects of Intellectual Property Rights (TRIPS), the Agreement on Trade-Related Investment Measures (TRIMS), and the Agreement on Subsidies and Countervailing Measures (SCM). In this respect, developing countries today face more difficulties than the previous developing countries (now developed) in devising and implementing industrial policies aimed at growing their economies.

Nonetheless, a closer look could make some developing countries identify a *de facto* industrial policy among some international arrangements, just as Bangladesh eventually did. The task to find and design such a *de facto* industrial policy should be tackled by local policy-makers and advisers of international development organizations or donor agencies. In this context, academics should also play a role in enlarging the policy space.

Additionally, unexpected and unpredictable events have been emerging in the world, such as Brexit and the US-China trade friction. These events may hinder some developing countries from promoting their economies. However, other developing countries may find a *de facto* industrial policy among them. Here also, academics may be able to play a role to aid developing countries.

Notes

1 Here, "textile products" include garment products.

2 According to GATT:

> If, within a period of sixty days after the request has been received by the participating exporting country or countries, there has been no agreement either on the request for export restraint or on any alternative solution, the requesting participating country may decline to accept imports for retention from the participating country ... of the cotton textile products causing or threatening to cause market disruption ...
>
> (GATT, 1962, Article 3.3)

3 According to GATT:

> The participating countries agree that ... the participating importing country ... shall take steps to ensure that the participating country's exports against which such measures are taken shall not be restrained more severely than the exports of any country not participating in this Arrangement which are causing, or threatening to cause, market disruption.
>
> (GATT, 1962, Article 6 (c))

4 Details of the conditions can be found in Annex A and B in GATT (1973).

5 GATT, Article 6 stipulates that

> [p]articipating countries shall not ... maintain restraints on trade in textile products originating in other participating countries which are imported under a system of temporary importation for re-export after processing ... [c]onsideration shall be given to special and differential treatment to re-imports into a participating country of textile products which that country has exported to another participating country for processing and subsequent reimportation ...
>
> (GATT, 1973, Articles 6.5 and 6.6)

6 According to GATT:

> The level below which imports or exports of textile products may not be restrained ... shall be the level of actual imports or exports ... during the twelve-month period terminating two months or, where data are not available, three months preceding the month in which the request for consultation is made ... Should the restraint measures remain in force for another twelve-month period, the level for that period shall not be lower than the level specified for the preceding twelve-month period, increased by not less than 6 per cent for products under restraint ... Where restraint is exercised for more than one product the participating countries agree that ... the agreed level for any one product may be exceeded by 7 per cent ...
>
> (GATT, 1973, Annex B, paragraphs 1 (a), 2 and 5)

7 According to the WTO:

> In cases where products of Chinese origin are being imported into the territory of any WTO Member in such increased quantities or under such conditions as to cause or threaten to cause market disruption to the domestic producers of like or directly competitive products, the WTO Member so affected may request consultations with China with a view to seeking a mutually satisfactory solution,

including whether the affected WTO Member should pursue application of a measure under the Agreement on Safeguards.

(WTO, 2001, Article 16.1)

8 Australia, Austria, Canada, Iceland, Liechtenstein, Norway, South Africa, Sweden, Switzerland, the UK, and the US were against it. Belgium, Brazil, Denmark, Federal Republic of Germany, Finland, France, Greece, Holy See, Ireland, Italy, Japan, Luxembourg, Monaco, Netherlands, New Zealand, Portugal, Republic of Viet-Nam, Rwanda, San Marino, Spain, Turkey, Uganda, and Venezuela opted for abstention (United Nations, 1964, Annex A.I.1, General Principle 8).

9 The Contracting Parties decided:

(a) that without prejudice to any other Article of the General Agreement, the provisions of Article I shall be waived for a period of ten years to the extent necessary to permit developed contracting parties ... to accord preferential tariff treatment to products originating in developing countries ...

(GATT, 1971)

10 The clause states that:

The Contracting Parties decide as follows: 1. Notwithstanding the provisions of Article I of the General Agreement, contracting parties may accord differential and more favourable treatment to developing countries, without according such treatment to other contracting parties; 2. The provisions of paragraph 1 apply to the following: (a) Preferential tariff treatment accorded by developed contracting parties to products originating in developing countries in accordance with the Generalized System of Preferences, ... (d) Special treatment on the least developed among the developing countries in the context of any general or specific measures in favour of developing countries.

(GATT, 1979)

11 It should be noted that the US provided 97.5 percent of duty-free market access to some LDC beneficiaries of the AGOA in 2015 (WTO, 2017, p. 29). In addition, the duty-free coverage in favor of LDCs in terms of import value varied over time (65.0 percent in 2012, 50.4 percent in 2014, and 39.7 percent in 2015, for example) (WTO, pp. 2014, 2016, 2017).

12 Bangladesh Bureau of Statistics (1985). The Bangladesh's fiscal year starts in July and ends in June of the subsequent year.

13 Cline estimates the consumer cost of protection in the US. The quotas and tariffs supposedly saved 214,200 apparel sector jobs at a price of $17,556 million in 1986 (1990, p. 191).

14 Mlachila and Yang (2004, p. 11) also note the same tariff rate was 12.8 percent in the US.

References

Bangladesh Bureau of Statistics. (1985). *Statistical yearbook of Bangladesh 1984–85.* Available at: databd.co/.../statistical-yearbook-of-bangladesh.
Bangladesh Bureau of Statistics. (2011). *Statistical yearbook of Bangladesh 2011.* Available at: databd.co/.../statistical-yearbook-of-bangladesh.
Bangladesh Bureau of Statistics. (2013). *Statistical yearbook of Bangladesh 2013.* Available at: databd.co/.../statistical-yearbook-of-bangladesh.

BGMEA (Bangladesh Garment Manufacturers and Exporters Association). (n.d.). Trade information. Available at: www.bgmea.com.bd/home/pages/TradeInformation.

Cline, W. R. (1990). *The future of world trade in textile and apparels.* Rev. edn. Washington, DC: Institute for International Economics.

Fukunishi, T., & Yamagata, T. (2014). *The garment industry in low income countries: An entry point of industrialization.* Basingstoke: IDE-JETRO, Palgrave Macmillan.

GATT (General Agreement on Tariffs and Trade). (1962). Long-Term Arrangement regarding international trade in cotton textiles, October 1, 1962.

GATT (General Agreement on Tariffs and Trade). (1971). Generalized system of preferences. Decision of 25 June 1971.

GATT (General Agreement on Tariffs and Trade). (1973). Arrangement regarding international trade in textiles, December 20, 1973.

GATT (General Agreement on Tariffs and Trade). (1979). Differential and more favourable treatment, reciprocity and fuller participation of developing countries, Decision of 28 November 1979.

GATT (General Agreement on Tariffs and Trade). (1981). Protocol extending the Arrangement regarding international trade in textiles, December 23, 1981.

GATT (General Agreement on Tariffs and Trade). (1986). Protocol extending the Arrangement regarding international trade in textiles, August 7, 1986.

GATT (General Agreement on Tariffs and Trade). (1994). Agreement on Textiles and Clothing, April 15, 1994.

Jolly, R., Emmerij, L., Ghai, D., & Lapeyre, F. (2004). *UN contributions to development thinking and practice.* Bloomington, IN: Indiana University Press.

Meier, G. M. (1995). *Leading issues in economic development,* 6th edn. New York: Oxford University Press,

Mlachila, M., & Yang, Y. (2004). The end of textiles quotas: A case study of the impact on Bangladesh. IMF Working Paper.

Naumann, E. (2006). The Multifibre Agreement—WTO Agreement on Textile and Clothing. TRALAC Working Paper No. 4/2006.

Quddus, M., & Rashid, S. (2000). *Entrepreneurs and economic development: The remarkable story of garment exports from Bangladesh.* Dhaka: University Press Limited.

Rahman, M. (2014). Trade benefits for least developed countries: The Bangladesh case— market access initiatives, limitations and policy recommendations. CDP Background Papers 018, United Nations, Department of Economics and Social Affairs.

Rhee, Y. W. (1990). The catalyst model of development: Lessons from Bangladesh's success with garment exports. *World Development,* 18(2), 333–346.

Stiglitz, J. E., & Greenwald, B. C. (2014). *Creating a learning society: A new approach to growth, development, and social progress.* New York: Columbia University Press.

United Nations. (1962). Cairo Declaration of developing countries. New York: United Nations.

United Nations. (1964). Proceedings of the United Nations Conference on Trade and Development, Vol. I, Final act and report, 23 March–16 June 1964. Geneva: United Nations.

United Nations. (1968). Proceedings of the United Nations Conference on Trade and Development, second session, New Delhi, 1 February–29 March 1968. New York: United Nations

United Nations. (2001). Duty and quota free market access for LDCs: An analysis of quad initiatives. Geneva: United Nations.

UNCTAD (United Nations Conference on Trade and Development). (2009). *Handbook on duty-free quota-free and rules of origin, Part I: Quad countries.* New York: United Nations.

UNCTAD. (United Nations Conference on Trade and Development). (2012) *Handbook on duty-free quota-free and rules of origin, Part II: Other developed countries' and developing countries' implementation of DFQF*. New York United Nations.

UNCTAD (United Nations Conference on Trade and Development). (2017). *The Least developed countries report 2016*. New York: United Nations.

World Bank. (2019). *World development indicators*. Washington, DC: World Bank.

WTO (World Trade Organization). (2001). Ministerial declaration. Adopted on 14 November 2001. WT/MIN (01) DEC/1. Geneva: World Trade Organization.

WTO (World Trade Organization). (2005). Doha Work Programme. Ministerial declaration. Adopted on 18 December 2005. WT/MIN (05)/DEC. Geneva: World Trade Organization.

WTO (World Trade Organization). (2017). Market access for products and services of export interest to least-developed countries, note by the Secretariat. WT/COMTD/LDC/W65/Rev.1. Geneva: World Trade Organization.

5 Towards pro-poor industrial policies in Indonesia

Progress, challenges, and future directions

Anang Gunawan, Rulyusa Pratikto, and Teguh Dartanto

5.1 Introduction

Industrialization plays a vital role in reducing poverty in developing countries. Compared to the traditional agricultural sector, the higher wages that are obtained from the manufacturing sector can significantly improve the labor wealth and pull down the poverty rate. However, the impact of industrialization on employment absorption and poverty reduction may be different in many countries. It depends on the stage of development, the type of industries, as well as the policy environment (Athukorala & Sen, 2015).

In Indonesia, industrialization has been seen as central to the development process since the 1950s. Nevertheless, during the early independence period of the 1950s to the mid-1960s, the performance of industrial development policies was relatively low due to political turmoil and economic issues (Thee, 2012). It was only after the mid-1960s that industrial development succeeded as trade and investment liberalization boosted foreign and domestic investment in the manufacturing sectors. Since that period, Indonesia's living standards have significantly improved, the incidence of poverty has significantly decreased, and inequality has been maintained at a low level (Hill, 1996).

In the aftermath of the Asian financial crisis (AFC) of 1997–1998, however, Indonesia began to deindustrialize. The share of manufacturing in the country's GDP experienced a significant decline from its peak at 29 percent in 2001 to 23 percent in 2017 (BPS, 2015). At the same time, poverty reduction was declining slowly and inequality was rising. In order to re-boost the manufacturing share of GDP and pursue sustained economic growth, Indonesia has been applying several industrial policies to promote domestic industries and labor welfare. These policies include encouraging political and macroeconomic stability to induce investments, minimum wage regulation, trade protection, and infrastructure development (Tijaja & Faisal, 2014).

What explains the success and failure of some of Indonesia's industrial policies on poverty reduction? The relationship between industrialization and poverty reduction has been of great interest to both scholars and policymakers. Therefore, this chapter aims to investigate which of Indonesia's industrial policies tend to be anti-poor or lack a pro-poor agenda, what the industrial development challenges are, and what kind of industrial policies should be adopted and implemented by Indonesia's policymakers.

We start by exploring the evolution of industrial policies that have been implemented in Indonesia. Specifically, this study will focus on trade orientation and protection, upstream-downstream linkages, minimum wage regulation, and infrastructure development. We will present some past studies, stylized facts, and empirical evidence to provide insight as to whether these policies are truly pro-poor or anti-poor. A brief summary of the development of industrialization in Indonesia, as well as the issue of structural transformation and its impacts on poverty, growth, and inequality, will also be investigated. We then analyze how to make inclusive industrial policies from the lessons learned from the East Asian national experiences, use human capital to support industrial policy, and discuss the Industrial Revolution 4.0. Finally, we summarize the essential findings and present some policy directions.

5.2 Historical perspective on industrial policies and implications for industrialization in Indonesia

Like most advanced countries that carry out industrialization policies in their development process, Indonesia has also put forward industrial policies in its national economic agenda since independence. After Indonesia's independence in 1945 up to the present day, the Indonesian government has implemented several industrial policies and paradigms in order to accelerate industrial development. However, since every government faces different challenges in developing the industrial manufacturing sector, the impact of industrial policies on economic growth, employment, inequality, and poverty reduction show a variety of different outcomes.

5.2.1 Early independence period (the early 1950s–1965)

From early independence until 1966, at least two central policies were implemented by the government to develop the industrial manufacturing sector (Poot, Kuyvenhoven, & Jansen, 1992). The first priority was focusing on the development of state-owned enterprises in the manufacturing sector. Some of the private and foreign enterprises owned by the Dutch were nationalized and became state enterprises. These state enterprises received some privileged policies from the government, such as bank credit, foreign exchange, and subsidies. However, the existence of raw material import restrictions coupled with political instability, a widening government deficit, and a high rate of inflation during that time created a poor environment for industrial development.

Another priority that aimed at developing the domestic manufacturing industry was promoting indigenous entrepreneurs. In order to quickly promote the indigenous entrepreneurs, the Indonesian government issued a regulation called the Benteng (Fortress) Program. This program was one of the important strategies that were included in the Urgency Development Plan or Urgency Industrial Plan released in 1951. This program was proposed in order to protect indigenous entrepreneurs who had difficulties in competing with non-indigenous entrepreneurs. Through this program, ease of access to import goods from abroad and cheap bank credit were facilitated for indigenous entrepreneurs (Siahaan, 1996). However, this program did not prove to be successful as many indigenous entrepreneurs were lacking the knowledge and capability to engage in the import activities addressed by this program.

No significant structural transformation from traditional agriculture to the modern industrial sector occurred during this period. As a result, the agriculture sector still dominated the national economy, while the manufacturing industry sector remained at the low level of around 8 percent in 1965. The average economic growth during the period was very low, around 3 percent per annum from 1951 to 1965. In terms of poverty alleviation, there was no significant reduction, and Indonesia at that time was still categorized as a low-income country.

5.2.2 The industrialization period (1966–1996)

Indonesia's modern industrialization started in 1966 when Suharto took power. During the 32 years of his reign, the government implemented some industrial strategies and approaches in order to boost industrial development: import-substituting industrialization, export-oriented industrialization, protection, and prioritizing particular chosen industries. In order to boost development, the government adopted regulations related to trade and investment liberalization at the beginning of the so-called "New Order" era.[1] These regulations, issued in the late 1960s, were proposed in order to stimulate and attract domestic and foreign private investors. These regulations, along with the world oil price increases starting in 1974, were the primary support for the rapid growth in Indonesia in the 1970s and resolved the most critical constraints for development during this period, which were a lack of government revenue and foreign exchange reserves (Booth, 1992; Booth & McCawley, 1981; Hill, 1997; Thee, 2012).

5.2.2.1 Import substituting industrialization

The import substituting industrialization (ISI) strategy in the late 1960s was the primary development paradigm implemented by policymakers for industrial development. The government selected some priority industries to be developed, which were dominated by state-owned enterprises. In parallel, the government also became selective in accepting foreign direct investment. Foreign companies were not allowed to invest in some particular sectors when the products could be fulfilled by domestic manufacturing production. Ishida (2003) examined the import ratio during the implementation of ISI and found that the import ratio for the overall manufacturing sector recorded a significant decline, particularly between 1980 and 1985.

ISI was mostly driven by the role of state-owned enterprises. Therefore, the industrial policy at that time was not concentrated on competitiveness, but focused on the achievement of production targets in order to fulfill domestic demand as well as create backward linkages (Tijaja & Faisal, 2014). The state-owned enterprises dominated in the areas of fertilizers, cement, oil refining, and some mining sectors. During the implementation of the import substitution policy, these state-owned enterprises had a great opportunity to either establish new factories or expand their capacity. On the other hand, the private sector played an important role in promoting ISI by developing the transport equipment and automobile industries.

5.2.2.2 *The protection era*

The implementation of import-substituting industrialization was supported by the adoption of protectionist policies. In the second half of the 1970s, the Indonesian government began to protect the domestic manufacturing sector from import competition by imposing import tariffs, particularly for products that had high domestic capacity and could fulfill local demand. The implementation of protection was also conducted by a non-tariff barrier such as local content. In general, the manufacturing sector received a positive impact from protection. In addition, the protection policies implemented during the import substitution period also helped some firms to improve their technological capacity and production processes, which became a significant factor in preparation for the export phase (Hill, 1997).

According to Hill (1997), at the beginning of the 1980s, many Indonesian economists started to consider the costs of protection. The national industries became less efficient due to being overprotected. The overprotection practices for a particular industry also allowed the entrepreneurs to produce similar products and created a lack of competitiveness within the industry. These practices had a negative impact on Indonesian industrial development, such as capital accumulation in particular industries or companies, a market monopoly or oligopoly, and industrial concentration.

Therefore, in the early 1980s, the government gradually shifted its policy from an inward-looking strategy to an outward-looking strategy. During that time, there was a significant liberalization in international trade policy in Indonesia through reducing tariffs and non-tariff barriers. On the other hand, the government provided incentives for foreign investors in order to attract investment from other countries through foreign direct investment (FDI). Since then, the industrialization paradigm in Indonesia has started to shift to being export-oriented.

5.2.2.3 *Export-oriented industrialization*

The transition from import–substitution industrialization to export-oriented industrialization in Indonesia led to some common policy changes. The first was exchange rate devaluation in order to increase or retain competitiveness. Second, there were significant reforms in the foreign trade regime, mainly the gradual import barrier reduction. The third was monetary and fiscal stabilization in order to control the inflation rate, to reduce capital market distortion, and to attract foreign and domestic savings.

In order to promote exports, Indonesia developed special export processing zones that are mostly located in the Java region near the government bureaucracy in Jakarta. Most export-led industries are low-skilled labor-intensive industries that produce textiles, garments, footwear, and resource-intensive products such as plywood and other wood products; therefore, this condition triggered urbanization in many rural areas.

5.2.2.4 Import substitution vs. export promotion and strategic industries development

The growth of manufacturing exports has decreased since 1993, along with the poor performance of labor- and resource-intensive manufactured exports such as textile, footwear, and wood products. In response to this challenge, the policymakers establish a "broad-based" strategy of industrialization for export promotion. This strategy aimed to promote various export-oriented industries beyond the main industries that had already been established. Instead of moving into an export-oriented strategy, the government still implemented the second phase of import substitution through the establishment of state-owned, upstream, basic, resource-processing industries (Thee, 2012).

Along with this policy, the government also developed "strategic industries" that were focused on achieving international competitiveness. This involved the establishment of high technology projects such as aircraft assembly. The performance of these industries was not as good as expected. These enterprises were fully protected and subsidized by the government and provided low profitability. Afterwards, during the Asian financial crisis of 1997–1998, the funds used for these industries were suspended according to the Government of Indonesia-International Monetary Fund Letter of Intent. It should be noted that the rise of strategic industries has transformed the industrial policy focus from the debate between import substitution and export promotion to an export-oriented strategy that is based on comparative advantage, combined with state-directed and state-funded technological innovation (Hill, 1997).

During the industrialization period, the incidence of poverty declined significantly. The poverty rate in 1996 was about one-third that of the early 1970s (see Table 5.1). Regardless of any other program implemented by the government that specifically aimed at poverty alleviation, industrial development made a major contribution to poverty reduction. The labor-intensive approach to developing industrialization during this period stimulated labor productivity growth. Furthermore, the significant decline in poverty in rural areas can also be explained by rapid urbanization as a consequence of industrial development (Suryahadi et al., 2011).

Table 5.1 Number and percentage of people living in poverty, 1970–1996

Year	Number of poor people (million)			Poverty rate (% of population)		
	Urban	Rural	Total	Urban	Rural	Total
Import-substituting industrialization period						
1970	n/a	n/a	70	n/a	n/a	60
1976	10.0	44.2	54.2	38.8	40.4	40.1
1978	8.3	38.9	47.2	30.8	33.4	33.3
1984	9.3	25.7	35.0	23.1	21.2	21.6
Export-oriented industrialization period						
1987	9.7	20.3	30.0	20.1	16.4	17.4
1990	9.4	17.8	27.2	16.8	14.3	15.1
1993	9.1	16.4	25.5	14.2	13.1	13.5
1996	7.2	15.3	22.5	9.7	12.3	11.3

5.2.3 The economic crisis (1997–1998)

During the Asian financial crisis of 1997 to 1998, government policies were focused on handling the severe socio-economic impact of the crisis. Therefore, there were no specific industrial policies implemented in order to increase and support the performance of the manufacturing sector. Since the economic crisis, the industrial sector's contribution to gross domestic product (GDP) has shown a negative pattern. The most severe impact on the manufacturing sector was in 1998 when the economy contracted by around 13.1 percent, and during the same time, the manufacturing sector declined by 11.4 percent (BPS, 2015).

The impact of the financial crisis in 1997 and 1998 on the manufacturing sector can be classified into two ways (Thee, 2000). The first effect was on capital outflow, which triggered a huge depreciation of the Indonesian rupiah along with monetary and fiscal policy tightening. In this case, sectors such as manufacturing, construction, and finance experienced the most contraction. In the context of the manufacturing sector, some companies suffered due to a rise in the cost of imported raw materials and the debt burden denominated in US dollars. The second way was through the change in relative prices due to currency depreciation. As a result, the high inflation rate led to a decline in purchasing power and demand by consumers for manufactured products. Moreover, workers in the real sector were laid off due to economic contraction, especially those in labor-intensive manufacturing industries as well as the banking and construction sectors.

The Asian financial crisis of 1997 to 1998 not only negatively affected the performance of the manufacturing sector, it also increased the number of poor people. Specifically, the increase in the informal employment sector and a decline in purchasing power parity consequently increased the number and percentage of poor people (Aswicahyono et al., 2010; Perdana & Maxwell, 2011). Table 5.2 shows that the increase in the number and percentage of poor people was higher in

Table 5.2 Number and percentage of poor during the Asian financial crisis, 1996–1999

Date	Number of poor people (in million)			Poverty rate (% of population)		
	Urban	Rural	Total	Urban	Rural	Total
Feb 96	9.42	24.59	34.01	13.39	19.78	17.47
Dec 98	17.60	31.90	49.50	21.92	25.72	24.20
Feb 99	15.64	32.33	47.97	19.41	26.03	23.43
Feb 00	12.31	26.43	38.74	14.60	22.38	19.14
Increase changes						
Feb 96–Dec 98	8.18	7.31	15.49	8.53	5.94	6.73
Decrease changes						
Dec 98–Feb 99	−1.96	0.43	−1.53	−2.51	0.31	−0.77
Dec 98–Feb 00	−5.29	−5.47	−10.76	−7.32	−3.34	−5.06

urban than rural areas from February 1996 to December 1998. The crisis greatly affected the increase of the poverty rate in the urban areas, and more specifically, for those located mainly in the Java region. This condition was because most manufacturing sectors were located in urban areas and the Java region. However, in February 2000, the number of poor people and poverty rate declined significantly. This improvement was caused by the Special Market Operation conducted by the government to control the price of rice as well as other social safety net programs (Suryahadi et al., 2011).

5.2.4 Macroeconomic stability and the recovery period (1999–2004)

In general, the economic recovery did not bring the performance of the manufacturing sector back to rates seen before the AFC in 1997–1998. The manufacturing sector had only been growing in low single digits since it began to recover in 1999. The business climate and domestic demand that still had not recovered from the crisis could not boost the growth of gross capital investment growth. The currency depreciation that occurred during the crisis had made the import price of final goods and raw material goods more expensive. In addition, this slow growth of the manufacturing sector can be associated mostly with business-unfriendly regulations, one of them being the minimum wage regulation.

5.2.4.1 The minimum wage regulation

Suryahadi et al. (2003) show that increases in minimum wages only positively impact the welfare of higher-income labor. These researchers stated that employment in unskilled labor tends to decrease when minimum wages increase, showing a shift in firms' preferences toward employment. That is, firms feel that they are better off when employing more skilled labor than unskilled labor since the skilled labor mostly has a level of wages that is higher than the regulation has stated. Therefore, this also implies that the policy is not preferential for the poor, which in turn can increase inequality.

Figure 5.1 presents stylized facts regarding the impact of a high increase of the minimum wage on poverty and inequality. By using provincial data from 2007 to 2015, it appears that the relationship is positive so that an increase in the minimum wage would make poverty and inequality rise. We argue that the main probable cause of this may stem from the use of minimum wage policy as a tool for political agendas.

Since most of the policymakers are politicians and they are likely to be opportunistic, they tend to use the minimum wage policy as a tool to increase their popularity, especially at election time. By raising (or promising a rise in) the minimum wage, their popularity also will increase among the workers. Therefore, we argue that at election time, relatively higher growth of minimum wages is likely to occur, which in turn may increase poverty and inequality.

In addition, Table 5.3 presents the results of our estimation regarding whether the election year (dummy period on election year) has a significant impact on minimum wage growth. Observations in Models (1) and (2) span from 2006 to 2015 in 429 cities and regencies across Indonesia, not including DKI Jakarta, North Kalimantan, and West Sulawesi provinces, which provided 4,290 observations. DKI Jakarta was excluded since the governor directly appoints the city mayor, making it the only region without mayoral/regent elections. North Kalimantan and West Sulawesi are relatively new provinces, so there were several crucial pieces of data that were not available, such as the unemployment and inflation rates. Model (3) excluded the regions that do not have their own wage board, thus making them somewhat irrelevant since the mayor/regent cannot decide nor propose the level of the minimum wage to the governor.

The estimation result confirmed our hypothesis, especially the results of Model (3). That is, at election time, the governor and mayor/regent who have their own wage board so that they can set the level of minimum wage, tend to increase the minimum wage level in the election period and the period after the election (shown by the lag variables of Gubernatorial and Mayor/Regent election). Therefore, we also agree with the argument presented by Suryahadi et al. (2003) that firms tend to switch their employees' requirements whenever minimum wage increases significantly. Rather than employing under-educated employees, they replace them with highly educated ones, assuming that the more highly educated employees will have higher productivity than the poorly educated ones. Wage levels of the highly educated, which are already higher than the minimum wage, make the highly educated employees preferable since a significant increase in the minimum wage would have a negligible effect on their wages.

These results, combined with the results of the Suryahadi et al. (2003) study, imply that the minimum wage policy may have a detrimental effect on poverty and inequality. A significant increase in minimum wage could lead to higher inequality and poverty since the increase negatively affects lower-educated employees. Those who manage to keep their job would have a higher wage, but

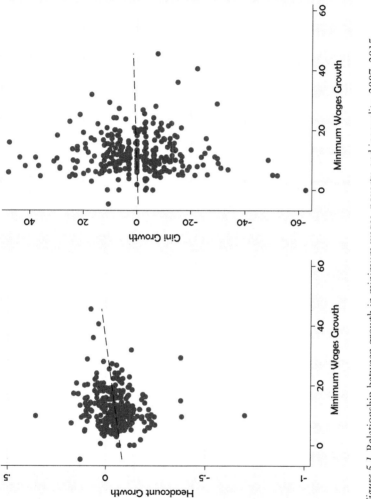

Figure 5.1 Relationship between growth in minimum wages, poverty, and inequality, 2007–2015

Table 5.3 The election cycles as a predictor of changes in the minimum wage

	Model (1)	Model (2)	Model (3)
Gubernatorial election	0.619**	1.068***	0.918**
	(0.283)	(0.288)	(0.458)
Mayor/Regent election	−0.377	−0.112	1.415***
	(0.254)	(0.259)	(0.425)
Lag Gubernatorial election		1.909***	3.046***
		(0.233)	(0.435)
Lag Mayor/Regent election		0.229	0.056
		(0.252)	(0.438)
GDP growth			0.063
			(0.047)
Unemployment rate			−0.337
			(0.252)
Inflation rate			0.643***
			(0.089)
R-squared	0.002	0.016	0.075
Prob > Chi-square	0.039	0.000	0.000
N	4290	4290	1616

most of them would lose their job or migrate to the informal sector and have to settle on lower wages. Even though the governor also sets the other types of the minimum wage, input and recommendations to the governor are given by the mayor or regent. Recommendations from the mayor or regent to the governor make use of input from the respective city or regency wage council, where the level of MWP (Minimum Wage Province) is also taken into consideration. However, not all cities and regencies have their own wage council, which may be due to low industry concentration in their areas. In this case, the minimum wage is equal to the level of MWP. Those cities and regencies that have their own wage council could have a higher minimum wage than the MWP.

The Regulation of the Minister of Manpower and Transmigration No. 7/2013 on Minimum Wages gives governors the power to set the minimum wage formally. This means that, even though the wage councils make recommendations, the governor may set the minimum wage higher or lower than the recommendation. Consequently, the minimum wage may serve the political interests of the governor (and to some extent the mayor/regent). The issue of the minimum wage has become a vehicle for gaining workers' votes in local elections. Several politicians have promised to increase the minimum wage significantly if they are elected (Tjandraningsih, 2015). This may also lead to unpredictable fluctuations in the minimum wage, which can make it difficult for a company to plan future operations and set prices.

Since the procedures could allow the governor and mayor/regent to abuse the minimum wage policy as a political tool, the central government has enacted changes to the wage regulation of PP (Peraturan Pemerintah/Government Regulation) No 78/2015. This new regulation states that the minimum wage increase must be anchored to the formula of the inflation rate plus economic growth. Even though the formal decision is still in the governors' hands, this change appears to have eliminated uncertainty for both entrepreneurs and laborers regarding the minimum wage increase.

5.2.5 Global shock and rapid globalization (2005–the present)

From 2005 to 2017, the manufacturing sectors grew at around 5 percent on average. This sluggish growth was followed by a decline of manufacturing share to GDP. Given that the recovery period had passed, but the industrial performance had still not shown a significant increase in its contribution to GDP. Basri and Rahardja (2010) argued that the declining trend of Indonesia's manufacturing sector during this period was also affected by the global economic crisis 2008–2009; thus, there was lower global demand for Indonesian products, which then resulted in the slow growth of Indonesia's exports. However, in the same period, other exporting countries such as China, India, South Korea, Singapore, and Vietnam impressively recorded more than 10 percent growth, while neighboring countries such as Thailand and Malaysia were experiencing 7.2 percent and 5.5 percent growth, respectively. Therefore, the figures imply that Indonesia was experiencing a further disengagement from international value chains.

Booth (2002) argues that even though both internal and external agriculture sector diversification is high, the linkage among sectors and regions remains weak. Therefore, Indonesia must strengthen the connectivity among regions and within regions in order to boost both vertical and horizontal integration among industries. As response to this issue, the important role of industrial development as the engine of growth was stated in the Long-Term National Development Plan 2005–2025. Under the plan, the integration of SMEs into value chains, either globally or locally, has been strengthening in order to create a strong upstream and downstream linkage as well as to create more balanced economic development within Java and abroad since linkages might occur among regions.

5.2.5.1 The Indonesian manufacturing sector in the global value chain

Kuncoro (2018) presents stylized facts regarding the sluggish growth of the manufacturing sector in Indonesia. Not only is the growth in a downward trend, but there are also indications of Indonesia's declining involvement in global supply chains. Examining the data of manufacturing exports and their distribution from 1991 to 2015, Kuncoro (2018) arrived at several conclusions. First, increases in food manufacturing shares (around 12 percent in 1991 and increasing to 35 percent in 2015) indicate that Indonesia took a relatively simple step to increase their exports. That is, the country capitalized on the commodity boom from 2004 to 2011 to serve as an easy path for them to increase their export performance. The commodity boom then induced an increase in food-manufacturing exports. While the average growth from 2000 to 2006 was around -5 percent, it increased significantly to around 14 percent from 2006 to 2013.

Nevertheless, the significant increase consisted of fewer overall products, where cooking palm oil serves as the primary commodity driving food manufacturing export performance. Second, although the share of machinery exports increased, from 6.4 percent in 1991 to 19.3 percent in 2015, its average growth was decreasing. While it experienced around 26 percent growth on average from 2000 to 2006, growth declined significantly to a mere 1–2 percent on average from 2006 to 2013. Third, Indonesian manufacturing has been experiencing the Dutch Disease phenomenon, where a boom in a primary commodity induces a disincentive for another export sector, in particular, machinery. This condition is an indication that Indonesian manufacturing has not been successful in exploiting the international value chain. In light of these events, the government has started to consider some policies regarding upstream-downstream linkages.

5.2.5.2 Upstream-downstream linkages

The absence of an industrial policy that creates sustainable linkages between the upstream and downstream industry is the particular policy that does not induce welfare growth of the poor. Indonesia's growth is heavily reliant on the commodities market, where linkages between the raw materials industry and the domestic industry are very weak. Most of the raw material or upstream products are being exported, arguably caused by low domestic demand, since there are limited middle and downstream industries for the commodities. A case in point is the natural rubber industry. Even though Indonesia is the second-highest rubber producer in the world after Thailand and has a high comparative advantage, the domestic downstream rubber industry is limited, giving no option for the upstream to supply their products to the domestic market. Thus, job creation for low- and middle-income families is also limited since the raw materials market does not have a spillover effect on manufacturing industry job creation.

In addition, global competition has increased significantly in recent years. In the regional context, Thailand and Vietnam have emerged as the main competitors for Indonesia in terms of crucial exports such as fabrics, footwear, and automotive parts, as well as the availability of low-skilled labor for industry. To increase industrial performance, recently, the government has focused on lowering the cost of doing business by tackling bottlenecks in ports and other trade facilities, improving the investment climate by promoting one-stop integrated services for business administration facilitation, and infrastructure development, mainly related to developing within-region and inter-regional connectivity. These activities are in line with the studies by Pratikto et al. (2016) and Kuncoro (2018), where both stated that one of the policies that can improve Indonesia's competitiveness is to develop better transport infrastructure with lower logistics costs.

5.2.5.3 Inter-regional infrastructure connectivity

The development of the transport infrastructure is crucial to create balanced and sustainable growth. Unfortunately, evidence shows that the condition of the transport infrastructure in Indonesia is underdeveloped, leading to high logistics costs. The World Bank's 2012 Logistic Performance Index ranked Indonesia 90th and 103th (out of 155 countries) for the quality of its road and port infrastructure, respectively; and 104th for the overall performance of the Quality of Trade and Transport-related Infrastructure (ASH Center, 2013). According to the World Bank (2016), in 2016, Indonesia's performance in this component has improved, although it is still one of the under-performers (ranked 84th). This condition is one of the particular issues that has been hampering Indonesia's economic and social development. The deficiency in the quality and quantity of the transport infrastructure contributes to a structural bottleneck and worsens domestic connectivity. This lack of infrastructure is a particular problem in the eastern Indonesian provinces, making it relatively costly for them to gain access to other regions.

A study by Pratikto et al. (2016) shows that the lack of adequate transport infrastructure, especially ports, leads to higher price levels in Eastern Indonesia relative to Western Indonesia. The high logistic cost causes investors to be reluctant to invest outside Java since the quantity and quality of transport infrastructure are very low. Therefore, even though the labor costs outside Java are relatively more competitive, firms are reluctant to invest in these regions, since their products must be transported to the region with the highest domestic market share, Java. As a consequence, this condition is hampering the effort of increasing real welfare and lowering poverty in Eastern Indonesia.

Therefore, developing interregional connectivity recently became a major focus of the government. In 2011, the government introduced the Master Plan for Acceleration and Expansion of Indonesia Economic Development (MP3EI). One of the goals of this plan is to accelerate industrial development through infrastructure development by promoting the participation of the private business sector through public-private partnerships (PPPs). However, this effort is facing some challenges, which are, first, the lack of institutional capacities, such as lack of financial information, the government contribution, and sharing of project risks, and, second, low interest to finance the infrastructure project by the domestic investors (Tijaja & Faisal, 2014).

At the end of 2015, the MP3EI no longer became a reference for industrial development under President Joko Widodo's administration. The development plan, including industrial and infrastructure development, has instead been included in the national medium-term development plan 2015–2019. Under this plan, the development paradigm has changed from focusing on development in the Java region to focusing on development in regions outside Java. Some massive infrastructure projects as well as industrial areas were planned to be developed outside Java. However, this plan is facing a challenge, especially regarding the constraints on the government budget. Inviting the private sectors through the scheme of PPP to tackle the budget constraints also has not yet been effective, since investment in infrastructure projects is considered a high-risk investment.

The high-risk investment is closely related to doubts about whether there is an effective demand for transport infrastructure. Investors have their doubts on the return on their investments since it is unclear whether the infrastructure projects will have high enough utility so that the revenue will be considered sufficient to make their investments feasible. The hesitations arise from the lack of sufficient demand for local goods and services due to Indonesia's low per capita income and the unequal distribution of that income (ASH Center, 2013). The unequal distribution of income has also contributed to unequal development, which leads to the lack of investment in infrastructure. Unequal development, especially in the eastern part of Indonesia, makes the investors hesitate regarding the utility of transport infrastructure since the sluggish development has resulted in lower availability of goods produced from Eastern Indonesia.

To sum up this section, Table 5.4 shows the summary of industrial policies and development in Indonesia since the independence period to the present day.

5.3 Structural transformation, industrialization, and the implications for poverty, growth, and inequality

The success story of the Indonesian economy is closely related to the structural transformation that happened in the economy during 1966–1996. During that period, Indonesia experienced an economic transition from the agriculture sector to the manufacturing and services sectors. The contribution of agriculture output to GDP and its share of employment decreased significantly, while the opposite has occurred in the manufacturing and services sectors. These extensive structural changes are both a cause and consequence of the exceptionally rapid economic growth that has enabled Indonesia to raise its living standards and reduce the poverty rate.

In the early 1970s, the industry[2] sector only contributed around 18 percent of Indonesia's GDP, of which around half of it was contributed by the manufacturing sector. After this, the contribution rose to around 43 percent of GDP in 1996 (25.6 percent was from the manufacturing sector) just before the Asian Financial Crisis occurred in 1997 and 1998. Simultaneously, the share of employment in manufacturing had significantly increased from just only 6 percent of the workforce in the 1960s to around 15 percent of the workforce in 1996. This significant development of the manufacturing industry in Indonesia, particularly in the 1980s, was supported by a combination of proper economic policy packages, which in turn contributed to substantial improvements in social welfare and a significant poverty reduction. After the AFC, however, industrial development showed the opposite pattern. The share of the manufacturing sector decreased gradually from around 29 percent of GDP in 2001 to only 23 percent of GDP in 2015 (see Figure 5.2).

Simultaneously, the poverty incidence also significantly declined from around 60 percent in 1970 to 11.3 percent in 1996 before the economic crisis hit Indonesia's economy in 1997. Dartanto and Otsubo (2016) observed that the Asian financial crisis in 1997–1998 caused almost 18.5 percent of the non-poor households to fall into poverty. The massive contraction happened in both the industry and service sectors just after the AFC in 1997–1998. The poverty rate in

Table 5.4 Industrial policies and industrialization in Indonesia since independence to the present

Time/period	1951–1966	1967–1985/6	1985/6–1996	1997–1999
Period of government	*President Soekarno*	*President Soeharto*		*President Bacharuddin Jusuf Habibie*
Political/economic incidents	• Military confrontation with Malaysia. • Conflict with Dutch about West Irian Province (now West Papua Province). • Budget deficit around 50 percent. • Hyperinflation around 135 percent (1964) and 600 percent (1965). • Cut from international commerce, technology and investment.	• Oil revenue: foreign exchange and state enterprises development. • Family Planning Program • Oil boom: "Dutch Disease Effect". • Oil price fall: prudent macroeconomic and "huge devaluations": 1st devaluation in 1978 2nd devaluation in 1983	• Oil price fall: prudent macroeconomic and "huge devaluations": 3rd devaluation in 1986 • Symptom of the Asian financial crisis: capital outflow	• The Asian financial crisis • Soeharto resigned as President • Reformation era • IMF financial assistance • Currency (IDR/USD) depreciation from 2,300 in Aug 97 to 15,000 by mid-98 • Timor-Leste Independence • Decentralization and Local Autonomy Regulation System
Indonesia's industrial development plans and related policies	• Economic/Industrial Urgency Plan. • Benteng (Fortress) Program.	• Trade Liberalization • Investment Liberalization • Foreign and Domestic Investment Law	• Five Year Development Plan (Repelita) IV to VI. • Banking Reform (Oct-1988) and Stock Market Reform (Dec 1988)	• Completing Five Year Development Plan (Repelita) VI. • Fixed to Managed Floating Exchange Rate System

(*continued*)

Table 5.4 Cont.

Time/period	1951–1966	1967–1985/6	1985/6–1996	1997–1999
Period of government	President Soekarno	President Soeharto	President Soeharto	President Bacharuddin Jusuf Habibie
	• First Five Year Development Plan 1956–1960 (terminated in 1958)—92 industrial projects, 42 completed, 30 had not even been started. • Eight Year Overall Development Plan—88 industrial projects.	• Five Year Development Plan (Repelita) I to III.	• "Strategies Industries", promoting selected strategic industries, such as PT. IPTN: aerospace industry and PT.PAL: shipbuilding industry.	• Leter of Intent (LoI) IMF • Subsidy budget for IPTN was stopped • Competition Law: Banning Monopolistic Practice and Unfair Competition • Banking Restructuration
Indonesia's industrial/development paradigm	• Interventionists and inward-looking strategy	• Import substituting industrialization • Protection	• Export oriented industrialization • Selected import substituting industrialization • Industrial subsidies for strategic industries	• Dual track industrial policies: • Outward-looking industrialization • Strategic industries
Industrial development progress	• Manufacturing share around 8 percent to GDP.	• Manufacturing share increased double to around 16 percent to GDP.	• Manufacturing share increased significantly from 16 percent in 1985 to around 25.6 percent to GDP in 1996.	• Manufacturing share to GDP slightly decreased to 25 percent in 1998.

• Manufacturing employment share around 6 percent to total employment.	• Manufacturing employment share around 8.3 percent to total employment in 1986.	• Manufacturing employment share increased to around 12.6 percent to total employment in 1996	• Manufacturing employment share dropped to around 11.4 percent to total employment in 1998, but then increased to 13 percent in 1999.
Impact on growth and poverty • Low economic growth. No significant poverty reduction. Indonesia was still categorized as a low-income country.	• High economic growth around 6.6 percent in average. • Significant decrease on poverty rate from around 60 percent (1970) to around 21.6 percent (1984)	• High economic growth around 6.8 percent in average. • Significant decrease on poverty rate to around 17.44 percent (1987) and around 11.3 percent (1996).	• Economic contracted by around -13.1 percent. • The poverty rate increased to 20.3 percent in 1999 (Feb) or 27.4 percent (new calculation on Feb 1999)

Time/period	*1999 (Oct) -2001 (July)*	*2001-2004*	*2005-2014*	*2015 ~*
Period of government	*President Abdurrahman Wahid*	*President Megawati Soekarnoputri*	*President Susilo Bambang Yudhoyono*	*President Joko Widodo*
Political/economic incidents	• Debt restructuration • Implementation of Decentralization System • Millennium Development Goals • Political instability: Impeachment of President Wahid.	• Rapid Globalization • The rise of China • Corruption Eradication Commission established.	• Global Financial Crisis 2008–2009 • Commodities Price Boom • ASEAN Economic Community • Direct Presidential Election	• Sustainable Development Goals (SDGs) Goal No.10 • Fuel subsidy remove • War Trade : US and China

(continued)

Table 5.4 Cont.

Time/period	1999 (Oct) -2001 (July)	2001-2004	2005-2014	2015 ~
Period of government	President Abdurrahman Wahid	President Megawati Soekarnoputri	President Susilo Bambang Yudhoyono	President Joko Widodo
Indonesia's industrial development plans and related policies	• Five Year Development Plan 2000 to 2004 (known as (PROPENAS) Program Pembangunan Nasional/National Development Program). • Labor Union Act • Minimum wages policy.	• Five Year Development Plan 2000 to 2004 (known as (PROPENAS) Program • Priority based Planning • Indonesia Labor Law	• Fuel Price Increases • Rice Import Ban • Master Plan for Acceleration and Expansion of Indonesia's Economic Development (MP3EI) • Long Term National Development Plan 2005–2025. • Five Year Development Plan I (2005–2009) and II (2010–2014)). • Fiscal Incentive (Investment incentives, tax holiday), non-fiscal incentive (Integrated One Stop, Indonesia National Standard) • National Industrial Policy and The New Industrial Bill • A new Mining Law	• Five Year Development Plan 2015–2019 (RPJMN III) and (RPJMN IV (2020–2024) • Master Plan of Industrial Development 2030 • Industrial Revolution 4.0: Making Indonesia 4.0 • Interregional connectivity: Infrastructure development

Indonesia's industrial/development paradigm	• Industrial policies were focused on macroeconomic stability and industrial recovery.	• Industrial policies were focused on macroeconomic stability and industrial recovery.	• Upstream-downstream linkages • Integration with Global Value Chain • Targeted industrial productivity and competitiveness. 　• Particular sectors 　• Special Economic Zones	• Targeted industrial productivity and competitiveness. • Targeted industrial location for regional equality. 　• More targeted SEZs 　• More targeted Industrial Parks
Industrial development progress	• Manufacturing share to GDP around 29.1 percent in 2001. • Manufacturing employment share around 13.3 percent to total employment in 2001	• Manufacturing share to GDP slightly decreased to 28.1 percent in 2004. • Manufacturing employment share around 12.4 percent to total employment in 2004	• Manufacturing share to GDP significantly decreased to 26.4 percent in 2009 and 21.1 percent in 2014. • Manufacturing employment share around 12.2 percent to total employment in 2009 and increased to 13.3 percent in 2014.	• Manufacturing share to GDP slightly decreased to around 20 percent in 2017. • Manufacturing employment share around 14.05 percent to total employment in 2017.
Impact on growth and poverty	• Economy grew at 0.80 percent in 1999 and 4.91 percent in 2000. • The poverty rate decreased to 18.4 percent in 2001	• Economy grew at an average annual rate of 4.5 percent. • The poverty rate decreased to 16.7 percent in 2004	• The annual rate of economic growth was around 5.7 percent. • The poverty rate can be eliminated to 14.15 percent in 2009 and 10.96 percent in Sept-2014	• Economy growing at an average annual rate of 5 percent. • The poverty rate decreased to 10.12 percent in 2017 and below 10 percent in 2018

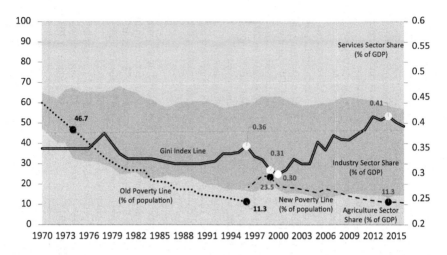

Figure 5.2 Structural transformation, poverty, and inequality trends, 1970–2015

urban areas, where most economic activities are located, jumped significantly by around 4.5 percent compared to the pre-crisis level. Since then, the incidence of poverty in Indonesia appears to be declining at a slower rate.

However, even though in the last decade, Indonesia has been able to create relatively high economic growth, inequality is rising and hampering poverty reduction. In the period 1996–1999, inequality (as measured by the Gini index) dropped slightly from 0.36 (1996) to 0.31 (1999) due to the Asian financial crisis that hit high-income households and reduced the income gap (Dartanto & Otsubo, 2016). Economic recovery after the crisis has initiated growing inequality in Indonesia since the welfare of the rich grows faster than that of the poor. Since the 1997–1998 economic crisis, the Gini index has been increasing, from around 0.30 in 2000 to approximately 0.41 in 2014. It is obvious that growth in Indonesia does not redistribute wealth to lower-income people. Since 1999, the income share held by the lowest 10 percent and 20 percent has been decreasing, whereas the opposite is true for the group in the highest 10 percent and 20 percent (World Bank, 2016).

Dartanto et al. (2018) found that Indonesia's experience is similar to that of other developing countries, in that there was an economic transition from an agriculture-oriented to a service-oriented economy before the industry sector matured. Fixed-effect estimations could be used to provide economic evidence that supports the notion that structural transformation leads to increases in inequality in Indonesia. The service sector's increasing share in the economy exacerbates inequality because the service sector is capital-intensive and high-skill-intensive. Therefore, only a few people enjoy the benefits of growth in this sector compared to growth in the agriculture or industry sectors.

Table 5.5 presents the estimation result of a study regarding structural transformation and its impact on inequality conducted by Dartanto et al. (2018). It shows that industry transformation from the agriculture to the service sector (Models (1)–(3)) will have a significant impact on increasing inequality. The explanation in this matter closely relates to the labor- and capital-intensive structure of the respective industries. While the agricultural sector tends to be labor-intensive, the service sector needs high-skill individuals and tends to be capital-intensive. Therefore, development in the service sector will benefit only middle- and upper-income families, while development in the agricultural and industrial sectors would have a more positive impact on increasing the welfare of lower-income families.

Furthermore, the results imply that increasing economic growth does not necessarily decrease inequality. The evidence presented here is further proof that the quality of Indonesia's growth is not yet promoting equality, as also presented by Dartanto and Patunru (2016). Therefore, the unfortunate exclusivity of economic growth should have attracted Indonesia's policymakers to create a microeconomic policy that promotes equality.

The results of the study also present a rather paradoxical conclusion. An increase in high school enrolment has an insignificant impact on decreasing inequality. Dartanto et al. (2018) stated that the results are in line with the logic that a rise in high school enrolment means that high-skilled labor likewise increases so that it would increase inequality. However, the seemingly neutral results of high school degree acquisition on inequality mean that it does not contribute to reducing inequality. This condition may be caused by high school graduates having a longer wait time to get jobs, so that they contribute the most to the unemployment rate.

Figure 5.3 shows the share of unemployment, where high school graduates contributed the most to the unemployment rate, which implies an oversupply or longer waiting time for graduates to get jobs. Therefore, increasing high school enrolment does not necessarily increase the income of the graduates, since they tend to be unemployed for a longer period of time compared to the other graduates. Figure 5.3 also presents interesting findings, where diploma graduates (vocational studies) have the lowest unemployment relative to the other graduates. In contrast to the high school graduates, this implies that the vocational graduates have some combination of higher demand, lower supply, and shorter waiting time to get jobs. Therefore, policies that promote the increase in the number of vocational studies graduates may serve as policies that create equality in economic growth. First, they may contribute to lowering inequality since most vocational studies graduates enter the industry sector, not services. Therefore, increasing high-skilled laborers through diploma graduates may serve as a path to lower inequality. Second, most vocational studies graduates come from middle-lower-income families. They likely prefer the diploma degree since it gives them specific skills that are needed by a specific industry with the expectation of a shorter waiting period to be employed.

Table 5.5 Structural transformation and income inequality: fixed effect estimations

Dependent variable	Inequality (Gini coefficient)					
Independent variables	Agriculture-industry transition			Agriculture-service transition		
	(1)	(2)	(3)	(4)	(5)	(6)
Agriculture share in GDP	-1.627*** (0.196)	-0.784** (0.339)	-0.789* (0.397)	-1.436*** (0.178)	-0.603** (0.238)	-0.408 (0.331)
Industrial share in GDP				-0.571*** (0.082)	-0.181 (0.117)	-0.139 (0.155)
Service share in GDP	0.689*** (0.100)	0.291 (0.188)	0.389* (0.221)			
Economic growth		0.069* (0.036)	0.086* (0.043)		0.069* (0.037)	0.063* (0.036)
Socio-demographic factors						
Poverty rate		-0.006*** (0.001)	-0.002 (0.003)		-0.006*** (0.001)	-0.004 (0.002)
Senior high school net enrolment			0.001 (0.000)			0.001* (0.000)
Log of foreign direct investment			0.004** (0.002)			0.005*** (0.002)
Government factors						
Infrastructure share in expense			-0.077** (0.033)			-0.073** (0.033)
Human capital share in expense			0.078 (0.092)			0.095 (0.109)
Intercept	0.309*** (0.039)	0.442*** (0.069)	0.261** (0.103)	0.873*** (0.064)	0.648*** (0.077)	0.471*** (0.119)
R-square (within)	0.513	0.567	0.502	0.495	0.559	0.481
F-stat (Wald-chi)	36.64***	40.13***	22.45***	34.17***	51.01***	25.08***
No. Obs.	288	288	171	288	288	171

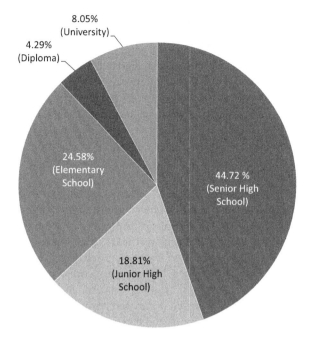

Figure 5.3 The average share of unemployment based on education, 2008–2015

Fortunately, the government of Indonesia's (GOI) vision and mission regarding the labor market and structural transformation in the future are in line with the results of this study. The GOI emphasizes the flexibility of the labor market and the development of an education curriculum that is relevant to industry's needs. This condition is then translated into education that puts emphasis on producing labor that has specific skills through training and education based on certain competencies. Therefore, promoting and developing vocational studies, certification, and training would have a positive impact not only on lowering unemployment but also on lowering inequality.

5.4 Making inclusive industrial policies: Challenges and future directions

5.4.1 Lesson learned from East Asian industrial policies: Japan, South Korea, and Taiwan

Few can argue against the idea that the presence of industrial policy is a necessary condition to create large-scale economic growth. However, industrial policy that only induces economic growth is not sufficient to guarantee that growth substantially will promote equality, especially in developing countries such as Indonesia.

Therefore, formulating inclusive industrial policy, which means policies that can give benefits to lower-income families, is important to generate quality economic growth.

Noland and Pack (2005) stated that in order to apply an industrial policy successfully, policymakers must first identify an existing market failure and devise the appropriate policy response. As has been explained in previous sections, there are several market failures in Indonesia that have resulted in outcomes not in line with the national interests. Several stylized facts have shown that even though Indonesia already has industrial policies that induce growth, they have not been pro-poor nor have they promoted equality. This has been shown by the sluggish improvement in poverty and inequality conditions, as well as local economic fragmentation and global disintegration.

Japan, South Korea, and Taiwan are regarded as primary examples of countries that have derived significant benefits from increasing integration with the international economy, without surrendering national autonomy in the economic or cultural spheres (Noland & Pack, 2005). Nevertheless, their success stories do not come easily; a variety of policies were applied and changed over time. However, there are some similarities between Japan, South Korea, and Taiwan. First, these countries promoted research and development heavily, whether by direct subsidies or by indirect subsidies carried out by the private sector. Second, they put more emphasis on policies that promoted exports. Weiss (2005) stated that by exporting, particularly in the case of the clothing and electronic sectors, East Asian firms gained knowledge of foreign designs and technologies. In the end, this stimulated them to upgrade their production to be in line with international compliance, thus enhancing productivity.

In formulating industrial policy that promotes inclusive growth, in Japan, Shimada (2016) identified that there were three important elements of productivity development. First, industrial development leads to the expansion of employment, which in turn may create unemployment of surplus personnel. Therefore, cooperation is needed between the public and private sectors in formulating policies that can channel the surplus, whether through job relocation or other measures. Second, a strategy for improving productivity should be agreed upon between labor and management by considering specific corporate circumstances. Third, the fruits of productivity must be distributed fairly among labor, management, and consumers. By enacting these measures, Japan has managed to transfer the relationship with its workforce from confrontational to constructive, something that can be learned by Indonesia as some of their industrial policy has resulted in a confrontational relationship between labor and firms (e.g., regarding the minimum wages policy).

As is also the case for the Japanese economy, the Korean "catching-up" program has been regarded as a success story of inclusive industrial policy. Similar to Japan, the Korean government supported the modernization and technological upgrading of domestic industries by promoting export and import controls, though these were implemented sequentially and gradually (OECD Development Centre, 2012). In the first stages of development, the Koreans focused on reverse engineering and learning from international best practices, and in later stages (since the 1970s), they have invested heavily in the creation of government institutes to enhance domestic capabilities. However, the "catching-up" did not result in equal distribution, especially from the perspective of regional development. Economic growth increased rapidly, but only for the capital region and the coastal areas since these locations were targeted as the center of industrial development. This has also been the case for the spatial dimension of industrial development in Indonesia that shows regional inequality in development, especially for the eastern part of Indonesia.

Therefore, since the late 1990s, the Korean government has enacted a paradigm shift policy, which promoted a regional development policy to balance the distribution of growth. The OECD Development Centre (2012) explained that during the first stage (1998–2003), the Korean government developed industrial clusters outside the capital region. In the second phase (2003–2008), the objective was to reduce disparities between regions by developing technoparks outside the capital region. This served as a stimulant for those interested in investing in these regions. In the third phase (2008–2011), regional development policy started to focus on mobilizing growth in the regions by increasing resource allocation. The current stage of regional development then shifted again, and more recently the government is focusing on identifying challenges and potentials of respective regions, while creating policies that optimize growth based on unique regional characteristics.

Wong et al. (2015) provide empirical evidence of Taiwan's industrial development experience over the past five decades. It shows that the state-led policy, institutional mechanisms, entrepreneurs, and collaboration platform play critical roles with respect to three developmental phases. These phases are: (1) achieving pro-poor growth; (2) achieving pro-domestic growth in high-tech industries; and (3) achieving pro-niche growth in terms of multi-stakeholder deliberation. Intarakumnerd and Liu (2019), in a somewhat similar manner, split Taiwan's economic development into four stages: (1) the import-substitution of labor-intensive industry; (2) export orientation with import substitution of intermediate goods; (3) liberalization and technological orientation; and (4) the economic globalization period. Therefore, both Wong et al. (2015) and Intarakumnerd and Liu (2019) imply that there is a need for gradual and sequential industrial development policy to achieve sustainable and equal growth.

Learning from the success of industrial policies from these economies, there are several conclusions that can be derived for Indonesia. First, these economies are similar in the sense of gradual and adaptive industrial policies. Over time, the paradigm of the policy is ever-changing based on their particular condition, but the goals are the same: making industrial policy bear fruits for all, whether through regional development or the active involvement of labor in a firm's strategic policy. Although in the first stages, they focused on how to boost growth rapidly, the latter stages focus on equality and inclusiveness. Second, whether it is in their early or later stages, export-led growth has been their main target since it acts as a stimulant for the industries to accept international standards, and thus constantly upgrade their domestic capabilities and technology. The governments of Japan, Korea, and Taiwan are actively endorsing and subsidizing the private sector, but they also apply strict regulations to the export-led private sector.

In general, these countries' experiences may be applied to the Indonesian economy. However, as Indonesia has its unique characteristics, not all of them can be replicated and expected to give the same positive outcomes. Kaur and Singh (2013) argue that Japan, South Korea, and Taiwan had pre-conditions that shaped industrial policy there within a broader social contract, such as relatively homogeneous populations, equitable distributions of income and education, and equity in access to healthcare. In this case, Indonesia is relatively different, especially in the respect that Indonesians are quite diverse. Fearon (2003) composed an index of ethnic and cultural diversity and Indonesia ranked as sixth most diverse among Asian countries, where only Malaysia is more diverse in the Southeast Asian region.

Easterly and Levine (1997), likewise, have argued that diversity has an effect of lowering economic growth. Taking the lesson from the Malaysian case, where in the early stage of Malaysia's development, the conflicts among ethnic groups were closely related to their industrial policy formulation. To relieve the conflict, Malaysia took the Bumiputra policy, where it increased the geographical distribution of the indigenous Malaysians so that they would have higher share of economic activity. However, this policy means that industrial development in Malaysia has been closely related to their political condition, where the politicians are mostly indigenous Malaysians, which Tai and Ku (2013) argue hinders their development. Therefore, Indonesia should take note of the Malaysian experience where equal distribution does not mean prioritizing particular ethnic groups, but giving them equal opportunity and managing industrial policy that should not be closely related to political cycles.

5.4.2 Human capital to support industrial policy

Another similarity between the success stories of industrial policy in East Asian countries, in particular, Japan, South Korea, and Taiwan, is their human capital development. More importantly, they have developed their education system based on their vision and mission of industrial development. For example, Taiwan's goal was to achieve pro-domestic growth in high-tech industries. Therefore, they established Hsinchu Science-based Industrial Park in 1980 and implemented a program for strengthening education, training, and recruitment of high-level science and technology personnel. The effectiveness of the program was then shown by the approximately 15 percent of Taiwan's university graduates who went overseas for graduate degrees throughout the 1980s–2000s (Intarakumnerd & Liu, 2019). Japan also customized its education system so that it produced both skilled and unskilled labor in its early development stages but still gave a fair distribution of resources among them.

Indonesia's main problem regarding human capital is its mismatch between education and job markets. According to Indonesia's result on the OECD

(2018) on Program for International Student Assessment (PISA) 2015, the performance of Indonesian students in science, mathematics, and reading is one of the lowest among PISA-participating countries, with an average ranking of 62 out of 69 countries. The low score implies that universities in Indonesia would have difficulties in optimizing their resources and performing research according to international standards. Furthermore, the low scores in math and science also mean that it is not ready to support industrial development, especially in light of the Industrial Revolution 4.0.

The GOI needs a strong policy to improve the quality of education; they must shift the paradigm from merely increasing the quantity of and access to education. In the future, the GOI should emphasize the flexibility of the labor market and the development of an educational curriculum that is relevant to industry's needs. This policy should also address education that focuses on producing labor that has specific skills through training based on certain competencies. Therefore, promoting and developing vocational studies, certification, and training would have a positive impact not only on lowering unemployment but also on lowering inequality.

5.4.3 Industrial Revolution 4.0 and the future of manufacturing industries in Indonesia

Industrial Revolution (IR) 4.0 combines technologies and techniques that will change the way products and services are produced. It includes major innovations in digital technology, cyber-physical systems, the Internet of Things, cloud computing, and cognitive computing (Hermann et al., 2016). This revolution is happening in all countries, and thus Indonesia needs to be well prepared to join the new trend. Therefore, the GOI prepared a roadmap, the so-called "Making Indonesia 4.0." In the roadmap, five industries will be prioritized in speeding up their manufacturing process according to the IR 4.0. These industries are food and beverages, chemicals, automotive, electronics, and the textile and apparel industries, which accounted for almost two-thirds of total manufacturing output in 2017.

The Ministry of Industry Republic of Indonesia (2017) stated that there are five challenges in the IR 4.0 implementation in Indonesia. First, there is a lack of the necessary digital infrastructure, such as high-speed fiber optics and cloud solutions to support new technologies. Second, the lack of skilled labor is combined with low productivity. Third, the manufacturing sector is dominated by local small and medium-sized enterprises with limited technological adoption. Fourth, government funding will likely continue to be insufficient to meet the increasing need to invest in new technologies and infrastructure. Fifth, underdeveloped domestic raw material processing facilities are causing a high dependency on imported raw materials by manufacturers.

Therefore, with regard to making inclusive industrial policy in the light of IR 4.0, the government needs to address these challenges. Note that with regard to the drivers of IR 4.0, the Indonesian economy is relatively large with a strong demand for the digital economy. In 2018, there were 90 million so-called millennials (age 20–34 years old),[3] and they were the key drivers demanding IR 4.0.

5.5 Conclusion

The impact of industrialization on employment absorption and poverty reduction is different in many countries. It depends on the stages of development of different types of industries as well as the policy environment. The success story of East Asian industrial policy shows that each country's policy was tailor-made under specific conditions. In the early Indonesian independence period (the 1950s–1960s), economic development relied mostly on potential domestic resources and human capital rather than attracting foreign investment, due to the strong nationalistic and anti-colonial sentiments. As also was the case for the Malaysian economy, in this period, the Indonesian government promoted indigenous entrepreneurs in their development. This proved to be unsuccessful as many indigenous entrepreneurs did not possess the knowledge and capability to adequately perform import activities.

As was also the case for the East Asian industrial policy in the early 1970s, the Indonesian government implemented import-substituting industrialization. However, the policy did not focus on increasing exports, rather it focused on production target achievement in order to fulfill domestic demand as well as create backward linkages. Therefore, the import-substituting policy did not translate into increased competitiveness. Although from the 1980s to the 1990s, Indonesia's manufacturing sector was the key driver for growth, and exports increased rapidly, in recent years, the situation has reverted to that of the early 1970s in the sense that it is fully dependent on domestic demand.

Therefore, based on historical perspectives and current conditions, there is some room for improvement for Indonesia's industrial policy so that it can support a fair distribution of growth and development.

1. Indonesia needs a strong industrial policy that translates into stimulus, regulation, and most importantly, strict and clear application regarding export-led industry. That is, the import-substituting industry must also be followed by export promotion. The importance of the export-led industry in this sense is that it will push the industry to accept international standards and adjust their production accordingly.
2. The minimum wage policy has proved to have a significant impact on both industry and labor welfare. It must be carefully implemented, and, most important of all, must eliminate the political interests of policymakers in the process of minimum wage setting.
3. The importance of market-education matching must be emphasized. The mismatch between jobs and education has led to a decline in Indonesia's competitiveness. Stakeholders must shift the paradigm from merely increasing the quantity of and access to education. In the future, the GOI should put

emphasis on flexibility in the labor market and the development of an educational curriculum that is relevant to industry needs.

4. A better transport infrastructure, especially ports, is essential to increase competitiveness, considering the current logistic performance of Indonesia. Not only increasing Indonesia's manufacturing competitiveness, developing transport infrastructure will also serve as a stimulus for investment to disperse and no longer only be concentrated in the capital region and the western part of Indonesia.

Notes

1 The New Order era is the term that represents the Soeharto regime from 1966 to 1998 in contrast to the rule of his predecessor, Soekarno, as his regime is known as the Old Order era.
2 The World Development Indicators' category 'Industry' includes mining and quarrying, manufacturing, utilities (electricity, gas, and water), and construction.
3 See www.thejakartapost.com/youth/2018/11/24/tech-savvy-millennials-redefining-workspaces.html (accessed March 8, 2020).

References

ASH Center. (2013). *The sum is greater than the parts: Doubling shared prosperity in Indonesia through local and global integration.* Cambridge, MA: Harvard University Press.

Aswicahyono, H., Hill, H., & Narjoko, D. (2010). Industrialization after a deep economic crisis: Indonesia. *Journal of Development Studies,* 46(6): 84–108.

Athukorala, P., & Sen, K. (2015). Industrialization, employment and poverty. *Working Papers in Trade and Development, 11.*

Basri, M, C., & Rahardja, S. (2010). The global financial crisis and Asian economies: impacts and trade policy responses. *ASEAN Economic Bulletin,* 27(1), 77–97.

Booth, A. (1992). *The oil boom and after: Indonesian economic policy and performance in the Soeharto era.* Kuala Lumpur: Oxford University Press.

Booth, A. (2002). The changing role of non-farm activities in agricultural households in Indonesia: Some insights from the agricultural censuses. *Bulletin of Indonesian Economic Studies,* 38(2), 179–200.

Booth, A., & McCawley, P. (1981). *The Indonesian economy during the Soeharto era.* Kuala Lumpur: Oxford University Press.

BPS. (2015). *Statistik 70 tahun Indonesia merdeka.* Jakarta: Badan Pusat Statistik.

Dartanto, T., & Otsubo, S. (2016). Intra-generation poverty dynamics in Indonesia: Households' welfare mobility before, during, and after the Asian financial crisis. JICA Working Paper.

Dartanto, T., & Patunru, A (2016). Examining the nexus of the poverty–growth–inequality triangle in Indonesia: Empirical evidence from province level data. In S. O. Thomas (Ed.), *Globalization and development: Country experiences.* (pp. 64–83). New York: Routledge.

Dartanto, T., Yuan, E. Z., & Sofiyandi, Y. (2018). Structural transformation and the dynamics of income equality in Indonesia: 1996–2014. In S. Paul (Ed.), *Kuznets beyond*

Kuznets: Structural transformation and income inequality in the era of globalization in Asia. Tokyo: ADB Institute.

Easterly, W., & Levine, R. (1997). Africa's growth tragedy: Policies and ethnic divisions. *The Quarterly Journal of Economics, 112*(4), 1203–1250.

Fearon, J. D. (2003). Ethnic and cultural diversity by country. *Journal of Economic Growth, 8*(2), 195–222.

Hermann, M., Pentek, T., & Otto, B. (2016). Design principles for Industry 4.0 scenarios. Paper presented at System Sciences (HICSS), 2016 49th Hawaii International Conference, Koloa, USA, IEEE.

Hill, H. (1996). *The Indonesian economy since 1966*. Cambridge: Cambridge University Press.

Hill, H. (1997). *Indonesia's industrial transformation*. Singapore: Institute of Southeast Asian Studies.

Intarakumnerd, P., & Liu, M.-C. (2019). Industrial technology upgrading and innovation policies: A comparison of Taiwan and Thailand. In K. Tsunekawa & Y. Todo (Eds.), *The emerging states at crossroads*. Singapore: Springer.

Ishida, M. (2003). Industrialization in Indonesia since the 1970s. IDE-JETRO Research Paper.

Kaur, I. N., & Singh, N. (2013). China, India and industrial policy for inclusive growth. Economics Department, University of California, Santa Cruz, CA, Working Paper, No. 710.

Kuncoro, A. (2018). Trends in the manufacturing sector under the Jokowi presidency: Legacies of past administrations. *Journal of Southeast Asian Economies, 35*(3), 402–424.

Ministry of Industry Republic of Indonesia. (2017). Bringing the Fourth Industrial Revolution to Indonesia. National Seminar–Outlook Industry 2018, 11 December 2017.

Noland, M., & Pack, H. (2005). The East Asian industrial policy experience: Implications for the Middle East. Peterson Institute for International Economics Working Paper Series, No. WP05-14.

OECD. (2018). *Programme for International Student Assessment (PISA) 2015 Results in focus*. Paris: OECD.

OECD Development Centre. (2012). *Industrial policy and territorial development: Lessons from Korea*. Paris: OECD Development Centre.

Perdana, A., & Maxwell, J. (2011). The evolution of poverty alleviation policies: ideas, issues and actors. In C. Manning & S. Sumarto (Eds.), *Employment, living standards and poverty in contemporary Indonesia*. Singapore: Institute of Southeast Asian Studies.

Poot, H., Kuyvenhoven, A., & Jansen, J. (1992). *Industrialization and trade in Indonesia*. Yogyakarta: Gadjah Mada University Press.

Pratikto, R., Ikhsan, M., Mahi, B. R., & Teguh, D. (2016). Tackling food price disparity through domestic connectivity. In *EAEA 2016 Conference Proceedings*. Bandung: The East Asian Economic Association.

Shimada, G. (2016). *Inclusive industrial development and Japan development aid - new opportunities for pro-poor regional cooperation through inclusive business in the Mekong region*. Conference paper for ADB Conference in Beijing.

Siahaan, B. (1996). *Industrialisasi di Indonesia: Dari Hutang Kehormatan sampai Banting Stir* [Industrialization in Indonesia: Since the debt of honour to the turn-around]. Jakarta: Pustaka Data.

Suryahadi, A., Raya, U. R., Marbun, D., & Yumna, A. (2011). Accelerating poverty and vulnerability reduction: Trends, opportunities and constraints. In C. Manning & S. Sumarto (Eds.), *Employment, living standards and poverty in contemporary Indonesia*. Singapore: Institute of Southeast Asian Studies.

Suryahadi, A., Widyanti, W., Perwira, D., & Sumarto, S. (2003). Minimum wage policy and its impact on employment in the urban formal sector. *Bulletin of Indonesian Economic Studies*, *39*(1), 29–50.

Tai, W. P., & Ku, S. (2013). State and industrial policy: Comparative political economic analysis of automotive industrial policies in Malaysia and Thailand. *JAS (Journal of ASEAN Studies)*, 1(1), 52–82.

Thee, K. W. (2000). The impact of the economic crisis on Indonesia's manufacturing sector. *The Developing Economies*, *38*(4), 420–453.

Thee, K. W. (2012). *Indonesia's economy since independence*. Singapore: Institute of Southeast Asian Studies.

Tijaja, J., & Faisal, M. (2014). Industrial policy in Indonesia: A global value chain perspective. ADB Economics Working Paper No. 411.

Tjandraningsih, I. (2015). *The minimum wage debate in decentralized Indonesia*. Jakarta: Akatiga Centre for Social Analysis.

Weiss, J. (2005). Export growth and industrial policy: Lessons from the East Asian Miracle experience. *ADB Institute Discussion Paper*, 26.

Wong, C.-Y., Hu, M.-C., & Shiu, J.-W. (2015). Governing the economic transition: How Taiwan transformed its industrial system to attain virtuous cycle development. *Review of Policy Research*, *32*(3), 365–387.

World Bank. (2016). *Indonesia's rising divide*. Washington, DC: The World Bank.

6 Industrial policy and development in Laos

Trade, industrial estates, and enterprise development

Souksavanh Vixathep and Alay Phonvisay

6.1 Introduction

Government intervention in the economy has long been a topic of debate and discussion in the political and academic spheres. In the history of economic development, governments in most developing countries that have successfully caught up with advanced economies and become industrialized have used industrial policy, in one or another way, to achieve their development goals and targets. Industrial policy is a tool that governments around the world use to intervene in economic activities, which encompass economic production, regulation of market functioning, trade and competition, education and training, innovation, and many other components.

Historically, the intervention of the state using industrial policy is considered an important step in the process of development, take-off, and long-run growth. In two classic examples, Germany in the late nineteenth century and Japan in the twentieth century became successful in the catch-up process with more developed countries, partly owing to active involvement of these countries' governments in the development of sound education and innovation systems. In the aftermath of World War II, several governments of developing countries used industrial policy to pursue industrialization. Successful cases that have been widely discussed and cited in the literature include the so-called Four Asian Tigers: South Korea, Taiwan, Singapore, and Hong Kong. The governments of these countries pursued active intervention in creating the initial conditions necessary for industrialization, comparative advantage, and targeted sectoral development, as well as supporting investment in education, skill training, innovation systems, trade liberalization, and many other areas (Di Maio, 2009; Wade, 2015). The formulation of appropriate industrial policies often requires certain preconditions and experiments by the government. In many cases, the successful implementation of policy packages has undergone trial-and-error processes and painful experiences, while the effectiveness of industrial policies has varied across countries.

In the period following the 2008 global financial crisis, income stagnation in industrialized countries occurred alongside a drastic fall in growth rates in developing countries, giving rise to the potential comeback of industrial policy and government intervention. The old policies involving import-substitution industrialization, selective subsidies, export subsidies, local content requirement, and quantitative restrictions on imports have faced severe criticism or been prohibited; yet, industrial policy has never disappeared in practice, but rather has changed names or content. For instance, in Latin America, industrial policies appear in the form of tax incentive policy, competitiveness policy, and small and medium-sized enterprises (SME) promotion policy. In East Asia, industrial policy comprises, for example, knowledge accumulation, production-scale expansion, innovation promotion, and SME promotion (see Di Maio, 2009; Wade, 2015). In this respect, all governments have an industrial policy. However, the striking difference between successful and unsuccessful cases is that governments that have successfully industrialized their economies tend to have formulated industrial policy consciously based on their prerequisites and specific conditions, and strictly implemented industrial policy for the benefit of the country. On the contrary, governments in unsuccessful cases often allowed their policy formulation to be influenced by groups with special interests to enable them to benefit from the country's industrial policy (see Stiglitz & Greenwald, 2014).

Turning to Laos,[1] since obtaining independence in 1975, the Government of Laos (GOL) has pursued socio-economic development and industrialization by formulating and implementing the so-called National Socio-Economic Development Plans (NSEDP), which encompass an industrial development plan. Lao industrial policy has been embedded in the National Socio-Economic Development Strategies, which form the core of the NSEDP. The NSEDP, therefore, can be viewed as the *de facto* industrial policy of the Lao government.

To date, there is no consensus globally on the definition of industrial policy. To a great extent, industrial policy can be understood as any government intervention or policy aimed at enhancing the business environment or changing the structure of economic activities (UNCTAD, 2016). In the literature, industrial policy is considered to include the following policies: (1) education and skill development policies; (2) targeted industrial support policies; (3) trade policies; (4) competition regulation policies; (5) sectoral competitiveness policies; (6) innovation and technology policies; and (7) competition regulation policies (Di Maio, 2009).

In a comprehensive definition of industrial policy, Warwick (2013) defines the horizontal industrial policy as government intervention that aims at enhancing the business environment or changing the economic structure toward sectors, technologies or tasks that would provide better prospects for economic growth and societal welfare (Warwick, 2013, p. 16). This definition of industrial policy is applied in this chapter and three policy components of Laos' industrial policy are discussed: (1) trade policy and trade liberalization; (2) industrial estate or special economic zone (SEZ) development policy; and (3) SME promotion policy.

The main objective of the chapter, therefore, is to examine the industrial policy of the Lao government from two aspects. First, this chapter discusses the historical development of Laos' NSEDP—the country's *de facto* industrial policy— after independence in 1975. Second, in an attempt to evaluate the contribution of industrial policy to economic development, the study focuses on three case studies: trade liberalization and comparative advantage; SEZ development; and SME promotion. For this purpose, this study uses previous and ongoing empirical studies conducted by the authors. The remainder of the chapter is as follows. Section 6.2 presents the historical evolution of development planning in Laos. The three case studies are presented in Section 6.3. Section 6.4 concludes and outlines some policy implications.

6.2 Industrial policy in Laos

In the development literature, industrial policy is often understood as "industrialization policy," "manufacturing strategy," "targeted sector policy," or more generally, "competitiveness or productivity policy," or "national strategy." For developing countries with inadequate infrastructure and a poor business environment, governments can include SEZ development in their industrial policies to attract investment in targeted industries (UNCTAD, 2016 ; Wade, 2015; Warwick, 2013). In the context of Laos, socio-economic development planning, which includes industrialization and modernization strategies, is *de facto* industrial policy. The formulation of industrial policy in Laos can be considered in two phases, namely, a centrally planned economy and a transition to a market economy (New Economic Mechanism, NEM, or *Chintanakan Mai*), as discussed in the following sections. A chronological overview of Laos' development plans is presented in the Appendix (Table 6.A1).

6.2.1 Central planning

During the first decade of independence 1975–1985, the GOL adopted a central planning system. The development plans and policies mainly focused on healing the economy from war-related damage and solving the food shortage problem. The one-year NSEDP, the first three-year NSEDP, and the first five-year NSEDP were adopted in 1976–1977, 1978–1980, and 1981–1985, respectively. These plans were aimed at the recovery of Laos' war-torn economy, improvement of agricultural production areas for food security, recovery and expansion of existing factories, and improvement of transportation infrastructure.

The first annual plan (1976–1977) provided guidelines for recovering agricultural and industrial production in order to move from a subsistence to a commodity-based economy. This plan also outlined economic reconstruction programs to improve people's living standards. A policy on cooperatives or agricultural collectivization was promoted in 1977, for it was strongly believed that this policy would enhance agricultural productivity and diminish slash-and-burn farming. The first three-year plan (1978–1980) was formulated to foster agricultural collectivization, which was the core policy for development. Moreover, this three-year plan emphasized the improvement of industrial facilities in order to increase agricultural production. During 1981–1985, the first five-year NSEDP was adopted by the Third Party Congress. The main objectives were to enhance agricultural and forestry production for food security, to improve existing and construct new industrial plants and factories, and to develop infrastructure, especially national roads (Nos 9 and 13) (LPTPCC, 2016). In this period, the GOL practically managed the entire economic system by formulating production targets, providing capital, technologies, and means of production, controlling prices, and distributing goods and services in the economy based on equitable principles.

6.2.2 The new economic mechanism

The second phase of development planning started in 1986, as the government embarked on a comprehensive reform program, the so called *Chintanakan Mai* or NEM, to move from a centrally planned economy to a market-oriented one following the collapse of the cooperative system. In this phase, the policy formulation can be further classified into two periods: (1) the inception period (1986–2000) and (2) the growth period (2000 onward) (see, e.g., Oraboune, 2011).

6.2.2.1 The inception period (1986–2000)

In 1986, the second five-year NSEDP (1986–1990) was adopted by the Fourth Party Congress. The main objectives were to build the necessary structure for growth in the agro-forestry, industrial, and service sectors; to improve existing laws and formulate new laws and regulations for the private sector; to adopt an open-door policy for foreign cooperation; to improve education, public health, and people's livelihoods; and to privatize state-owned enterprises (SOEs). The third NSEDP (1991–1995) was developed to continue the implementation of these reform policies. The highlights of this plan included the transformation from a subsistence economy to commodity production; emphasis on the role of foreign investment and open-door cooperation; and promulgation of the Business Law in 1994 to ensure a level playing field for all types of businesses. The fourth NSEDP (1996–2000) was aimed at implementing eight national priority programs (food production, commercial production, stabilization of shifting cultivation and resettlement of shifting cultivators, rural development, infrastructure development, foreign economic relations, human resource development, and services development, specifically, tourism, trade, banking, and finance) and at expanding cooperation with the regional and international communities. The specific policies in this fourth NSEDP were to improve and expand existing industries (cement, beverages, tobacco, and food processing) and to establish new industries (bio-fertilizers, vegetable oil extraction, and sugar production). Moreover, the policy promoted so-called small industry and handicraft, environmental protection, and rural development. In 1997, Laos became a member of the Association of Southeast Asian Nations (ASEAN), which has deepened the country's integration into the regional economy (CPI, 1986, 1991, 1996).

6.2.2.2 The growth period (2000 onward)

In the second period of the open-door policy, the development policies became clearer and more systematic. The goals of the fifth NSEDP (2001–2005) were to ensure social order and political stability; achieve rapid and sustainable economic growth; reduce the number of poor households by 50 percent; ensure food security for the population; provide appropriate alternatives to shifting culti-vation; strengthen the organization and enhance the efficiency of SOEs; and develop skilled labor at various levels to accommodate the industrialization and modernization process.

In particular, there was significant industrial policy design during this period. The Industrialization and Modernization Strategy (2001–2020) was formulated. The strategy (2001–2020) was divided into three phases. Phase I (2001–2005) was to prepare for and enhance the competitiveness of existing industries for sur-vival upon the implementation of the ASEAN Free Trade Agreement (AFTA) in 2008. Phase II (2006–2010) was to continue the improvement of the pre-requisite conditions (governance and administration, human resources, economic infrastructure, and macroeconomic stability) for the industrial sector. Phase III (2011–2020) was to complete the establishment of the prerequisites for industri-alization and modernization and to establish leading industries (electricity, wood processing, tourism, mining, and construction materials) (CPI, 2001, 2002). Also in this period, an SME promotion and development policy was formulated and the first SEZ was established in Savannakhet Province.

In the most recent three NSEDPs (2006–2010, 2011–2015, and 2016–2020), including the current (eighth) plan, the major policy targets are to eliminate slash-and-burn cultivation practices, further develop the agricultural sector, achieve sig-nificant poverty reduction and sustainable growth, strengthen the capacity of the private sector, achieve industrialization and modernization to graduate from the least-developed country (LDC) status by 2020, promote enterprise development (particularly, productivity-enhancing innovation activities), promote efficient use of natural resources, develop land-link transportation networks, and ensure pol-itical stability, peace, and order in society. Moreover, a 10-year Socio-Economic Development Strategy (2016–2025) contains seven strategies for industrializa-tion and modernization (CPI, 2006; MPI, 2011, 2016). Furthermore, Vision 2020 and Vision 2030 are long-term industrial policies through which the GOL has established the direction and priority sectors for socio-economic develop-ment, and has implemented industrial policy in the medium and long terms.

6.3 Impact of industrial policy on economic development

Policy assessment is an intrinsic complex issue. It attempts to establish a causal relationship between policy implementation with overall impacts and to measure additionality or net positive outcomes. This study is an attempt to provide an ex-post or impact evaluation of industrial policy using quantitative and qualitative approaches. A quantitative impact evaluation that is closer to Step 4–Step 6 in the "Six Steps to Heaven" methodology would provide a more holistic evaluation of the SME promotion policy of the GOL (Cowie, 2012). To evaluate the impact of industrial policy on economic development, three policy components are discussed in this case study: trade policy, development of SEZs, and promotion of

SMEs. These three components are among the priorities of the GOL for socio-economic development.

6.3.1 Overview of the Lao economy

With a population of 6.6 million, Laos is traditionally an agriculture-based economy. After embarking on economic reforms in the late 1980s, the economy grew steadily from US$1.5 billion in 1984 to US$11.1 billion in 2016 (a seven-fold increase) and is gradually moving from agriculture to industry and services. The share of the agricultural sector in gross domestic product (GDP) declined from 49 percent in 2000 to 20 percent in 2016, while the shares of the industrial and service sectors increased from 19 percent to 32 percent and from 32 percent to 48 percent, respectively. With regard to employment, the primary sector, including the agriculture and extraction industries, provides employment opportunities for most of the labor force. For example, of roughly 3.1 million people in the labor force in 2010, about 71 percent (36 percent of the population) were engaged in agriculture and 8 percent in mining and quarrying (ADB, 2017; World Bank, 2017).

Table 6.1 presents an overview of the Lao economy for the period 1985–2016. On average, economic growth accelerated following the start of the NEM in 1986. Derived from 2017 Key Indicators of the Asian Development Bank, GDP grew at an annual rate of more than 7.2 percent during 2000–2016, compared to 4.5 percent in the second half of the 1980s. Over the same period, per capita real GDP increased from US$432 to US$1,643. In terms of sectoral contribution, in 2016, the agricultural sector contributed 2.8 percent of the GDP growth rate of 7.0 percent, the industrial sector 12.0 percent, and the service sector 4.7 percent (ADB, 2017). In the same vein, imports and exports (trade) have recorded an upward trend in both value (real terms) and share of GDP. Although the growth of exports and imports has fluctuated, the figures imply an expansion in international trade over the last two decades. Similarly, saving and investment as well as external borrowing have all increased. In summary, the indicators in Table 6.1 suggest a positive development in economic growth and integration of the country over the period under discussion.

6.3.2 Trade policy and comparative advantage

In line with the trend of outward-looking policy adopted across developing and transition economies in the 1980s and 1990s, trade liberalization has been included in the economic reform and development policy of the Lao government. Trade reform in Laos is divided into three phases: (1) a closed economy with central control (1975–1985); (2) transition to a market economy (1986–2000); and (3) an open economy with an open-door policy (2000 onward) (see, e.g., Douangboupha, 2010; Nishimura et al., 2016; Otani & Pham, 1996; Vixathep, 2011).

Table 6.1 Overview of the macro economy

Description	1985	1990	1995	2000	2005	2010	1015	2016
GDP (USD million, 2010 prices)	1,594	1,967	2,656	3,582	4,848	7,128	10,374	11,102
Per capita GDP (USD, 2010 prices)	432	462	547	672	843	1,141	1,557	1,643
GDP annual growth rate (%)	5.07	4.47[a]	6.19[b]	6.17[c]	6.24[d]	8.01[e]	7.79[f]	7.02[h]
Trade/GDP (%)	13.8	35.85	60.55	74.31	80.66	74.22	74.76	68.45
Exports/GDP (%)	4.04	11.33	23.22	30.1	34.16	35.81	30.96	29.34
Imports/GDP (%)	9.77	24.52	37.33	44.21	46.5	38.41	43.8	39.11
Exports (USD million, 2000 prices)	584	412	435[b]	521[c]	558[d]	483[e]	531[f]	n.a.
Imports (USD million, 2000 prices)	641	614	599[b]	765[c]	772[d]	711[e]	645[f]	n.a.
Export growth rate (%)	22.72	8.19	33.65	1.7	12.59	28.94	10.08	21.06[h]
Import growth rate (%)	19.14	-1.84	29.56	-1.36	12.86	19.51	21.15	-9.43[h]
Gross saving/GDP (%)	3.41	-0.61[g]	15.18	2.44	10.79	18.57	12.16	n.a.
Gross investment/GDP (%)	7.04	13.50[g]	n.a.	13.93	23.08	25	28.16	26.42
External debt/GDP (%)	26.25	204.38	122.38	146.2	119.85	91.26	90.43	89.04
Total population	6.59 million (as of July 1, 2016)							

Notes: 1. "n.a." means the data are not available. 2. The superscript denotes: a) average of 1986–1990; b) average of 1991–1995; c) average of 1996–2000; d) average of 2001–2005; e) average of 2006–2010; f) average of 2011–2015; g) value of 1988; and h) value of 2016

Source: Compiled by the authors; data are from Key Indicators (various issues), Asian Development Bank; World Development Indicators (various issues), World Bank.

Prior to the introduction of economic reform, the growth strategy pursued by the government was inward-oriented. Trade mainly occurred with countries of the Council for Mutual Economic Assistance (COMECON)[2] in a framework of bilateral economic assistance. In the second half of the 1980s, together with the launch of the NEM, trade liberalization was implemented gradually. In the initial reform stage, the tax and trade system put more emphasis on administrative controls than on facilitation and tariffs. Trade reform encompassed the gradual removal of price controls in retail trade and agricultural procurement, the introduction of a market-oriented trading system and the necessary legal framework for a market economy, SOE reform in the decision-making process; and launch of a structural reform program with assistance of the World Bank and the International Monetary Fund. The GOL carried out several reforms in subsequent years. By the mid-1990s, the maximum tariff rate was reduced from 150 percent to 40 percent (Fane, 2006; Fukase & Martin, 1999; Otani & Pham, 1996; see Table 6.2 for more details).

At the regional level, the government made a bold step toward trade liberalization by joining the ASEAN in 1997, and subsequently, Laos has participated in the AFTA and implemented the Common Effective Preferential Tariff (CEPT) scheme. Within the scope of the CEPT scheme, tariffs on manufactured and processed agricultural products were reduced to 0–5 percent by 2008, import tariffs were gradually reduced, import and export licensing procedures were simplified, and quantitative restrictions and non-tariff barriers were eliminated. In addition, Laos applied for World Trade Organization (WTO) membership in 1997 and officially became a member in 2013 (Fukase & Martin, 1999; Vixathep, 2011).

In the current open-economy era, trade and investment as well as economic integration have remained important components of Lao industrial policy. They have been incorporated into the recent development plans (NSEDP7 and NSEDP8) and are considered one of the main strategic interventions of the government. In particular, the strategies to change Laos from a land-locked to a land-linked country and the regional cooperation framework in ASEAN Economic Community (AEC) 2015 are important components of the recent development policy. A chronological summary of trade reform and its gradual inclusion in industrial policy is presented in Table 6.2.

6.3.2.1 Impact of trade reform on the Lao economy

In the literature, particularly in the Neoliberal School, there is a widespread theoretical assumption and empirical and political conclusion that free trade is favorable to growth. However, once this strict assumption for trade analysis is relaxed, the gains from trade could be marginal and free trade might not be desirable. Recently, questions have arisen about the causal relationship between openness and growth, including even the reverse assumption about free trade (Stiglitz & Greenwald, 2014). The views on the impact of trade liberalization on economic growth and development are far from achieving consensus. In view

Table 6.2 Summary of trade and investment reforms in Laos

Time	Reforms/policies
1975	Gained independence and end of colonial era
1978	Removal of some restrictions on private sector activity but international trade still under state control
1981–1985	Experiments in decentralizing selected state-owned enterprises (SOEs); small private trading allowed; further reforms in prices, wages, and salaries
1986	Introduction of the New Economic Mechanism (*Chintanakan Mai*)
1986–1987	Low degree of liberalization of internal trade; less intervention of administrative units in small trading companies; elimination of restrictions on provincial trade and rice movement; broadening of economic relations with foreign countries; expansion of trade in convertible currencies
1988	Rationalization of tariff structure; reduction in import tariff rates
1986–1989	Relaxation of most controls on retail prices and agricultural procurement prices, giving autonomy to SOEs in decision making on business; private sector allowed to trade in all commodities (except strategic goods); requirement to impose submission of trade plans to the State Committee for Foreign Economic Relations
1988	Abolition of the multiple and fixed exchange rate system; introduction of a single rate system (closer to the parallel market); promulgation of law on foreign direct investment (FDI)
1989	Introduction of export quota on high-quality timber
1990	Reduction of list of strategic goods exportable only by state companies
1991	Partial liberalization of international trade (elimination of quantitative restrictions and specific licensing requirements for most goods)
Mid-1990s	Dominance of non-tariff barriers (quotas), but tariff structure partly simplified (12 tariff rates); revision of law on FDI (simplification of profit tax)
1995	Maximum rate decreased from 100% to 40% that included six bands (5%, 10%, 15%, 20%, 30%, and 40%); abolition of restrictive export licensing for domestic user protection; simplification of import-licensing system
1997	Joined ASEAN and committed to full implementation of the ASEAN Economic Community Blueprint by 2015; application for access to the World Trade Organization (WTO) (July 16, 1997)
2004	Revision of law on FDI (extension of investment term for foreign investors to 50 years and 75 years under special circumstances)
2010	Trade policy in NSEDP7: Promotion of domestic production of goods with potential for export; enhancement of economic and trade integration; approval of unification of foreign investment law and domestic investment law into one
2013	Formal membership of WTO on February 2 (as the 158th member country)
2016	Current trade policy in NSEDP8: Trade development embedded in the regional cooperation framework, for example, the ASEAN Economic Community 2015; application of multilateral trade policy to promote modernization and integration; development of infrastructure and markets to open and strengthen regional and domestic trade, particularly along the east–west corridor; and broadening sharing of market information with domestic and foreign investors

Sources: Adapted from Vixathep (2011, p. 30, Table A2); compiled by the authors from various sources (Otani & Pham, 1996; Martin, 2001; Fane, 2006; Douangboupha, 2010; Onphanhdala & Suruga, 2010; MPI, 2011, 2016; WTO home page (www.wto.org)).

of evaluating the impact of trade policy reform on economic development, this section considers the changes in the patterns of external trade and the evolution of revealed comparative advantage (RCA)[3] of Laos during the transition and open-door periods (1985–2015). The discussion of trade patterns and RCA for the period 1985–2005 largely refers to the findings of Vixathep (2011).[4]

Over the last three decades, Laos's international trade has expanded steadily, with exports increasing from US$21 million in 1985 to more than US$3 billion in 2016 and imports from US$61 million to US$3.4 billion. However, the patterns of trade have changed relatively little. Exports have been dominated by unprocessed agricultural products (coffee and spices), resource-based commodities (wood products and copper), and labor-intensive industrial products (apparel and clothing items). Recently, some machinery and transportation equipment have entered export markets with noticeable shares (Table 6.3). Imports, on the other hand, have been dominated by beverages, material inputs and equipment, fuels, minerals, machinery, and vehicles (Table 6.4). With regard to the destinations of exports and sources of imports, the major trade partners of Laos, namely, Thailand, China, and Vietnam, have not changed over the period under study. The combined value of exports and imports of these countries comprises between 85 percent and 92 percent of Laos' exports and imports, respectively.

Vixathep (2011) applies three indicators—the ratio of high RCA products[5] to total ranked products,[6] the trend of standard deviation of the RCA index, and the Spearman rank correlation coefficients—to evaluate the diversification of exports. All measures imply that the structure of exports has been rigid and little diversification has occurred (Table 6.5). Some intra-industry diversification and specialization are evident only in simple commodities (e.g. simple wood items and apparel products). The findings suggest that the conditions, including the skill levels of the Lao labor force, would still be inadequate for more sophisticated products with higher added value. In spite of the fact that Laos' international trade is affected by several factors, including domestic and foreign countries' trade policies and internal and external conditions, the findings in Vixathep (2011) imply that trade liberalization, as a component of industrial policy, has so far not yielded a positive impact on the country's competitiveness, which had been expected by policymakers. In the same vein, Douangboupha (2010) maintains that Laos' economic growth is influenced by several factors, including internal and external factors, socio-political and economic factors, and trade policy, but it is a challenging task to account for the impact of trade policy reform on growth (for more discussions and suggestions on trade reform, see World Bank. (2006)).

6.3.3 Special economic zones

The second component of industrial policy analyzed in this study is the development of SEZs and their impact on economic development. Industrial estate development is a key component of industrial policy in East Asia. Faced with obstacles and capacity limitations to development (both physical and institutional factors), some latecomer countries in East Asia implemented industrial estate development as part of their industrialization policies (e.g., the world's first export-processing

Table 6.3 Commodity composition of exports (% share, value in USD million)

Description	SITC	1985	1990	1995	2000	2005	2010	2015	2016
Food and live animals	0	54.82	4.31	10.14	7.33	5.92	19.12	12.64	20.4
Beverages and tobacco	1	-	-	0.41	0.06	0.21	1.37	8.35	8.42
Crude materials, inedible, except fuels	2	37.93	77.04	40.49	33.94	29.69	31.61	27.29	28.15
Mineral fuels, lubricants	3	-	0.05	0.25	0.4	11.25	0.87	0.18	0.24
Animal and vegetable oils and fats	4	-	-	0	0	0	0	0	0.01
Chemicals and related products, n.e.s.	5	0.1	0.08	1.74	0.04	0.28	1.18	6.78	5.67
Manufactured goods (class. by material)	6	4.01	7.43	8.68	1.21	16.05	26.85	19.83	13.68
Machinery & transportation equipment	7	0.91	0.98	0.26	18.16	1.43	1.4	12.09	12.35
Miscellaneous manufactured articles	8	1.13	10.11	37.45	36.81	31.4	11.12	7.75	6.92
Other commodities and transactions	9	1.11	1.43	0.3	2.01	3.14	6.47	5.1	4.16
Total commodity exports (USD mil, 2000 prices)		21	63	202	349	600	1,591	2,739	3,004

Notes: 1 Owing to lack of an import unit value index for Laos, a corresponding index of developing Asian countries was used for 1985–2000 (base year=2000), and a corresponding index of Southeast Asian countries was used for 2005–2016 (base year=2000). 2 For 1985, some partners reported only the total value of bilateral trade with Laos. Hence, the value of total exports used for calculating the shares was lower than the values reported in this table. However, the composition is assumed to persist. 3 'n.e.s.' denotes not elsewhere specified. 4 SITC stands for Standard International Trade Classification of the UN.

Source: Compiled by the authors (data are from the UN Comtrade online database).

Table 6.4 Commodity composition of imports (% share, value in USD million)

Description	SITC	1985	1990	1995	2000	2005	2010	2015	2016
Food and live animals	0	6.56	10.08	8.68	6.89	8.67	6.02	4.18	7.38
Beverages and tobacco	1	0.74	0.83	8.88	6.86	5.27	5.12	0.95	5.77
Crude materials, inedible, except fuels	2	0.14	0.25	0.25	2.38	0.83	0.5	0.97	1.04
Mineral fuels, lubricants	3	19.55	5.57	7.83	11.7	18.35	25.29	20.1	14.98
Animal and vegetable oils and fats	4	0.06	0.23	0.26	0.28	0.3	0.21	0.12	0.09
Chemicals and related products, n.e.s.	5	10.06	8.76	6.53	6.39	7.6	6.81	5.94	5.3
Manufactured goods (class. by material)	6	22.55	18.79	21.62	22.94	20.98	17.66	22.16	18.94
Machinery & transportation equipment	7	28.8	46.86	35.27	35.82	29.93	30.84	41.62	41.66
Miscellaneous manufactured articles	8	8.26	6.79	6.11	4.92	5.2	3.42	3.85	3.1
Other commodities and transactions	9	3.28	1.88	4.62	1.67	2.75	4.13	0.11	1.73
Total commodity exports (USD mil, 2000 prices)		61	120	534	602	1,020	1,341	2,975	3,394

Notes: 1 Owing to lack of an import unit value index for Laos, a corresponding index of developing Asian countries was used for 1985–2000 (base year=2000), and a corresponding index of Southeast Asian countries was used for 2005–2016 (base year=2000). 2 'n.e.s.' denotes not elsewhere specified.
Source: Compiled by the authors (data are from the UN Comtrade online database).

Table 6.5 Ratio of revealed comparative advantage and net export indexes and standard deviation

RCA index	1985	1990	1995	2000	2005
High RCA products (A)	8	20	23	22	33
Total ranked products (B)	39	86	98	116	178
Ratio of high RCA products to total (A)/(B)	0.21	0.23	0.23	0.19	0.19
Total share of high RCA products (% share)	42.2	96.2	96.03	96.5	93.12
Standard deviation	0.95	1.07	1.3	1.39	1.37
Sample size	39	86	98	116	178
NE Index	*1985*	*1990*	*1995*	*2000*	*2005*
High NEI products (A)	11	24	26	25	34
Total ranked products (B)	30	78	92	111	175
Ratio of high NEI products to total (A)/(B)	0.37	0.31	0.28	0.23	0.19
Total share of high NEI products (% share)	42.16	94.67	95.2	77.82	89.24
Standard deviation	0.85	0.78	0.79	0.72	0.67
Sample size	30	78	92	111	175

Notes: 1 The ratio of high RCA products to total ranked products does not increase over the period under study. 2 A downward trend of the standard deviation of the index of RCA implies a diversification of exports. The standard deviation of RCA and NEI indexes of Laos does not decline.

Source: Vixathep (2011, p. 17, Table 8).

zone was developed in Taiwan). Industrial estate development has become a key policy tool to attract FDI in the East Asian region (Ohno, 2013).

The development of SEZs in Laos illustrates the industrial agglomeration process at the early stage of cluster development. At the current stage of development, the GOL does not have sufficient resources to provide an attractive investment climate to investors across the entire country. Hence, SEZ development is a viable option to offer good business conditions to attract FDI in targeted sectors. From the onset of Laos' economic reform, SEZ development has been one of the government's development priorities. An SEZ is an area or zone that is developed for specific purposes, such as to promote government-targeted industrial sectors and rapid economic development. An SEZ is governed by a specific set of laws and regulations, which differ from those in other investment areas and grants special privileges to business operations.

The SEZ concept used in Laos emerged from a feasibility study for the construction of the 2nd Lao–Thai Friendship Bridge in Savannakhet Province presented by the Japan International Cooperation Agency in 2000. Furthermore, the Decree on Management Regulations and Incentive Policies for the Savan-Seno SEZ (Decree No. 177/PM) was legislated. The decree was subsequently used as model for other SEZs. The aim of Savan-Seno SEZ development was to attract and promote domestic and foreign investment along road No. 9 from the

Friendship Bridge in Savannakhet to Vietnam, in the fields of production, export, trade, tourism, services, warehousing, and in-transit passenger and goods transportation. The Lao Government decided to construct the Savan-Seno SEZ as an experimental site by investing in the construction of basic infrastructure of the zone (GOL, 2003; Phonvisay et al., 2017).

In 2004, the GOL enacted the Law on the Promotion of Domestic Investment (No. 10/NA) and the Law on the Promotion of Foreign Investment (No. 11/NA) to create a sound environment and conditions for domestic and foreign investment; and to enable investors to undertake business activities in a speedy and convenient manner. The GOL has made continuing efforts to establish a good environment to support SEZ development and amended and unified the two laws into the Law on Investment Promotion (LIP) No. 02/NA in 2009.

The LIP classifies SEZs into two types: SEZs and specific economic zones. On the one hand, an SEZ is an area that the government has designated to develop into a new modern town as a place to attract domestic and foreign investment—with an area of at least 1,000 hectares (ha), special promotion policy, and an autonomous economic and financial system. An SEZ is managed by an SEZ management board and an SEZ economic executive board. The resident population in a special zone does not have to resettle. They can participate in the SEZ activities in order to develop the zone; raise their income; and achieve sustainable security and environment. An SEZ may be established by combining different specific economic zones.

On the other hand, a specific economic zone refers to an area delineated by the government as an industrial zone, a production-for-export zone, a tourism zone, a duty-free zone, a technology and information development zone, or a border trade zone, among others. The establishment of a specific economic zone is based on the specific characteristics of the zone: its development, production, and services. The territory of a specific economic zone is clearly demarcated and no people live there; the zone is managed by an economic executive board via a one-seal mechanism (GOL, 2009; SEZ Secretariat Office, 2012).

In 2010, the Prime Minister's Decree on Special Economic Zones was issued, which serves as a legal framework to promote SEZ investment. In the same year, the National Committee and the Secretariat Office to the National Committee for Special Economic Zones were established to lead the development and management of all SEZs in Laos. These two government bodies have been assigned to establish a competitive SEZ legal system and guidelines, formulate the open-door policy for SEZ development in all sectors in the country, set up SEZs based on a market-driven method, simplify investment and business operation processes by creating a one-stop service, and develop SEZs based on equity, accountability, sustainability, and environmental preservation (Nishimura et al., 2016). Since mid-2016, however, SEZs have been placed under the direct supervision of the Ministry of Planning and Investment (MPI) and the National Committee for Special Economic Zones.

The primary goals of establishing SEZs in Laos are to create more jobs for local people, transfer skills and technology from foreign to local staff, increase government revenue, and contribute to economic growth. Since the establishment of the Savan-Seno SEZ in 2003, 11 more SEZs have been approved for development, including 4 SEZs and 8 specific economic zones. At the time of writing, all 12 SEZs were classified as SEZs (Table 6.6).

Based on our interviews with officials of the SEZ Secretariat Office, the 12 SEZs occupy about 19,621 ha of land area in total. With combined investment planned by 295 firms of US$6.8 billion, the SEZs could create 15,544 jobs.[7] With regard to type of investment, 38 percent are in services, 28 percent in manufacturing, and 34 percent in trade and logistics. By the end of 2016, the overall investment in these SEZs was US$1.62 billion, comprising US$1.3 billion from zone developers, US$329.5 million from joint ventures (investors), and US$23.9 million from the Lao government. The figures reveal that in the last decade, SEZ development has been driven by the private sector, especially foreign developers and investors. Nonetheless, in the fiscal year 2015–2016, the share of investment by the GOL and investors in SEZ development has increased remarkably, whereas that of zone developers has fallen drastically. This trend reflects the expanded role in participation of the GOL and investors in developing the Champasack and Luangprabang SEZs, which were officially established in the same fiscal year (Table 6.7).

In terms of registered capital, to date, a total amount of US$8.22 billion has been recorded, of which foreign, domestic, and joint investments each have roughly one-third. Furthermore, the top-five leading foreign investors in SEZs during 2003–2016 were from China, Thailand, Vietnam, the US, and Japan (Table 6.8). With regard to the number of investors and invested capital, the distribution is rather uneven across the economic zones. The large differences in distribution—from Savan-Seno with 74 firms and Golden Triangle with 59 firms to Dongphosy with only 2 investors—most likely arise from the configuration of the zones, including location, infrastructure development, provision of incentives, and marketing strategy of individual developers (Table 6.6).

6.3.3.1 Impact of special economic zone development on the Lao economy

As a case study for industrial estate development, a survey of the cross-border impact of and collaboration with Thai SEZs was conducted in September–October 2016 (for more details, see Phonvisay et al., 2017). For data collection, the study applies a semi-structured interview approach to interview the stakeholders of both Lao and Thai SEZs. However, the discussion in this section is mainly based on the survey results of the Lao component. The stakeholders on the Lao side include government bodies in charge of SEZs at the ministerial and provincial levels (MPI, Ministry of Labor and Social Welfare, Management Committee of VITA Park; Saysettha SEZ, Golden Triangle, and Provincial Departments of Industry and Commerce and Departments of Planning and Investment of Savannakhet and Bokeo Provinces, SEZ Secretary Office, SEZ developers, and representatives of investors in SEZs).

Table 6.6 Special economic zones in Laos (as at end of 2016)

No.	Special/specific economic zone	Location	Establishment year	Estimated investment (USD mil)	Sector	Number of enterprises (2003–2015)
1	Savan-Seno SEZ	Savannakhet Province	2003	74	Industrial zone	74
2	Boten SEZ	Luangnamtha Province	2003 (Upgraded 2012)	500	Trade and logistics	14
3	Golden Triangle	Bokeo Province	2007 (Upgraded 2014)	1,000	Tourist and new urban center	59
4	VITA Park	Vientiane capital	2009 (Upgraded 2010)	43	Industrial zone	38
5	Phoukyo SEZ	Khammuane Province	2011	708	Industrial zone	16
6	Saysettha SEZ	Vientiane capital	2010 (Upgraded 2011)	128	Industrial zone	9
7	Thatluang SEZ	Vientiane capital	2011	1,600	Tourist and new urban center	13
8	Long Thanh SEZ	Vientiane capital	2008 (Upgraded 2012)	1,000	Tourist and new urban center	4
9	Dongphosy SEZ	Vientiane capital	2009 (Upgraded 2012)	50	Trade and logistics	2
10	Thakhek SEZ	Khammuane Province	2012	80	Trade and logistics	18
11	Champasack SEZ	Champasack Province	2015	493	Industrial zone	8
12	LuangPrabang SEZ	LuangPrabang Province	2016	1,200	Tourist and new urban center	-

Note: "Upgraded" in column 4 indicates the year in which a "specific economic zone" was upgraded to a "special economic zone."

Source: SEZ Secretariat Office (2016).

Table 6.7 Actual investment in SEZs by investor type, 2003–September 2016

Sector	Actual invested capital (2003–2016) (USD million)	% share	Actual invested capital (2015–2016) (USD million)	% share
Government	23.9	1.47	17.3	20.2
Zone developer	1,270.20	78.23	34.6	40.31
Investors	329.5	20.3	33.9	39.49
Total	1,623.70	100	85.8	100

Source: SEZ Secretariat Office (2016).

Table 6.8 Investment in SEZs by country, 2003–September 2016

No.	Country	Number of enterprises	Registered capital (USD million)	% share
1	China	134	1,551.50	58.18
2	Thailand	29	523.3	19.62
3	Japan	21	28	1.05
4	Malaysia	6	17.7	0.67
5	France	5	1.9	0.07
6	Vietnam	2	302.5	11.34
7	Australia	2	0.5	0.02
8	the Netherlands	2	1	0.04
9	South Korea	3	1.8	0.07
10	Germany	1	0.1	0.004
11	Denmark	1	0.5	0.02
12	US	1	235.5	8.83
13	Hong Kong	1	2	0.07
14	Belgium	1	0.5	0.02
	Total	209	2,666.80	100
I	Foreign	209	2,666.80	32.4
II	Domestic	63	2,736.80	33.3
III	Joint domestic/foreign	23	2,815.60	34.3
	Total	295	8,219.30	100

Source: SEZ Secretariat Office (2016).

The contribution of SEZs to the Lao economy is evaluated based on their direct impact, which includes employment generation, import–export activities, and fiscal contribution. First, with regard to job creation, to date, 7,180 Lao laborers and 8,364 foreign laborers have found employment in the 12 SEZs. It is worth noting that Savan-Seno SEZ and VITA Park employ most of the domestic labor force in SEZs (74.2 percent), whereas the Golden Triangle engages most foreign workers in the economic zones (87.7 percent). These three SEZs together employ 84.6 percent of the country's total workforce in the economic zones (15,544 people) (Table 6.9). The high ratio of foreign-labor employment

Table 6.9 Employment in SEZs in 2016 (people, % share)

No.	SEZ	Laotians	Foreigners	Total
1	Savan-Seno SEZ	4,128 (57.5)	101 (1.2)	4,229 (27.2)
2	Boten SEZ	212 (3.0)	429 (5.1)	641 (4.1)
3	Golden Triangle	338 (4.7)	7,336 (87.7)	7,674 (49.4)
4	VITA Park	1,198 (16.7)	52 (0.6)	1,250 (8.0)
5	Saysettha SEZ	82 (1.1)	132 (1.6)	214 (1.4)
6	Dongphosy SEZ	42 (0.6)	14 (0.2)	56 (0.4)
7	Phoukyo SEZ	60 (0.8)	12 (0.1)	72 (0.5)
8	Thatluang SEZ	112 (1.6)	93 (1.1)	205 (1.3)
9	Long Thanh SEZ	489 (6.8)	96 (1.1)	517 (3.3)
10	Thakhek SEZ	50 (0.7)	96 (1.1)	146 (0.9)
11	Champasack SEZ	469 (6.5)	71 (0.8)	540 (3.5)
12	LuangPrabang SEZ	–	–	–
	Total	7,180 (100)	8,364 (100)	15,544 (100)

Note: Percentage shares are in parentheses.

Source: Compiled by the authors (data are from SEZ Secretariat Office, 2016).

in Golden Triangle may be attributed to the facts that the zone is still in its early stage of development and thereby requires a large number of workers for construction work and infrastructure development, and that Bokeo Province is incapable of supplying local human resources to meet the labor demand in the zone.

Second, over the period 2003–2016, the accumulated amount of exports by SEZs was US$352 million and that of imports was nearly US$1.2 billion. In particular, Savan-Seno, VITA Park, and Champasack SEZ recorded export activities, whereas the service-based economic zones appear to concentrate more on import activities, such as construction materials for infrastructure development and consumer goods for service provision in the zones, or the investors in those zones are not yet ready for export activities (Table 6.10). Moreover, it is revealed from Table 6.10 that most SEZ trade activities started only recently. Specifically, the ratio of imports, exports, and trade (sum of imports and exports) in 2015–2016 to that of the entire period of SEZ development (2003–2016) is about 79.2 percent in all cases. This fact implies there is a relatively long period of investment, development, and preparation for business operations in economic zones or industrial estates, which, in turn, has implications for the implementation of industrial policy.

Third, in terms of contribution to the country's output, SEZs have shown an upward trend in the share of GDP. For example, the percentage share of output of SEZs in GDP was 0.3 percent in 2013. The figure increased to more than 1.0 percent in 2014 and is expected to be around 3 percent in 2015. Since the establishment of the first SEZ in 2003, the GOL has collected US$16.5 million in tax revenues, of which it earned US$4.2 million tax on concession contract agreements in the fiscal year 2015–2016 alone (Table 6.11). Upon the expiration

Table 6.10 Imports and exports of SEZs, 2003–2016

No.	SEZ	2003–2016		2015–2016	
		Export value (USD million)	*Import value (USD million)*	*Export value (USD million)*	*Import value (USD million)*
1	Savan-Seno SEZ	310.2	287.7	259.1	196.2
2	VITA Park	38.3	59.4	18	15.6
3	Champasack SEZ	3.6	4.9	1.5	1.6
4	Boten SEZ	–	4.6	–	1.1
5	Golden Triangle	–	7.4	–	5.9
6	Saysettha SEZ	–	744.1	–	691.1
7	Thatluang SEZ	–	10.6	–	1.4
8	Long Thanh SEZ	–	31.4	–	0.6
9	Dongphosy SEZ	–	0.09	–	0.03
10	Thakhek SEZ	–	5.7	–	2.5
	Total	352.2	1,155.90	278.6	916

Source: SEZ Secretariat Office (2016).

Table 6.11 Tax revenue from SEZs, 2003–2016

No.	SEZ	*Tax revenue 2003–2016 (USD 1,000)*	*Tax revenue 2015–2016 (USD 1,000)*
1	Savan-Seno SEZ	1,535.20	369
2	Boten SEZ	12.3	n.a.
3	Golden Triangle	9,941.60	3,069.50
4	VITA Park	729.7	374.6
5	Saysettha SEZ	201	105.7
6	Dongphosy SEZ	280.4	60.7
7	Phoukyo SEZ	7	7
8	Thatluang SEZ	11.5	11.5
9	Long Thanh SEZ	1,527.60	172.6
10	Thakhek SEZ	2,121.50	n.a.
11	Champasack SEZ	16.3	13.8
12	LuangPrabang SEZ	–	–
	Total	16,475.00	4,184.50

Notes: 1. Tax revenue is based on concession contract agreement; 2. "n.a." denotes that the data are not available.

Source: SEZ Secretariat Office (2016).

of the tax holiday periods, this contribution is expected to increase sharply (SEZ Secretariat Office, 2016).

In summary, over the 2003–2016 period of development, the SEZs and specific economic zones have made a significant direct contribution to the national economy in generating employment opportunities for Lao and foreign labor forces (15,544 people), trade (US$1.5 billion), and tax revenue to the government (US$16.5 million). However, owing to financial and technical limitations in our research, the indirect impact (i.e., contribution to output and employment through the supply chain and outsourcing) and catalytic impact (i.e., wider economic benefits or enhancement of productivity and technical spillovers from SEZs) cannot be captured in the study. In this respect, the interview survey reveals some outsourcing of production and skill training for the Lao labor force by SEZ firms to local suppliers, which, if appropriately promoted, would enhance the indirect and catalytic effects of SEZ development on the Lao economy.

6.3.4 Small and medium-sized enterprises

The third component of industrial policy analyzed in this study is the development of SMEs, which is a very common component of industrial policy around the world. However, among developing and developed countries, the targets of SME promotion differ markedly. For developing countries, SME promotion policy covers all sizes of firms and sectors with simple procedures for poverty reduction (generation of income and employment), while for developed countries, the policy targets the establishment of high-performing SMEs aimed at enhancing internal value and innovation (Ohno, 2013, pp. 80–81). In Southeast Asia, development of SMEs has been included in the AEC Blueprint of the ASEAN as a component of equitable economic development. This development reflects the importance that the governments of ASEAN countries attach to SMEs in the pursuit of economic development. As in most developing countries, in Laos, SMEs form the backbone of the manufacturing sector in terms of number of firms and employment generation. SME development has drawn significant interest from both the government and the international community.

Turning to SME[8] promotion in Laos, since the promulgation of the Business Law in 1994, the role of SMEs has become increasingly significant for economic development. The first SME promotion policy was formulated in the fourth five-year NSEDP (1996–2000), in which SMEs were referred to as "small industry and handicraft business." The role of SMEs was fully recognized in the fifth NSEDP (2001–2005). The Prime Minister's Decree on the Promotion and Development of Small and Medium-Sized Enterprises (No. 42/PM) in 2004 formulated the overall framework for defining the directions and policies, the establishment of the SME support fund and organizations, and regulations, practices and measures to promote and develop SMEs in the country. Following this decree, the policy on supporting SMEs has been embedded in the subsequent five-year NSEDPs. For example, the major goal of the sixth NSEDP (2006–2010) for the development of SMEs was to promote their rapid expansion.

From the seventh NSEDP (2011–2015) onward, policy on promoting SMEs has been included in the enterprise development section. Seven policy areas (prioritized directions) serve as a reference for formulating a strategy and work plan for the promotion and development of SMEs. This strategy includes: (1) improving the regulatory environment and public administration of economic activities; (2) improving access to finance; (3) encouraging the formation of new enterprises; (4) increasing the provision of support and business development services; (5) enhancing business linkages between large enterprises and SMEs; (6) promoting productivity enhancement aimed at upgrading the quality and standard of products and services of SMEs; and (7) enhancing access to markets and enlarging markets for SMEs.

The seventh NSEDP emphasizes that the strategy requires SMEs to upgrade and modernize, so that they can be integrated into the production system. Moreover, they should be able to trade their products with other locales, provinces, and countries. They are expected to compete under the AFTA. Moreover, encouraging SMEs, cooperative enterprises, and household enterprises to use newer technologies in order to improve their productivity and enhance their effectiveness is stated as a goal in the same NSEDP. In 2011, the Decree on the Promotion and Development of Small and Medium-Sized Enterprises (No. 42/PM) was upgraded to the Law on the Promotion of Small and Medium-Sized Enterprises, No. 11/NA.

With regard to policy implementation, under Decree No. 42/PM, the Small and Medium-Sized Enterprise Promotion and Development Office, which acts as the secretariat, was established in the Ministry of Industry and Commerce[9] and was subsequently promoted to the Department of Small and Medium-Sized Enterprise Promotion (DOSMEP). The DOSMEP has the function of formulating strategies and work plans for the promotion of SMEs. In addition, the Small and Medium-Sized Enterprise Promotion and Development Committee (SMEPDC) was established based on the Prime Minister's Decision No. 23/PM. The SMEPDC—a government body with 25 members from the public and private sectors—is responsible for SME-related tasks at the central level and provides advice to the government on issues related to the promotion and development of SMEs (for more details, see Vixathep, 2017). Table 6.12 presents a summary of SME development plans and changes in policy priority for the periods 2006–2010, 2011–2015, and 2016–2020. Table 6.12 highlights the change in ranking of key policy priorities to reflect the rapidly changing developments in contemporary domestic, regional, and global markets. Increasing emphasis is being given to policies on improving SME competitiveness.

6.3.4.1 Impact of SME development on the Lao economy

The discussion on the development of SMEs and their contribution to economic development in this section focuses on the establishment of SMEs, the generation of employment opportunities, and government policy on successful entrepreneurship. The discussion is largely based on recent empirical studies: a study on human capital and innovation in Laos' SMEs (see Phonvisay & Vixathep, 2018); and two studies on entrepreneurial human and social capital and government policy in SME development (see Matsunaga & Vixathep, 2019; Vixathep, 2017). The former study applies primary data from a questionnaire survey on SMEs in Vientiane Capital, conducted in March–May 2016. The two latter studies use firm data extracted from the 2008 and 2012 enterprise surveys conducted by the

Table 6.12 Overview of SME development policy priorities

Policy priorities	NSEDP (2006–2010)	NSEDP (2011–2015)	NSEDP (2016–2020)
1	Create an enabling regulatory and administrative environment	Improve the regulatory environment and public administration of economic activities	Promote productivity, technology, and innovation
2	Enhance competitiveness	Improve access to finance	Enhance access to finance for SMEs
3	Expand domestic and international markets	Form new enterprises	Enhance access to business development services
4	Improve access to finance	Increase the provision of support and business development services	Enhance SME access to and expansion of domestic and international markets
5	Encourage and create favorable conditions for the establishment of business organizations	Enhance business linkages between large enterprises and SMEs	Create and develop entrepreneurs
6	Enhance entrepreneurial attitudes and characteristics within the society	Promote productivity enhancement for upgrading the quality and standard of products and services of SMEs	Create an enabling environment for establishing and operating SME business
7	Enhance the promotion and development of SMEs at the central and local levels	Enhance access to markets and enlarge markets for SMEs	

Source: Department of SMEs, Ministry of Industry and Commerce, Government of Lao PDR.

GIZ[10] in the Lao-German Programme on Human Resource Development for a Market Economy (GIZ, 2014; GTZ, 2010).

According to data derived from the MPI, in the initial central planning period (1975–1985), the number of SMEs was very small and the expansion was very slow, increasing from 229 to 440 enterprises. However, after the launch of economic reforms in the late 1980s, SMEs in Laos experienced rapid growth, and the number of enterprises increased from 1,986 (1986–1990) to 10,631 (1996–2000) and 44,916 (2006–2010) (LSB, 2015, p. 12, Table 5). The share of SMEs in the total number of firms in Laos is approximately 99 percent.

If enterprises are categorized by number of employees, about 107,223 firms (86.1 percent) are classified as micro enterprises and 17,295 firms (13.9 percent) as SMEs[11] in 2013 (Table 6.13, Row 22–23). The micro enterprises create roughly 276,441 jobs (59 percent) and the larger category of SMEs generate

Table 6.13 Employment in SMEs in Laos (people)

No.	Economic activities	Micro enterprises	SMEs	Total
1	Agriculture, forestry, and fishery	4,820	8,059	12,879
2	Mining	212	2,979	3,191
3	Manufacturing	32,246	50,096	82,342
4	Electricity and gas	89	1,760	1,849
5	Waste management	277	1,337	1,614
6	Construction	590	9,075	9,665
7	Wholesale and retail	180,836	57,354	238,190
8	Transportation and storage facilities	8,000	4,883	12,883
9	Hotels, services, and restaurants	31,004	29,434	60,438
10	Information and communication	707	3,209	3,916
11	Finance and insurance	732	5,376	6,108
12	Property and real estate	1,384	1,311	2,695
13	Professional, science, and technology	811	1,707	2,518
14	Management	1,700	3,314	5,014
15	Security service	5	166	171
16	Education	293	6,848	7,141
17	Health and social security	913	919	1,832
18	Art, entertainment, and leisure	1,645	3,686	5,331
19	Other services	10,177	2,648	12,825
	Total size of the labor force (people)	276,441	194,161	470,602
	Percentage share	58.7	41	100
	Number of enterprises	107,223	17,295	124,518
	Percentage share (%)	86.1	13.9	100

Source: Data are provided by MPI upon the request of the authors. The information is extracted from the data of the 2013 Economic Census.

about 194,161 jobs (41 percent) of the total 470,602 jobs created by micro, small, and medium-sized enterprises. The wholesale and retail sector generates 238,190 jobs, the manufacturing industry 82,342 jobs, and the hotel and restaurant industry 60,438 jobs, respectively (Table 6.13). It is worth noting that among these three sectors/industries, SMEs have generated more employment opportunities in manufacturing, while micro enterprises dominate job creation in wholesale and retail and in hotels and restaurants. It can be observed that the SME sector has contributed more significantly to the generation of employment opportunities than the SEZs have, while the latter have contributed more significantly to international trade and tax revenue.

With regard to human capital and innovation, the findings in Phonvisay and Vixathep (2018) reveal that owners' education induces innovation activities, thereby implying the importance of entrepreneurial human capital on innovation in SME development.

The discussion on the impact of government policy is derived from the findings in Vixathep (2017) and Matsunaga and Vixathep (2019), in which the "impact of government policy" is considered as the perception of entrepreneurs toward

Table 6.14 Sign and significance of government assistance for SMEs (extracted from full regressions)

Dependent variable: Business turnover of SMEs in 2008 or 2012	Results from 2008 survey of GTZ		Results from 2012 survey of GIZ	
	Ordered Probit models without education and firm size interaction terms	*Ordered Probit models with education and firm size interaction terms*	*Ordered Probit models without education and firm size interaction terms*	*Ordered Probit models with education and firm size interaction terms*
Usefulness of assistance of central government (2008/2012)	-0.06 (0.16) (not significant)	–0.06 (0.16) (not significant)	0.07 (0.15) (not significant)	0.07 (0.15) (not significant)
Usefulness of assistance of local authorities (2008/2012)	0.07 (0.16) (not significant)	0.07 (0.16) (not significant)	0.01 (0.16) (not significant)	0.02 (0.16) (not significant)
Usefulness of assistance of central government (2006/2010)	0.04 (0.15) (not significant)	0.03 (0.15) (not significant)	0.05 (0.09) (not significant)	0.03 (0.04) (not significant)
Usefulness of assistance of local authorities (2006/2010)	–0.002 (0.16) (not significant)	0.004 (0.16) (not significant)	0.10 (0.08) (not significant)	0.01 (0.05) (not significant)

Notes: 1. The dependent variable is business turnover of SMEs in 2008 or 2012, classified into five categories. 2. The variable of impact of government policy is a dummy variable (0 = very unhelpful, unhelpful; 1 = neutral, helpful, very helpful). 3. The interaction terms in the table are dummy variables that are generated by multiplication of human capital and firm-size dummy variables. 4. The figures reported in the table are extracted from the ordered Probit estimations for 2006 and 2008, separately. 5. Owing to space limitations, the full tables for individual cases are not reported, but are available upon request to the authors. 6. Standard errors are in parentheses. No single coefficient is statistically significant.

Source: Adapted from Vixathep (2017, p. 46, Table 5) for 2008, unpublished result by authors for 2012.

the business facilitation for SMEs of the central government and local authorities in 2006 and 2008, and 2010 and 2012, respectively. The studies reveal that government assistance for SME development at both central and provincial levels did not achieve satisfactory results for businesses during 2008–2012. This result has been confirmed with the empirical analyses based on the survey data (see Table 6.14). The finding implies that the SME promotion policies have not achieved the government target of promoting SME development. This is a very important issue for the formulation and implementation of industrial policy. Nevertheless, it is important to note that the survey question about and the resulting inference on satisfaction with government facilitation are based on the subjective perceptions of entrepreneurs and that these perceptions improved during 2008–2012. Therefore, comprehensive research that applies more objective approaches is necessary to shed light upon the complex issue of SME promotion (Vixathep, 2017).

Further findings from the aforementioned empirical studies suggest that entrepreneurial human capital (e.g., formal and vocational education and work experience) and social capital (e.g., participation in business associations and public–private dialogue) tend to enhance successful entrepreneurship or innovation activities in SMEs. These findings pertain to the importance of human and social capital and entrepreneurship promotion in economic development (Bosma et al., 2004; Van Praag & Cramer, 2001; Vixathep & Matsunaga, 2015).

6.4 Conclusion

The Lao economy has experienced high growth over the past decade. However, in order to mitigate resource dependency of growth and achieve sustainable improvement in living standards, appropriate industrialization is indispensable for economic development. This chapter has discussed industrial policy in Laos by reviewing the chronological evolution of the NSEDP—Laos' *de facto* industrial policy—since its independence in 1975, and by examining the contribution of industrial policy to economic development in three areas: international trade, industrial estate, and enterprise development.

The evolution of industrial policy in Laos has undergone two phases: a centrally planned economy and a transition to a market-oriented economy. In the central planning period (1975–1985), development planning and policy formulation were largely concentrated on restoring the economy from war-related damage and dealing with the food shortage problem. During this decade, the Lao government introduced a one-year, a three-year, and the first five-year NSEPDs, and practically managed the entire economic system.

The second phase started in 1986 with an economic reform program, the NEM, passing through a preparation period (1986–2000) and continuing to a growth period (2000 onward). During the transition to a market economy, there have been seven five-year NSEDPs, including the current eighth NSEDP in its final year. The goals of the NSEDPs have included, but not been limited to, social order and political stability, reduction of mass poverty, development of the agricultural sector, rapid economic growth, integration into the regional and global economy, industrialization and modernization, inclusive and sustainable growth, development of land-link transportation networks, progression from LDC status by 2020, and long-term direction and priority sectors for economic development (Vision 2020 and Vision 2030).

The impact of industrial policy on economic development has been discussed in detail in three case studies of policy components in this chapter. The first policy component under study is trade policy. Trade reform in Laos was discussed in three phases, namely, a closed economy with central control (1975–1985), the transition to market economy (1986–2000), and the open economy with the open-door policy (2000 onward). The weight of Lao's international trade has changed from COMECON countries to ASEAN and East Asian trade partners. Integration into the regional economy (i.e., joining ASEAN) and the global economy (i.e., joining the WTO) has resulted in consolidation of tariff lines, the reduction of tariffs on manufactured and processed agricultural products, and the removal of quantitative restrictions and non-tariff barriers. Trade policy has been incorporated into the NSEDPs and regional cooperation framework, that is, the AEC 2015. International trade has grown remarkably, both in monetary terms and percentage share of GDP. However, the change in trade structure has been marginal and trade has been largely concentrated in unprocessed agricultural products, resource-based products, and products of labor-intensive industries. By all measures, there has been little diversification of trade, while specialization has tended to occur in simple product lines. The findings imply that the conditions, including the skill levels of the labor force, remain inadequate for more sophisticated products with higher added value, and that trade policy has so far not yet achieved the expected positive impact in the area of trade and the country's competitiveness.

The second policy component is industrial estate development. The first SEZ, the Savan-Seno SEZ, was established by a government decree (Decree No. 177/PM) in 2003. Since then, 11 more specific economic zones and SEZs have been established. Upon upgrading of the former zone type to the latter, there were 12 SEZs in Laos at the time of writing. The contribution of SEZs to the Lao economy has been evaluated from three respects, namely, the generation of job opportunities, the contribution to trade and foreign currency earnings, and the contribution to the government's tax revenue (direct impact). Over a long period of development, the SEZs have been found to have some direct impact on the national economy (e.g., the share of SEZ trade in "trade of goods and services" in 2016 was about 11 percent). Although the indirect and catalytic impacts have not been addressed in the study, the study has revealed some spillovers from SEZs to domestic firms outside the zones, which could enhance the indirect and catalytic effects if appropriately promoted.

The third policy component is enterprise development (SME development). The Enterprise Law promulgated in 1994 established private SMEs as legal entities. The first SME promotion policy was formulated in the fourth NSEDP (1996–2000). From the seventh NSEDP (2011–2015), the policy on promoting SMEs has been included in the enterprise development section and contains seven policy areas that serve as a reference for formulating a strategy and a work plan for the promotion and development of SMEs. The evaluation of the impact of SME promotion on economic development has addressed issues related to the establishment of SMEs, the generation of employment opportunities, and the government policy on successful entrepreneurship. In the central planning period, there were very few SMEs and their number grew very slowly. Following the reforms in the late 1980s, SMEs have experienced rapid growth in the number of enterprises and now comprise practically 99 percent of the total number of firms in the country. This sector has made a more significant impact on employment generation than the SEZ sector has. In terms of policy analysis, in spite of a sound SME promotion policy, actual implementation—at both central and provincial levels—has yet to make any significant impact on SME development. Furthermore, the results have revealed that entrepreneurial human and social capital is crucial to enhancing successful entrepreneurship and innovation activities in SMEs.

In summary, the three case studies have highlighted the importance of sound industrial policy with well-coordinated policy components (e.g., trade, SEZ development, enterprise development, and FDI). More work is necessary to improve capacity building for government officers, thereby enhancing effective policy implementation. The policy analysis has revealed that the quality and appropriateness of education and training are a crucial factor in diversifying trade and moving up the value-added ladder, enhancing the direct, indirect, and catalytic impacts of SEZ development, and promoting SME development and successful entrepreneurship. Government policies targeting education and training should aim for quality enhancement and the appropriateness of industrial policy formulation for market demand. The findings pertain to the importance of human resource development, entrepreneurship promotion, and effective coordination among stakeholders and policy components for economic development. Finally, notwithstanding this positive trend, a potential hindrance to the development of SEZs in near future could be the labor shortage that might be accelerated due to rapid economic development in neighboring countries and increasing labor mobility in the region.

Appendix

Table 6.A1 Overview of development plans of the Government of Lao PDR

No.	Time period	Development plan
	Central planning (centrally planned economic system)	
1	1976–1977	One-year National Socio-Economic Development Plan (NSEDP)
2	1978–1980	Three-year NSEDP
3	1981–1985	First five-year NSEDP (NSEDP1)
	Market-oriented economy (New Economic Mechanism, Chintanakan Mai)	
4	1986–1990	Second five-year NSEDP (NSEDP2)
5	1991–1995	Third five-year NSEDP (NSEDP3)
6	1996–2000	Fourth five-year NSEDP (NSEDP4)
7	2001–2005	Fifth five-year NSEDP (NSEDP5)
8	2006–2010	Sixth five-year NSEDP (NSEDP6)
9	2011–2015	Seventh five-year NSEDP (NSEDP7)
10	2016–2020	Eighth five-year NSEDP (NSEDP8) [current development plan]

Notes

1 The full name of the country is the Lao People's Democratic Republic (Lao PDR).
2 COMECON was established in January 1949 by representatives of six former socialist countries: Bulgaria, Czechoslovakia, Hungary, Poland, Romania, and the former Soviet Union.
3 In the study by Vixathep (2011), two trade performance indexes—Balassa's RCA index and the net export index (NEI)—are applied for the analysis. Following Balassa (1965), the RCA index is defined as the ratio between (a) the share of a country's commodity exports in the commodity exports of the world, and (b) the share of the country's total exports in the total exports of the world:

$$RCA_{i,t} = \frac{X_{i,j} / X_{w,j}}{X_{i,tot} / X_{w,tot}} = \frac{X_{i,j} / X_{w,tot}}{X_{i,j} / X_{w,tot}}$$

where $RCA_{i,t}$ denotes the RCA index of country i in commodity group j, $X_{i,j}$ is country i's exports of commodity group j, $X_{w,j}$ represents the world's exports of commodity group j, $X_{i,tot}$ stands for country j's total exports, and $X_{w,tot}$ denotes total exports of the world.

Following UNIDO (1982), the NEI index is defined as the ratio of a country's net exports (exports minus imports) to the country's total trade (exports plus imports):

$$NEI_{i,t} = \frac{X_{i,j} - M_{i,j}}{X_{i,j} + M_{i,j}}$$

4 Due to unavailability of trade figures for Laos for 1985–2005, the study uses trade data reported by major trade partners of Laos in the UN Comtrade database. The RCA and NEI indexes are calculated for all available commodities at the three-digit level of Standard International Trade Classification (SITC) of the United Nations.
5 High RCA products are those with an index of RCA of greater than unity (greater than 0 for the NEI index), referring to export commodities that have achieved comparative advantage in export markets.
6 "Total ranked products" means all available export commodities of Laos, for which data are available in the UN Comtrade database.
7 See Table 6.9 for detailed information on employment in SEZs.
8 For definitions of SMEs in Laos and selected Asian economies, see Vixathep (2017), Section 2.2 and p. 35, footnote 6.
9 Prior to 2006, the secretariat was located in the Ministry of Industry and Handicraft.
10 The name 'Deutsche Gesellschaft für Technische Zusammenarbeit (GTZ)' has been changed to 'Deutsche Gesellschaft für Internationale Zusammenarbeit (GIZ)'.
11 Typically, SMEs include micro, small, and medium-sized enterprises.

References

ADB (Asian Development Bank). (2017). *Key indicators for Asian and the Pacific 2017*. Available at: www.adb.org/publications/series/key-indicators-for-asia-and-the-pacific/ (accessed March 28, 2018).

Balassa, B. (1965). Trade liberalization and 'revealed' comparative advantage. *Manchester School of Economic and Social Studies*, 32, 99–125.

Berisha, G., & Pula, S. J. (2015). Defining small and medium enterprises: A critical review. *Academic Journal of Business, Administration, Law and Social Sciences*, 1(1), 17–28.

Bosma, N. S., Van Praag, C. M., Thurik, A. R., & De Wit, G. (2004). The value of human and social capital investments for the business performance of startups. *Small Business Economics*, 23(3), 227–236.

CPI (Committee for Planning and Investment). (1986). *The second national socio-economic development plan (1986–1990)*. Vientiane: Committee of Planning and Investment (CPI), Government of Lao PDR.

CPI (Committee for Planning and Investment). (1991). *The third five-year national socio-economic development plan (1991–1995)*. Vientiane: Committee of Planning and Investment (CPI), Government of Lao PDR.

CPI (Committee for Planning and Investment). (1996). *The fourth five-year national socio-economic development plan (1996–2000)*. Vientiane: Committee of Planning and Investment (CPI), Government of Lao PDR.

CPI (Committee for Planning and Investment). (2001). *The fifth five-year national socio-economic development plan (2001–2005)*. Vientiane: Committee of Planning and Investment (CPI), Government of Lao PDR.

CPI (Committee for Planning and Investment). (2002). *Strategy for industrialization and modernization (2001–2020)*. Vientiane: Committee of Planning and Investment (CPI), Government of Lao PDR.

CPI (Committee for Planning and Investment). (2006). *The sixth five-year national socio-economic development plan (2006–2010)*. Vientiane: Committee of Planning and Investment (CPI), Government of Lao PDR.

Cowie, P. (2012). SME policy evaluation: Current issues and future challenges. In R. A. Blackburn & M. T. Schaper (Eds.), *Government, SMEs and entrepreneurship development: Policy, practice and challenges* (pp. 243–256). Surrey: Gower Publishing Limited.

Di Maio, M. (2009). Industrial policies in developing countries: History and perspectives. In M. Cimoli, G. Doci, & J. E. Stiglitz (Eds.), *Industrial policy and development* (pp. 107–143). Oxford: Oxford University Press.

Douangboupha, L. (2010). Effects of trade policy reforms on economic growth: The case of the Lao P.D.R. *Lao Trade Research Digest*, 1(1), 59–96.

Fane, G. (2006). Trade liberalization and poverty reduction in Lao PDR. *Journal of the Asia Pacific Economy*, 11(2), 213–226.

Fukase, E., & Martin, W. (1999). *Economic effects of joining the ASEAN Free Trade Area (AFTA): The case of the Lao People's Democratic Republic*. Washington, DC: World Bank.

GIZ (Deutsche Gesellschaft für Internationale Zusammenarbeit). (2014). HRDME Enterprise Survey 2013 for Lao PDR. Vientiane.

GTZ (Deutsche Gesellschaft für Technische Zusammenarbeit). (2010). Enterprise survey 2009: Main report. Lao-German Programme on Human Resource Development for a Market Economy (HRDME). Vientiane.

GOL (Government of Lao PDR). (2003). Decree on the management regulations and incentive policies regarding the Savan-Seno Special Economic Zone. Vientiane: Lao People's Democratic Republic.

GOL (Government of Lao PDR). (2009). Law on Investment Promotion. Vientiane: Lao People's Democratic Republic.

LSB (Lao Statistics Bureau). (2015). Report of Economic Census II, 2013. Ministry of Planning and Investment. Vientiane: Lao Uniprint Ltd. [Report in Lao language].

LPTPCC (Lao Propaganda and Training of the Party Central Committee). (2016). Forty years of implementing Lao National Social-Economic Development Plan of Lao PDR. *Communist Review*, September 12. Available at: http://laos.tapchicongsan.org.vn/ Home/Doi-ngoai-va-hoi-nhap/2016/374/Story.aspx (accessed January 29, 2018).

Martin, W. (2001). Trade policy reform in the East Asian transition economies. World Bank, Policy Research Working Paper, No. 2535. Available at: http://documents. worldbank.org/curated/en/865921468760507338/pdf/multi-page.pdf (accessed March 28, 2018).

Matsunaga, N., & Vixathep, S. (2019). Laos' economic development and small and medium enterprise policy. *Journal of Economics and Business Administration*, 220(4), 1–20 [in Japanese].

MPI (Ministry of Planning and Investment). (2011). The seventh five-year national socio-economic development plan (2011–2015). Vientiane: Ministry of Planning and Investment (MPI).

MPI (Ministry of Planning and Investment). (2016). The eighth five-year national socio-economic development plan (2016–2020). Vientiane: Ministry of Planning and Investment (MPI).

Nishimura, H., Kimura, F., Ambashi, M., & Keola, S. (2016). *Lao PDR at the cross-roads: Industrial development strategies 2016–2030*. Jakarta: Economic Research Institute for ASEAN and East Asia.

Ohno, K. (2013). *Learning to industrialize: From given growth to policy-added value creation*. London: Routledge.

Onphanhdala, P., & Suruga, T. (2010). FDI and investment climate in Lao P.D.R. *Lao Trade Research Digest*, 1(1), 31–58.

Oraboune, S. (2011). Lao PDR's industrial development policy and intermediate good trade. In M. Kagami (Ed.), *Intermediate goods trade in East Asia: Economic deepening through FTAs/EPAs*, BRC Research Report No. 5 (266–296). Bangkok: IDE-JETRO.

Otani, I., & Pham, C. D. (1996). The Lao PDR: Systemic transformation and adjustment. IMF Occasional Paper No. 137.

Phonvisay, A., Thipphavong, V., & Manolom, T. (2017). Cross-border impact of Thailand's SEZs on Laos' SEZs and collaboration in the midst of regional integration. *Lao Trade Research Digest*, 6, 42–66.

Phonvisay, A., & Vixathep, S. (2018). Determinants of innovation in Laos: A survey of micro and small businesses in Vientiane. *Journal of Economics and Business Administration*, 218(5), 77–92.

SEZ Secretariat Office. (2012). Development strategy for the special economic zone (2011–2020). Vientiane: Special Economic Zone (SEZ) Committee, Government Office.SEZ Secretariat Office. (2016). *Annual report*. Vientiane: Special Economic Zone (SEZ) Committee, Government Office.

Stiglitz, J. E., & Greenwald, B. C. (2014). The role of industrial and trade policy in creating a learning society. In J. E. Stiglitz & B. C. Greenwald (Eds.), *Creating a learning society* (pp. 369–400). New York: Columbia University Press.

UNCTAD. (2016). *Structural transformation and industrial policy*. New York: United Nations Conference on Trade and Development (UNCTAD).

UNIDO. (1982). *Changing patterns of trade in world industry: An empirical study on revealed comparative advantage*. Vienna: United Nations Industrial Development Organization (UNIDO).

Van Praag, C. M., & Cramer, J. S. (2001). The roots of entrepreneurship and labor demand: Individual ability and low risk aversion. *Economica*, 68(269), 45–62.

Vixathep, S. (2011). Trade liberalization and comparative advantage dynamics in Lao PDR. *Lao Trade Research Digest*, 2(1), pp. 1–33.

Vixathep, S. (2017). Entrepreneurship, human and social capital, and government policy in small and medium enterprise development in Laos. *Japan Social Innovation Journal*, 7(1), 33–50.

Vixathep, S., & Matsunaga, N. (2015). Entrepreneurial human and social capital in small businesses in Vietnam: An extended analysis. Working Paper No. 29, Kobe University, April, 2015. Available at: www.research.kobe-u.ac.jp/gsics-publication/gwps/2014-29.pdf (accessed January 30, 2018).

Wade, R. (2015). The role of industrial policy in developing countries. In A. Calcagno, S. Dullien, A. Márquez-Velázquez, N. Maystre, & J. Priewe (Eds.), *Rethinking development strategies after the financial crisis* (vol. 1). Berlin: United Nations Conference on Trade and Development and Fachhochschule für Technik und Wirtschaft.

Warwick, K. (2013). Beyond industrial policy: Emerging issues and new trends. OECD Science, Technology and Industry Policy Papers, No. 2, http://dx.doi.org/10.1787/5k4869clw0xp-en.

World Bank. (2006). *Building export competitiveness in Laos: Summary report.* Washington, DC: World Bank.

World Bank (2017). World Development Indicators 2017. Available at: http://data.worldbank.org/ (accessed March 28, 2018).

7 Promoting local SMEs through GVCs

A framework and case study of Laotian SMEs

Chanhphasouk Vidavong and
Shigeru Thomas Otsubo

7.1 Introduction

According to UNCTAD's *World Investment Report 2013*, global value chains (GVCs) coordinated by multinational corporations (MNCs) account for roughly 80 percent of global trade, and this value-added in trade contributes about 30 percent on average to the GDP in developing countries (UNCTAD, 2013). While an extension of the GVC network would be conducive to job creation and income growth in developing countries, participation in GVCs should also bring about an upgrading of supply capacity on the part of local firms. For the local small and medium-sized enterprises (SMEs) that have only limited exposure to global business practices, GVC participation could provide access to new technologies, innovations, and markets. This, in turn, should lead to improvements in productivity and competitiveness. In reality, however, benefits to local firms are not automatically created, and proper facilitation by the state and conscious efforts by local firms to upgrade their capacities are called for. This chapter introduces the roles of GVCs in developing countries, and explores challenges and opportunities for local firms focusing on SMEs. This chapter then presents the main findings from a field survey-based case study of SMEs in Laos, in order to understand in a realistic manner, the challenges that local SMEs in developing countries face.

There are currently several obstacles to Lao business development. For instance, only 12.1 percent of Lao businesses have access to formal finance, and only approximately 10 percent of firms use computers for IT work. This situation is further exacerbated by a lack of local institutional support. Consequently, fewer than 2 percent of businesses in Laos can integrate into the global markets as exporters; and of these, 0.51 percent of firms perform as direct exporting firms and 1.44 percent of firms act as suppliers to both domestic and international markets (calculation based on LSB, 2015). Thus, SMEs participating or being selected to be part of GVCs should operate with specific policy support for each particular economy. Therefore, this chapter aims to shed light on four key questions to be addressed. First, can GVCs promote local SME performance in Laos? This question seeks to examine the role of GVCs in local SMEs. Second, what are the current concerns and benefits of GVC participation for Lao SMEs? The current concerns of local firms are defined along with raising awareness regarding the benefits of SMEs from GVC participation. Third, how can SMEs participate in GVCs? The characteristics of SMEs that probably engage in GVCs are identified in order to recommend necessary preparations for local SMEs to satisfy these prerequisites. Finally, does the quality of local institutions matter for GVC participation by local SMEs? Findings from these questions and related analyses should lead us to discover important policy implications.

7.2 SMEs' development in Laos and constraints

> The small and medium-sized enterprises (SMEs) are independent enterprises that are legally registered and operated according to the prevailing laws of the Lao People's Democratic Republic, and classified into the size categories according to the business sector, the annual average number of employees, the total assets and the annual turnover.
>
> (National Assembly, 2011)

Table 7.1 presents the definition of SMEs in Laos.

SME promotion and development have been a significant issue in Laos in many aspects. For instance, Decree 42/PM to the Law on Promotion SMEs, No. 11/NA, dated December 21, 2011, became the effective law of the Lao PDR. Second, a service network to provide consulting on business development has been established by the Lao National Chamber of Commerce and Industry (LNCCI) to enhance SMEs' startups, productivity, market information, and innovation. Third, low-interest-rate loans for SMEs have been launched, supported by multiple donors, to enable SMEs to grow. Fourth, the registration system of enterprises and regulations has been improved in order to facilitate business activities. As a consequence, the permanent business license replaced older renewable ones. Fifth, a dialogue between government and business sectors at every level under the Lao Business Forum has been arranged. This creates an excellent opportunity for discussions among relevant stakeholders on Lao business development. Furthermore, the promotion of SME participation in the

Table 7.1 Definition of small and medium-sized enterprises (SMEs) in Laos

Category	Average annual no. of employees	Total assets in kip	Annual turnover in kip
Small	< 20	≤ 250 million	≤ 400 million
Medium	< 100	≤ 1.2 billion	≤ 1 billion

Source: Prime Minister's Office, 2004, Decree 42/PM, dated April 20, 2004.

global value chains both at home and in the global markets was identified as one of the key SME promotion policies in several public documents, in particular, the Small and Medium Enterprise Development Plan 2016–2020 (Prime Minister's Office, 2017). Finally, Lao PDR has established more than ten Special Economic Zones (SEZs). These have been conscious attempts on the part of the Lao government to encourage local SMEs' linkages to export activities and activities in the SEZs.

SMEs account for a large part of total employment in Laos. According to the economic census held in 2006 and 2013 in Lao PDR, SMEs contributed approximately 80 percent of job creation during this period. However, SME productivity has been relatively low compared to productivity of larger firms. Based on the economic census in 2013, approximately 65 percent of the total number of firms are informal businesses (LSB, 2015). Consequently, SMEs encounter several constraints, namely, costly registration, high tax rates, and difficult access to financial institutions for business growth in Laos (WB, 2019). Even though some SMEs can access the low-interest rate loan programs for start-up and business expansion, this is not diversified and is still limited to areas in Vientiane, the nation's capital. How to receive loans is still not understood by many SMEs due to their insufficient knowledge and the lack of information disseminated from stakeholders. These limitations impede SMEs' financial access and undermine start-up businesses, growth, and competition against other firms in surrounding countries and the global economy.

Furthermore, several concerns indicate that Lao businesses, especially SMEs, cannot compete in the global markets. For instance, according to the World Bank (2019b), in the human capital index (HCI), Laos had a score of 0.452 in 2017 that was low even compared to other ASEAN latecomers, such as Vietnam (0.67), Cambodia (0.49), and Myanmar (0.47). This reflects the low labor productivity of firms. Additionally, firms offering formal training are somewhat uncommon in Laos as the percentage of firms offering formal training programs for their permanent employees were only 6.5 percent of total firms in 2016, relatively low compared to Vietnam (22.2 percent in 2015) and Cambodia (22.2 percent in 2016). Only 3.4 percent (2016) of firms in Laos spend money on research and development (R&D), while firms in Vietnam and Cambodia are actively investing in R&D with a higher share at 15.7 percent (2015) and 12.3 percent (2016), respectively.

The economic census also presents crucial facts such as Lao businesses have concerns about low managerial capacity and that the country has a high proportion of informal businesses. Approximately 81.9 percent of firms are operating business activities without any accounting system applied to record their sales and expenditures. Regarding paying taxes, 64.1 percent of firms pay lump-sum payments. 6.9 percent of firms do not pay taxes. According to the World Bank's *Doing Business Report* in 2019, firms seem to suffer from high costs, complicated procedures, and uneven government performance, especially in the phase of business start-ups (World Bank, 2019a).

7.3 Theories and frameworks for analyses

7.3.1 The Smile Curve approach

Seminal scholars developed the conceptual U-shaped or Smile Curve (e.g., Gereffi, 1994, 1999; Gereffi & Fernandez-Stark, 2016; Shen, Liu, & Deng, 2016; Ye, Meng, & Wei, 2015;) as shown in Figure 7.1. It describes the stages of production from pre-production or intangible activities at the upstream level (e.g., R&D, design) to assembling production or the tangible activities at the midstream level (e.g., input, intermediate goods, and manufacturing), and to post-production or intangible activities (downstream, namely, distribution, marketing, and services). Firms in developing countries often participate in a supply chain with little value-added creation or thin profit due to the lack of capacity for capital-intensive insertion. Meanwhile, firms in advanced countries concentrate on pre- and post-production activities such as R&D, design, branding, distribution, marketing, and after-sales services.

Ye et al. (2015) examined an inter-country input-output model in order to classify the existing connections among producers and consumers in GVCs. This facilitates a more precise understanding of the Smile Curve by mapping country and industry positions with degrees of GVC participation. It uses data from 1995 to 2011 of world input-output tables in order to trace exports of electrical and optical equipment from China and Mexico, and exports of automobiles from

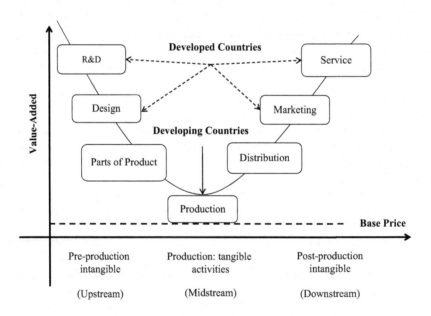

Figure 7.1 The Smile Curve

Source: Modified from Gereffi & Stark (2016, p. 14) and Shen et al. (2016, p. 7).

Japan and Germany. Although only three observable final products are selected, there are various industries (and countries) involved. The findings confirm that GVCs' activities do not always perform as U-shaped. Furthermore, a country with a high speed of technology upgrading can gain more in terms of value-added.

Shen et al. (2016) also attempted to prove that developing countries have the chance to gain a higher profit relative to developed countries at the production stages. Their study commenced with a firm profit maximization approach of three phases of the supply chains to establish the theoretical background from a mathematical modeling approach. The results conclude remarkably that countries in the midstream are not always the losers. The productivity gap and the entire cost gap effects can accurately explain who might lose or win. It means that labor productivity must be high enough to compensate for the whole costs. Finally, production and service with low costs and high productivity inevitably rely on technological capacity and economic incentives supported by proper institutions.

7.3.2 GVC participation and functional upgrading

Policymakers and entrepreneurs need to understand upgrading contexts for GVCs in order to formulate a pragmatic policy and to improve firms' competitiveness (Gereffi et al., 2005; Gereffi & Sturgeon, 2013; Humphrey & Schmitz, 2001, 2002; Kaplinsky & Morris, 2001). Gereffi (1999) and Kaplinsky and Morris (2001) pointed out how to upgrade by commencing with the process, product, functional, chain, and channel upgrading, respectively. In developing countries, in particular, SMEs should concentrate on appropriate strategic pathways to upgrade capabilities, e.g., types of innovation (Branzei & Vertinsky, 2006). Focusing on GVC upgrading refers to the explicit transformation from original equipment assembling (OEA) production with a few value-added proportions under contract with a global buyer to become an original equipment manufacturer (OEM) by using a buyer's symbol (as shown in Figure 7.2). Then, firms

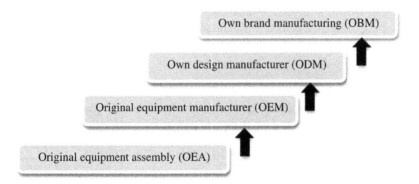

Figure 7.2 Stages in GVCs' functional upgrading
Source: Based on Gereffi (1999); and Kaplinsky and Morris (2001).

attempt further to become an own design manufacturer (ODM) by developing and designing the line of products directly to customers. Finally, firms constitute their brand of so-called own brand manufacturing (OBM) and become the lead firm (Gereffi, 1999). Previous episodes of successful GVC participation initiated upgrading from low value-adding activities to own brand, for instance, such as those observed in Taiwan, South Korea, and later in China. They engaged in global production networks from original equipment assembly with low value-added at first, moving up to the status of lead firms while some of their products have already moved to their own brand. The well-known cases of the achievements in GVC upgrading can be found with the development of Huawei, Acer, Hyundai, and Samsung.

If the curvature of the Smile Curve deepens, it creates larger differences in gains among participants in different stages of the production process. On the other hand, if the curve becomes flatter, this signifies a more equal distribution of gains among participants at different stages of the production stream. If firms in developing countries start at the lower value-added midstream of this production process, industrial upgrading can take place conceptually either horizontally or vertically, as Figure 7.3 shows. In Figure 7.3, a vertical/upward shift of the Smile Curve from SC1 to SC2 represents the case where all firms in different production streams simultaneously upgrade product and process by the same degree of productivity and efficiency gains. It means that firms at all stages of the production stream can be better off, including firms in developing countries operating mainly in the midstream. The second case of production upgrading can take place, as indicated by the horizontal expansion of the Smile Curve from SC1 to SC3. This flattening of the Smile Curve can emerge if the firms at the midstream-stage materialize production upgrading at a faster pace as compared to that among firms in the other streams. With this development, firms in the midstream can contribute higher value-added with heightened productivity. In this way, the firms in developing countries located predominantly in the midstream of the production process can obtain higher value-added and profits even if they are constrained to the midstream stage of production. Furthermore, this upgrading of the firms' capacity should also give rise to the possibilities of firms in developing countries gradually extending the scope of their activities into upstream and downstream, that is, a functional upgrading.

7.3.3 Roles of GVCs in promoting SMEs and impediments

Various opportunities for SMEs can be gained by economic integration. For instance, participation in global value chains (GVCs) can accelerate the growth of SMEs (Kim & Hemmert, 2016; Lefebvre, Lefebvre, & Bourgault, 1998; Lu & Beamish, 2001; Musteen, Francis, & Datta, 2010; Nazar & Saleem, 2009) and small firms (Brouthers & Nakos, 2005). SMEs can gain from GVC participation by learning-by-doing, innovation capacity improvement, technology transfer, and human capital upgrading (Harvie & Charoenrat, 2015; Vidavong, 2019).

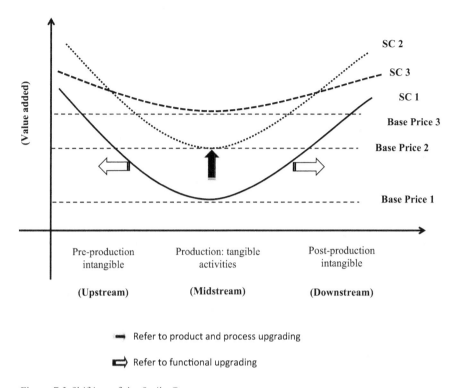

Figure 7.3 Shifting of the Smile Curve
Note: SC = Smile Curve.
Source: Based on Ohno (2013); and Ye et al. (2015).

Moreover, firms participating in GVCs with links to upstream and downstream partners show a significant growth potential (UNCTAD, 2010).

SMEs can commence GVC participation with a simple form such as acting as a supplier of intermediate inputs under subcontract with buyers instead of direct exports with more complicated processes (Lim & Kimura, 2010). Yuhua and Bayhaqi (2013) summarize that GVC participation enables SMEs to improve technical capacity, production and operational efficiencies, and demand for their existing products and services. It also provides reachable cooperation with upstream and downstream firms. Firms participating in GVCs, in either a direct or indirect form, enjoy mostly positive impacts on their business. For instance, Prete, Giovannetti, and Marvasi (2017) confirm that GVC participation has a positive impact on productivity gains for North African firms. Van Biesebroeck (2005) shows that exporting activities raise the productivity of manufacturing SMEs in Sub-Saharan Africa. Abe (2015) finds the same for Asian SMEs. The WTO (2016) indicates that GVC players perform better than non-GVC players.

Furthermore, participating SMEs tend to enjoy more stable growth than non-participants via better business diffusion and upgrading prospects (Navas-Aleman, 2011). Van Biesebroeck (2005), Giroud, Simona, and Giroud (2011), Jaklic, Dikova, Burger, and Kuncic (2016), and Prete et al. (2017) confirm that GVC participation has a positive impact on business performance.

However, SMEs are disadvantaged in GVCs compared to large firms (Abonyi, 2005; Vaaland & Heide, 2007; Yener, Dogruoglu, & Ergum, 2014). Thus, participation in GVCs remains a challenge for SMEs, especially in developing countries. Government assistance (e.g., market access, technology, marketing, and financial support) profoundly influences the ability of SME to access the global market (Cardoza, Fornes, Farber, Duarte, & Gutierrez, 2016). Better institutions with regard to trade policies, reforms in trade facilitation, and reduction in non-tariff barriers enable local firms to integrate into the global market (Deng & Zhang, 2018; Descotes et al., 2011; Hoekman & Nicita, 2011; Iwanow & Kirkpatrick, 2007; Kiss & Danis, 2008; Portugal-Perez & Wilson, 2011). In contrast, adverse regulations and inconsistent legal frameworks harm SMEs in their international business activities.

In terms of technology transfer through foreign direct investment (FDIs), at least one study finds that it was not promoted well even in the case of Chinese industries (Hu, Jefferson, & Jinchang, 2005). China's automotive industry, in its initial integration into the global production network, seems to have been confined to low value-added activities (Li, Kong, & Zhang, 2015). Abonyi (2005) shows that SMEs in low-income countries are dominated by lower-tier suppliers in GVCs. These studies imply that SMEs should improve their international competitiveness through R&D, quality control, and skill development. However, SMEs in developing countries cannot meet these challenges all by themselves due to their limited capabilities. This can lead to economic and social instability, increased unemployment, and widening income inequality. The needs of facilitation by the public sector, firm's own efforts, and proper public-private partnerships in dealing with obstacles that local SMEs face in their process of internationalization and technology upgrading are well documented and recognized.

7.3.4 Impact of GVC participation on local wages

Regarding the average wages of local firms participating in GVCs, some seminal studies find positive impacts, while some others find negative impacts. For instance, based on the survey of export processing zones (EPZs) in Madagascar, Cling, Razafindrakoto, and Roubaud (2009) show that wages in EPZs are lower than in other areas. Romero (1995) and Kusago and Tzannatos (1998) elucidate insignificantly different wages between two groups by comparing the firms in an Asian export processing zone with the firms outside. However, Robertson, Sitalaksmi, Ismalina, and Fitrady (2009) present two case studies and empirical analyses based on the National Labor Force Survey (1988–2004) in Indonesia, showing that FDI firms provide better working conditions compared to local firms. Neak and Robertson (2009) use a socio-economic survey in Cambodia and indicate that working conditions and wages seem to be better in the garment sector (export-oriented) than in agriculture. Robertson and Trigueros-Arguello (2009) with the use of a household survey of El Salvador for 1995–2005, and Marcouiller and Robertson (2009) with the use of a Honduran enterprise survey in 2001–2004, present similar findings. Kabeer and Mahmud (2004) find that garment workers in Bangladeshi export processing zones (EPZs) have 70 percent higher average income than workers in non-EPZ sections. Kabeer and Tran (2003) and Nadvi and Thoburn (2004) report that Vietnamese garment sector workers employed in joint-venture firms can earn higher average wages relative to those in local small private garment businesses.

7.3.5 *Factors in GVCs' extension and SMEs' participation*

Two main fundamental theories of GVC growth are reviewed: internal factors (resource endowment and firm efficiency) and external factors (market access and institution). First, commercial firms seek to enter economies that abound in low-cost primary inputs, intermediate inputs, productive labor, advanced technology, and strong demand. For instance, in the case of China, its market size is significantly attractive to multinational corporations (Onkvisit & Shaw, 2009). The neo-Hecksher-Ohlin approach explains that firm-specific advantages in technologies and skills enable firms to integrate into the global market (Lall, 1986; Wakelin, 1998; Wilmore, 1992; Ye et al., 2015). At the firm level in developing economies, the main factors permitting the firms to have access to export markets are innovations and learning processes to acquire technological capabilities (Bell & Pavitt, 1993; Iammarino, Padilla-Perez, & Tunzelmann, 2008; Lall, 1992). Furthermore, participation in global markets requires reductions in production costs and the formation of efficient supply chains. A well-organized supply chain for sourcing inputs, often with just-in-time delivery of products, helps firms to reduce procurement costs. Low transaction costs and economies of scale are conducive to agglomeration and cooperation among corporations. Furthermore, new trade theories assert that the firms that produce efficiency can export and invest overseas (Helpman et al., 2004; Melitz, 2003).

Second, easier market access and better institutions can trigger GVCs' access to those economies. A conducive business environment, trade facilitation with lower tariff and non-tariff barriers, sufficient market information, multi-modal transportation, and good logistics systems with well-developed infrastructure can attract new investments by GVCs. MNCs have expanded enormously in the form of supply chains and increased regional flows of FDIs in Asia, starting in the 1980s due to trade liberalization, an export-oriented strategy, and information and communication technology (ICT) development (ESCAP, 2009). Some developing countries, especially the least developed countries, have gained access to global markets by using the generalized scheme of preferences (GSPs) to export their products.

Additionally, local institutions play a crucial role in enhancing SMEs' integration in the global market. A lack of government assistance (market access, technology, marketing, and financial support), adverse regulations, and inconsistent legal frameworks profoundly impede the ability of SMEs to access the global market (Cardoza et al., 2016). For local firms to improve technology in specific production processes, institutional support from the public sector is imperative. Conducive trade policies, trade facilitation reforms, and reductions in non-tariff barriers significantly enhance local firms' access to the global market (Deng & Zhang, 2018; Descotes et al., 2011; Hoekman & Nicita, 2011; Iwanow & Kirkpatrick, 2007; Kiss & Danis, 2008; Portugal-Perez & Wilson, 2011).

In summary, extensions of GVCs into local economies and local SMEs' participation in GVCs can be promoted both through internal factors (firm characteristics, managerial capacity, financial liquidity, innovation, and technical capabilities) and external factors (local institutions, business environment, trade facilitation). In Section 7.4, we present a case study of SMEs in Laos in order to evaluate the significance of these aforementioned factors in explaining their participation in GVCs and their exporting activities. Unlike the former studies that focused only on manufacturing sectors, this case study includes firms in service sectors in addition to those in manufacturing. Furthermore, there are few empirical studies that investigate the relationship between local institutional performance and SMEs' participation in GVCs. The empirical analyses try to estimate the significance of the factors presented in determining both the direct and indirect (through GVCs) exporting activities of SMEs in Laos, based on the data collected through the author's field surveys.

7.4 Model and data

7.4.1 Impacts of GVC participation on SMEs' performance

In examining the roles of GVCs on business performance, Lu, Wang, and Zhu (2018) emphasize many dimensions, for instance, output, productivity, wages, employment, and capital investment. Prete et al. (2017) examine the impact of GVCs on labor productivity in both total output and net-output, and total factor productivity. Based on the literature review, this chapter focuses on business performance, namely, total sales, productivity, current assets, employment, innovations, human capital development, and wages. Therefore, this study can be considered a modified version of Prete et al. (2017) and Lu et al. (2018). The variables used for the impact assessments in this study are as follows:

- *Labor productivity (lnPR):* Labor productivity is the total sales divided by total employment and used in a logarithm. This is an approximation of labor productivity given the lack of precise procurement data and total hours worked.
- *Capital per worker (lnCW):* Current assets (machinery, factory, vehicles, warehouses) divided by total employees are used as proxies for capital-labor

ratios, and used in a logarithm (US$). The study uses reported (in accounting books) values without any further adjustments.

- *Internal firm capacity (IFC)*: This index represents a firm's human capacity is composed of the following seven variables: (1) skill intensity (proportion of employees with vocational school and above educational attainments); (2) CEO's education levels; (3) managers' education levels, taking values from 1 to 4 (1 = vocational or lower, 2 = bachelor, 3 = master; and 4 = PhD); (4) CEOs' age; (5) managers' ages (years); (6) CEOs' experience' and (7) managers' experience of working with MNCs (years).
- *Innovation capacity (INC)*: This is an index that combines the following three indicators: (1) ratios of R&D expenditures to total sales; (2) ratios of IT expenditures to total sales, both taking values from 0–4 (0 = 0%, 1 = <0.5%, 2 = 0.5–0.99%, 3 = 1–2%, and 4 = >2%); and (3) technology upgrading—purchasing new machines or improving existing ones in recent years—taking values from 0–4 (0 refers to not improved or upgraded at all, and 4 refers to very much improved or upgraded). Standardized scores are computed for each of these three indicators and aggregated to a composite index.
- *GVC participation (DGVC)*: A dummy variable that takes the value of 1 for the firms engaging in GVCs, 0 otherwise. It is hypothesized that the firms participating in GVCs tend to have better performance than non-participating firms.
- *Firm age (LnFA)*: This denotes the number of years in business, used in a logarithm. It is expected that the experience of doing business enhances a firm's capacity through learning-by-doing effects.
- *Joint venture (DJV)*: A dummy variable that takes the value of 1 for the firms that share ownership with foreign firms/investors, 0 otherwise. It is expected that the joint venture promotes local firms' performance through transfers of production and managerial technologies.
- *Finance access (DAF)*: A dummy variable that takes the value of 1 for the firm that has access to finances from financial institutions, 0 otherwise.
- *Service (DSS) and Agriculture (DSA)*: Sector dummies for service or agricultural sectors. Sector dummies are used in order to take care of the unexplained gaps among sectors.
- *Location (DLC and lnDIS)*: DLC is a location dummy that takes the value of 1 for the firms located in the Vientiane capital area, 0 otherwise. *lnDIS* refers to the distance from a firm's place to the nearest special economic zones (SEZs), and used in a logarithm. It is used as an instrument in the instrumental variable estimations (2SLS).

7.4.2 Determinants of SMEs' participation in GVCs

A logit model is estimated in order to analyze factors affecting the probability of local SMEs participating in GVCs in Lao PDR. Various explanatory variables that represent firm characteristics are largely drawn from the studies by Harvie, Narjoko and Oum (2010), Srinivasan and Archana (2011), Arudchelvan and

Wignaraja (2015), and Wignaraja (2013). The logit model used in this study can be described as Equation (7.1):

$$GVC_i = \ln\left(\frac{P_i}{1-p_i}\right) = \gamma 0 + \lambda' X_i + \eta_i \tag{7.1}$$

where GVC_i takes the value of 1 for the firms participating in GVCs, 0 otherwise.

GVC_i = 1, Probability = P_i

GVC_i = 0, Probability = $1 - P_i$

$0 \leq P_i \leq 1$

X_i is a set of explanatory variables that include firms' characteristics (internal factors) and external factors such as local institutional performance. λ'refers to the vector of coefficients. η_i is an error term that captures the effects of unknown factors, measurement errors, and other unobservable disturbances.

Using the estimated coefficients and each firm's characters (internal and external factors), firm i's probability to participate in GVCs can be estimated as Equation (7.2):

$$P_i = \frac{1}{\left(1 + e^{-GVC_i}\right)} = \frac{1}{\left[1 + e^{-\left(\gamma_0 + \lambda' X_i + \vartheta_i\right)}\right]} \tag{7.2}$$

The marginal effects of explanatory variables on the probability of participation can also be estimated.

Seminal literature tries to find the determinants of firms' exporting activities with cross-country, firm-level studies (Hoekman & Nicita, 2011; Iwanow & Kirkpatrick, 2007; Oura, Zilber, & Lopes, 2016; Portugal-Perez & Wilson, 2011; Sterlacchini, 2001). Furthermore, the relationship between firm sizes and exporting activities is examined at the firm level by Kumar and Siddharthan (1994), Zhao and Li (1997), Wignaraja (2002), and Srinivasan and Archana (2011). Some studies focus on SMEs' exports (Kim & Hemmert, 2016; Lefebvre et al., 1998; Lu & Beamish, 2001; Musteen, Francis, & Datta, 2010; Nazar & Saleem, 2009). Some focus on small firms' exports (Brouthers & Nakos, 2005). Van Dijk (2002), Harvie et al. (2010), Srinivasan and Archana (2011), Wignaraja (2013), and Arudchelvan and Wignaraja (2015) conducted econometric analyses to identify determinants of SMEs' participation in the global production networks. Furthermore, Kiss and Danis (2008) and Deng and Zhang (2018) analyze the relationship between institutions and internationalization. Descotes et al. (2011) and Deng and Zhang (2018) focus on institutions and SMEs' exports.

Drawing on these earlier studies, the following variables are used in this analysis:

- *Firms' size*: This consists of total employees (LnL) and registered capital (LnRC) in US dollars. They are used in logarithm form. A larger firm has economies of scale that lead to lower production costs with higher total sales. Most seminal studies show that large firms are more competitive than others in global markets. It is hypothesized that a larger firm has a better chance of participating in GVCs.
- *Innovation capacity (INC)*: This is defined in the same way as INC in Section 7.4.1. A firm with a higher innovation capacity is expected to have a higher probability of participating in GVCs as it naturally enjoys higher productivity and competitiveness in the global markets.
- *Internal firm capacity (IFC)*: This is defined in the same way as IFC in Section 7.4.1. Firms with better strategies and higher capacity are more likely to capture opportunities in the new global markets. Therefore, higher IFC with higher human capital is hypothesized to increase the probabilities of SMEs' participation in GVCs.
- *CEO's field of study (DFE)*: A dummy variable for the CEO's field of study. It takes the value of 1 if it is relevant to business administration, 0 otherwise. It is assumed that CEOs who graduated with degrees in business administration or other relevant fields conducive to entrepreneurship are more likely to approach global production networks.
- *Quality of local institutions (QLI)*: This reflects the number and degree of impediments that firms face with respect to the quality of local institutions, as reported by the respondents. It takes the values from 0–3, 0 is the best, while 3 is the worst. In the field survey, firms are requested to select the difficulties that they face from the following institutional categories: lack of government assistance, high tariffs, low efficiency of government, complicated import-export procedures, and unclear tax collection. Ineffective government assistance, adverse regulations, and inconsistent legal frameworks impede the probability of SMEs' direct access to global markets or participation in GVCs.
- *Firm age (LnFA)*: This is defined in the same way as LnFA in Section 7.4.1. It is expected that the experience of doing business enhances a firm's capacity through learning-by-doing effects. Thus, firms with more years of business operations may have higher probabilities of GVC participation.
- *Joint venture (DJV)*: Defined in the same way as DJV in Section 7.4.1. A dummy variable takes the value of 1 for the firms that share ownership with foreign firms/investors, 0 otherwise. This provides alternatives for a local firm to enter foreign markets through intelligent market information, closer relationship with parent firms, and know-how to trade with technical efficiency.
- *Location (DLC)*: Defined in the same way as DLC in Section 7.4.1. DLC is a location dummy that takes the value of 1 for the firms located in the Vientiane capital area, 0 otherwise. Firms located in the capital area may have a greater chance of participating in international business activities due to better infrastructure, market information, and business support.

- *Manufacturing (DSM) and agriculture (DSA)*: Sector dummies for service or agricultural sectors. Unlike the sector dummies presented in Section 7.4.1, the service sector is chosen to be the base sector. Sector dummies are used in order to take care of the unexplained gaps among sectors in accessing global markets.

- *Average English proficiency (AEP)*: This takes values from 1–5, with 5 representing the highest proficiency in English. A firm with higher English proficiency can better communicate and negotiate with (potential) foreign business partners, and therefore has a higher probability of entering foreign markets.

- *Business exchanges with suppliers (DRS)*: A dummy variable takes the value of 1 if a firm has active business exchanges with suppliers, 0 otherwise. Firms that have active business exchanges such as through R&D activities, training, and market information sharing with business partners may have higher chances of exporting, directly or through GVCs.

7.4.3 Data

This study uses data collected by the author's field survey that includes 135 firms. The target groups of firms are classified into two types by screening secondary firm data provided by the Ministry of Industry and Commerce (MOIC) of the Laotian government, and by inquiring with firms with cross-border business activities about their local business partners. Type (1) firms are the firms participating in GVCs, and they are further divided into indirect and direct participants. The indirect participants are the firms that have a connection with large firms (FDI, MNC, joint venture firms located in Laos) that operate international businesses, GVCs in a narrow sense. After requesting and receiving those large firms' lists of local business partners, we identified local SMEs that operate as parts/components suppliers and/or as service providers to them for our field survey. In this study, local exporting firms that are screened from the lists given by MoIC are also included in the group of GVC participants.

Type (2) firms are the non-exporting (non-GVC participating) firms that serve the domestic market. Among non-exporting firms, the firms selected in Type (2) are the ones that share similar characteristics to Type (1) firms in terms of firm size and other business characteristics. Therefore, Type (2) firms are the controlled samples for comparative analyses. There are two steps in proceeding in Type (2).

First, the study identified formal firms (registered businesses) in the form of SMEs that do not engage in international business activities in specific target areas (prominent cities of three provinces and the capital, Vientiane). In the second step, the research attempted to classify those identified firms into sector groups that roughly match those in the Type (1) group. A random sampling method was applied to select samples among Type (2) candidates. In the field, however, some firms were additionally selected for Type (2) based on self-selection and snowballing methods as they seem to be as good compared to the relevant Type (1) firms.

A single survey format was developed that contained an explanation regarding GVC participation. The initial survey was conducted in mid-2015 by the author and colleagues (supported by MOIC). However, approximately 30 percent of the desired data was missing. The second follow-up survey was conducted in 2017 in order to obtain the missing data. The research attempted to be consistent with data collected at two different time points, by asking only for missing data related to the year 2015, and by making proper adjustments for changes in the macro-economic environment between these two-time points. Most of the missing data in the first survey was related to the financial statements of the firms. Firms were selected nation-wide, namely, from the capital city of Vientiane (27.41 percent), Luang Prabang (37.04 percent), Savannakhet (23.70 percent), and Champasack (11.85 percent) provinces. Some 82.4 percent of the respondents to the questionnaire were directors, managers, and owners. For some firms in big cities, interviews and questionnaire surveys were conducted on separate days. In local provinces, most firms could be interviewed on the visiting day with assistance from the staff of the provincial offices of the Department of Industry and Commerce.

7.5 Results and discussion

7.5.1 Benefits of SMEs' participation in GVCs

According to the data collected during the field survey conducted in 2015, about 63 percent of SMEs participating in GVCs actively invest in technology upgrading, 46 percent of the firms surveyed receive technical assistance from outside in terms of R&D, marketing, training, and information exchange, and 72 percent of the total sample are SME participating in GVCs. This indicates that SMEs in global production networks have better chances of receiving support from local institutions and international businesses. Moreover, they can join in R&D activities with lead firms and have access to the available technologies. Consequently, firms participating in GVCs have a better chance of absorbing technology transfers from their business partners, as shown in Table 7.2, for instance, by training employees, designing a new product, conducting R&D, using patents and licenses, and accessing new market information. Indeed, it can be suggested that lead firms may invest in R&D and share some of their fruits with their business partners (SMEs). On the other hand, it is notable that firms participating in GVCs outperform non-participating firms in many aspects such as in terms of average growth in total sales, profits, and assets as shown in Figure 7.4.

7.5.2 Constraints that SMEs face

Table 7.3 shows the top 10 constraints that firms face, as reported by the sample firms surveyed. Results are presented for all firms, firms participating in GVCs, and firms not participating in GVCs. For the entire group of firms, unclear custom collection, lack of labor, high electricity costs, high tariffs, lack of policy support

Table 7.2 Firms exchanging business activities with their main customers and suppliers

No	Exchanges of business activities	Main customer (C)		Main supplier (S)	
		Total (%)	Firms in GVC (%)	Total (%)	Firms in GVC (%)
1	Receiving training from the main C/S	23.7	71.88	17.04	73.91
2	Providing any training to the main corporate C/S	17.04	60.87	14.81	55
3	Designing a new product with the main corporate C/S	22.96	58.06	27.41	59.46
4	Patents and licensing of C/S	27.41	64.86	26.67	66.67
5	The main corporate C/S conduct R&D together	35.56	66.67	29.63	67.5
6	The main corporate C/S assist your firm for new market analysis	34.07	65.22	26.67	61.11
Average		26.79	64.59	23.71	63.94

Source: Author's calculation based on own survey conducted in 2015.

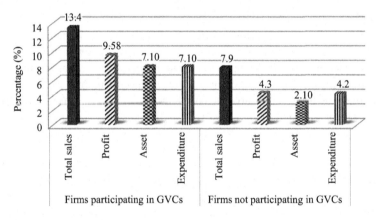

Figure 7.4 Business performance in terms of average growth, 2011–2014
Source: Author's drawing based on survey conducted in 2015.

from government, lack of capital, low-skilled labor, financial access difficulty, lack of experts, and high transport and communication costs were pointed out, with this order representing the frequency of impediments that these firms face.

Table 7.3 also shows that frequencies of various constraints cited are different between the group of firms participating in GVCs and the group of non-participating firms. The firms participating in GVCs cited, more frequently, lack of labor, unclear custom collection, high tariffs, high electricity costs, and lack of experts. The firms not participating in GVCs raised issues related to unclear

Table 7.3 Top 10 constraints that firms face

No	All firms	Participating firms in GVCs	Non-participating firms in GVCs
1	Unclear custom collection	Lack of labor	Unclear custom collection
2	Shortage of labor	Unclear custom collection	High electricity costs
3	High electricity costs	High tariffs	Lack of policy support from government
4	High tariffs	High electricity costs	Shortage of labor
5	Lack of policy support from government	Lack of experts	Lack of capital
6	Lack of capital	High transport and communication costs	Financial access difficulty
7	Low-skilled labor	Low-skilled labor	Low-skilled labor
8	Financial access difficulty	Lack of policy support from government	High tariffs
9	Lack of experts	Lack of capital	High transport and communication costs
10	High transport and communication costs	Financial access difficulty	Poor cooperation among line-government agencies

Source: Author's tabulation based on a survey conducted in 2015.

custom collection, high electricity costs, lack of policy support from government, and shortage of labor. This group of firms also cited poor coordination among government's line ministries. It is furthermore observed that only 20 percent of all firms in this group have access to financial institutions. Consequently, the difficulty they face in accessing financial institutions is ranked higher among firms not participating in GVCs.

7.5.3 Regression results

7.5.3.1 Impact of GVC participation on SMEs' performance

Table 7.4 shows the impacts of GVC participation on SMEs' performance in terms of labor productivity, total sales, current assets, employment, innovation capacity, internal firm capacity, and average wages. Regression results are reported in three panels in Table 7.4: Panel A, without controlling for covariates; Panel B, with controlling for a small set of covariates (sector, location); and Panel C, with controlling for a broader set of covariates (sector, location, experience, ownership). These regression analyses of the impacts, as represented by the set of dependent variables shown in the first row in Table 7.4, of GVC participation are conducted by taking into account the endogeneity issue between a dependent variable and GVC participation dummy (DGVC). An instrumental variable (distance from firm's place to the closest special economic zone, in logarithm) is used in the 2SLS regressions.

Table 7.4 Impact of GVCs' participation on SMEs' performance

Dependent variables	Labor productivity	Total sale	Current asset	Employees	Innovation capacity	Firm capacity	Average wages
	lnPR	lnTS	lnCA	lnL	INC	IFC	LnW
Panel A: Without controlling for covariates							
GVC participation	0.553	3.297**	2.603*	3.026**	5.139*	13.00**	0.685
	-1.041	-1.557	-1.469	-1.307	-2.639	-5.872	-0.619
Panel B: With controlling for small set of covariates (sector, location)							
GVC participation	-1.138	2.492**	3.701**	3.714***	1.517	1.514	0.162
	-0.949	-1.164	-1.55	-1.332	-1.563	-2.653	-0.483
Dummy, agriculture	0.775**	0.67	0.381	0.014	0.636	2.434**	0.236
	-0.348	-0.427	-0.569	-0.489	-0.574	-0.974	-0.177
Dummy, service	0.576**	-0.115	-0.148	-0.615*	0.326	2.455***	0.188
	-0.253	-0.31	-0.413	-0.355	-0.417	-0.708	-0.129
Dummy, location	0.575**	0.224	-0.354	-0.284	1.131***	3.758***	0.179
	-0.248	-0.304	-0.405	-0.348	-0.408	-0.693	-0.126
Panel C: With controlling for larger set of covariates (sector, location, experience, ownership)							
GVC participation	-0.831	2.279**	3 557***	3.176***	1.49	3.15	0.248
	-0.736	-0.902	-1.23	-0.944	-1.269	-2.125	-0.398
Dummy, agriculture	0.763**	0.817**	0.543	0.19	0.532	1.841**	0.254
	-0.316	-0.387	-0.528	-0.405	-0.544	-0.912	-0.171
Dummy, service	0.621***	0.013	-0.036	-0.518*	0.328	2.399***	0.218*
	-0.235	-0.288	-0.393	-0.301	-0.405	-0.678	-0.127
Dummy, location	0.489**	0.156	-0.364	-0.272	0.975**	3.149***	0.151
	-0.235	-0.288	-0.393	-0.302	-0.405	-0.679	-0.127

Firm age	0.215	0.177	0.079	-0.018	0.252	1.169***	0.079
	-0.141	-0.173	-0.235	-0.181	-0.243	-0.407	-0.076
Dummy, joint venture	-0.079	-0.718*	-0.674	-0.715*	0.154	1.437	-0.114
	-0.333	-0.408	-0.556	-0.427	-0.574	-0.961	-0.18
Dummy, finance access	-0.092	0.063	-0.181	0.158	0.626	1.013	-0.063
	-0.259	-0.317	-0.432	-0.332	-0.446	-0.746	-0.14
Observations	135	135	135	135	135	135	135
Anderson	11.07	11.07	11.07	11.07	11.07	11.07	11.07
Stock-Yogo	11.34	11.34	11.34	11.34	11.34	11.34	11.34
Sargan statistic	0	0	0	0	0	0	0

Note: *** $p<0.01$, ** $p<0.05$, * $p<0.1$; the standard errors are reported in parentheses; an endogenous (DGVC) and instrument variable (distance from firm's place to the nearest SEZs) are applied (2SLS).

Source: Author's calculation based on data collected during field survey in 2015.

The results presented in Panel A show the differences observed in this set of dependent variables between the two groups of firms, i.e., participating and non-participating firms in GVCs. Firms participating in GVCs, as compared to the non-participating firms, have significantly higher values in total sales, current assets, number of employees, innovations, and human resources. However, differences in labor productivity or wages are not observed. Those results, however, should be carefully interpreted as the study cannot identify the direction of causality. It may be the case that GVCs tend to choose local firms with certain sizes of operation and with certain levels of innovation and internal human capital capacities for their local partners, rather than those values actually representing local firms' performance. The fact that no significant differences are observed between the two groups in labor productivity or average wages seems to point to a lack of the virtuous circle of GVCs, higher labor productivity, and higher wages in the current state of integration in Laos.

Panel B shows the results obtained with controls for sectors (agriculture, service, and manufacturing) and for firm's location (either in the Vientiane capital area or not). After controlling for these small covariates, the significance of GVC participation dummy disappears for the dependent variables of innovation capacity and internal human capital capacity. These results indicate that while GVC participation is associated with higher values of total sales, current assets, and employment, the differences in firms' internal human capital capacity is more likely to be explained by sector and locational gaps. Innovation capacity seems to depend on location, being in the capital area or not.

In Panel C, regression coefficients with controls for a larger set of covariates such as firm age, joint venture, and access to finances are estimated. The results are consistent with those reported in Panel B. Firm experience is significantly associated with a firm's higher internal human capital capacity, either a firm participates in GVCs or not.

For average wages that many are concerned with, this study only picks up a positive sector wage gap for service. In summary, the study does not find the formation of a virtuous circle of local firms' participation in GVCs except for the fact that participation in a GVC and firm's operational sizes are positively correlated, even after controlling for other factors. These results suggest the importance of proper facilitation for positive qualitative impacts of GVC participation of local firms, in addition to the possible size effects that may lead to economies of scale or cluster formation.

7.5.3.2 Determinants of SMEs' participation in GVCs

Table 7.5 reports the results from the logit-model regression analyses for the determinants of SMEs' participation in GVCs. In line with the findings from the previous section, a firm's size, both in terms of a total number of employees and registered capital, is significant as a positive determinant of SMEs' participation in GVCs (Column 1). Results reported in Column (2) show that internal firm capacity, along with a firm's size, can explain the probability of a firm's participation in GVCs. Partial results reported in Column (3) show that, among the

Table 7.5 Determinants of SMEs' participation in GVCs

Variables	Column (1)	Column (2)	Column (3)	Column (4)	Column (5)	Column (6)
Total employees	0.166***	0.149***	–	0.161***	0.171***	0.169***
	–0.046	–0.047	–	–0.047	–0.047	–0.057
Registered capital	0.052*	0.055*	–	0.047*	0.038	0.045
	–0.028	–0.029	–	–0.028	–0.029	–0.037
Internal firm	–	0.023**	–	–	–	–
capacity	–	–0.012	–	–	–	–
Innovation	–	–	–	–	–	–0.026
capacity	–	–	–	–	–	–0.031
CEO's education	–	–	0.113*	0.081	0.001	0.046
	–	–	–0.063	–0.063	–0.041	–0.074
CEO's field of	–	–	–	–	0.160*	0.182*
study	–	–	–	–	–0.093	–0.107
Skill intensity	–	–	0.056	0.045	0.063	0.05
	–	–	–0.052	–0.055	–0.054	–0.066
CEO's experience	–	–	–	–	0.057	0.135
in MNCs	–	–	–	–	–0.042	–0.164
Quality of local	–	–	–	–	–	–0.158***
institutions	–	–	–	–	–	–0.049
Firm's age	–	–	–	–	–	0.058
	–	–	–	–	–	–0.064
Dummy, joint	–	–	–	–	–	0.348***
venture	–	–	–	–	–	–0.08
Dummy, location	–	–	–	–	–	0.151
	–	–	–	–	–	–0.11
Dummy,	–	–	–	–	–	–0.12
manufacturing	–	–	–	–	–	–0.134
Dummy,	–	–	–	–	–	–0.278*
agriculture	–	–	–	–	–	–0.167
English	–	–	–	–	–	–0.095
proficiency	–	–	–	–	–	–0.067
Dummy,	–	–	–	–	–	0.235**
relationship	–	–	–	–	–	–0.105
with suppliers						
Observations	135	135	135	135	135	135
Pseudo R2	0.125	0.146	0.036	0.143	0.162	0.275
Log-likelihood	–79.54	–77.572	–87.778	–77.889	–76.158	–65.87
LR chi2	22.63	26.57	6.656	25.94	29.4	49.97
Prob(F-statistic)	0	0	0.037	0	0	0

Notes: *** $p<0.01$, ** $p<0.05$, * $p<0.1$; the standard errors are reported in parentheses. The service sector is used as the base for the sector dummies. The figures represent the marginal effect obtained by estimating a logit model.

Source: Author's calculation based on data collected during field survey in 2015.

components of the internal firm capacity (IFC) index, CEOs' education level is significant, but workers' skill/education levels are not significant. This may reflect the current situation in Laos, where GVCs tend to choose firms/factories with a relatively large pool of unskilled workers for their local partners.

When the estimation combines firm size and education in the same model (Column 4), the weak significance of education levels disappears as the size effects dominate. However, CEO's educational field of study (either related to business administration or not) survives as a determinant of a firm's participation in GVCs (Column 5).

Column (6) reports the results from the estimation with controls for other firm characteristics such as sectors, ownership, firm age, access to finances, location, English proficiency, business exchanges, and quality of local institutions. In addition to the robust firm-size variable (total employment), significance is found for joint venture, the quality of local institutions, firms' exchanges with suppliers, and CEOs' fields of education. The importance of improving the quality of local institutions, including regulations, policy support, and infrastructure, is also supported by the findings of the obstacles faced by the local firms reported in Table 7.3. The significance of ownership (joint venture) dummy suggests that, at the initial stages of engagement, a local firm can form a joint venture with local subsidiaries of foreign firms to enter the international markets. Firms that have active business exchanges with business partners, in particular with suppliers, are more likely to participate in GVCs. This set of findings should serve as a good guide in designing proper facilitation policies for local SMEs' participation in GVCs and foreign markets.

7.6 Conclusion

In terms of business performance, total sales, current assets, employment, innovation, and internal firm capacity (human capital), have a positive effect from GVC participation. However, the labor-productivity and wages results suggest that SMEs participating in GVCs are no different from non-participating firms by 2SLS regression. This reflects the reality of those SMEs with relatively large employment size that engage in low-productive and labor-intensive work while providing low incentives. The outcome of the econometric exercise is substantially consistent with the descriptive analysis that the quality of local institutions matters for local SME participation in GVCs. Furthermore, the results suggest that firm size, foreign ownership (joint venture), the CEO's education background, service sector, and good relationship with suppliers positively affect the probability of SMEs tapping into GVCs.

For faster Lao SME development, the government should intervene in local SMEs in the initial stage of GVC participation. To ensure long-term effects, innovation and human resource development must be upgraded along with appropriate incentives, in particular, wages. Raising awareness of SMEs on innovation improvement and cluster constitution, policy reforms, factor markets, and targeted SMEs policies are crucial factors to further SME development. Customs schemes with practical action, trade policy, export promotion initiatives, and special effective financial schemes are likewise crucial factors for SME participation in GVCs. Furthermore, problem supply-side factors such as difficulty accessing finance, high electricity costs, inadequate transportation and communication, shortage of labor, and workers' inadequate education must be overcome. Additionally, behind-the-border issues, namely, unclear corporate tax collection, lack of government support, inefficient cooperation among line-government-agency, and complicated import-export procurements all play their part. Reducing these bottlenecks at the firm and country level would assist in encouraging the full potential of SME participation in GVCs in the future.

Therefore, Laotian employees should have a better chance to upgrade their knowledge and skills in order to cope with new technology. Innovation transmission policies are still in their early stages; they should be more diversified and selective. External agencies should be able to evaluate trade facilitation activities implemented regularly and independently. Lastly, cluster constitution should be fostered along with frequent monitoring by stakeholders.

Acknowledgments

This chapter draws on C. Vidavong (2019), "Can global value chains (GVCs) promote local small and medium-sized enterprises (SMEs) and pro-poor development in Laos?," PhD dissertation, submitted to Nagoya University, with revisions and additions.

References

Abe, M. (2015). SMEs' participation in global value chains: Changes and opportunities. In ADBI & ADB (Eds.), *Integrating SMEs into global value chain: Challenges and policy actions in Asia* (pp. 27–65). Mandaluyong, the Philippines: Asian Development Bank.

Abonyi, G. (2005). Transformation of global production, trade, and investment: Global value chains and international production networks. Paper presented to Expert Group Meeting on SMEs' Participation in Global and Regional Supply Chains, UNESCAP, Bangkok, November.

Arudchelvan, M., & Wignaraja, G. (2015). SME internationalization through global value chains and free trade agreements: Malaysian evidence. ADBI Working Paper Series, No. 515.

Bell, M., & Pavitt, K. (1993). Technological accumulation and industrial growth: Contrast between developed and developing countries. *Industrial and Corporate Change*, 2(2), 157–210.

Branzei, O., & Vertinsky, I. (2006). Strategic pathways to product innovation capabilities in SMEs. *Journal of Business Venturing*, 21(1), 75–105.

Brouthers, L. E., & Nakos, G. (2005). The role of systematic international market selection on small firm's export performance. *Journal of Small Business Management*, 43(4), 363–381.

Cardoza, G., Fornes, G. G., Farber, V., Duarte, R. G., & Gutierrez, J. R. (2016). Barriers and public policies affecting the international expansion of Latin American SMEs: Evidence from Brazil, Colombia, and Peru. *Journal of Business Research*, 69(6), 2030–2039.

Cling, J. P., Razafindrakoto, M., & Roubaud, F. (2009). Export processing zones in Madagascar: The impact of the dismantling of clothing quotas on employment and labor standards. In R. Robertson, D. Brown, G. Pierre, & M. L. Sanchez-Puerta

(Eds.), *Globalization, wages, and the quality of jobs* (pp. 237–64). Washington, DC: World Bank.

Deng, P., & Zhang, S. (2018). Institutional quality and internationalization of emerging market firms: Focusing on Chinese SMEs. *Journal of Business Research, 92*, 279–289.

Descotes, R. M., Walliser, B., Holzmuller, H., & Guo, X. (2011). Capturing institutional home country conditions for exporting SMEs. *Journal of Business Research, 64*(12), 1303–1310.

ESCAP. (2009). *Globalization of production and the competitiveness of small and medium-sized enterprises in Asia and the Pacific: Trends and prospects.* Studies in Trade and Investment, No. 65. Bangkok: United Nations.

Gereffi, G. (1994). The organization of buyer-driven global commodity chains: How US retailers shape overseas production networks. In G. Gereffi & M. Korzeniewicz (Eds.), *Commodity chains and global capitalism.* London: Praeger.

Gereffi, G. (1999). International trade and industrial upgrading in the apparel commodity chain. *Journal of International Economics, 48*(1), 37–70.

Gereffi, G., & Fernandez-Stark, K. (2016). *Global value chain analysis: A primer* (2nd ed.). Durham, NC: Duke University, Center on Globalization, Governance & Competitiveness (CGGC).

Gereffi, G., Humphrey, J., & Sturgeon, T. (2005). The governance of global value chains. *Review of International Political Economy, 12*(1), 78–104.

Gereffi, G., & Kaplinsky, R. (2001). Introduction: Globalization, value chains and development. *IDS Bulletin, 32*(3), 1–8.

Gereffi, G., & Sturgeon, T. (2013). Global value chain-oriented industrial policy: The role of emerging economies. In D. K. Elms, & P. Low (Eds.), *Global value chains in a changing world* (pp. 328–360). Geneva: World Trade Organization.

Giroud, A., Simona, G. L., & Giroud, A. (2011). Knowledge transfer from TNCs and upgrading for domestic firms: The Polish automotive sector. *World Development, 40*(4), 796–807.

Harvie, C., & Charoenrat, T. (2015). SMEs and the rise of global value chain. In ADBI & ADB (Eds.), *Integrating SMEs into global value chain: Challenges and policy actions in Asia,* (pp.1–26). Mandaluyong, the Philippines: Asian Development Bank.

Harvie, C., Narjoko, D., & Oum, S. (2010). Firm characteristic determinants of SME participation in production networks. Discussion Paper Series 2010–11. Jakarta Economic Research Institute for ASEAN and East Asia (ERIA).

Helpman, E., Melitz, M. J., & Yeaple, S. R. (2004). Export versus FDI with heterogeneous firms. *American Economic Review, 94*(1), 300–316.

Hoekman, B., & Nicita, A. (2011). Trade policy, trade costs, and developing country trade. *World Development, 39*(12), 2069–2079.

Hu, A. G. Z., Jefferson, G. H., & Jinchang, Q. (2005). R&D and technology transfer: Firm-level evidence from China industry. *The Review of Economics and Statistics, 87*(4), 780–786.

Humphrey, J., & Schmitz, H. (2001). Governance in global value chains. *Institute of Development Studies Bulletin, 32*(3). Available at: www.ids.ac.uk/files/humphrey_schmitz_32_3.pdf

Humphrey, J., & Schmitz, H. (2002). How does insertion in global value chains affect upgrading in industrial clusters? *Regional Studies, 36*(9), 1017–1027.

Iammarino, S., Padilla-Perez, R., & Tunzelmann, N. V. (2008). Technological capabilities and global-local interactions: The electronics industry in two Mexican regions. *World Development, 36*(10), 1980–2003.

Iwanow, T., & Kirkpatrick, C. (2007). Trade facilitation, regulatory quality and export performance. *Journal of International Development, 19*(6), 735–753.

Jaklic, A., Dikova, D., Burger, A., & Kuncic, A. (2016). What is beneficial for first-time SME-exports from a transition economy: A diversified or a focused export-strategy? *Journal of World Business, 51*(2), 185–199.

Kabeer, N., & Mahmud, S. (2004). Globalization, gender and poverty: Bangladeshi women workers in export and local markets. *Journal of International Development, 16*(1), 93–109.

Kabeer, N., & Tran, T. V. A. (2003). Global production, local markets: Gender, poverty and export manufacture in Vietnam. Mimeo. Brighton: Institute of Development Studies.

Kaplinsky, R., & Morris, M (2001). *A handbook for value chain research.* Institute of Development Studies, University of Sussex. Available at: www.ids.ac.uk and www.prism.uct.ac.za/papers/VchNov01.pdf.

Kim, J. J., & Hemmert, M. (2016). What drives the export performance of small and medium-sized enterprises subcontracting firms?. A study of Korean manufacturers. *International Business Review, 25*(2), 511–521.

Kiss, A. N., & Danis, W. M. (2008). Country institutional context, social networks, and new venture internationalization speed. *European Management Journal, 26*(6), 388–399.

Kumar, N., & Siddharthan, N. S. (1994). Technology, firm size and export behavior in developing countries: The case of Indian enterprises. *The Journal of Development Studies, 31*(2), 289–309.

Kusago, T., & Tzannatos, Z. (1998). Export processing zones: A review in need of update. World Bank Group, Social Protection Discussion Paper Series, No. SP 9802.

Lall, S. (1986). Technological development and export performance in LDCs: Leading engineering and chemical firms in India. *Review of World Economics (Weltwirtschaftliches Archiv), 122*(1), 80–92.

Lall, S. (1992). Technological capabilities and industrialization. *World Development, 20*(2), 165–186.

Lefebvre, E., Lefebvre, L. A., & Bourgault, M. (1998). R&D-related capabilities as determinants of export performance. *Small Business Economics, 10*(4), 365–377.

Li, Y., Kong, X. X., & Zhang, M. (2015). Industrial upgrading in global production networks: The case of the Chinese automotive industry. ERIA-DP-2015-07, Economic Research Institute for ASEAN and East Asia. Available at: www.eria.org/ERIA-DP-2015-07.pdf.

Lim, H., & Kimura, F. (2010). The internationalization of small and medium enterprises in regional and global value chains. ADBI Working Paper Series No. 231.

LSB (Lao Statistic Bureau). (2015). *Economic census II, 2013: Report.* Vientiane Capital: Lao Statistic Bureau, Ministry of Planning and Investment.

Lu, J. W., & Beamish, P. W. (2001). The internationalization and performance of SMEs. *Strategic Management Journal, 22*(6–7), 565–586.

Lu, Y., Wang, J., & Zhu, L. (2018). Place-based policies, creation and agglomeration economies: Evidence from China's economic zone program. *American Economic Journal: Economic Policy, 11*(3), 325–360.

Marcouiller, D., & Robertson, R. (2009). *Globalization and working conditions: Evidence from Honduras.* In R. Robertson, D. Brown, G. Pierre, & M. Sanchez-Puerta (Eds.), *Globalization, wages, and the quality of jobs* (pp. 175–201). Washington, DC: The World Bank.

Melitz, M. J. (2003). The impact of trade on intra-industry reallocations and aggregate industry productivity. *Econometrica*, *71*(6), 1695–1725.

Musteen, M., Francis, J., & Datta, D. K. (2010). The influence of international networks on internationalization speed and performance: A study of Czech SMEs. *Journal of World Business*, *45*(3), 197–205.

Nadvi, K. & Thoburn, J. (2004). Vietnam in the global garment and textile value chain: Impacts on firms and workers. *Journal of International Development*, *16*(1), 111–123.

National Assembly (NA). (2011). Law on the promotion small and medium-sized enterprises. Vientiane Capital, Lao PDR: NO: 011/N.A, dated December 21, 2011.

Navas-Aleman, L. (2011). The impact of operating in multiple value chains for upgrading: The case of the Brazilian furniture and footwear industries. *World Development*, *39*(8), 1386–1397.

Nazar, M. S., & Saleem, H. M. N. (2009). Firm-level determinants of export performance. *International Business & Economics Research Journal*, *8*(2), 105–112.

Neak, S., & Robertson, R. (2009). Globalization and working conditions: Evidence from Cambodia. In R. Robertson, D. Brown, G. Pierre, & M. Sanchez-Puerta (Eds.), *Globalization, wages, and the quality of jobs* (pp. 97–129). Washington, DC: The World Bank.

Ohno, K. (2013). *Learning to industrialize: From given growth to policy-aided value creation*. London: Routledge-GRIPS Development Forum Studies.

Onkvisit, A., & Shaw, J. J. (2009). Nature of international marketing. In A. Onkvisit & J. J. Shaw (Eds.), *International marketing: Strategy and theory* (pp. 3–28). London: Routledge.

Oura, M. M., Zilber, S. N., & Lopes, E. L. (2016). Innovation capacity, international experience and export performance of SMEs in Brazil. *International Business Review*, *25*(4), 921–932.

Portugal-Perez, A., & Wilson, J. S. (2011). Export performance and trade facilitation reform: Hard and soft infrastructure. *World Development*, *40*(7), 1295–1307.

Prete, D. D., Giovannetti, G., & Marvasi, E. (2017). Global value chains participation and productivity gains for North African firms. *Review of World Economics*, *153*(4), 675–701.

Prime Minister's Office. (2004). Decree on small and medium-sized enterprise. Vientiane Capital: Prime Minister's Office, No. 42/PM, dated April 20, 2004.

Prime Minister's Office. (2017). Decree on Small and Medium Enterprise Development Plan 2016–2020. Vientiane, Lao PDR: Prime Minister's Office, No.253/PM, dated August 18, 2017.

Robertson, R., Sitalaksmi, S., Ismalina, P., & Fitrady, A. (2009). Globalization and working conditions: Evidence from Indonesia. In R. Robertson, D. Brown, G. Pierre, & M. Sanchez-Puerta (Eds.), *Globalization, wages, and the quality of jobs* (pp. 203–236). Washington, DC: The World Bank.

Robertson, R., & Trigueros-Arguello, A. (2009). The effects of globalization on working conditions: El Salvador, 1995–2005. In R. Robertson, D. Brown, G. Pierre, & M. Sanchez-Puerta (Eds.), *Globalization, wages, and the quality of jobs* (pp. 131–173). Washington, DC: The World Bank.

Romero, A. T. (1995). Labor standards and export processing zones: Situation and pressures for change. *Development Policy Review*, *13*(3), 247–276.

Shen, J. H., Liu, X., & Deng, M. (2016). An elementary theoretical approach to the "smiling curve" with implications for "outsourcing industrialization." Available at: https://ssrn.com/abstract=2878762 or http://dx.doi.org/10.2139/ssrn.2864895.

Srinivasan, T. N., & Archana, V. (2011). Determinants of export decision of firms. *Economic and Political Weekly, 46*(7), 49–58.

Sterlacchini, A. (2001). The determinants of export performance: A firm-level study of Italian manufacturing. *Review of World Economics, 137*(3), 450–472.

UNCTAD. (2010). *Integrating developing countries' SMEs into global value chains.* New York: United Nations.

UNCTAD. (2013). *World investment report 2013: Global value chain world: Investment and trade for development.* New York: United Nations.

Vaaland, T. I., & Heide, M. (2007). Can the SME survive the supply chain challenges? *Supply Chain Management: An International Journal, 12*(1), 20–31.

Van Biesebroeck, J. (2005). Exporting raises productivity in Sub-Saharan Africa manufacturing firms. *Journal of International Economics, 67*(2), 373–391.

Van Dijk, M. (2002). The determinants of export performance in developing countries: The case of Indonesian manufacturing. ECIS (Eindhoven Centre for Innovation Studies) Working Paper Series, 200201.

Vidavong, C. (2019). Roles of global value chains (GVCs) in promoting small and medium-sized enterprises (SMEs) in Laos. *Forum of International Development Studies, 50*(2), 1–20.

Wakelin, K. (1998). Innovation and export behavior at the firm level. *Research Policy, 26*(7–8), 829–841.

Wignaraja, G. (2002). Firm size, technological capabilities and market-oriented policies in Mauritius. *Oxford Development Studies, 30*(1), 87–104.

Wignaraja, G. (2013). Can SMEs participate in global production network? Evidence from ASEAN firms. In K. E. Elms, & P. Low (Eds.), *Global value chains in a changing world* (pp. 279–313). Geneva: World Trade Organization.

Wilmore, L. (1992). Transnationals and foreign trade: Evidence from Brazil. *Journal of Development Studies, 28*(2), 314–335.

World Bank. (2019a). *Doing business report 2019.* Washington, DC: World Bank. Available at: www.doingbusiness.org/.

World Bank. (2019b). *World development indicators.* Available at: https://databank. worldbank.org/data/ reports.aspx?source=world-development-indicators.

WTO. (2016). *World trade report 2016: Leveling the trading yield to SMEs.* Available at: www.wto.org/english/res_e/booksp_e/world_trade_ report16_e.pdf.

Ye, M., Meng, B., & Wei, S. J. 2015. Measuring smile curves in global value chains. IDE Discussion Paper No. 530. Chiba City, Japan: IDE–JETRO. Available at: www.ide. go.jp/English/Publish/Download/Dp/530.html

Yener, M., Dogruoglu, B., & Ergum, S. (2014). Challenges of internationalization for SMEs and overcoming these challenges: A case study from Turkey. *Procedia-Social and Behavioral Sciences, 150*, 2–11.

Yuhua, Z., & Bayhaqi A. (2013). SMEs' Participation in global production chains APEC Policy Support Unit, Issues Paper No .3.

Zhao, H., & Li, H. (1997). R&D and exports: An empirical analysis of Chinese manufacturing firms. *The Journal of High Technology Management Research, 8*(1), 89–105.

8 The role of Thailand's industrial promotion policies in ASEAN

Chalaiporn Amonvatana

8.1 Introduction

Economic cooperation and integration have always been an issue for countries in Southeast Asia. The Association of South East Asian Nations (ASEAN) was first established with the objectives to promote and cooperate on the issues of peace, security, economy, knowledge, society, and cultures on the ground of equality and mutual benefits among ASEAN member countries. Under the Bangkok Declaration signed on August 8, 1967, Indonesia, Malaysia, the Philippines, Singapore, and Thailand were the first five countries to join ASEAN. Later, another five countries, namely, Brunei Darussalam, Cambodia, Lao PDR, Myanmar, and Vietnam, joined ASEAN. Since 2010, ASEAN has consisted of 10 member countries.

In 2002, the Singaporean Prime Minister proposed the idea of an ASEAN Economic Community (AEC) at the ASEAN Summit held in Cambodia. The leaders of ASEAN agreed on this project in the following year at the ASEAN Summit held in Indonesia. Several attempts had been made in the direction of regional cooperation and regional community building. The ASEAN Free Trade Area (AFTA), signed in 1992, the ASEAN Framework Agreement on Services (AFAS), signed in 1995, and the ASEAN Investment Area (AIA), signed in 1998, are the major building blocks to support the AEC.

As the AEC is now fully effective, the Thai government is obliged to help increase the region's competitiveness. The AEC Blueprint has attracted attention from academics and researchers but a lot of attention has been on the impact of the AEC Blueprint on individual countries. For Thailand, economic growth is one clear positive result of economic integration. The empirical studies also suggest that the poverty reduction is related to economic growth (Jitsuchon, 2006; Krongkaew et al., 2006; Warr, 2004). However, what has been questionable is the relationship between economic growth and income disparity, especially between Bangkok and other regions. More importantly, what has been understudied is the impact of the industrial policy of the particular country on the growth and development of ASEAN as a whole. Surveying the existing literature, this chapter looks at two levels of Thailand's industrial policy. First, it aims to analyze whether the policies that the Thai government adopted help close the poverty gap or have instead created a wider gap and worsened Thailand's regional disparities. Second, it aims at examining whether the policies initiated by the Thai government have promoted ASEAN regional growth and development. To deepen our understanding, Section 8.2 describes the background of each ASEAN member country and identifies its strengths and weaknesses. Section 8.3 discusses the development of Thailand's and other member countries' industrial policies in the AEC context, covering the period from the 1990s to the 2010s. Section 8.4 analyzes the opportunities and challenges to Thailand's industrial promotion from economic integration under AEC. These sections taken together help evaluate Thailand's industrial policies in the AEC context in the final section.

8.2 Background of the ASEAN member countries

ASEAN is one of the world's largest markets after China and India. The total geographical area of the ASEAN member countries is 4,479,128 km² and the total population, as of 2018, is 654.28 million. As a region, the annual GDP of ASEAN grew at 4.7 percent in 2015 and is expected to grow at 5.1 percent in 2018 according to the Asian Development Bank. Considering the economic performance of ten ASEAN member countries during 2012–2016, we find out that an overall economic growth of ASEAN was relatively high with an average of 3.0–8.0 percent (excluding Brunei Darussalam) compared to the world economic growth rate at 2.65 percent. Despite high economic growth, the GDP per capita of ASEAN member countries is highly differentiated. According to the World Bank (2016), Cambodia, Indonesia, Lao PDR, Myanmar, the Philippines, and Vietnam are classified as lower-middle-income countries (US$1,035–4,085). Thailand and Malaysia are classified as upper-middle-income countries (US$4,085–12,615). Brunei Darussalam and Singapore are classified as high-income (US$2,615 or more). During 2012–2016, while Singapore had the highest GDP per capita at US$54,677.38, Cambodia had the lowest GDP per capita at US$974.84.

Moreover, the average inflation rate of most ASEAN member countries was quite low around 1.0–4.0 percent. This mild inflation can help stimulate the spending and investment. This is contrast to Indonesia and Myanmar, which had relatively high inflation rates, and Brunei, which faced deflation. With regards to the unemployment rate, Cambodia had the lowest unemployment at 0.22 percent and the Philippines had the highest unemployment rate at 6.57 percent. However, the average unemployment rate of member countries is still low at only 2.92 percent, compared to the global unemployment rate at an average of 5.0–6.0 percent. A summary of the ASEAN key indicators is shown in Table 8.1.

Despite the quite impressive economic performance of ASEAN, ASEAN countries face pervasive and deep-rooted corruption problems. Considering the corruption perception index of 2016, almost all the ASEAN member countries scored less than 40 out of 100, which meant a high level of corruption was observed in these countries. Singapore was the only country that had an outstanding score of 84 out of 100.

Table 8.1 ASEAN key indicators

Country	Total land area (km²)	Total population in 2018 (million)	GDP growth rate (annual, %) average 2012–2916	GDP/capita (US$) average 2012–2016	Inflation, consumer price index (annual, %) average 2012–2016	Unemployment rate (%) average 2012–2016	Corruption perception index: CPI in 2016
Brunei Darussalam	5,765	0.43**	−1.36**	33,584.94	−0.10**	1.78	58
Cambodia	181,035	16.24	7.14	974.84**	2.79	0.22**	21**
Indonesia	1,904,443*	266.79*	5.35	3,541.40	5.48	5.96	37
Lao PDR	236,800	6.96	7.57*	1,991.60	3.53	1.39	30
Malaysia	330,800	32.04	4.2	10,371.34	2.22	3.12	49
Myanmar	676,600	53.85	7.46	1,263.42	6.12*	5.1	28
the Philippines	298,170	106.51	6.58	2,802.89	2.69	6.57*	35
Singapore	710**	5.79	3.27	54,677.38*	1.38	2.38	84*
Thailand	513,115	69.18	3.41	5,644.70	1.46	0.7	35
Vietnam	331,690	96.49	5.91	1,606.68	4.05	1.98	33
Total	4,479,128	654.28	4.953	11645.92	2.962	2.92	–

Note: * maximum, ** minimum

8.2.1 *Economic fundamentals of ASEAN member countries*

ASEAN is a group of countries characterized by diversity. Each country has its own way of conducting business, different laws and regulations, uneven economic development, and is different in culture and social context. Although some countries, such as Thailand and Lao PDR, share quite similar cultures, their economic development is totally different.

8.2.1.1 *Thailand*

Thailand has experienced an economic boom and bust along with its economic development as illustrated in Figure 8.1. Thai economy sharply rose to its peak from 1986 to 1989 after the industrial policy changed from import-substitution policy to export-led growth policy. With this rapid growth, the Thai economy established a strong foundation and many scholars categorized Thailand as the future fifth tiger in Asia, following Hong Kong, Singapore, South Korea, and Taiwan. Unfortunately, Thailand was severely affected by the financial crisis in 1997. As indicated by the World Bank, the economy collapsed with an annual percentage growth rate at -2.8 in 1997 and reached its all-time low at -7.6 in 1998. The economy began to recover in 1999. Thailand experienced moderate growth since then until the global financial crisis took place in 2008. Economic growth was hit during 2007–2008 due to the limit on international trade. After a short period of recovery, another major problem that negatively affected Thai economic growth was severe flooding in 2011 and political instability in 2013–2014.

Over 2012–2016, Thailand's average economic growth was 3.41 percent and its GDP per capita was US$5,645. The average unemployment rate was very low at 0.70 percent during the same period, the second lowest rate in ASEAN

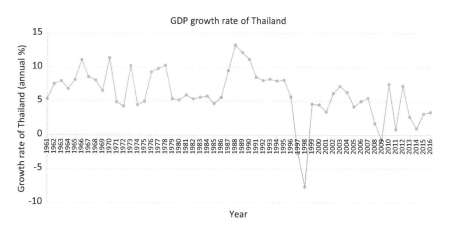

Figure 8.1 GDP growth rate of Thailand, 1961–2016
Source: National Economic and Social Development Board.

after Cambodia. With regards to geographic location, Thailand has an advantage of being a center in various areas, such as aviation, trade, and investment. Its domestic transport system links easily with neighboring countries by road, rail, and flights. Thailand has become the production base for automobiles, electronics, and agricultural products. It is also rich in resources for food products. The main industries are in the export sector, which included automobiles and parts, computers, rubber, jewelry and accessories, plastic resin, petroleum products, electrical circuits, chemical products, and rice.

An overview of the economic fundamentals of other ASEAN member countries is explained below (Amonvatana, 2015).

8.2.1.2 Brunei Darussalam

Although it has the smallest population, the average GDP per capita was US$33,584.94 during 2012–2016, the second highest in ASEAN after Singapore. It is a rich petroleum-exporting country with a GDP growth rate of -1.36 percent. Its major sources of income come from oil and natural gas. The major export destinations consist of Japan, Malaysia, the United Kingdom, and the United States. Manufacturing imports include industrial products, automobiles, tools and machinery, electrical appliances, and agricultural imports comprise rice and fruits.

8.2.1.3 Cambodia

Cambodia shares a border with Lao PDR, Thailand, and the bay of Thailand, and Vietnam. Over 2012–2016, its average economic growth was 7.14 percent but the GDP per capita was only US$97,484, the lowest in ASEAN. Textiles, construction, agriculture, and tourism are the major sectors that drive the Cambodian economy. Cambodia had the lowest unemployment rate in ASEAN. Nevertheless, the corruption perception index scored 21 points, the lowest among ASEAN member countries.

8.2.1.4 Indonesia

Indonesia has a large consumer market, especially the Muslim consumer market, because it is the largest country in ASEAN in terms of the total land area and population. The size of its GDP is also the largest in ASEAN. Indonesia benefits from various canals that expedite water transportation between oceans, as it is located in the Southeast Asia region that connects the Pacific and the Indian Ocean, between Asia and Australia. The main industries are petroleum and natural gas and mining.

8.2.1.5 Lao PDR

Lao PDR is a landlocked country bordered by five countries that have growing economies, including China, Cambodia, Myanmar, Thailand, and Vietnam. Lao

PDR has biodiversity in energy, electricity, and natural resources, such as water and minerals that are important for a production base. During 2012–2016, the average GDP growth rate was 7.57 percent, the highest rate in ASEAN. Its major source of revenue comes from the electricity business.

8.2.1.6 Malaysia

From 2012 to 2016, Malaysia's average GDP per capita was US$10,371.34, the third largest in ASEAN after Brunei Darussalam and Singapore. The average economic growth was 4.2 percent over the same period. The major industries in Malaysia can be divided into three groups. The first group is the financial institutions. The two dominant Malaysian financial institutions that have branches all over Asia-Pacific are Malayan Banking Berhad or Maybank and Commerce International Merchant Bankers or CIMB. The second group is petroleum and natural gas. Malaysia is the third largest petroleum producer and the second largest natural gas provider in Asia-Pacific. The third group is tourism, which highly promoted by the Malaysian government. In addition to these groups, Malaysia is the center of internationally recognized Halal food manufacturing.

8.2.1.7 Myanmar

Myanmar is an emerging and developing economy with average GDP per capita of US$1,263.42 during 2012–2016. Myanmar has a large consumer market in Asia. It has the advantage of geography because it borders China and India, the two neighbors with the largest consumer and labor markets in Asia. Myanmar's geography and climate are suitable for agriculture. It is also rich in natural resources. The main industries are agriculture, rubber, zinc mining, textiles, electricity, footwear, and fishery. Its GDP growth primarily comes from the agricultural sector. The major export products consist of rice, seeds, wooden products, and fisheries products.

8.2.1.8 The Philippines

The Philippines is a sovereign island country with the average GDP growth rate of 6.58 percent during 2012–2016. The average GDP per capita was US$2,802.89. The Philippines had a chronic problem with the high unemployment rate of 6.57 percent, the highest rate in ASEAN. The major exports include electronic parts, machinery, textiles, and automobiles.

8.2.1.9 Singapore

Of the ASEAN member countries, Singapore is the smallest country in terms of total land area and the second smallest in terms of population. This small open economy depends extensively on international trade. It is an economic center in the region and the world, with very strong sectors in service, high technology production, and innovative products. Compared to other ASEAN member countries, its basic infrastructure, transportation, and logistics systems are more advanced. The GDP per capita is as high as US$54,677.38 with moderate GDP growth rate of 3.27 percent during 2012–2016. The unemployment rate was quite low at 2.38 percent. Singapore primarily exports machinery, chemical products, and clothing and garments. Not only is Singapore's economic performance impressive, the corruption perception index scored 84 points, the highest in ASEAN.

8.2.1.10 Vietnam

Vietnam has grown continuously in the last decade. Due to fiscal stabilization and continuous inflows of foreign direct investments, its economic growth was impressive with an average of 5.91 percent with average GDP per capita of US$1,607 over 2012–2016. Vietnam also benefits from its geographic location that connects it to China, Cambodia, and Laos by land. The main export products of Vietnam are crude oil, textiles, footwear, fisheries products, and electronics.

8.2.2 Strengths and weaknesses of the ASEAN member countries

To determine the appropriate industrial policy for Thailand in an AEC context, the strengths and weaknesses of Thailand and other ASEAN member countries need to be analyzed. From the perspective of AEC, it is obvious that Thailand's strength is its strategic location. Thailand is located at the center of the region, which connects it to various countries either by land or by sea, making Thailand a center of many economic activities. Additionally, Thailand has developed a good and convenient transport system that can be linked with other countries. It is also rich in resources for food production.

Despite several strengths that Thailand has, political instability has become one of the major weaknesses for Thailand during the past decade. The Thai political regime has fluctuated between democratic election, coup, and revolution since the 1930s. This political instability has adversely affected Thai economic performance as evidenced in the recent political turmoil during 2013–2014 (Sethapramote, 2014). Household consumption, for instance, shrank due to loss of consumer confidence and uncertainty about the economic and political situation. Income from the tourism industry also dropped. Another weakness of Thailand is the labor situation as it is lacking in terms of skilled labor and the workforce is illiterate in foreign languages. In comparison to other ASEAN member countries, the minimum wage in Thailand is relatively high (Philippines' National Wage and Productivity Commission, 2010). The Philippines has the highest daily minimum wage in the region at US$5.75–10.05, followed by Thailand. The daily minimum wage of Thailand is US$9.02–9.32. The third highest daily minimum wage is Malaysia at US$7.27–7.90. This is contrary to the case of CLMV (Cambodia, Lao PDR, Myanmar, and Vietnam) and Indonesia, which have a daily minimum wage as low as US$2–5. Meanwhile, Singapore and Brunei Darussalam do not set a standard of minimum wages. Last but not least, Thailand also has the problem of infringement of intellectual property rights.

Other ASEAN member countries have strengths and weaknesses as shown in Table 8.2. According to Table 8.2, it is seen that Malaysia and Singapore share similar strengths in terms of relatively high level of GDP per capita, stable politics, high security, and numbers of skilled labor. On the other hand, Cambodia, Indonesia, Lao PDR, Myanmar, and Thailand have similarities in terms of

Table 8.2 Strengths and weaknesses of other ASEAN member countries

Country	Strengths	Weaknesses
Brunei Darussalam	Wealth from exporting petroleum	Small consumer market
	High GDP per capita, second highest in ASEAN	Labor shortage
	High purchasing power and economic security	
Cambodia	Lowest wage in ASEAN	Public utility system in the process of development
	Convenience link with other countries	High transportation cost
	Rich and diverse natural resources	Lack of skilled labor
	Available resources that promote investment in electricity business	Unclear regulations in exports and imports
	Important base in agricultural production	Lack of data collection and statistics and research analysis
		Lack of credibility in systems in finance, banking and judicial process
		High cost of electricity
Indonesia	Largest population in ASEAN	Poor basic infrastructure and logistics system
	Large labor force and cheap wages	Limited transportation modes and high reliance on water transportation
	Large market and the largest Muslim consumer market	Lack of quality labor
	High purchasing power and demand for quality products	High military spending due to long land and seas borders
	Many nation-wide large ports	Frequent natural disasters
	Rich and diverse natural resources	Complex process of civil servant system and bureaucracy
Lao PDR	Small market	Landlocked country with mountains and plateaus
	Rich in biodiversity in energy, electricity, and natural resources	Inconvenient transportation
	Low wages, second lowest in ASEAN	Lack of basic infrastructure
	Political stability	Instability of Laos kip (currency)

(*continued*)

Table 8.2 Cont.

Country	Strengths	Weaknesses
Malaysia	High GDP per capita	Small consumer market due to small population size
	Rich and advantage in Energy	Lack of skilled labor
	Integrated infrastructure system and logistics management system	High investment and labor cost
	Skilled, discipline, and quality labor force	Social inequality between Chinese and Malay people
	Continual and clear developing plan and policies	
	High literacy in English	
Myanmar	Large consumer market	Poor basic infrastructure system
	Easy border access to China and India	Uncertainties in politics, policies and skirmishes with minority groups
	Low wages	Lack of skilled labor
	Advantage in geography	Lack of marketing and financial data
	Abundant natural resources	
	Weather suitable for agriculture	
the Philippines	Large population	Location far away from ASEAN member countries
	Large and potential consumer markets	High labor cost
	Large labor force with technology knowledge	Lack of unskilled labor
	Good literacy in English	Insecurity in life and assets
	Rich in natural resources	Lack of basic infrastructure
Singapore	Highest GDP per capita in ASEAN	Small consumer market
	Shipping center of the world	
	Efficient logistics system	High business operation and cost of living
	Free trade policy with no import duties	Dependence on raw materials
	Political stability and security	Low marriage and birth rates
	Skilled labor with high education and literacy in English	Country moving fastest toward an elderly society
Vietnam	Location that links China and Southeast Asia	Unprepared and insufficient infrastructure and utility
	Large and potential consumer market with high purchasing power	High logistics and time costs
	Low wages	High land and office rent costs
	Political stability	Unclear laws and regulations
	Quality population and willing to learn new knowledge	
	Good education system	
	Rich in seafood, crude oil, and natural gas	

richness and diversity of natural resources but with inadequate skilled labor and technology. Brunei Darussalam, the Philippines, and Vietnam have the benefit of having workforces that literate in foreign languages. Still, Brunei Darussalam has a problem with labor shortages while the Philippines and Vietnam face a problem from lack of infrastructure and utility and the high cost of conducting business.

It is obvious that the strength of ASEAN is low labor cost with abundant and diversity of natural resources. The consumer market of ASEAN is also large. These factors taken together will attract investors from all over the world to invest in ASEAN. Nonetheless, ASEAN remains weak due to its lack of skilled labor, such as the case of Cambodia, Indonesia, Myanmar, and Thailand. Unprepared and poor basic infrastructure and logistics problems, including high logistics cost and slow logistics, are observed in ASEAN as well.

8.3 Industrial policies in the AEC context

8.3.1 Thailand

ASEAN has always been the core of Thailand's foreign policy since Thailand signed the Bangkok Declaration in 1967. Thailand was also involved in establishing the ASEAN Free Trade Area (AFTA) with the aim of enhancing the ASEAN region's competitive advantage in 1992. AFTA is regarded as the first step toward AEC. Furthermore, Thailand actively participated in the drafting of the ASEAN Charter and initiated the working plan to establish AEC or the AEC Blueprint. The AEC Blueprint was first implemented in 2015.

According to the AEC Blueprint, the key characteristics of the AEC include a single market and production base, a highly competitive economic region, a region of equitable economic development, and a region fully integrated into the global economy. As of December 2015, ASEAN in general had completed measures under the AEC Blueprint of 93.9 percent out of total of 506 measures (Department of ASEAN Affairs, 2017, p. 1). Significant progress was made in integrating into a single market and production. Upon achieving AEC Blueprint 2015, ASEAN developed the AEC Blueprint 2025.

In promoting a single market and production base, Thailand and the other member countries have to commit to five core elements. The first core element is the free flow of goods. Through AFTA, member countries have to gradually eliminate import duties on products on the Inclusion List (IL) and the Sensitive List (SL), such as coffee, potatoes, dried coconuts, and flowers, from 5 percent to 0 percent from January 1, 2010 onwards. In accordance with such a commitment, Thailand reduced the duties on 8,287 products in IL to 0 percent since January 1, 2010. Thailand also decreased the duties of 13 products in SL to 5 percent since January 1, 2010 (Ministry of Foreign Affairs, 2011). To qualify for such a privilege, the products have to on both the export country and import country's lists and at least 40 percent has to be produced in one of the ASEAN member countries.

The second core element is the free flow of services. ASEAN member countries has to permit ASEAN investors to hold shares of no less than 70 percent of the service providers in the Priority Integration Sector (PIS) and remove any restriction on market access. This sector includes e-ASEAN (telecommunications and computers), healthcare, tourism, and air freight in 2010. For the logistics sector, ASEAN investors should be allowed to hold shares of no less than 51 percent. Last but not least, the member countries have to permit ASEAN investors to hold shares of no less than 70 percent in the non-priority services sector. As of April 2018, Thailand, as represented by the Ministry of Commerce, is in negotiation with other member countries to draft a framework agreement on services to allow ASEAN investors to invest in services to at least 70 percent of total shares in particular ASEAN member countries.

The third core element is the free flow of investment. ASEAN signed the Framework Agreement on the ASEAN Investment Area (AIA) in 1998. This agreement aims to transform ASEAN into an attractive area for investment for both ASEAN investors and external investors. Later in 2009, the AIA was developed as the ASEAN Comprehensive Investment Agreement (ACIA) with a broader context to include ASEAN Investment Guarantee Agreement (IGA). The member countries are allowed to liberalize investments with conditions, through a reservation list. For Thailand, the Council on International Economic Policy assigned the Board of Investment (BOI) to take the lead in drafting the reservation list in cooperation with the private sector in 2008. According to the BOI, the reservation list will be based on the reservation list stipulated under foreign business law.

The fourth core element is the free flow of capital. This means strengthening the ASEAN capital market development and integration, which is under the Ministry of Finance and the Securities and Exchange Commission of Thailand, and allowing greater capital mobility, which is under the direct responsibility of the Bank of Thailand.

Finally, the last core element is the free flow of skilled labor. The ASEAN member countries have to facilitate the movement of natural persons involved in trade of goods and services and investment. With respect to this element, the ASEAN member countries agreed to establish the framework for national skilled labor, as well as establish the Mutual Recognition Arrangement Framework (MRA Framework) on professional services.

In addition to these core elements, Thailand is committed to cooperating with other member countries on priority integration sectors, as well as the agricultural sector.

Thailand successfully completed the task under the AEC Blueprint up to 96.0 percent (Ministry of Foreign Affairs, 2017). By adopting the AEC Blueprint, Thailand is committed to liberalizing goods and service markets, as well as investment in other ASEAN member countries. Thailand also agrees to provide economic cooperation and amend its domestic laws, where necessary, to accommodate the aim to transform ASEAN into a single market and production base.

In addition to the commitments made under the AEC Blueprint, the Thai government has introduced various policies to promote regional cooperation and support economic expansion in the AEC. The Thai government also encourages domestic investment, focusing on basic infrastructure and logistics. The AEC allows Thailand to grasp an opportunity to be the logistics hub of ASEAN due to its strategic location at the center of the ASEAN member countries. Examples of policies to develop local capacity and upgrade Thailand's logistics include developing more rail routes in Bangkok and its suburbs and developing rail infrastructure to link Thailand to its neighboring countries. The efficiency of air freight and land transport has also been enhanced through Thailand's Transport Infrastructure Development Strategy 2015–2022.

Accompanying the development in infrastructure and logistics, the Thai government launched policies to promote business activities and investment with neighboring countries and attract foreign direct investment. The first policy is the special economic zones (SEZ), which was implemented in 2015. The SEZ were selected based on the proximity of the provinces to the neighboring countries in terms of trade, economy, and investment. The Ministry of Finance and the BOI offer both tax and non-tax incentives to the investors who invest in SEZ and provides a One-Stop-Service System (OSS) to speed up the registration process for business. The SEZ policy has two phases and covers 10 provinces that are in proximity to neighboring countries. The first phase was 2016 to 2017, covering Mukdahan, Song khla, Sa Kaeo, Tak, and Trat. The second phase is 2018–2019, covering Chiang Rai, Kanchanaburi, Narathiwat, Nong Khai, and Nakhon Phanom.

Another policy is the Eastern Economic Corridor (EEC), the future technology base. The EEC is the development of the Eastern Seaboard, which has played a significant role in Thailand's economy for over 30 years. Many of high-value goods, including petro-chemical industries and automobiles, are manufactured on the Eastern Seaboard. In an attempt to achieve Thailand 4.0 policy, the Thai government decided to invest large sum of money to develop Eastern Seaboard to be the EEC (Poovanich, 2016). The EEC also covers three eastern provinces of Thailand: Chonburi, Chachoengsao, and Rayong. This project will focus on 10 targeted industries, which are divided into First 5 S-Curve industries, such as next-generation automotive and intelligent electronics, and New 5 S-Curve industries, such as robotics and automation, and biofuels. The EEC has the ultimate goal of transforming the Thai economy into an innovation-driven economy following the Thailand 4.0 policy. The investors in EEC will also receive tax benefits.

The focus of Thailand's industrial policy expands beyond domestic investment to cover investment abroad. Since the labor wages in Thailand are higher than those of its surrounding countries and the ASEAN has prospects for high growth, the BOI recommends that Thai businesses should expand their production base to other ASEAN member countries with low wages and abundant labor and resources (BOI 2017). Active market access in the ASEAN member countries can yield benefits for Thai products in the regional market when ASEAN is transformed into a single market.

To achieve the goals of the AEC, all member countries have to move in the same direction. In addition to the policy initiatives by the Thai government to support economic integration under the AEC, we also find similar efforts on the other ASEAN member countries. Most countries' policies emphasize attracting foreign direct investment rather than promoting domestic investors to invest abroad as exemplified below.

8.3.2 *Brunei Darussalam*

Brunei Darussalam has accelerated its economic infrastructure under the long-term plan called "Wawasan 2035-Vision Brunei 2035" (Business Information Center, 2017). This plan aims to create economic diversity and reduce revenue reliance on the export of petroleum and natural gas. The government of Brunei Darussalam permits foreign investors to co-invest in the basic infrastructure development project for the Halal-related industry, as well as the tourism industry and industry downstream from petroleum and natural gas. Moreover, its industrial policy is moving toward economic integration by allowing foreigners to hold shares in specific businesses up to 100 percent. For businesses in the food industry and industry that uses domestic input, previously foreigners could not hold more shares than 70 percent. Other industrial policies include tax incentives and investment incentives for pioneer industries.

8.3.3 *Cambodia*

Because the revenue of the country relies heavily on the export of some industries, such as the textiles, the government aims to diversify the risk from relying on such exports by promoting other industries through four strategic plans. The strategic plan of the government is to strengthen the investment environment, to reduce the cost of conducting business in Cambodia, to expand market access through trade agreements, and to develop the agricultural sector and the basic infrastructure in rural areas. The government also is trying to promote foreign direct investment by allowing foreign investors to invest in any form of business without restriction on nationality. Furthermore, if foreign investors invest in a qualified investment project, they are entitled to tax benefits. Cambodia also provides tax benefits for investment in special economic zones or export processing zones.

8.3.4 *Indonesia*

Because of the financial crisis in 1997, many foreign investors had withdrawn their money from Indonesia. By 2002, the Indonesian economy had recovered and foreign investors started to invest in Indonesia again. To ensure the smoothness of industrial development, the Indonesian government has launched the Master Plan: Acceleration and Expansion of Indonesia Economic Development 2011–2025 (MP3EI). Under this new framework, the government aims to push forward selected industries, including agriculture, rubber, energy and petroleum, mining, fishery, tourism, and telecommunications. Furthermore, an Economic

Corridor has been established to accommodate the new framework. Moreover, in order to attract foreign investors for FDI, the Indonesian government has designated investment priority sectors that can receive investment benefit from the government.

8.3.5 Lao PDR

The government of Lao PDR has heavily promoted investment in the country through various measures. First, Lao PDR has revised and updated its las to favor investors. For example, the limitation on the length of time that investors could conduct general business in Lao PDR was revoked. For concession businesses, including electrical power and mining, the period can be extended for no longer than 99 years. The Lao PDR government also shortened the timeframe for processing related to foreign investment. Second, special economic zones/specific economic zones have been established in Lao PDR. Moreover, a one-stop-service was set up to accommodate investors and disseminate information for the investors. Third, investment benefits, as well as tax benefits, such as exemption from profit tax, raw material import duty exemption, and export duty exemption, will be granted to particular businesses. Fourth, the government also promoted public-private partnerships to invest in designated areas through investment benefits and tax benefits, such as import duty exemption, information facilitation, land utilization, and honorary citizen status.

8.3.6 Malaysia

The government of Malaysia has provided investment incentives both directly and indirectly under its laws, covering all industries in the country. The Malaysian Investment Development Authority (MIDA) provides investment benefits to investors in two ways. First, investors with pioneer status can be exempted from corporate income tax of 70 percent for 5 years. In addition to this, the capital allowance, as well as accumulated losses occurred during the pioneer status can be counted as tax deductions. Second, regardless of pioneer status, investors can receive investment tax allowance. Sixty percent of the qualifying capital expenditure, which is specified by MIDA and occurs within the first 5 years, can be used as a tax deduction. Apart from the benefits provided by MIDA, investors can also receive the benefit from investing in the Economic Corridor, including the East Coast Economic Region, Iskandar Malaysia, the Northern Corridor Economic Region, the Sabah Development Corridor, and the Sarawak Corridor for Renewable Energy.

8.3.7 Myanmar

The economy of Myanmar had been closed for many decades until the Myanmar government decided to open the economy in 1988. The Myanmar economy has changed from having solely the state as the owner of all industries to having increased level of foreign investment. The major proportion of investment is in the petroleum and natural gas industry, followed by the energy industry, telecommunications, and mining, respectively. Most investors come from China, Singapore, Thailand, Hong Kong, and the United Kingdom, in that order. After opening the economy, the government tried to increase domestic investment through the relaxation of investment regulations, shortening the registration process, bringing in foreign specialists for business development in private sector, and finally providing investment incentives. Also, a special economic zone has been formed as an industrial zone like its neighboring countries, including Thailand.

8.3.8 The Philippines

According to the Philippines Development Plan 2014–2016, the development objectives cover increasing job opportunities in the country through the development of the manufacturing and services sectors, supporting activities with high value-added, promoting linkages between small and medium-sized enterprises, as well as strengthening regional and global cooperation. In order to achieve these objectives, not only has the government tried to stimulate economic activities from all sectors through incentives from the Board of Investment but it has also developed technology and industrial clusters and supported the development of a niche market in the Philippines. Investment benefit is provided either based on the type of business, which has to be listed under the investment priorities plan, or based on the location of the business, which has to be located in the Philippines Economic Zone.

8.3.9 Singapore

Singapore is the most developed country in ASEAN. In addition to its well-developed basic infrastructure, its industrial policy facilitates investment in the country and abroad. Singapore treats domestic investors and foreign investors equally. This is evident in the investment laws that allow foreigners to hold shares up to 100 percent in almost every type of business (Fiscal Policy Research Institute Foundation, 2016). The businesses that Singapore wants to promote for domestic investment include building-cleaning and landscaping businesses, arts, entertainment, and recreation, food and beverages, and aircraft leasing and aircraft rentables business. The exceptions are in broadcasting and radio frequency businesses and newspapers, which permit the foreigners to hold shares of no more than 49 percent and of no more than 5 percent, respectively. Moreover, the industrial policy of Singapore also places emphasis on research and development (R&D). Singapore encourages foreign businesses to establish their regional headquarters or global headquarters in Singapore so that Singapore can gain know-how and technology from those businesses (Department of Trade Negotiations, 2014). On the other hand, Singapore also encourages domestic investors to invest abroad to expand their production base.

8.3.10 *Vietnam*

Vietnam recently introduced a reform of the economy moving from a centrally planned socialist system to economic liberalization. The role of the private sector was enhanced through the establishment of joint stock companies. Investment opportunities in Vietnam have also been liberalized, focusing on foreign investment with high technology and investment in mountain or underdeveloped rural areas. Accompanied by tax benefits and investment benefits, the Vietnamese government will provide labor training and land privileges to investors who invest in the special economic zone, either in the export processing zone, the industrial park, or the high-tech zone. For instance, the investors will be entitled to sublease the land in the special economic zone and have a right on such land similar to the right of the landowner.

8.4 Opportunities and challenges to Thailand's industrial promotion

8.4.1 *Opportunities*

The AEC creates both opportunities and challenges to Thailand. The opportunity is clear that if ASEAN member countries are successfully integrated as prescribed by the AEC Blueprint. Thailand, as represented by AEC, will have more economic bargaining power against non-ASEAN countries. This is because AEC will lead to a large and competitive regional market. The AEC not only creates opportunities for ASEAN as a whole, but it also creates various opportunities for Thailand individually. For investment, although ASEAN member countries eagerly implement industrial promotion, the policies that are implemented by the Thai government can still attract foreign investors. Comparing the industrial promotion policy of Thailand with that of Indonesia, Malaysia, and the Philippines, Thailand offers more tax benefits and other benefits than these countries.

More importantly, the AEC can help Thailand deal with rising wages and labor shortages efficiently. Thailand can utilize the strengths of its neighboring countries to attract foreign investors to maintain their supply chain in Thailand. This opportunity can be illustrated by the Thailand-Plus-One project initiated by the Japanese government. Under this project, due to increased labor costs and labor shortages in Thailand, the Japanese manufacturers in Thailand expanded their supply chain to CLMV (Cambodia, Laos, Myanmar, and Vietnam) at a lower cost. However, they only shifted their labor-intensive processes to low-cost production sites in CLMV. They continued to keep the main production bases in Thailand. The Japanese automobile manufacturers and electronic devices producers are examples of businesses that join this project. According to Economic Intelligence Center of Siam Commercial Bank (2016), the Thailand-Plus-One project benefits all stakeholders. Japanese manufacturers can reduce their costs and increase profits. For CLMV, the expansion of the supply chain network helps create jobs and brings technology advances and know-how to these countries through Japanese foreign direct investment. Thailand itself can continue to enjoy the benefit of Japanese foreign direct investment.

The Japanese companies changed the role of their production bases in Thailand to be able to respond to the changing demands of the local markets in CLMV (Oizumi & Soejima, 2015, pp. 10–12). As the production bases in Thailand increase in significance, it is likely that the Japanese parent companies will provide more support activities. Moreover, Thailand can gain more technological transfer and know-how as major Japanese automotive and part manufacturers have already announced their plans to strengthen development functions at the production bases in Thailand. This includes an expansion of R&D functions in Thailand. For example, Mitsubishi Motors has established a test course to the same standard as in the Japanese parent company with the aim of enhancing R&D capabilities (Oizumi & Soejima, 2015, pp. 10–12). In this respect, workers in the industrial areas can benefit from skill, knowledge, and capability development. Maintaining the manufacturing site implies that the workers in such areas do not have to lose their jobs. With AEC and investment incentives, Thailand can attract foreign direct investment by promoting itself as the center for supply chain through its advantage of its geographic location.

The AEC brings closer ties between Thailand and its neighboring countries economically. Together with foreign investment in Thailand, it is an opportunity for Thailand to actively expand its market to the ASEAN member countries and gain the benefit from low wages and rich resources in those countries. Thai businesses can also enjoy investment benefits and a reduction in trade barriers as ASEAN member countries are focusing on attracting foreign investors through investment incentives and decreases in tariff and non-tariff barriers so as to achieve the AEC Blueprint.

The BOI, for instance, recommends that Thai businesses should establish their production base in Indonesia in order to sell products in Indonesia domestically instead of exporting the product from Thailand to Indonesia. This is because the domestic market in Indonesia is large and growing, especially on the island of Java. Moreover, Indonesia has good distribution channels. Thai businesses can hire local distributors to help distribute and promote the products in the domestic market. The prospect product is automotive parts.

CLVM is also a good choice for investment. Examples are as follows. According to the Trading Policy and Strategy Office under the Ministry of Commerce (2016, p. 6), Lao PDR is an interesting country to invest in agriculture and processed agricultural products. The reasons include the abundant natural resources and plenty of land suitable for agriculture, as well as the Generalized System of Preference (GSP) right of Lao PDR to export to a global market.

Besides, the BOI points out that Thai businesses should invest in Myanmar due to increased liberalization of Myanmar's economy and investment promotion from the government (BOI, 2017). However, nowadays, already a lot of foreign investors are interested in Myanmar. In order for Thai businesses to penetrate Myanmar's market, a trading partnership is essential. The targeted trading partner is the middle class in the big cities.

CLMV has become important in Thailand's export sector. According to the Ministry of Commerce, the first major export destination for Thailand is ASEAN-5 at 17.0 percent followed by CLMV at 9.1 percent. The main exported products to CLMV consist of oil-related products, automobiles and automotive parts, beverages, steel and iron, and chemical products. The trading activities that occurred in Thailand's border areas with CLMV have contributed to Thailand's regional development in terms of increased income and poverty reduction.

According to the study by the Asian Development Bank (ADB) and the International Labour Organization (ILO), the integration as an economic community can generate regional economic growth of 7.1 percent. The economic community can also create job opportunities for as many as 14 million by 2025, especially in the services sector and the transport and logistics sector.

8.4.2 Challenges

The AEC has brought about challenges to Thailand's industrial promotion in three aspects: labor, investment, and R&D and innovation. The challenge to labor comes from the shortage of skilled labor to meet the needs of industry and investors. The Thai workforce is mostly illiterate in foreign languages as well. According to the AEC, Thailand is inferior to Malaysia and Singapore in terms of skilled labor. This is because the workforce in Malaysia and Singapore has the advantage of language skills and a higher level of education, which allow them to deal with sophisticated work win high technology business. It is a big challenge for the Thai government to develop local capabilities as this problem has been found in Thailand for a long time. What Thailand possesses is low-skilled labor but Thailand also faces a challenge from the countries with lower wages, such as CLMV, and a bigger workforce, such as Indonesia. If the existing foreign investors decide to move the whole production site from Thailand to Thailand's neighboring countries, it will definitely affect Thailand's regional development due to increased unemployment. Additionally, it will emphasize regional disparity because the workers from such areas have a tendency to migrate to other regions, especially Bangkok and its suburbs, to find jobs.

The second challenge relates to investment and industrial factor. Despite the fact that Thailand heavily promotes the investment in New S-Curve industries, the level of investment in New S-Curve industries is still low. Investment continues to be concentrated around First S-Curve industries. This implies that the industrial policies previously adopted by Thailand cannot strengthen local capabilities to meet the needs of investors and yield the outcome the government intends. This is also linked to the lack of skilled labor, as mentioned earlier. With respect to New S-Curve industries, Indonesia, Malaysia, and the Philippines have higher potential than Thailand due to their readiness in innovation, education, and training.

The third challenge is technological development and innovation. Despite foreign direct investment in Thailand, the level of technology in Thailand remains moderate. According to the Global Competitiveness Report conducted by World Economic Forum, Thailand ranked 63rd for technological readiness during 2016–2017, lower than the previous year when it ranked the 58th. While other ASEAN member countries, such as Malaysia, have successfully built up their technological capabilities, Thailand is struggling with R&D and innovation to develop and create added value to its products. Inadequate technological advances and lack of innovation are considered to be one of the main factors that trap Thailand as a middle-income country. In the long term, relying solely on foreign direct investment will not make Thailand a high-income country. This has to be incorporated with the success of Thailand to enhance its technological capabilities together with the skill, knowledge, and capability of the workforce and basic infrastructure.

To maximize the opportunities from AEC and deal with the challenges, the Thai government issued the Twelfth National Economic and Social Development Plan. The plan creates a framework for the country's development from 2017 to 2021. This plan encompasses both the strengthening of human capital's potential and the development of science, technology, research, and innovation. Aiming to solve the problem of the workforce, the Ministry of Industry has set three strategies under the Twelfth Development Plan. The strategies consist of enhancing the human capital's potential, alleviating inequality in society, and strengthening the economy and its competitiveness. The Ministry of Industry has used information technology to help manage the workforce and increase the performance of the workforce in accordance with the Thailand 4.0 umbrella. Furthermore, the Ministry of Finance has developed a 20-year strategic framework for human resource development (2017–2036). The goal of this strategic framework is to add value to the workforce and help the country to tackle the middle-income gap and inequality.

With regards to technology and innovation development, the Twelfth Development Plan aims to push Thailand forward to be an innovative country by using the developed countries, such as South Korea, Japan, Sweden, and the United States, as a role model. To achieve the goal, this plan focuses on using knowledge in science, R&D, technology, and innovation from both the public and the private sectors.

Under this strategy, the government came up with three development guidelines. First, R&D investment, social adoption, and commercialization should be promoted. The targeted recipients include (1) the competent industries, such as food technology and medical technology; (2) the group that can cause a leap in growth from R&D and technology, such as medical hubs and aviation technology; and (3) society to promote inclusive growth and quality of life, such as educational technology and technology for the disabled and the elderly. The second guideline is to develop technopreneurs. The technopreneurs will be main players in technology and innovation development. Third, an appropriate environment for the promotion of science, technology, research, and innovation in relation to human resources, science and technology infrastructure, and management systems. The examples include the enhancement of researcher capability and speeding up the development of researchers in specific areas, such as production engineers and data scientists. Additionally, research and studies in accordance with area and provincial development should be promoted so as to upgrade the provinces' capability.

8.5 Evaluating Thailand's industrial policies in the AEC context

8.5.1 Impact on Thailand's regional development

The data used to evaluate the industrial policies, which the Thai government previously implemented to support AEC, is the GDP growth rate and poverty data based on region. Within the AEC context, of particular concern is the lack of Thailand's regional development. Even though many studies claim that economic growth leads to poverty reduction, whether it will result in a smaller poverty gap or enhance regional growth and development has to be analyzed.

Thai economic growth fluctuated from 1961 to 2016 as shown in Figure 8.1. In 2016, the Thai economy grew at 3.2 percent (Bank of Thailand, 2016, p. 1). The factors contributing to economic growth consisted of the manufacturing sector and the agricultural sector, which both grew at 0.9 percent (Office of Industrial Economics, 2016, p. 4). Private consumption grew at 3.5 percent. Private investment grew at a slow pace at 1.4 percent because some investors were waiting for the detail of Eastern Economic Corridor Act, which was expected to be promulgated in 2018. According to the Bank of Thailand's yearly report on economic and monetary conditions (2016, p. 30), private investment was concentrated in the services sector and the public utility sector. The investment in the manufacturing sector had not fully recovered despite the tax reduction offered by the government to promote domestic investment. Investment slightly expanded only in some export-related industries, such as electronics and the electrical appliances industry and the automobile and automotive parts industry. Meanwhile, the government expenditure was one of the key drivers for economic recovery. The government expenditure has expanded continuously, especially investment in basic infrastructure on transport (Bank of Thailand, 2016, p. 32).

According to the reports by the Office of Industrial Economics (2015, 2016), the numbers in the workforce dropped from 39.16 million in 2015 to 37.14 million in 2016. Employment figures also declined from 38.87 million to 37.14 million. Even though the overall employment declined, the employment in the manufacturing sector rose from 6.31 million to 6.4 million over the same period.

Above all, despite a cycle of boom and bust, the overall economic growth rate from the First National Development Plan (1961–1966) to the Eighth National Development Plan (1996–2001) has an average of 6.7 percent annually.

The poverty and income distribution reflect the outcome of the industrial policies implemented on Thailand's regional development. According to the National Economic and Social Development Board (NESDB), the poverty line has gradually increased from 881 baht per person per month in 1988 to 1,555 baht in 2000 and further increased to 2,644 baht in 2015. The poverty gap also portrays the same trend. In Thailand, the poverty gap constantly declined from 11.46 in 2000 to 1.14 in 2015. The headcount ratio sharply declined from 42.33 percent to 7.2 percent in 2015.[1] We can see that the fluctuation in economic growth does not directly lead to the fluctuation in poverty alleviation. Nonetheless, looking at the big picture, as long as Thailand can maintain the annual percentage growth rate at an average of no less than 3 percent, the poverty rate is likely to fall.

Over time, Thailand has successfully reduced the numbers of the poor and inequality in income at the national level. The economic growth was unfavorable to the Thai poor during 1981–2000. The income disparity had a worsening trend. For instance, the Gini index increased from 0.38 in 1981 to 0.43 in 2000.[2] After the recovery of the economy from the financial crisis, since 2000, economic growth has helped the poor more than proportionately. The Gini index has continuously declined to 0.38 again in 2013.

Looking at the regional level, the disparity is observed. Figure 8.2 indicates that northeastern region has always been the region with the highest headcount ratio while Bangkok has always been the region with the lowest headcount ratio (NESDB 2015, pp. 7–8). Despite the sharp decline in headcount ratio in all regions from 1988–2015, the headcount ratio in the northeastern region was five times the headcount ratio in Bangkok. In 2015, the poor were highly concentrated in the northeastern region, the southern region, and the northern region with the headcount ratio of 10.30 percent, 9.92 percent, and 8.78 percent, respectively. The headcount ratio in Bangkok was very low at 2.01 percent.

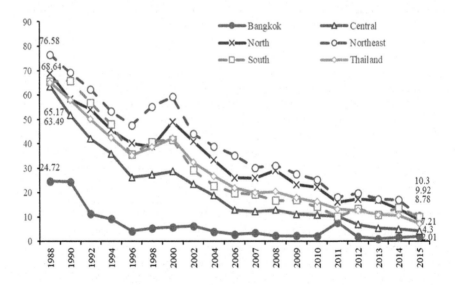

Figure 8.2 Concentration of poverty by region
Source: National Economic and Social Development Board.

In detail, the urban poor together with the rural poor significantly dropped over 1988–2015, except in a few years in the midst of the financial crisis in the late 1990s, as illustrated in Figure 8.3 and Figure 8.4. Both the numbers of urban poor and rural poor decreased at a similar pace. This is different from the period of 1962–1986, when the urban poor numbers had decreased a lot faster

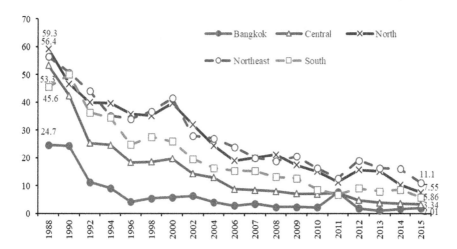

Figure 8.3 Head count ratio in urban area by region
Source: National Economic and Social Development Board.

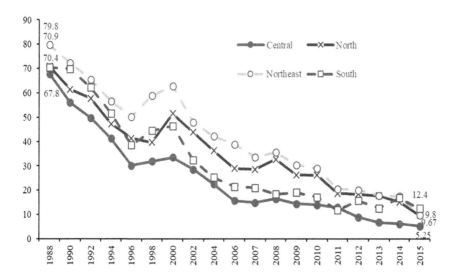

Figure 8.4 Head count ratio in rural area by region
Source: National Economic and Social Development Board.

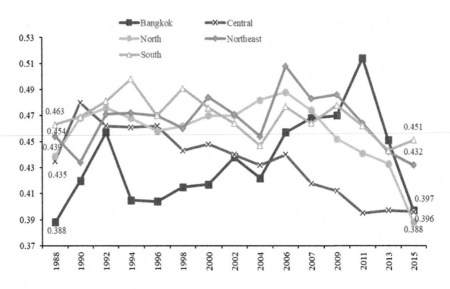

Figure 8.5 Gini index of Thailand by region
Source: National Economic and Social Development Board.

than those of the rural poor (Krongkaew, 1993; Warr, 2004). This data reflects that the pro-poor growth policy, which used to be more favorable to the urban people, has shifted to focus on both the urban poor and rural poor since the late 1980s. However, it should be noted that although the urban areas and rural areas have been the beneficiaries of the government's promoting policy, the disparity remains evident between regions.

According to Figure 8.5, income inequality in Thailand's regions has shown different patterns to some extent. In effect, this means that the government policies did not have a countrywide effect in terms of inequality reduction. For example, while the Gini index of Bangkok significantly increased from 1996 to 2011, the Gini index of the central region moved in the opposite direction with a gradual decline during the same period.

8.5.2 Impact on ASEAN

In the last several years, the ASEAN member countries have made efforts to promote economic integration. However, it turns out that the problem of inequality in some member countries is worsening. Figure 8.6 depicts the Gini index of the ASEAN member countries, excluding Singapore and Brunei Darussalam, due to lack of available data. On one hand, the Gini index of Thailand and the Philippines has an upward trend during 2000–2015. The Gini index of the Philippines, for instance, dropped from 0.43 in 2000 to 0.40 in 2015. On the other hand, Lao PDR and Malaysia had higher levels of Gini index. Comparing the data in 2000

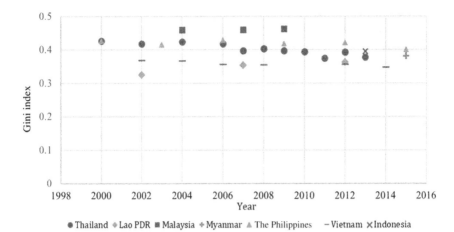

Figure 8.6 Gini index in selected countries

with 2012, the Gini index of Lao PDR increased from 0.33 to 0.36. Meanwhile, Malaysia's Gini index rose from 0.46 in 2004 to 0.47 in 2009. Nonetheless, the trend of the Gini index in Indonesia and Myanmar cannot be analyzed because of limited available data.

At this stage, various differences are seen among ASEAN member countries. Although their regional growth is relatively impressive, there are milestones to be achieved in order to form the economic community. Moreover, limited efforts are clearly seen in relation to ASEAN's regional development as a whole because the member countries are focusing on solving their own domestic problems. The industrial policies in most member countries specifically place emphasis on how to build local capabilities and what investment benefit should be provided in order to maximize the opportunity provided by the AEC. Little mention is made in the industrial policies about how countries should contribute to regional development, not only economically but also socially and politically.

8.6 Conclusion

For more than four decades, Thailand has followed industrial policies to strengthen its economic performance and level of competitiveness. At present, economic integration in the AEC is the new concern for both the government and the private sector. The government has introduced several projects, including the SEZ and EEC, as well as strategies to enhance local capabilities, particularly in technology and innovation. Also, the government encourages Thai investors to invest in neighboring countries, such as CLMV. Nonetheless, it cannot be denied that economic growth can create a wider disparity in the country, if the policies are not well managed. It should be kept in mind that not only does economic growth drive the poor to be richer but it also drives the rich to be richer too. This disparity is also evident in the regional aspect. It is a challenge for the government to create a good balance between economic integration and Thailand's regional development.

Notes

1 Head count ratio, sometimes known as poverty incidence, refers to the proportion of a population consuming below the poverty line.
2 The Gini index is a popular measure of the level of income inequality. The lower the level of Gini index, the lower level of income inequality. If Gini index equals 1, there is perfect inequality.

References

Amonvatana, C. (2015). New era of regional connectivity in ASEAN and the role of Japan. Paper presented at the conference in Nagoya, Japan, May 14.

Bank of Thailand. (2016). Yearly report on economic and monetary conditions. Bangkok: Bank of Thailand.

BOI (Board of Investment). (2017). BOI recommends Thai businesses to expand their investment in ASEAN (in Thai). Press release, no. 107.

BOI (Board of Investment). (n.d.) ASEAN agreement on investment (in Thai). Available at: www.boi.go.th/upload/การเปิดเสรีการลงทุนภายใต้%20ACIA%20%28revised%29_52346.pdf (accessed March 15, 2018).

Business Information Center. (2017). Investment in Brunei Darussalam. Available at: http://globthailand.com/brunei_0002 (accessed March 15, 2018).

Department of ASEAN Affairs. (2017). The development of ASEAN Economic Community (AEC). Available at: www.mfa.go.th/asean/contents/files/other-20170419-093427-318548.pdf (accessed April 20, 2018).

Department of Trade Negotiations. (2014). Information on investment in Singapore (in Thai). Available at: ww.thaifta.com/ThaiFTA/Portals/0/investment_sg2557.pdf (accessed March 15, 2018).

Economic Intelligence Center. (2016). Japan's "Thailand-plus-one" revisited: a business opportunity in the Mekong sub-region. *Bangkok Post*, April 4. Available at: www.scbeic.com/en/detail/product/2176 (accessed April 20, 2018).

Fiscal Policy Research Institute Foundation. (2016). Situation of foreign direct investment in ASEAN (in Thai). Available at: www.fpri.or.th/wp/?p=1481#.Wr5wB4hubIW (accessed March 15, 2018).

Jitsuchon, S. (2006). Sources of pro-poorness of Thailand's economic growth. *Thammasat Economic Journal*, 24(3), 68–107.

Krongkaew, M. (1993). Income distribution and poverty. In P. Warr (Ed.), *The Thai economy in transition*. Cambridge: Cambridge University Press.

Krongkaew, M., Chamnivickorn, S., & Nitithanprapas, I. (2006). Economic growth, employment, and poverty reduction linkages: The case of Thailand. Issues in Employment and Poverty Discussion Paper No. 20.

NESDB (National Economic and Social Development Board). (2015). Report on poverty and inequality in Thailand (in Thai). Bangkok.

Office of Industrial Economics. (2015). Quarterly report on industrial economy: Q4/ 2015 (October-December) (in Thai). Bangkok.

Office of Industrial Economics. (2016). Report on industrial economy in 2016 and trend in 2017 (in Thai). Bangkok.

Oizumi, K. & Soejima, K. (2015). Expanding regional supply chains in the ASEAN economic community: The potential for building science cities in Thailand. *Pacific Business and Industries*, 15, 2–23.

Poovanich, P. (2016). The development of Eastern Economic Corridor and the future of Thai construction business (in Thai). Available at: www.gsb.or.th/getattachment/ 8de08880-ff05-4c8a-afca-930df9d84f0c/Hot_Issue_EEC_final.aspx (accessed March 15, 2018).

Philippines' National Wage and Productivity Commission. (2010). *Minimum wage in ASEAN countries*. Manila:

Sethapramote, Y. (2014). The economic consequences of Thailand's political crisis. *The Nation*. March 28. Available at: www.nationmultimedia.com/business/The-economic-consequences-of-Thailands-political-c-30230268.html (accessed April 20, 2018).

Warr, P. (2004). Globalization, growth, and poverty reduction in Thailand. *ASEAN Economic Bulletin*, 2(1), 1–18.

9 Thailand's industrial policy

Its history and recent development

Nalitra Thaiprasert and Phanida Roidoung

9.1 Evidence of economic and industrial policies in Thailand

9.1.1 Historical background

Thailand's economic and industrial policies can be dated back to the times of Pridi Phanomyong (1900–1983) and Field Marshal Plaek Phibunsongkram (1879–1964) (hereafter referred to as Phibun). Pridi was the leader of the 1932 revolution, the founder of Thammasat University in 1934, and the seventh Prime Minister of Thailand (1946). Phibun was the third Prime Minister of Thailand (the country was called Siam before 1939) in 1938–1944 and 1948–1957. Through most of their time in power, Thailand was very unstable: facing the 1932 revolution, the abdication of King Rama the Seventh (1935), the Japanese Occupation during World War II (1941–1945), the declaration of war by Thailand on the Allies (1942), the anti-Japanese resistance of the *Seri Thai* movement (1942–1945), and the death of King Rama the Eighth (1946). The power struggles between Pridi's and Phibun's allies continued for almost two decades after the 1932 revolution.

In 1933, Pridi had proposed a radical economic plan which called for the nationalization of all land and labor. He proposed that the government should directly manage the agricultural and industrial sectors and create economic development plans, every citizen should become civil servants or government employees, and the government must provide welfare to all citizens (Bunnag, 1957). However, the plan was rejected not only by the royalists but also by his allies who did not believe in socialism. As a result, Pridi had to seek temporary exile for one year.

Phibun was a nationalist leader who issued the *Cultural Mandates* to encourage all Thais to use the Thai language and adopted Western attire and manners to become more civilized. As prime minister, he signed a military alliance with Japan in 1941 and declared war on Britain and the United States in 1942. In terms of economic policy, Phibun believed that investment should be done by the government. He imposed anti-Chinese immigrant policies by encouraging Thai citizens to refrain from doing business with Chinese immigrants to reduce their economic power. He used various measures to restrict the economic domination of the Thai market by those of Chinese descent. This created rent-seeking opportunities for the generals and the Thai elite groups to extract profits from Chinese businesses in exchange for their protection. Phibun also often called Chinese businesspeople Communists to deprive them of their livelihoods (Satitniramai, 2013, pp. 31–35). Phibun also limited other foreigners' involvement in Thailand's economy. He encouraged Thai citizens to become businesspeople. He set an example by setting up *Thai Niyom* (literally, favoring Thai) company as the headquarters to gather agricultural and home-based manufacturing products made by Thai citizens through its subsidiary *Provincial* companies. The *Thai Niyom* company also acted as the country's exporter, importer, and domestic distributor. Hence, it was a channel for Phibun's government to monopolize Thailand's economy and trade and promote the nationalist economy (Fineman, 1997, pp. 75–76; Petchprasert, 1981, p. 86; Ruamsilp, 1978, pp. 107–108).

However, in Phibun's second premiership after World War II, he changed his political strategy to favor the US as he feared the influence of Communist ideology and wanted military assistance from the Americans to support his internal political survival (Satitniramai, 2013, p. 25). As a result, the US transferred $10 million to his government in 1950, following its entry into the Korean War (Fineman, 1997, pp. 101–114). Furthermore, in the same year, the US, under the Griffin Mission, also gave another $11.4 million of economic assistance to Thailand with the agreement that Thailand must maintain the stability of its currency and exchange rate, and remove trade and investment barriers (Pattamanant, 1983, p. 32). However, Phibun did not comply with this economic agreement with the US as he realized that the Americans could not afford to cut ties with Thailand while fighting Communism in Asia (Satitniramai, 2013, p. 24). He encouraged the build-up of state-owned enterprises (SOEs), such as *Kao Thai* (literally, Thai Rice) company, Thai Industry Promotion company, a tobacco factory, a textile factory, an oil distilling factory, a water transportation company, and an alcoholic beverage distributor (Natsupha & Janevitkarn, 1981, p. 234; Skinner, 1958, pp. 186–188). In 1954, the US asked Phibun to sign the Guaranty of Private Investment Agreement which made the Thai government recognize the transfer to the US of any right, title, interest, or compensation for loss of any person whom the American government had guaranteed in assets, currency, credits, or other property (Buranapluke & Bunnag, 1978, p. 209). Following the signing of this Agreement, Phibun issued the Industrial Promotion Act, B.E. 2497 (1954) which clearly stated the promotion of private and foreign investments in Thailand. However, this Act was not exercised broadly as only one American company (Foremost Dairies) was promoted under the law (UN, ECAFE, 1956, p. 166, cited in Sudchai, 1986, p. 67). In addition, Phibun gave investment promotion to two SOEs out of six companies selected (from the total of 93 that applied) and set up the Economic Promotion of the Nation company in 1954, which had a reputation for rent-seeking by the elite Rajchakru sect (Siamwalla, 1976, p. 65). These events greatly disappointed the American government. Furthermore, Phibun issued the Establishment of Government Organizations Act, B.E. 2496 (1953), allowing the government to use the state budget to subsidize SOEs (Kanajanadul, 1976, p. 81). Hence, the amount of foreign investment in Thailand declined from around 2.5 billion baht in 1938 to only 600 million baht in 1954 (Collis, 1942, p. 10; Jacob, 1961, p. 237), while investment by Thai citizens increased by only 220 million baht between 1955 and 1958 (Ingram, 1971, pp. 316–317). Moreover, Phibun announced a list of occupations and businesses to be reserved by law for only Thai citizens (such as barbers) or those in which Thai citizens must have at least three-quarters of shareholder rights (such as a sawmill) (Skinner, 1958, pp. 186–188). In sum, during his time in office, Phibun was an avid supporter of the anti-Communist, anti-Chinese movements but at the same time was an anti-free market and anti-capitalist leader who sought American support for his own political gain.

It could be concluded that both Pridi's and Phibun's policies toward the Thai economy were pro-nationalist, but they had different contexts as Pridi was not against Chinese businesses. Both also did not believe in capitalism and the free market. However, Pridi devoted himself to promoting democracy for Thailand but Phibun was a tenacious dictator who tried to cling on to power.

In 1957, Field Marshal Sarit Dhanaraj (1908–1963) staged a coup d'état against Phibun. This was the turning point in Thailand's economic and industrial policies as well as the Thai-American relationship. Sarit was supported by the US after World War II to fight against Communism in Asia. This external factor played an important role in Sarit's move toward capitalism. Since the end of World War II and the rise of China's Communist influence in Asia in the 1950s, the US had set Thailand as its strategic point to contain Communism and as an important trade ally. The US had poured plenty of foreign aid into Thailand through the United States Agency for International Development (USAID) to build the infrastructure, especially the road network system to the northeast, and to promote capitalism in the country (Fineman, 1997). Sarit deepened his admiration for the United States when he met President Eisenhower and other important executive leaders in 1958. While in America, Sarit proposed three programs to the US government: (1) the Economic Assistance Program; (2) the Military Assistance Program; and (3) the Anti-Communism Program; all these programs provided large amounts of assistance funds to Thailand and made the US Thailand's main economic and military ally for two decades (Satitniramai, 2013, pp. 26–29). After returning to Thailand, Sarit came to be a great promoter of capitalism and private investment for the Americans (Pattamanant, 1983). In addition, the US provided other technical assistance to the Thai government, such as an agreement in 1956 between the Thai government and the Public Administration Service of Chicago to reform the public budget and financial system, which led to the establishment of the Public Budget Act, B.E. 2502 (1959) (Satitniramai, 2013, p. 51). The Thai government was also able to send its civil servants to study in the US on both short- and long-term programs with financial help from American agencies, such as the Fulbright and Rockefeller scholarships. As of 1986, almost 40 percent of the high-ranking civil servants had received their education at American universities (Satitniramai, 2013, pp. 68–69).

Two other external factors influenced Sarit's move toward pro-capitalism. The first was the influence of the World Bank's policy on the economy. The second factor was the emergence of Chinese Communism that affected the geopolitics of Asia. In the case of the World Bank, the organization was the representative of the capitalist world which was backed by the US to promote the free market, capital investment, trade liberalization, and a pro-capitalism development paradigm to developing countries around the world. The World Bank's involvement with Thailand's economy started with the Phibun government. When the World Bank came to Thailand to give loans for infrastructure projects, it realized the dominance of Thai government over many industries in the country. Hence, when Sarit became the new leader, the World Bank hastily sent its staff to conduct an economic survey of Thailand during 1957–1958 and later published its report called "Public Development Program for Thailand," which criticized Phibun's nationalist economic development plan and proposed Thailand should set up new government agencies and a budget system to oversee the country's economic development. The World Bank's report also encouraged Sarit's government to open up the country to foreign investors, establish the National Economic Development Board (NEDB) to take over the country's development plans and create the Board of Investment (BOI) to promote private and foreign investments in Thailand (Dilokvitayarat, 1983, p. 88). Also, the World Bank proposed restructuring the Ministry of Industry (MOI) to assist the investment promotion policy, reform the national economic agencies, and create other new economic agencies. The influence of the World Bank was evident in the drafting of the National Economic Development Board Act, B.E. 2502 (1959), the Industrial Finance Corporation of Thailand Act, B.E. 2502 (1959), the Investment Promotion for Industry Act, B.E. 2505 (1962), which was the bedrock of the BOI, and the National Statistical Office (1963) (Attakorn, 1964; Dilokvitayarat, 1983, pp. 88–89).

Regarding the role of China, the spread of Communist ideology became the accelerator to Sarit's actions toward capitalism and pro-America as Sarit himself greatly despised Communism, claiming that it was a threat to the nation, to religion, and to the king.

Sarit's motivation to promote private investment and capitalism also has its roots in the internal power struggle between the two major elite groups in the country: the Rajchakru sect and the SisaoThewes sect. During Phibun's premiership, the Rajchakru sect had won control over 104 SOEs under various ministries, mostly in the MOI and Ministry of Agriculture, while the SisaoThewes sect, which was led by Sarit, controlled only six SOEs under the Ministry of Defense (Pattamanant, 1983, p. 37). Hence, by privatizing SOEs, Sarit could gradually reduce the power of the Rajchakru sect and build his economic power over privatized firms (Satitniramai, 2013, pp. 62–63; Sudchai, 1986, p. 90).

9.2 Sarit's government's interventions in the context of industrial policy

The foundation of Thailand's industrial policy was Sarit Dhanaraj's capitalist policy, although the implementation of the policy experienced a long lag, resistance to change, conflict of interests, rent-seeking, and corruption (Pattamanant, 1983;

Satitniramai, 2013). During his premiership, Sarit was able to issue numerous laws and regulations and set up several governmental and semi-governmental agencies to support his capitalist policy, as he had created the centralization of power to himself (absolutism) and entrusted technocrats to maintain the stability of the macroeconomic policies. He institutionalized the position of prime minister by making 15 important government agencies and departments report directly to the Office of the Prime Minister (OPM) in 1959 (Satitniramai, 2013, pp. 64–67). Sarit also promoted infrastructure development and maintained internal security to support the development of capitalism and the free market economy in Thailand. Section 9.2 explains these direct and indirect interventions of Sarit's capitalist policy.

9.2.1 Direct intervention through laws and regulations

The Coup d'état Proclamation number 33, B.E. 2501 (1958) by Sarit clearly stated the goals and broad policies regarding the promotion of domestic investment, that the government would not build new manufacturing factories to compete with those of the private sector or transfer them to control of the government. The private owners of industries being promoted would receive:

- An import tariff reduction for their imports of machinery, equipment, and important raw materials;
- Income tax exemption from selling their products for at least 2 years, but not to exceed 5 years;
- Export tariff exemption for their products needed to export;
- Protection from competition from imports and investment of similar products which are produced domestically;
- No increase in taxes.

Also, they could send foreign exchange linked to the capital investment or profit out of the country, bring skilled workers into the country, and receive an attenuation of the immigration law.

Following this, in the Coup d'état Proclamation number 43, B.E. 2502 (1959), Sarit added the list of industries qualified to receive this promotion, such as the manufacturers of consumer goods and the manufacturers of construction materials. Additionally, in the Coup d'état Proclamation number 47, B.E. 2502 (1959), Sarit gave foreign investors under the forms of limited company or registered company the right to own industrial land of a suitable amount, but soon after he revised the statement from "suitable amount" to "unlimited" in the Coup d'état Proclamation number 49, B.E. 2502 (1959) (Sudchai, 1986, pp. 107–112).

Before long, the government issued the Investment Promotion for Industry Act, B.E. 2503 (1960) and B.E. 2505 (1962). The former listed 123 types of industries, ranging from steel mills to hotel sectors, which qualified for industrial promotion. The latter had similar contents as the Coup d'état Proclamation number 33, B.E. 2501 (1958), with some minor changes, that the government will exempt Thai and foreign investors from the following taxes:

- Import tariff for all kinds of machines and equipment;
- Commercial tax for all kinds of machines and equipment imported;
- Export tariff for exported products;
- Income tax for five years (changed from 2–5 years);
- Import tariff for raw materials for five years according to types of industries (100 percent exemption for industries necessary for economic development, 50 percent exemption for industries important but less necessary for economic development, and 25 percent exemption for other industries).

Also, the Thai and foreign investors could send foreign exchange out of Thailand more freely under the B.E. 2505 Act. Furthermore, the government issued the Reduction or Exemption of Import Tariff for Promoted Industries Act, B.E. 2503 (1960) and B.E. 2504 (1961) to confirm the statement in the Coup d'état Proclamation number 33, B.E. 2501 (1958) regarding the industrial promotion issue (Sudchai, 1986, pp. 112–121). Hence, these interventions had given the means to Thai and foreign investors alike to invest in Thailand much more freely.

9.2.2 Direct intervention through the creation of governmental and semi-governmental agencies for economic development and support to technocrats

In 1959, several governmental and semi-governmental agencies were created by Sarit to support his advocacy of capitalism and the free market. Important examples of these agencies are the National Economic Development Board (NEDB), the Board of Investment (BOI), the Fiscal Policy Office (FPO), the Bureau of the Budget (BB), and the Industrial Finance Corporation of Thailand (IFCT),

The NEDB (later the name changed to the National Economic and Social Development Board: NESDB, in 1972) was founded under the National Economic Development Board Act, B.E. 2502 (1959) to make long-term economic and social development plans and adjust those plans accordingly with help from various ministries and departments. It also had the responsibility of evaluating economic development projects for governmental agencies and deciding on investment budgets for the SOEs. The NEDB was under the OPM, making it one of the most significant government agencies in Thailand. The law set the prime minister as the chairman of the NEDB and the deputy prime minister as the vice-chairman. The board members were appointed by the Cabinet and the executives of the NEDB were led by a secretary-general and had a three-year term of office. The NEDB issued Thailand's first economic development plan (1961–1966) with the following aims:

- To increase the national income per capita;
- To increase capital accumulation;

- To add value to major agricultural products and major manufacturing and mining products;
- To increase electricity production;
- To build more highways and improve existing roads;
- To improve logistics, transportation, healthcare, and the education system;
- To increase export and import values and maintain the balance of payments;
- To create a friendly atmosphere for macroeconomic stability;
- To increase the government budget for economic development;
- To allocate the government budget from foreign borrowing and foreign aid.

Thus, the NEDB was involved in every macroeconomic issue as it was the main policymaking and assessing agency.

The BOI was created in 1959 before the Investment Promotion for Industry Act, B.E. 2503 (1960) and B.E. 2505 (1962) were issued to support it. The BOI was also set up under the OPM. Although Phibun did try several measures to promote the country's industries, such as setting up the MOI in 1954, and issued the Industrial Promotion Act, B.E. 2497 (1954), the result was far from impressive as there were only 11 factories selected for promotion, with four of them SOEs (Boonyaked, 1964, p. 133). Sarit selected 27 experts from various fields, ranging from military officers, academics, and politicians to run the BOI and appointed the ministers of finance, foreign affairs, agriculture, economics, and industry as the consultation board. Like Sarit's other interventions, the BOI's duty was to assist only private investors, not the government agencies or the SOEs. The establishment of the BOI led to a significant increase in privately-owned companies as 217 new factories were promoted from 1959 to 1963, with a total registered capital of 1.75 billion baht and a total investment of 5.22 billion baht, and the employment of around 28,000 workers (Boonyaked, 1964, p. 137). The industries which received the BOI promotion ranged from cement, sugar refinery, chemical fertilizer, hotels, cooking flours, steel mills, automobiles, monosodium glutamate, factories for hemp sack, textiles, and cotton yarn (Attakorn, 1964, p. 84).

The FPO is a department under the Ministry of Finance, which was founded in 1961, following the dissolution of the Division of Fiscal Policy and the Division of Statistics. It had to adopt modern expertise in public finance and the formulation of fiscal policy. The history of the BB could be dated back to the reign of King Rama V. However, the modern BB was founded in 1959 to be under the OPM through the technical advice from the US for Thailand to have modern budget practices. Interestingly, Puey Ungphakorn, who was a highly respected technocrat, was appointed the first Director-General of the BB in 1959 and the FPO in 1961 at the same time while he was the Governor of the Bank of Thailand (BOT). Hence, during that time Thailand's monetary policy, fiscal policy, and budget policy were tightly connected.

The IFCT was founded in 1959 under the Industrial Finance Corporation of Thailand Act, B.E. 2502 (1959) to give financial support to Thai investors both in Thailand and abroad. The IFCT was created to assist during the setting-up, expansion, development, and operation of private companies. Although the IFCT was not a governmental agency, the Thai government did guarantee corporate loans from both domestic and foreign sources. Besides, several Thai commercial banks were the major shareholders of the IFCT with the support of the BOT. It also received support from the World Bank through the International Monetary Fund (IMF) as the latter bought around 13 percent of the IFCT shares. The IMF's support of the IFCT was a channel for the World Bank, under the guidance of the US, to promote capitalism in developing countries (Sudchai, 1986, p. 134; Supinit, 1970, p. 134). Sarit's government went so far to give interest-free loans to several private companies, mostly the ones being promoted under the BOI, and, in 1962, his government approved another 20 million baht loan with a very low interest rate and long-term repayment condition to those companies. With Sarit's full support, the IFCT received a total of $2.5 million (around 50 million baht) loan from the World Bank, and gained a good reputation from American commercial banks that resulted in them receiving substantial investment capital, and they took in another 11 million Deutschmark (around 55 million baht) from a German credit institution (Hongladdarom, 1964, p. 126). From 1959 to 1968, the IFCT allocated a total of 345 million baht to 95 private companies in various sectors (IFCT, 1967, p. 1093). As a result, private investors in Thailand were very satisfied with Sarit's capitalist policy and his management of the country. Unfortunately, the IFCT discontinued its previous mission and was merged with the Thai Military Bank (TMB) and the Thai Danu Bank in 2004. Unlike the IFCT, the TMB did not provide any specific loans to the promoted businesses (TMB Bank, 2017).

Thailand was able to maintain macroeconomic stability for a long time (until the East Asian Financial Crisis in 1997) because of the competency and credibility of the technocrats in the macro agencies mentioned above, under the leadership of the BOT. Sarit entrusted technocrats from these agencies to oversee the country's macroeconomic policies and protected them from the abuses of bureaucrats (Satitniramai, 2013, p. 98). The goals of these technocrats were to create sound monetary policy, fiscal policy, and economic development to provide macroeconomic stability (Satitniramai, 2013, pp. 69–73). The main actor among these competent technocrats was Puey Ungphakorn, as he was entrusted with many roles in those macro agencies. Also, Sarit had appointed several economic advisors and scholars who believed in *laissez-faire* to manage Thailand's economy. These technocrats played an important role in the drafting of Thailand's first Economic Development Plan (1961–1966) which advocated capitalism and a free market in the country (Sudchai, 1986, pp. 93–100).

The BOT played an important role in stabilizing the Thai baht. In 1955, it decided to eliminate the dual (or multiple) exchange rate system by keeping the free market exchange rate and dropping the government-controlled exchange rate used during Phibun's government to reduce arbitrage, speculation, and rent-seeking. It also created the foreign-exchange reserve system to help maintain the value of Thai baht (Satitniramai, 2013, p. 43). As a result, the Thai baht moved in a very narrow band of 20.40 to 20.80 baht per one US dollar in 1963, the year Thailand accepted the IMF's rule of the plus or minus 1 percent of parity by intervening in its foreign exchange market (Hongladdarom, 1964, p. 128; Satitniramai, 2013, p. 72). This policy received praise from foreign investors whose exchange rate risk was greatly reduced. Also, the BOT regularly bought or issued promissory notes at a small discount from exporters and firms which needed credit to buy raw materials. The promissory notes issued by the BOT could be used as collateral for loans from commercial banks at a 7 percent interest rate. This policy greatly helped investors to access credit and smooth their operations (Sudchai, 1986, p. 155). With all these sound management policies, since 1947, Thailand did not face any severe inflation problems until the first oil shock in 1973 (Satitniramai, 2013, pp. 36, 72–73). Furthermore, the BOT had tried to maintain the stability of the commercial banking sector in Thailand, such as setting the proper reserve ratio, the loan risk diversification ratio, and the asset liquidity ratio, as it realized that this sector was the source of capital investment in the country. The BOT fought hard to establish the Commercial Bank Act, B.E. 2505 (1962) which led Thailand's commercial banks to become the bedrock of the country's funding for economic investment until the East Asian Financial Crisis in 1997 (Satitniramai, 2013, pp. 80–92).

9.2.3 Indirect intervention through infrastructure development

In addition to direct intervention, Sarit had improved Thailand's infrastructure substantially with financial support from the US government and the World Bank. The infrastructures being improved by Sarit were:

1   *Hydroelectric power generation.* In every region, numerous dams and reservoirs were built in the 1960s. This new source of electricity could greatly support the rise of industrialization around Bangkok and later in other major regional hubs. Additionally, a by-product from building hydroelectric power sources was access to the irrigation system by some fortunate Thai farmers (Petchprasert, 1981, p. 98).
2   *The road and rail systems.* With funding support from the American government to fight Communism to the east of Thailand, the national highway networks branching in all directions had increased to a total of 9,115 kilometers during Sarit's premiership (Veerawan, 1964, p. 110). With the modernization of the road networks, firms could easily access raw materials and their customers, which helped to spur industrialization. Additionally, Sarit also increased the rail network by 112 kilometers through funding from the World Bank (Attakorn, 1964, p. 81; Ketboonchu, 1974, p. 47), though the railway development was not as efficient as the road network development.
3   *The telephone system.* Vast telephone networks were set up in Bangkok and the regional provinces as the numbers of landlines increased from 38,238 in 1959 to 54,350 in 1963, a 42.1 percent increase (Sudchai, 1986, p. 150).

The improvement in the telephone network helped businesses reduce communication time and substantially increase their productivity.

4 *The survey of mineral resources.* As industrialization had progressed, more mineral resources were demanded by more firms. Sarit's government supported the surveys of both metallic and nonmetallic minerals and set up mineral development centers to give technical support to miners (Attakorn, 1964, pp. 96–97).

9.2.4 Indirect intervention through internal security improvement and political stability

Sarit Thanaraj was best known for his dictatorial style in managing Thailand's politics and internal security. During his premiership, the existing labor unions in Thailand were dissolved and new ones were completely banned. Sarit viewed labor unions as a source of disruption between workers and their employers which hindered investment and industrialization and he thought unions could be used as a channel to promote Communism in Thailand. In 1958, he then repealed the Labor Act, B.E. 2499 (1956) previously set up by Phibun (Ramkomut, 1977, p. 23).

Also, Sarit ordered through the Coup d'état Proclamation number 17, B.E. 2501 (1958) the shut-down of numerous newspapers and arrested their editors who criticized him and his government by claiming there were threats of Communism in the country (Noibuatip, 1974; Sudchai, 1986, pp. 163–171). He also dissolved parliament through the Coup d'état Proclamation number 3, B.E. 2501 (1958) and dissolved 31 political parties through the Coup d'état Proclamation number 8, B.E. 2501 (1958) (Sudchai, 1986, pp. 172–181).

Furthermore, he regularly ordered the deployment of military personnel or civil servants to survey the rural villages under the so-called "community development" projects to improve the living conditions of the rural population and maintain internal security at the same time (Sudchai, 1986, pp. 181–201). Hence, it is no exaggeration to conclude that Thailand's industrialization and stability were created at the expense of its development of human rights and civil liberty, the improvement of the quality of life of Thai workers, and the progress of its democratic system.

9.3 The role of ethnic Chinese capital and commercial banks

Unlike Phibun, Sarit welcomed the role of Chinese entrepreneurs in the Thai economy. It is undeniable that ethnic Chinese business networks have played an important role in much of Thailand's economic dynamism. One area of their dominance is in the commercial banking sector as a result of the change in the regulations. With the promulgation of the Commercial Banking Act, B.E. 2505 (1962), the government began prudential regulation of banks. But government intervention in the banking sector quickly moved beyond prudential regulation as the government then banned new bank entry, severely limited foreign bank expansion, and undermined the operations of informal credit markets (Hewison 1989, p. 283). The major consequences of these policies were the rapid growth in bank deposits, the equally rapid development of a small number of family-owned commercial banks, a decline in the importance of foreign-controlled banks and significant concentration in the banking industry. Taken together, these outcomes virtually guaranteed easy availability of credit to a small number of Thai entrepreneurs (Rock, 2001, p. 269).

Before the liberalization of the financial market in the 1990s, businesses in Thailand could rely only on commercial banks as sources of capital investment. Financial support from the government, such as the IFCT, was limited. Hence, commercial banks played an important role in allocating capital funds and deciding which sectors should be promoted at a specific point in time (Siamwalla, 2001, pp. 3–4). For example, during the early 1970s, the Saha Union Group set up 10 firms producing yarn and sewing thread. At the request of the Bangkok Bank, the group also took over the country's largest spinning and weaving operation: Thai Durable Textile. By the mid-1980s, the Saha Union's Textile Company was the second largest spinning operation in the country (Rock, 2001, p. 270). Furthermore, when their Japanese joint venture partners refused to remove restrictions on Saha Union's entry into the textile export markets in the late 1970s, the company used its personal ties to the Bangkok Bank to gain access to a soft loan to buy out its Japanese partners (Rock, 2001, p. 271).

In conclusion, Thailand's commercial banking sector was the only private sector which had tremendous power to protect its self-interest and counterbalance the power of technocrats and it was highly protected by the elites in power (Satitniramai, 2013, pp. 98–99, 166–167). However, it is important to note that the role of Thai commercial banks was still quite limited as they were not assigned by the government a direct role to oversee businesses, as was the case of the major banks in Japan.

9.4 Subsequent industrial policies and the role of Japan

9.4.1 Government interventions during import-substitution industrialization in the 1960s–1970s

Although pro-capitalism and the open economy were policies encouraged by Sarit Thanarat in the late 1950s to the early 1960s, Thailand had also adopted import-substitution industrialization (ISI) in the late 1960s to the 1970s. Between 1974 and 1978, tariffs were raised on 53 industrial categories and reduced on only 19 categories. Average rates of nominal protection of import-substituting activities increased from 24.8 percent to up to 50.8 percent (World Bank, 1980, p. ii).

The World Bank (1980) had argued in its 1980 report on "industrial development strategy in Thailand" that the BOI's promotions to reduce import duties and business taxes on inputs of promoted firms, the increases in the scope of the import control law, and the imposition of local content requirements (LCR) on several products, including automobiles and motorcycles, all had further raised the protection of import-substituting activities. It further contended that BOI's import protection had not been compensated for by export incentives as duty, and tax exemptions only partially relieved the burden of customs duties and indirect taxes on export production. Export credits were limited in scope and the subsidy did not attain 1 percent of the value of manufactured exports. Also, promoted firms encountered considerable difficulties in administration and the growth of the exports of several products was restricted by the application of export control (World Bank, 1980, pp. ii–iii).

For example, in the case of the automobile industry, the Thai government used LCR to protect its local market and at the same time promoted inward foreign direct investment into vehicle and auto parts production (Natsuda & Thoburn, 2013, p. 413). The LCR was implemented from 1975 and progressively raised, particularly on pick-up trucks, up to the early 1990s, as part of an industry-specific policy to localize production. Also, a ban on passenger car imports was imposed from 1978 to 1991 (Natsuda & Thoburn, 2013, p. 421).

The main reason that Thailand used the ISI policy was due to the deteriorating trade deficit, especially after the mid-1960s with annual increases averaging 10.2 percent between 1960 and 1973 and these amounted to 5 percent of GDP in 1973. Also, the quadrupling of oil prices between 1973 and 1978 and the doubling of oil prices between 1978 and 1980 made Thailand experience a current account deficit of around 9–10 percent of GDP in 1980 (World Bank, 1980, p. i). Furthermore, due to the end of the Vietnam War in 1975, Thailand's balance of payments was adversely affected by the decline in earnings from foreign exchange and transfers from the US (World Bank, 1980, p. i). At the same time, the growth of Thai exports had slowed down due to the near exhaustion of uncultivated land which constrained further expansion of agricultural exports, the quota limits on textile and clothing exports under the International Multi-Fiber Agreement, the surge of domestic inflation rates, and the depreciation of the Japanese yen (World Bank, 1980, p. ii).

The World Bank (1980) claims that the cost of Thailand's ISI policy to reduce the trade deficit was higher than its earnings from export activities and government revenues. The reasons are because the ISI policy tended to promote capital-intensive industries which limited employment creation, it tended to favor large-scale industries over small- and medium-sized enterprises (SMEs) as well as favoring firms in Bangkok over those in the outlying regions. Furthermore, there was a lack of economies of scale in producing for the small domestic market, domestic production costs were higher than the cost of comparable imports, and credit rationing was applied by Thai commercial banks which discriminated against SMEs and regional firms. In sum, by favoring high-cost import substitution and capital-intensive activities, these measures impeded efficient industrial growth, export expansion, industrial employment enlargement, the growth of small- and medium-scale industry and primary activities, and regional industrial development at this time (World Bank, 1980, p. iii).

On the other hand, the neo-statists, such as Rock (2001), claim that Thailand's ISI was highly effective and long-standing, especially in agricultural markets, such as the stabilization of rice prices at a low level through a variable export tax which had contributed to the emergence of a large export-oriented agro-processing industry once the government began offering promotional privileges to them. Rock maintains that there are equally important examples of successful selective interventions during first-stage ISI in the 1960s as well as in second-stage ISI in the 1970s, and the promotion of non-traditional manufacturing exports and non-traditional agro-industry exports during the 1980s (Rock, 2001, pp. 268–269). He also argues that systematic government policy bias favoring large firms and a few entrepreneurs is also evident in industrial policy. Between 1959 and 1980, government requirements for promotional privileges, such as BOI business tax exemptions on imported capital goods and raw materials, tariff protection on local production and tax holidays and IFCT's subsidized credit all favored large firms (Rock, 2001, p. 269). He claims that these large infant industries did graduate into export production industries, such as the Sukree Group and the Saha Union Group in the textile industry, the CP Group in agro-industry and diesel engines for agricultural machinery sector (Rock, 2001, pp. 270, 271, 272).

9.4.2 Government intervention during export-oriented industrialization since the mid-1980s and the role of Japan

Since the mid-1980s, Thailand has been extensively involved in East Asia's industrial production and development due to the change in Japan's manufacturing production strategy as a result of the Plaza Accord in 1985. The Accord was an agreement between Japan, the US, France, the United Kingdom, and West Germany to lower the US trade deficit by making the Japanese yen and German Deutschmark appreciate against the US dollar. The agreement led to a rapid appreciation of the yen and the currencies of the four Newly Industrializing Economies (NIEs: South Korea, Taiwan, Hong Kong, and Singapore), which had close manufacturing supply chains with Japanese manufacturing firms. These appreciations resulted in the lower competitiveness of exports from these economies and the restructuring of manufacturing industrial production and investment in Japan and the NIEs. As a result, Thailand, Malaysia, and Indonesia became more attractive to investors from Japan and the NIEs (Figure 9.1), resulting in a boom in manufacturing industrial production in Southeast Asia (Chukiatkhajorn & Thaiprasert, 2014; Jomo, 2001, p. 11). This pattern of structural change in East Asia was predicted by Akamatsu's Flying Geese model and further elaborated by Kojima (2000). Hence, Thailand turned away from its ISI policy to the promotion of export-oriented industrialization (EOI) policy.

In addition to the restructuring of manufacturing industrial production in Asia, the use of ISI policy was limited following the Uruguay Round trade negotiations (1986–1994) under the World Trade Organization (WTO) as member

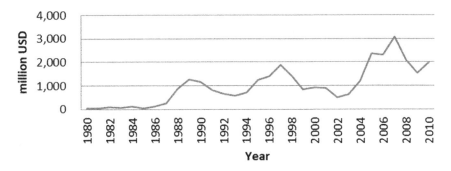

Figure 9.1 Foreign direct investment from Japan to Thailand
Source: JETRO.

Table 9.1 Foreign direct investment to Thailand, 1983–1991 (million baht)

Year/country	1983	1984	1985	1986	1987	1988	1989	1990	1991
Japan	2,431	2,588	1,531	3,049	3,268	14,607	18,761	27,930	15,593
USA	1,265	3,730	2,368	1,293	1,815	3,184	5,220	6,154	5,918
Europe	2,124	469	475	593	986	2,294	4,080	4,410	4,214
Singapore	555	1,120	1,125	403	535	1,572	2,688	6,135	6,468
Hong Kong	870	334	647	955	796	2,794	5,715	7,027	11,565
South Korea	20	4	4	4	22	304	254	487	295

Source: Bank of Thailand.

countries were not able to use government intervention and protectionist policies to drive their industrialization as they had previously done. The most comprehensive plan of tariff restructuring was proposed in 1990 and implemented in 1995 and 1997. This involved tariff reduction and rationalization, wherein maximum tariffs were reduced from 100 percent to 30 percent (Jongwanich & Kohpaiboon, 2008, p. 6). Also, the Thai government abolished its LCR in many manufacturing industries in 2000 (Natsuda & Thoburn, 2013, p. 413).

As mentioned before, Thailand had been providing investment incentives through the BOI since the early 1960s. Besides the BOI industrial promotions, the government used other measures to support the EOI policy, such as the tariff exemption/drawback (Section 19 of the Customs Laws) administered by the Department of Customs, and the tax rebate scheme of the Fiscal Policy Office. In response to the policy environment in Thailand, FDI inflows have increased noticeably since the late 1980s (Table 9.1). The dollar value of Foreign Direct Investment (FDI) net inflows increased from annual averages of $0.3 billion during the period 1981–1985 to $1.4 billion and $1.8 billion during the period 1987–1990 and 1991–1995, respectively (Jongwanich & Kohpaiboon, 2008, p. 6).

Table 9.2 Thailand's export index, 1985–1996

Year	1985	1989	1990	1992	1993	1994	1995	1996
Export Index	10.13	29.08	33.4	47.02	53.53	65.54	81.84	80.8

Source: World Bank

However, it is important to note that Thailand's industrial policy was far from creating national champion firms. According to interviews with high-ranking officials from the MOI and the BOI, it was mentioned that it would be unwise to create national champion firms since they require extensive government support and protection, and the pressure to upgrade technology constantly to compete globally is very intense. Furthermore, the size of the Thai market was too small to achieve the economies of scale. It is wiser to attract FDI of world-renowned firms that can bring in the latest state-of-the-art technology to the country and create the first- and second-tier backward-linkage Thai firms (C. Kaewsaeng, pers. comm., July 20, 2017; S. Harnhiran, pers. comm., August 3, 2017). As Natsuda and Thoburn (2013) put it, the Thai government has focused more on selecting national "product champions," as in the case of automobile industry, the government helped the automobile product champions, i.e., pick-up trucks, by setting lower excise tax rates to create market demand for them (2013, p. 414).

The EOI policy changed the structure of Thailand's exports from primary commodity-based to manufacturing-based exports as the share of manufacturing exports to total exports increased from about 30 percent in the early 1980s to around 75 percent in 1996. Since the early 1990s, machinery, electronics and electrical appliances, transportation equipment, and completely built vehicles have become the important export items (Jongwanich & Kohpaiboon, 2008, p. 3). The policy contributed to a remarkable economic performance in Thailand. Between 1981 and 1996, the average annual growth of real GDP was 7.9 percent and exports grew at an annual rate of 21 percent (Table 9.2). The level of GDP per capita in 1996 was more than six times that in 1960 and the share of exports to GDP increased from 23 percent in the early 1980s to 48 percent in 1996 (Jongwanich & Kohpaiboon, 2008, p. 3).

Thailand continued to adopt the EOI policy even after the 1997 East Asian financial and economic crises. However, from the period of 2006 to 2019, the unstable political system, coupled with Thailand's inability to upgrade its technology and the skills of its workforce, and the depletion of its cheap labor and natural resources have led Thailand to fall into the so-called "middle-income trap." Without proper adjustments, Thailand will continue to face low growth rate and income as a result of its decline in competitiveness, domestic investment, and FDI inflows.

Table 9.3 Chronological events contributing to the development of Thailand's economic and industrial policies

Period	Event
1933 Pridi Phanomyong	A proposal to nationalize all land and labor (rejected)
1938 Plaek Phibunsongkram	Setting up Thai Niyom (lit. favoring Thai) company to promote economic nationalism and limit Chinese immigrants' and foreigners' involvement in Thailand's economy
1950 Plaek Phibunsongkram	Thailand received economic assistance from the U.S. with the agreement that Thailand must maintain the stability of its currency and exchange rate, and remove trade and investment barriers (not fully complied)
1953 Plaek Phibunsongkram	Establishment of Government Organizations (State-Owned Enterprise) Act B.E. 2496, allowing the government to use a public budget to subsidize SOEs
1954 Plaek Phibunsongkram	Industrial Promotion Act, B.E. 2497 to promote private and foreign investments in Thailand (not broadly exercised)
1955 Plaek Phibunsongkram	Bank of Thailand (BOT) eliminated the dual (or multiple) exchange rate system and created the foreign-exchange reserve system.
1957–1963 Sarit Dhanaraj	American influence (through the World Bank) due to the containment of communism in Asia, a turning point of Thailand's economic and industrial policies to move toward capitalism (free market, capital investment, trade liberalization, private investment, major infrastructure development, and technical assistance)
	Technocrats were entrusted to create soundness in monetary policy, fiscal policy, and economic development to provide macroeconomic stability.
1958 Sarit Dhanaraj	Coup d'état Proclamation number 33, B.E. 2501 (1958), to promote domestic investment
1959 Sarit Dhanaraj	Coup d'état Proclamation number 43, B.E. 2502 (1959), to add a list of industries qualified for the promotion
	Coup d'état Proclamation number 47, B.E. 2502 (1959), foreign investors under the forms of a limited company or registered company earned rights to own industrial land in a suitable amount
	Coup d'état Proclamation number 49, B.E. 2502 (1959), to change foreign land ownership from "suitable amount" to "unlimited"
	Public Budget Act, B.E. 2502 (1959)
	National Economic Development Board Act, B.E. 2502 (1959)
	Industrial Finance Corporation of Thailand Act, B.E. 2502 (1959)
	Sarit institutionalized the prime-ministership by making 15 important government agencies and departments report directly to the Office of the Prime Minister (OPM), such as:

(*continued*)

Table 9.3 Cont.

Period	Event
	• Board of Investment (BOI) was created to promote privately-owned companies • Bureau of the Budget (BB) was created to have modern budget practices • Industrial Finance Corporation of Thailand (IFCT) was created under the Industrial Finance Corporation of Thailand Act, B.E. 2502 (1959) to give financial support to Thai investors both in Thailand and abroad
1960–1962 Sarit Dhanaraj	Investment Promotion for Industry Act, B.E. 2503 (1960) and B.E. 2505 (1962), to support the establishment of BOI, give tax and tariff exemption to Thai and foreign investors for specified categories, allow foreign exchange outflow, list out 123 types of industries qualified for the industrial promotion Reduction or Exemption of Import Tariff for Promoted Industries Act, B.E. 2503 (1960) and B.E. 2504 (1961), to support the industrial promotion The Fiscal Policy Office (FPO) under the Ministry of Finance was created in 1961 to adopt modern expertise in public finance and formulation of fiscal policy The first Economic Development Plan (1961–1966) was drafted to advocate capitalism and free market Commercial Bank Act, B.E. 2505 (1962), to promote Thailand's commercial banks to become the funding source for economic investment
The late 1960s to 1970s Ten Prime Ministers	Adoption of Import-Substitution Industrialization (ISI) policy to raise the protection of import-substituting activities. Capital intensive large-scale industries, non-traditional manufacturing exports, and non-traditional agro-industry exports had benefited from ISI at the expense of SMEs and regional firms
The mid-1980s to 1997 Eight Prime Ministers	The Japanese influence on the restructuring of manufacturing industrial production in Asia and the adoption of export-oriented industrialization (EOI) policy The EOI policy changed the structure of Thailand's exports from primary commodity-based to manufacturing-based exports and FDI inflows have increased noticeably since the late 1980s Thailand faced the East Asian financial and economic crises in 1997
1997–present (2019) Eight Prime Ministers	Adoption of EOI continues

9.5 Recent national socio-economic plans and their connections to industrial promotion policies

The Thai governments from the past to the present have identified several policies to support economic and industrial development. For instance, Prime Minister Thaksin Shinawatra placed science, technology, and innovation forcefully on the policy agenda. His Science and Technology (S&T) Strategic Plan (2004–2013) identified four national priority core technologies: information and communi-cation technology (ICT), biotechnology, materials technology, and nanotech-nology, and pointed to five major strategies: the cluster development linked to strengthening the National Innovation System (NIS), the development of S&T human resources, the development of S&T infrastructure, the enhancement of public S&T awareness, and improvements to the S&T management system (Lauridsen, 2009, p. 414). Also, the Harvard economist, Michael Porter and his associates were hired by Thaksin's government to identify established and emerging clusters (automotive, fashion, food, tourism, and software) to be the so-called targeted industries for Thailand (Lauridsen, 2009, p. 415).

Other examples of the economic and industrial development policies from other Thai governments are Prime Minister Chuan Leekpai's proposal in 1997 to increase the potential of Special Economic Zones and industrial competitiveness, Prime Minister Abhisit Vejjajiva's proposal in 2008 to increase industrial product-ivity, Prime Minister Yingluck Shinawattra's proposal in 2013 of the two trillion baht infrastructure (logistics and transportation) development project (Thailand Future Foundation, 2013). These policies were not unique but were proposed by different sets of executive power as new bodies of government often want to take the credit for their policy initiatives (Table 9.3). Since industrial promotion policies from the past to the present largely overlapped, this section will discuss only the most recent policy initiatives under the government of Prime Minister Prayuth Chan-ocha.

9.5.1 *Government initiatives*

The present Thai government has created a 20-year national strategy, 2017–2036, to use as the country's development guidelines and plan for the country's sustainable social and economic development. The National Economic and Social Development Plan has required every ministry to set up, follow, and correspond to the 20-year national strategies.

The 20-year national strategic plan consists of six areas, six primary strategies, and four supporting strategies. The six areas are: (1) security; (2) competitiveness enhancement; (3) human resource development; (4) social equality; (5) green growth; and (6) rebalancing public sector development. The six primary strat-egies seek to enhance and develop the potential of human capital; to ensure justice and reduce social disparities; to strengthen the economy and enhance competitiveness on a sustainable basis; to promote green growth for sustainable development; to bring about national stability for national development toward prosperity and sustainability; and to enhance the efficiency of public sector management and promote good governance. As for the four supporting strategies for efficient national development, they involve infrastructure development and the logistics system; science and technology, research, and innovation; urban, regional, and economic zone development; and international cooperation for development (NESDB, 2017a).

9.5.1.1 *The Twelfth National Economic and Social Development Plan (2017–2021)*

The Twelfth National Economic and Social Development Plan (2017–2021) has been worked out in keeping with the 20-year national strategy. It focuses on the philosophy of the sufficiency economy, which has become the guiding light of the country's development since the Ninth Plan, beginning in 2006. The philosophy aims to change the priority of economic policy from growth to social development. The main objective is to bring about people's happiness and well-being. It has been followed as a shared value by the Thai people, has guided the transformation to a new national management system, based on the goals of efficiency, quality of life, and sustainability. The Twelfth Plan is geared to reduce income disparity and poverty, to strengthen the Thai economy and enhance the country's competitiveness, to promote natural capital and environmental quality, and further boost the confidence of Thailand in the international community.

Industrial development policy has been composed in the third strategy of the Twelfth Plan, which focuses on economic strength and sustainable competitiveness. Thailand's economic growth has remained unsatisfactory for several consecutive years. These are the result of the global economic downturn, domestic limitations hindering the improvement of the country's productivity and competitiveness, and the slow growth of the country's basic economic foundations. The developments during 2017–2021 will, therefore, emphasize the realization of the country's economic potential, and build the country's stability. For instance, exports have great potential to expand and become an important mechanism to drive the Thai economy. Thailand's productivity should increase, and both public-private investment and public-private partnerships should grow continuously. More citizens and entrepreneurs should be included in the tax base. The agriculture sector should focus on sustainable farming and increase farmers' incomes. Industrial areas should move toward becoming eco-industrial towns. Thailand's revenue from tourism due to its international competitiveness should continue to increase. SMEs should play a greater role in economic systems, and the financial sector should become more efficient (NESDB, 2017b).

9.5.1.2 *The Ministry of Industry's (MOI) Strategic Plan (2017–2021)*

The MOI's Strategic Plan (2017–2021) has outlined the direction of Thailand's industrial development and is used as a guideline for the ministry's operations. The conceptual framework of the plan is derived from the relevant development of the industries, industrial policies, and related plans at both national and ministerial levels (MOI, 2017).

The MOI has the following aims:

- to promote and cultivate entrepreneurs' strength and competitiveness in the global market;
- to improve and develop the industrial ecosystem to facilitate the transformation toward the Thailand 4.0 policy;
- to promote environmentally friendly production in the industrial sector;
- to coordinate and integrate the works of related organizations, both internal and external, to achieve common development goals.

The MOI sets four major strategies to drive industrial development. It is important to create balance, stability, and sustainability in the manufacturing sector. The promotion and development of industries by applying science, technology, and innovation (STI) will result in productivity, value creation, and standard improvement. Also, enhancing and strengthening the competitiveness of Thai entrepreneurs in the global economy can be accomplished by building up the enabling factors, which are laws and regulations, improving the ease of doing business, creating clusters and networks, as well as supporting policies and plans for each specific sector. These enabling factors will help induce the necessary investments and reduce business obstacles. Also, the promotion of socially and environmentally friendly production can be achieved through smart regulation, knowledge sharing, and public participation.

9.5.1.3 *Thailand 4.0: A new economic model of industrial development*

Thailand 4.0 is an economic model for 2017–2021. It will enable Thailand to overcome the challenges of the middle-income trap, the growing income inequality, and unbalanced development by transforming the country into an innovation-driven economy achieving upper-income status with a stronger and more balanced economic foundation. According to the 20-year National Strategic Plan, the government has been planning to strengthen the local economy and will further improve Thailand's connection to global markets. This will be done by strengthening the economy through the "Sufficiency Economy" approach and collaborating with the public and private sectors, as well as academic institutions.

To achieve Thailand 4.0, the Thai government is targeting ten industries which have been divided into two groups: (1) First S-Curve: the upgrading of five existing high potential industries (Agriculture and Food, Tourism, Automotive, Electrical and Electronics, and Petrochemicals) by using research and development, and high technology and innovation, coupled with (2) New S-Curve: the development of five new industries (Automation and Robotics, Aerospace, Digital, Bio-Energy and Bio-Chemicals, and Medical and Healthcare). These will be carried out by transforming Thailand's comparative advantage, including the country's rich biodiversity and cultural diversity, to create a competitive advantage focusing on "Science, Technology, Innovation and Creativity" (Suchinai, 2017).

This policy development does not involve jumping into new industries and leaving existing ones behind. The focus is on making the necessary modifications to create balanced and sustainable growth and improve the country's social and economic foundations, thereby increasing the living standards for all Thais. Thailand 4.0 will connect and strengthen the core of upstream targeted industries, startups, and small and medium-sized enterprises.

To ensure Thailand 4.0's success, the government will work together with the public and private sectors, academic institutions, and civil society to put the right mechanisms in place, to cover all aspects such as investments in physical, logistics and digital infrastructure, human capital, education, government support, targeted industries development, and the Eastern Economic Corridor (EEC). Thailand 4.0 demonstrates the Thai government's determination to move the country forward by reforming the country's economic structure and enhancing the country's competitiveness through attractive policies to increase foreign investment in the targeted industries and promote the country as a regional trading and investment hub. This is an ambitious but necessary step forward for Thailand. The government claims that Thailand 4.0 will enable the country to continue on a solid economic footing by providing sustainable growth and development and reducing disparities in society. Moving to Thailand 4.0 will bring the country tremendous opportunities for both Thai and international investors (BOI, 2017).

9.5.1.4 The Eastern Economic Corridor (EEC): The main potential growth engine

The EEC project has been initiated to continue the success of Thailand's Eastern Seaboard, which has been the centerpiece of the Thai economy, connecting trade and investment with the rest of the world and supporting the digital economy. The area, comprising of the three provinces of Chachoengsao, Chonburi, and Rayong, is rich in energy resources, manufacturing of raw materials, and human resources of professionals and high-skilled labor in ASEAN. The EEC project will create investments in infrastructure, industrial, and social projects, which will, in turn, strengthen economic and social development, not only for Thailand but also other neighboring countries through interconnectivity (Kasemsarn, 2018).

The development of the EEC is part of the constitutionally-mandated 20-Year National Strategy of Thailand and is governed by the EEC Act of May 15, 2018, which would be the first of its kind in Thailand's history, where the entire focus would be on a regional-specific development. With these excellent facilities, the EEC is the most suitable location for investment to drive the ASEAN economy. For the development and realization of the EEC, the Thai government will ensure the continuity of both private and public investments and aim to generate $45 billion (1.7 trillion baht) in the first 5 years (2018–2022). The Thai government hopes to complete the EEC project by 2021, thereby developing the eastern provinces into the hub of technological manufacturing and services with strong connectivity to its ASEAN neighbors and beyond.

The EEC development scheme contains several privileges as follows:

- Exemption from corporate income tax for up to 13 years;
- Exemption from import duties on machinery, raw or essential materials that are imported for use in production and R&D;
- Matching grants for investment, R&D, innovation development and human resources development in targeted industries;
- Permission to own land for BOI-promoted projects;
- The right to take up the state's land lease agreement for 50 years, and renewable upon approval for a further 49 years;
- The lowest personal income tax rate (17 percent) in ASEAN for executives, specialists, and researchers who are qualified by the Director-general of Revenue Department, under the law which related to the nation's competitiveness enhancement in the promoted businesses or the Investment Promotion Act;
- A one-stop service center to facilitate foreign investors which provides useful information and issues permits for trading, export, and import in one location;
- An attractive five-year work visa for investors, specialists, and scientists (EECO, 2018a).

The government expects the funding to come from a mixture of state funds, public-private partnerships, and foreign direct investment. To make the EEC into a Special Economic Zone, the Thai government has identified five core areas, as follows: (1) increased, improved and integrated infrastructure; (2) target industries; (3) business industrial clusters and innovation hubs; (4) creation of new cities and communities through smart urban planning; and (5) regional tourism (Royal Thai Embassy, 2018).

The major focus area of the EEC is to improve existing connectivity by air, land, rail, and sea, and to foster manufacturing and innovation. Priority is given to various infrastructure projects, such as U-Tapao airport, the TG MRO Campus (Thai airways' Maintenance, Repair and Overhaul hub), high-speed rail linking three airports, Laem Chabang port phase 3, Map Ta Phut port phase 3, and double-track rail lines. By 2020, the EEC is expected to generate 5 percent of GDP, tax revenue of up to 100 billion baht per year, lower logistics cost by 400 billion baht, create 100,000 jobs a year, attract 1.5 times more tourists, and 1.8 times higher tourism revenue (EECO, 2017).

9.5.2 Public-private partnerships

Due to the annual budget limit on the country's investment, the Thai government is trying to increase PPPs as alternative additional sources of funding to fill the gap. PPPs can be expanded and improve the delivery of services and the operation of the infrastructure by tapping into the expertise and efficiency of the private sector, mobilizing private capital to facilitate the cost-effective delivery of infrastructure and services, directly responding to customers' needs, and enabling a more efficient use of resources by improving the identification of long-term risks and their allocation.

9.5.2.1 *The Public-Private Partnership (PPP) Act, B.E. 2562 (2019: Revised Version)*

The PPP Act is the designated center of the State Enterprise Policy Office (SEPO) under the Ministry of Finance and as the center of the PPP coordinating body, which also provides a secretariat for the high-level PPP Policy Committee. Thailand had the first PPP legal framework in 1992 called the Public-Private in State Undertaking Act (PPSU). The PPSU Act focused on private participation in government services through concessions. However, there were lots of obstructions to project approval, thus the government revised the PPP framework and named it the Private Investment in State Undertaking Act (PISU) in 2013, which emphasized the PPP investment promotion in the areas of contract standardization, guidance for small projects, a precise timeframe for projects and other restrictions. Nonetheless, the PISU Act had major concerns over the scope of PPP, clarification on partnership principles, problem-solving measures, and lack of PPP promotions, which caused project delays and decreased the interest of the private sector. Therefore, the government decided to revise the PISU Act and enacted the Public-Private Partnership (PPP) Act in March 2019 with related subordinate legislation regulations to be issued under this Act later (SEPO, 2019a).

The PPP Act 2019 emphasizes the private sector's participation in the transparency and accountability process, its innovation and knowledge transfers to government entities, and extra support measures from related agencies. It encompasses the PPP application aimed at infrastructure-related investment, building a relationship between public and private parties based on fair partnership principles, providing a mechanism to tackle challenges throughout the PPP process, and providing PPP promotions to projects under monetary and fiscal discipline. Under this Act, PPP projects must be worth 5 billion baht or more, which includes: (1) the economic sector: public infrastructure investment, i.e., transportation, water management, energy and telecommunications; (2) the social sector: public services investment, i.e., healthcare, education, and social welfare; and (3) other sectors specified under the royal decree. For a project to be selected under the 2019 Act, it must first conduct an appraisal with assistance from approved consultants. This must include public-sector comparators and a risk management plan. Project approval is sought from the SEPO and the PPP Policy Committee (SEPO, 2019b).

The increase in public-private participation will create substantial benefits for the government; in the economic and social sectors, especially on the whole life costing, value for money, risk-sharing and service improvement; and infrastructure investment from facilitating the infrastructure base to supporting industries and businesses in infrastructure development. Nevertheless, if a budget fund

Table 9.4 The PPP process

	Normal track	PPP Fast Track	PPP-EEC Track
PPP feasibility study	8–10 months	3.5 months	3.5–4.5 months
Project appraisal	6–8 months	4 months	
Tender evaluation and contract award	5–7 months	1.5 months	4.5–5.5 months
Total estimated time required	25 months	9 months	8–10 months

Source: State Enterprise Policy Office (SEPO, 2015) and Eastern Economic Corridor Office (EECO, 2018b).

or a government loan, subsidy or guarantee is required in a PPP project, the Council of Ministers must also approve the project. There is no evidence that a proper accounting process has been developed by the Ministry of Finance to deal with contingent liabilities. Thus far, infrastructure development under stimulus measures has been recorded under an off-budget account. There is a need to better integrate financial commitments for infrastructure into budgetary reporting. Since PPP is a risk-sharing plan between the government and the private sector, it is necessary to identify the risk and responsibility. Also, political stability and continuous policy implementation are the fundamental factors in creating an environment for investment and increasing investor confidence. Furthermore, it is necessary to publicize the PPP concept and procedure to government entities and the private sector to create a clear and smooth project implementation.

9.5.2.2 PPP Fast Track

The PPP Fast Track process is an attempt by the Thai government to eliminate red tape and the bottlenecks commonly associated with the approval and development of infrastructure projects (PwC Thailand, 2018). The PPP Fast track was announced by the PPP Policy Committee in 2015, and the PPP-EEC track was announced by the EEC Policy Committee in 2017. The PPP Fast Track allows the PPP Policy Committee to focus their efforts on strategically important projects which in turn shortens the time required for approval and development of the projects (SEPO, 2015). The PPP Fast Track and the PPP-EEC Scheme will reduce the PPP process, project preparation, the working team set-up and contract drafting, from 25 months to 8–10 months (Table 9.4).

9.5.2.3 PPP implementation for industrial development

EEC is one of the most attractive PPP projects for industrial development. The SEPO and related agencies have collectively developed rules, regulations, conditions, and processes for PPPs and direct private investment to better facilitate important investments in the EEC. These allow projects to be implemented and maintained freely and transparently, including the dissemination of information and auditing of private sector investments. Also, measures have been set to expedite overall project approval processes by allowing them to occur in parallel, which reduces the timelines to 8–10 months (EECO, 2018b). These regulations apply to investment projects deemed priority as determined by the EEC Policy Committee. The government is also trying to encourage private investors through the PPP-EEC track for industrial development in the EEC area. The government has identified an EEC project list, timeframe, market sounding and appropriate government subsidies, i.e., corporate income tax exemption, machinery, and raw material import tax exemption, and landowners' rights.

9.6 Conclusion

It is important to note that the Thai government from the past to the present has never officially announced any industrial policy for the country. Hence, Thailand's industrial policy seems to follow the so-called "market-friendly approach" more than a fully-fledged industrial policy as used in countries like South Korea or Taiwan. Besides, Thailand does not have a distinct ministry like the Ministry of Economy, Trade and Industry (METI) of Japan or the Ministry of the International Trade and Industry (MITI) of Malaysia to handle the industrial policy.

The arguments related to industrial policy of Thailand can be separated into two major sides: neo-liberals who believe that the Thai government lacks the institutional skills necessary for effective sectoral interventions (Christensen et al, 1993), and the neo-statists who believe that the Thai government interventions since Sarit's rule, the ISI period, and the EOI period have been selective, extensive, and effective (Jomo, 2001; Rock, 2001).

Neo-liberals claim that Thai government agencies did not have the capability to supervise each industry rigorously or instruct the private sector through industrial policy, and although Thailand has had great macroeconomic policies, it has poor microeconomic policies conducted at the ministry level (Satitniramai, 2013, pp. 93, 96). Nevertheless, the rising role of commercial banks in the 1960s until 1997 could be intentionally designed by the technocrats to avoid rent-seeking from public agencies through capital allocation (Satitniramai, 2013, p. 95). According to Evans (1995), Thailand merely changed from a "Predatory State," which was extractive and rent-seeking, to become an "Intermediate State," which succeeded in only some aspects of its management, i.e., macroeconomic policies, but failed to improve state agencies at the micro-level or ministry level. Hence, Thailand has failed to achieve the status of "Development State" as it regularly produces conflicting and short-sighted policies. Nevertheless, the "Intermediate State" of Thailand was strong enough to jump-start the capital accumulation led by the private sector and the government was willing to receive ideas, inputs, and feedback from the private sector which allowed policies to be carried out more realistically (Satitniramai, 2013, pp. 96, 100–101).

The neo-statists, on the other hand, argue that without successful government interventions, Thailand's large infant industries would not have graduated into export production industries. The interventions have contributed to the success, though it is far from perfect, of the Thai industries today (Jomo, 2001; Rock, 2001).

As Thailand's industrial development is still evolving, arguments from both sides are crucial for policymakers to review, rethink, and redesign the future of Thailand's economic and industrial policies to reduce gaps and become more inclusive, pro-poor, and sustainable.

References

In Thai

Attakorn, B. (1964). Sarit Thanarat's development projects. In The Cabinet (Ed.), *Biography of Sarit Thanarat*. Bangkok: The Cabinet.

BOI. (2017). *Opportunities Thailand: Innovation-driven economy*. Bangkok: BOI.

Boonyaked, T. (1964). Sarit Thanarat's investment promotion for industry. In The Cabinet (Ed.), *Biography of Sarit Thanarat*. Bangkok: The Cabinet.

Bunnag, D. (1957). *The statesman Pridi Phanomyong*. Bangkok: Sermvitbannakarn.

Buranapluke, C., & Bunnag, P. (1978). *A study on political effects of Thai-American relationship (1920–1963)*. Bangkok: Chulalongkorn University.

Chukiatkhajorn, P., & Thaiprasert, N. (2014). *Effects of Japanese economic crisis on inflows of foreign direct investment from Japan to ASEAN 4 and 3 Newly Industrialized Economies* (Master's thesis). Chiang Mai University, Chiang Mai, Thailand

Dilokvitayarat, L. (1983) Evolution of development thoughts: Political economic demonstration. *Economic Review*, 6(2), 83–97.

EECO. (2017). EEC press conference. Bangkok: EECO.

EECO. (2018a). Investment benefits on EEC. Available at: www.eeco.or.th/en/investment/investment-privileges/investment-benefits-on-eec

EECO. (2018b). Public-Private Partnership. Available at: www.eeco.or.th/en/content/public-private-partnerships

Hongladdarom, S. (1964). Sarit Thanarat's economic and fiscal policies. In The Cabinet (Ed.), *Biography of Sarit Thanarat*. Bangkok: The Cabinet.

IFCT (Industrial Finance Corporation of Thailand). (1967). IFCT and economic development. *Commerce News Special Edition*, 20 August.

Kanajanadul, W. (1976). Challenges and future of Thai state-owned enterprises. *Development Administration Journal*, 16(1), 79–105.

Kasemsarn, T. (2018). *Eastern Economic Corridor (EEC): Industry focus*. Bangkok: KPMG Thailand.

Ketboonchu, K. (1974). *World Bank and economic development in Thailand* (Master's thesis). Chulalongkorn University, Bangkok, Thailand.

MOI. (2017). *The Ministry of Industry's Strategic Plan (2017–2021)*. Bangkok: MOI.

Natsupha, C., & Janevitkarn, M. (1981). Evolution of ideology in Thai society. In C, Natsupha et al. *Economics and History of Thailand*. Bangkok: Sarngsan.

NESDB. (2017a). *20-year National Strategy (2017–2036)*. Bangkok: NESDB.

NESDB. (2017b). *The Twelfth National Economic and Social Development Plan (2017–2021)*. Bangkok: NESDB.

Noibuatip, S. (1974). *The history of bloody democracy*. Bangkok: Siam Publisher.

Pattamanant, U. (1983). *The U.S. and Thai economic policy (1960–1970)* (Master's thesis). Chulalongkorn University, Bangkok, Thailand

Petchprasert, N. (1981). Expansion of capitalism in Thailand from 1945 to present. In S. Manarangsan (Ed.), *Expansion of capitalism in Thailand from 1945 to present*. Bangkok: Sarngsan.

PwC Thailand. (2018). *Infrastructure developments and public private partnerships in Thailand: A 2018 update*. Bangkok: PwC Thailand.

Ramkomut, C. (1977). *Laborers and strikes in Thailand* (Master's thesis). Chulalongkorn University, Bangkok, Thailand.

Royal Thai Embassy. (2018). Thailand's Eastern Economic Corridor (EEC): Opportunities for investment. Available at: https://thaiindia.net/recent-economic-policies/item/3451-thai-eastern-economic-corridor-eec.html

Ruamsilp, P. (1978). *Phibunsongkram's economic development policies from 1938 to 1944* (Master's thesis). Chulalongkorn University, Bangkok, Thailand.

Satitniramai, A. (2013). *Thai state and economic reform*. Nonthaburi: Same Sky Books.

SEPO. (2015). PPP Fast Track. Bangkok: SEPO.

SEPO. (2019a). Public Private Partnership in Thailand. Bangkok: SEPO.

SEPO. (2019b). Public Private Partnership Act 2019. Bangkok: SEPO.

Siamwalla, A. (1976). Structures and relationship among economic entities in Thailand. In R. Thanapornpan (Ed.), *Society and economy*. Bangkok: Thammasat University.

Suchinai, H. (2017). *Investment opportunities in Thailand*. Bangkok: The Office of Board of Investment.

Sudchai, C. (1986). *Thailand's economic development policy during the Sarit government, 1958–1963*. Bangkok: Silpakorn University.

Supinit, W. (1970). The World Bank. In *Economic Prognostication Trade College*, 1970–1971, 117–135.

Thailand Future Foundation. (2013). The two-trillion project and future of Thailand. Thailand Future Forum No. 3. Bangkok: Thailand Future Foundation.

TMB Bank. (2017, June 29). About TMB Bank. Available at: www.tmbbank.com/about

Veerawan, A. (1964). Sarit Thanarat's fiscal and finance management. In The Cabinet (Ed.), *Biography of Sarit Thanarat*. Bangkok: The Cabinet.

In English

Christensen, S. et al. (1993). *The lessons of East Asia: Thailand, the institutional and political underpinnings of growth*. Washington, DC: World Bank.

Collis, H. C. (1942). *Foreign capital in Southeast Asia*. New York: Institute of Pacific Relations.

Evans, P. (1995). *Embedded autonomy: States and industrial transformation*. Princeton, NJ: Princeton University Press.

Fineman, D. (1997). *A special relationship: The United States and military government in Thailand, 1947–1958*. Honolulu: University of Hawaii Press.

Hewison, K. (1989). *Bankers and bureaucrats: Capital and the role of the state in Thailand*. New Haven, CT: Yale University Southeast Asia Studies.

Ingram, J. C. (1971). *Economic change in Thailand 1850–1970*. Stanford, CA: Stanford University Press.

Jacob, E. (1961). *Agrarian unrest in Southeast Asia*. Bombay: Asia Publishing House.

Jomo, K. S. (2001). *Southeast Asia's industrialization: Industrial policy, capabilities and sustainability*. New York: Palgrave.

Jongwanich, J., & Kohpaiboon, A. (2008). Private investment: trends and determinants in Thailand. *World Development, 36*(10), 1709–1724.

Kojima. K. (2000). The "flying geese" model of Asian economic development: Origin, theoretical extensions, and regional policy implications. *Journal of Asian Economics, 11,* 375–401.

Lauridsen, L. S. (2009) The policies and politics of industrial upgrading in Thailand during the Thaksin era (2001–2006). *Asian Politics & Policy, 1*(3), 409–434.

Natsuda, K., & Thoburn, J. (2013). Industrial policy and the development of the automotive industry in Thailand. *Journal of the Asia Pacific Economy, 18*(3), 413–437.

Rock, M. T. (2001). Selective industrial policy and manufacturing export success in Thailand. In K. S. Jomo (Ed.), *Southeast Asia's industrialization: Industrial policy, capabilities and sustainability* (pp. 263–282). New York: Palgrave.

Siamwalla, A. (2001). *Picking up the pieces: Bank and corporate restructuring in post-1997 Thailand*. Bangkok: Thailand Development Research Institute.

Skinner, G. W. (1958). *Leadership and power in the Chinese community of Thailand*. Ithaca, NY: Cornell University Press.

World Bank. (1980). *Industrial development strategy in Thailand*. Washington, DC: World Bank.

10 The process of change in the economic development model of the Pacific Island Countries under the influence of globalization

Tetsuo Umemura

10.1 Introduction

Small Island Developing States (SIDS) are facing difficulties in their social and economic development. The United Nations Office of the High Representative for the Least Developed Countries, Landlocked Developing Countries and Small Island Developing States points out:

> SIDS tend to confront similar constraints in their sustainable development efforts, such as a (1) narrow resource base depriving them of the benefits of economies of scale; (2) small domestic markets and heavy dependence on a few external and remote markets; (3) high costs for energy, infrastructure, transportation, communication, and servicing; (4) long distances from export markets and import resources; (5) low and irregular international traffic volumes; (6) little resilience to natural disasters; (7) growing populations; high volatility of economic growth; (8) limited opportunities for the private sector and a proportionately large reliance of their economies on their public sector; and (9) fragile natural environments.

These constraints have been discussed by researchers who have tried to identify the typical economic and social model of small island countries.

Bertram and Watters (1985) called the development system of small Pacific Island Countries MIRAB, an acronym for Migration (MI), Remittances (R), Foreign Aid (A), and the Public Bureaucracy (B). These factors distinguish several important socio-economic characteristics of island countries. After the concept of the MIRAB model, Guthunz and Krosigk (1996) discussed another model, which is known as "TouRAB." Instead of the Migrant factor, the factor is Tourism, given as "Tou" in the model. Many island countries rely heavily on inbound tourism, and it becomes an engine of their economies. In addition, Baldacchino (2006) introduced the PROFIT model. PROFIT is an acronym for "People considerations affecting citizenship, residence and employment rights (P); Resource management (R); Overseas engagement and ultrarational recognition (O); Finance (F) and Transportation (T)." This model also explains the characteristics of small island countries. Finally, McElroy (2006) took notice of tourism activities in small island countries with the so-called SITEs (Small Island Tourism Economies) model. This model focuses on tourism-driven island economies instead of migration, remittance, aid, and bureaucracy.

This chapter focuses on nine Pacific Island Countries, namely. Republic of Fiji (hereafter FJI), Republic of Kiribati (hereafter KIR), Republic of the Marshall Islands (hereafter MHL), Federated States of Micronesia (hereafter FSM), Republic of Palau (hereafter PLW), Independent State of Samoa (hereafter SAM), Solomon Islands (hereafter SLB), Kingdom of Tonga (hereafter TON), and the Republic of Vanuatu (hereafter VUT). These countries achieved their independence after World War II.

Instead of "Migration," "Remittance," "Foreign Aid," and "Bureaucracy," international trade, both export commodities and export destinations, and inbound tourism are examined as the economic development factors for Pacific Island Countries. These factors have been influenced by the former colonial powers or administrative countries such as the United Kingdom, France, Germany, the United States, Australia, New Zealand, and Japan.

The aforementioned developed countries supported many Pacific Island Countries after World War II, not only through Official Development Assistance or Aid (ODA) but also through preferential treatment in the import of commodities from the small island countries. Moreover, international trade with SIDS has been affected by the globalization of the world economy that started around 1995. Exports actually drive economic growth, and affect the industrial structures of island countries.

Another factor is international tourism, which is the fastest-growing sector in recent years, and can be considered as the export of services. Due to the high economic growth of emerging and developing economies combined with globalization, the demand for international tourism has been increasing. It means that the growth rate of international tourism is higher than the growth rate of world GDP. Historically, Pacific Island Countries are one of the better-known tourist destinations around the world. This chapter also discusses how international trade and inbound tourism affect industrial structural change in Pacific Island Countries, validates historical trade statistics, and presents a panel analysis.

10.2 Literature review and historical background of the Pacific Island Countries

The most popular model of the island countries is MIRAB by Bertram and Watters (1985). In this model, five small island countries were included: Cook Islands (self-governing in free association of New Zealand, hereafter Cook or COK), Tokelau Islands (self-administering territory of New Zealand), Niue (self-governing in free association with New Zealand), Republic of Kiribati, and Tuvalu (parliamentary democracy under a constitutional monarchy; a Commonwealth realm).[1]

Table 10.1 Profile of small island countries in the MIRAB study

	Area (km²)	Population (1981)	Sea area (000 km²)**	(1) GNP per capita (USD, 1983)**	(2) Aid per capita (USD, 1983)**	Ratio (2)/(1) (%)
Cook Island	240	17,751	1,830	1,360	423	31
Kiribati	712	60,133*	3,550	460	275	60
Niue	259	3,281	390	1,080(a)	1,867	173
Tokelau Island	10	1,572	290	560	900	160
Tuvalu	26	8,154*	900	570(a)	525	92

Note: *: World Development Indicators. **: Pacific Economic Bulletin (a) 1980.

Source: South Pacific Commission (1985); World Bank. World Development Indicator database.

These five countries in the MIRAB study were very small in terms of economy and population, especially Tokelau and Tuvalu. Table 10.1 shows their land area, population, sea area, GNP per capita (1), aid per capita (2), and the ratio of (2) divided by (1) in 1983. Niue and Tokelau recorded a ratio of 173 percent and 160 percent, respectively. Cook and Kiribati also heavily relied on foreign aid at 31 percent and 60 percent. Around the 1980s, foreign aid was vital for most small island countries so that the MIRAB model was proposed. Currently, these small island countries still need economic and technical assistance through associations or other types of relations with developed countries such as New Zealand, Australia, Japan, and the UK.

In his ongoing research, Bertram (1999) classified Samoa, Tonga, FSM, and other island countries using the MIRAB model. Samoa and Tonga have relied on workers' remittance, and FSM had heavily relied on foreign aid. He also mentioned that Fiji, Papua New Guinea (hereafter PNG), and the Solomon Islands are excluded from the MIRAB model because these countries had not heavily relied on foreign aid or workers' remittance. Even though there is a trade deficit, the imports of these countries have been financed by their export of goods. The situation of this international trade means these countries were considered to be relatively economically independent countries compared with the other island countries.

The "TouRAB" model discussed by Guthunz and Krosigk (1996), focuses on four countries: Tonga, the Maldives, the Seychelles, and Martinique (Table 10.2). Tonga is in the South Pacific, the Seychelles and the Maldives are in the Indian Ocean, and Martinique is in the Caribbean. These researchers were focusing on the economic aspects of tourism in these island countries.

This study made two important points:

> One reaches a rather skeptical conclusion in the case of small island states, due, in particular, to their relatively fragile economies, ecological vulnerability, and socio-cultural characteristics. However, tourism can constitute

Table 10.2 Tourism in Tonga, the Maldives, the Seychelles, and Martinique

Island	Inhabitants (thousands, 1991)	Tourists (thousand, 1990)	Receipt (million $US, 1990)	Tourists per km²	Tourists per inhabitant
Tonga	97	21	9	0.22	28
the Maldives	221	195	85	0.88	650
the Seychelles	72	104	120	1.44	229
Martinique	364	282	240	0.77	255

Source: Guthunz & Krosigk (1996), p. 20.

one element in a new "world of choices," in which small island states try to maximize the various elements of interdependence.

(Guthunz & Krosigk, 1996, p. 33)

Even though island countries are fragile in many aspects, international tourism can be a pillar for their economy. Nowadays, international tourism plays a vital role, especially in small countries with limited resources. Almost all island countries have a Ministry of Tourism or related government organization to promote inbound tourism.

The second point is that:

> Islands in the sun have a lot to offer in this regard, especially the tropical ones which have always been a metaphor for paradise, a place of refuge, peace and tranquillity, exotic and authentic nature, and innocent and friendly natives an image of island.

(Guthunz & Krosigk, 1996, p. 34)

These images can be an essential tourism resource for small island countries, and it boosts recent inbound tourism.

The next model is the PROFIT model put forward by Baldacchino (2006). PROFIT means "People considerations affecting citizenship, residence and employment rights (P); Resource management (R); Overseas engagement and ultranational recognition (O); Finance (F) and Transportation (T)" (Baldacchino, 2006, p. 54). The differences between the MIRAB and PROFIT models are shown in Table 10.3.

The bottom line is that the MIRAB model is rather pessimistic, but the PROFIT model is not. The point to note is that the PROFIT model includes not only the Pacific Island Countries but also African and Caribbean Island Countries so that the conclusions of the PROFIT model are not fully applicable to common characteristics of the Pacific Island Countries.

McElroy (2006) developed the Small Island Tourists Economies (SITEs) model, which focuses on tourism-driven island economies. The study focused

Table 10.3 Characteristics of the MIRAB and PROFIT models

MIRAB	PROFIT
Migration (out)	Migration (in/out)
Remittances (high)	Remittances (low/medium)
Aid (high)	Aid (low/nil)
Bureaucracy (high)	Bureaucracy (medium/high)
Resource management (low/nil)	Resource management (medium/high)
(Para-)Diplomacy (subsidy-driven)	(Para-)Diplomacy (procedure-driven)
Finance management (low)	Finance management (medium/high)
Transportation management (low)	Transportation management (medium/high)
Manufactures (low)	Manufactures (medium)

Note: "In and out" means in-migration and out-migration. "high," "medium," and "low" mean relative dependency level.

Source: Baldacchino (2006), p. 54, Table 1.

on islands with less than 1 million population or less than 5,000 km² of land area. The author calculated the Tourism Penetration Ratio (TPI) for 36 island countries and regions of the Pacific, Africa, and the Caribbean. TPI scores consist of: (1) average visitor spending per island resident; (2) average daily visitor density per 1,000 population; and (3) rooms per square kilometer. These indicators are converted into an index using the formula below.

TPI = {(indicator value of the specific country) minus (minimum value of the country set)} divide by {(maximum value) minus (minimum value of the country set)}

The TPI score was calculated for the unweighted average of the three indicators. McElroy (2006, p. 76) concluded that "for small island economies, tourism is a viable engine of growth." This means that inbound tourism is the foundation of economic growth for island countries. Inbound tourism equals international tourism receipts, which is an export of services in terms of international economics. Since it is rather difficult for small island countries to export goods, to receive foreign tourists means service export and they are able to earn foreign exchange for their economies.

There are four significant models for small island countries: MIRAB, TouRAB, PROFIT, and SITEs. The differences among these models are discussed by Baldacchino and Bertram (2009). In their article, previous studies of small island countries are divided into two categories, "Optimistic tone" and "Pessimistic tone." Figure 10.1 illustrates the development models of small island countries with their component factors.

The MIRAB model, which has a pessimistic tone, consists of "Aid," "Geostrategic rents," and "Remittances." On the other hand, the PROFIT model, which has an optimistic tone, consists of "Niche manufactures," "High-value

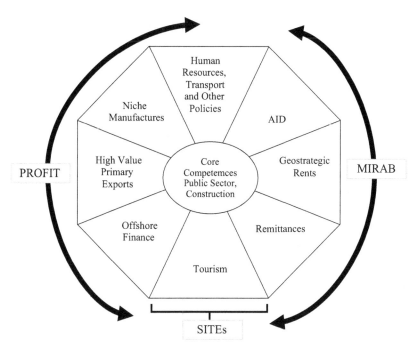

Figure 10.1 Spinning the wheel: the structures of small economies
Source: Baldacchino & Bertram (2009, Figure 2, p. 152) partially modified.

primary exports," and "Offshore finance." These factors indicate the potentiality of island countries. The SITEs model consists only of "Tourism."

Baldacchino and Bertram (2009) presented a threefold taxonomy, in which 65 small economies, including island countries and regions, were categorized using the MIRAB, PROFIT, and SITEs models. Thus, they highlighted the common characteristics of island countries via a thorough, global investigation. However, their discussion does not consider the geopolitical and historical factors for each country. Also, another difficulty is mixing island countries not only in the Pacific but also in the Indian Ocean and the Caribbean. Applying the categorization of Baldacchino and Bertram (2009) to the sample countries of this chapter, Figure 10.2 was created.

Five countries, Kiribati, the Marshall Islands, Micronesia, Samoa, and Tonga, are grouped in the MIRAB model. The Solomon Islands are categorized in overlapping between MIRAB and PROFIT. Two countries, Fiji and Vanuatu, are classified as overlapping with the PROFIT and the SITEs model.

In this chapter, geopolitical and historical factors are considered to investigate the typical characteristics of the Pacific Island Countries with a focus on the export of goods and tourism.

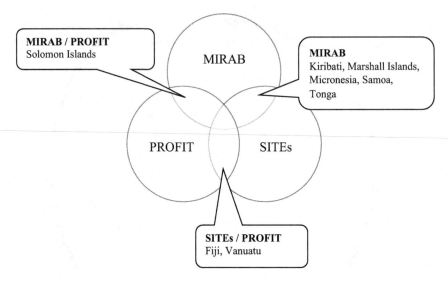

Figure 10.2 Classification of the small Pacific Island Countries
Source: Based on Baldacchino and Bertram (2009, p. 152, Figure 1).

10.3 Export analysis of the Pacific Island Countries

In this section, nine Pacific Island Countries, Fiji, Kiribati, the Marshall Islands, Micronesia, Palau, Samoa, the Solomon Islands, and Vanuatu, are examined in terms of merchandise exports (exports of goods /export commodities) to see the progress of industrial development. Island countries consist of small lands and vast marine areas, so that after World War II to the 1980s, their primary industries were fisheries and agriculture, namely, natural tropical foods such as bananas, pineapples, mangos, taro, and cassava. Plantation products, such as coffee, sugar, and tea, were also produced. A subsistence economy was dominant for all island countries. Fishing was mostly for coastal fish, not deep-sea fishing.

After World War II and until independence, these countries received foreign aid from their former colonial powers or administrative countries, such as the USA, Australia, New Zealand, and Japan. This financial support and technical assistance were intended to contribute to economic and social development, and manufacturing industry.

Based on historical evidence, the first stage of their development of the industry sector was primary industries, mainly fisheries. For example, from 1972 to 1989, the Japanese company Solomon Taiyo, now Maruha Nichiro Cooperation, operated a seafood factory to produce canned fish with Japanese technical assistance in the Solomon Islands. At present, the major export commodities from the Solomon Islands are still fish-related. Another case was the Pacific Fishing Company Pte Ltd (PAFCO) in Fiji. It was established with the

Fijian and Japanese governments in 1963 and operated until 1987. According to PAFCO:[2] "The principal activities of the company were Tuna loin processing and Tuna canning for local and overseas markets." Economic and technical assistance for the fisheries sector in the Pacific Islands Countries came from the EU, the USA, and Japan. In terms of the manufacturing sector, a Japanese affiliated firm, the Yazaki Australia Vaitele Factory, opened in Apia, the capital of Samoa, in 1991 and produced wire harnesses, which are automotive parts, until 2016. After the factory closed, the total number of exports from Samoa decreased sharply. A more detailed historical background of the Pacific Islands is shown in Table 10. A1 in the Appendix.

10.3.1 Commodity exports from Pacific Island Countries in 1975 and 1985

Commodities exported from island countries reflect their natural resources, historic plantations, and foreign aid. Fiji and the Solomon Islands were colonized in the 1800s, and Kiribati was colonized after World War I by the UK. As an effect of colonization in Fiji, for example, 65.7 percent of their export commodities in 1975 was sugar (Table 10.4). The dominant industry was naturally sugar cane cultivation and sugar processing. In 2018, the export structure changed, and sugar was exported to Spain, China, and the UK as just 6 percent of total exports.[3] Other Pacific Island Countries also have had a similar experience after becoming independent, starting in Samoa (1962) to most recently Palau (1994). In this way, the experience of colonization or occupation affects the industrial structure, mostly the primary industries.

Table 10.4 compares the shares of principal export commodities from six South Pacific Island Countries in 1975 and 1985. There are some notable characteristics of an individual country's exports. Based on these export statistics, the industrial structure and development levels can be observed.

In Fiji, sugar exports were dominant in both years, but its share decreased from 67.5 percent to 41.2 percent. The shares of exports of tuna and gold increased, and this indicated a diversification of export commodities in Fiji. Kiribati depended entirely on phosphate exports in 1975, making up 96 percent of its total exports, but copra exports replaced phosphate in 1985, representing 77.9 percent. As it has run out of phosphate, there now is no manufacturing industry in Kiribati. Samoa is a compelling case. Cocoa and copra exports were dominant in 1975, but then the focus changed to coconut oil and palm oil. Cocoa seemed to be a trace of the plantation legacy. To produce copra does not require advanced manufacturing technology, however, over the ten years since 1975, the technology level seemed to improve so that coconut oil, which is a manufacturing product, could be made and exported. Another observation is that Samoa introduced palm oil trees, a non-native species, to produce palm oil.[4] These days, palm oil is mostly used in processed foods like vegetable oil. By doing this, Samoa can be considered as attempting to become a more industrialized country. The Solomon Islands seemed to be stagnant in terms of technology improvement. Their main export items were copra, wood, and fish in 1975, and

Table 10.4 Comparison of principal export commodities in six countries, 1975 and 1985 (%)

Commodity	Fiji		Kiribati		Samoa		Solomon Islands		Tonga		Vannatu	
	1975	1985	1975	1985	1975	1985	1975	1985	1975	1985	1975	1985
Tuna	0.1	4.3		16.8			20.8	27.3			32.7	0.0
Bananas	0.0	0.0			1.2	1.4			8.1	3.9		
Coconuts		0.0			1.9	7.8			7.5	8.0		
Sugar, honey, etc.	67.5	41.2										
Coffee		0.0										0.6
Cocoa		0.2			26.0	6.5	0.9	4.8			5.0	4.1
Feed stuff for animals	0.4	0.5										
Copra	3.6	2.8	3	77.9	57.3	4.2	76.2	22.6	67.4	1.2	42.8	42.7
Coconut oil						43.2				35.2		
Palm oil						34.2						
Wood and manufactures thereof	1.1	1.1			3.3	2.3	26.9	23.8			0.2	4.3
Phosphate			96									
Metalliferous ores and scrap	0.1	0.1					0.2	0.8	0.0		8.6	
Coral, shells, etc.	0.1	0.2					1.4	0.8	0.0		1.2	0.7
Gold	6.1	8.0										
Coverage of total exports	79	59	100	95	90	100	127	80	83	48	90	52

Note: The coverage of the Solomon Islands in 1975 might be a statistical error.

Source: Compiled from Oversea Trade (South Pacific Commission) various issues.

the export structure had not much changed in 1985. Only the shares of cocoa and tuna exports had increased. According to statistics, the technological level in Tonga seems to have improved since the main export item changed from copra to coconut oil over these ten years. In the case of Vanuatu, tuna and copra exports were dominant in 1975 at 42.8 percent, yet while it still depended on copra exports in 1985 with 42.7 percent, the share of tuna exports sharply dropped to zero.

Considering the coverage of total exports; the shares of principal commodities decreased in all countries apart from Samoa from 1975 to 1985, which means the export structure was diversified in the span of ten years. Though some countries showed evidence of manufacturing technology improvement, there still were limited manufacturing products as shown by observing the change in their export commodities. Eventually, the Pacific Island Countries became dependent on primary industry during the 1970s and the 1980s, and this tendency has continued until the present day (see Tables 10.A2 and 10.A3 in the Appendix).

10.3.2 Changing export destinations in the Pacific Island Countries

10.3.2.1 Export destination analysis of the Republic of Fiji

Figure 10.3 shows the share of Fiji's main export destinations from 1970 to 2018. The line shows the export coverage of the six main export destinations.

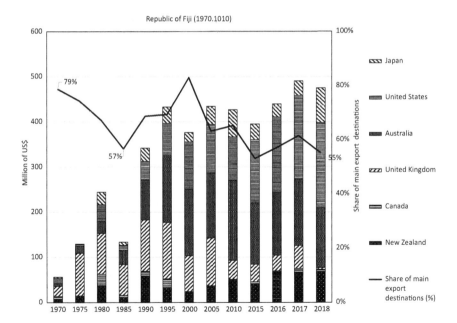

Figure 10.3 Export destination share in Fiji
Source: Based on Direction of Trade Statistics database (IMF).

The date at the top of indicates Independence Day. Fiji became independent on October 10, 1970, from the UK. During colonization, both sugar cane cultivation and sugar processing were the only industries. In overall exports, the biggest export destination was the UK with 31 percent, and the second destination was the US, with 16 percent in 1970. The other export destinations were Canada (12 percent), Australia (9 percent), New Zealand (7 percent), and Japan (4 percent). The total share of these export destinations was 79 percent. In 2018, the most significant share of export destinations was the US with 21.7 percent, and the most considerable export commodity was mineral water. The percentage of other destinations was Australia (15.6 percent), Japan (9 percent), and New Zealand (7.9 percent). These shares covered 54 percent of the total exports from Fiji. Comparing 1970 and 2018, the export share of the UK decreased from 16 percent to only 0.5 percent, and the main export commodities also changed from sugar and coconut production to mineral water and fishery products. After independence, the sugar industry played a vital role in Fiji's economy, but the focus has changed to fishery products and the famous "Fiji Water." The number of export destinations has increased; that means the export destinations are diversifying, which is the better direction in terms of trade policy.

10.3.2.2 Export destination analysis of Republic of Kiribati

Figure 10.4 shows the export destinations of Kiribati from 2000 to 2018. The UK colonized Kiribati after World War I, then it was occupied by the UK and the US after World War II. Kiribati became independent on July 12, 1979. At that time, the major export destinations were France (48 percent), New Zealand (37 percent), and the UK (15 percent) in 1979 (SPC 1979). A full 99.9 percent of the export commodities was phosphate, and once this resource had been depleted, the main export commodity changed to coconuts which caused the total amount of exports to decrease sharply. According to the COMTRADE database, there was no manufacturing product to export in recent years. Looking at the number of export destinations, it increased from five countries (France, New Zealand, the UK, the US, and Japan) with the coverage of 100 percent in 1979 to 30 countries in 2018, which means Kiribati is also diversifying its export destinations.

According to the COMTRADE database, the major export item in 2017 was fishery products, which represented 95 percent of all commodities and was exported to Thailand, Mexico, the Philippines, Japan, Korea, and the US. In Kiribati, export destinations have increased, but the range of export commodities is still very limited. Only exported fishery production contributes to its economy.

10.3.2.3 Export destination analysis of the Marshall Islands

The Marshall Islands became independent on October 21, 1986, from being a UN Trust Territory administered by the US. MHL has a compact of free association with the US, and a US military base is located on the Kwajalein atoll. In the maritime border, political and economic relationships with the US are strong, and the MHL government depends heavily on financial support.

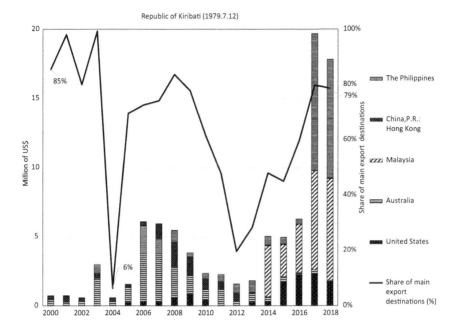

Figure 10.4 Export destination share in Kiribati
Source: Based on Direction of Trade Statistics database (IMF).

Regarding international trade, the total amount of exports has been fluctuating. The major export items in 2000 were fishery products exported to Thailand, with 49 percent of total exports (Figure 10.5). Major export destinations in 2000 were the UK, France, and Germany. These export destinations changed to Korea, Cyprus, and the Netherlands in 2018. The share of fishery products exported in 2000 was 52 percent, but decreased to 11 percent in 2018. The main export destinations were China and Thailand. However, the most crucial export commodity was "Passenger and cargo ships" exported to Korea, Cyprus, the Netherlands, Germany, and Poland as flag-of-convenience ships.[5] The total number of ships exported accounted for 62 percent of the total exports. According to fleet statistics by UNCTAD, in 2019, MHL is the second biggest flag of registration country for merchant fleets followed by Panama. Vanuatu also exports ships as flag-of-convenience ships. This movement seems to be a new development strategy for island countries with limited resources.

10.3.2.4 Export destination analysis of the Federated States of Micronesia (FSM)

FSM consists of four states: Yap, Chuuk, Pohnpei, and Kosrae. Japan occupied FSM during World War I. After World War II, FSM was occupied by the US and became a UN Trust Territory, followed by independence on November 3, 1986.

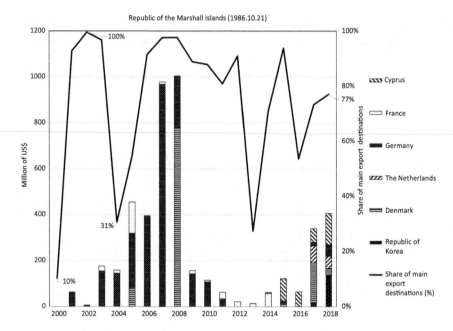

Figure 10.5 Export destination share in the Marshall Islands
Source: Based on Direction of Trade Statistics database (IMF).

FSM and the US have a compact agreement. Based on the agreement, FSM has received financial assistance, and the government heavily relies on it. This is because there is no industry and most of the economy is subsistence.

In 2000, the major export commodity of FSM was also fishery products, with 77 percent of total exports, and the destinations were Thailand and Japan (Figure 10.6). In 2018, the share of exports of fishery products increased to 97 percent of exports, and the major export destinations were Thailand (44.6 percent), Guam (14.1 percent), China (14.0 percent), and Japan (11.9 percent). The total amount of export in 2000 was US$6.42 million and increased to US$153.81 million, which means a 240 percent increase.

There is a very limited manufacturing sector in FSM, and the only hope is Nan Madol, an archeological site located in the Pohnpei state, which was registered as a World Heritage Site in 2016 so that tourism might become a new pillar of the economy.

10.3.2.5 Export destination analysis of Palau

Palau, like FSM, was occupied by Germany in the 1800s, and was then held by Japan during World War I. After World War II, Palau became a UN Trust Territory. Palau spent an extended period prior to reaching its independence.

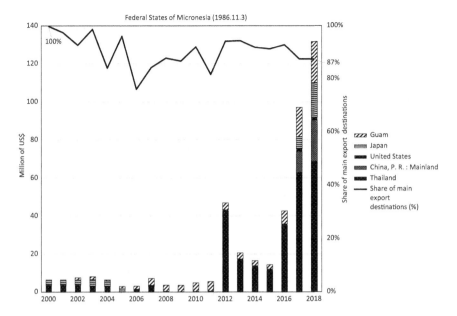

Figure 10.6 Export destination share in the Federated States of Micronesia
Source: Based on Direction of Trade Statistics database (IMF).

Finally, it was independent on October 1st, 1994, making it the most recent year of autonomy among the Pacific Island Countries.

In 2000, Palau exported a total amount of US$2.56 million, and the largest export destination was Japan (54 percent) and the second was the US (12 percent) (Figure 10.7). The main export commodity was fishery products. Japan was the main export destination for Palau and this tendency has continued. Of the export share in 2018, Japan was 78.1 percent, Panama was 4.7 percent, and the US was 2.7 percent. Palau also has been receiving financial assistance from the US under the Compact of Free Association, like FSM and the Marshall Islands. The Japanese government also has given ODA to Palau. The range of export commodities is very limited in Palau, and international tourism is the staple foreign exchange earner.

Although the Marshall Islands, Micronesia, and Palau are all categorized as the Micronesian region, their political status and surrounding geopolitical circumstances are strongly affected by the US, starting from World War II. Because they are located are in the Northern Hemisphere, the line from Hawaii to the Philippines over these countries is strategically crucial to the US.

10.3.2.6 Export destination analysis of Samoa

The Independent State of Samoa, previously "Western Samoa," was the first Pacific Island Country to become independent. Samoa was a UN Trust Territory

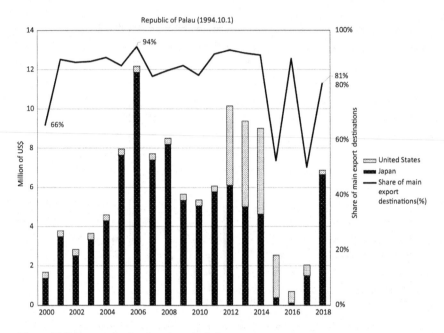

Figure 10.7 Export destination share in Palau
Source: Based on Direction of Trade Statistics database (IMF).

of New Zealand after World War I, and on January 1, 1962, Samoa became independent.

Major export commodities were copra and cocoa, representing around 80 percent of total exports in the 1960s. Samoa manufactured wire harnesses, an automotive part, using an Australian manufacturing factory operated via a Japanese affiliate company, Yazaki. From 1991 to 2016, the most critical manufacturing exports product were wire harnesses (Figure 10.8). In 1995, the total amount of exports sharply increased from US$3.98 million to US$60.90 million, which is about a 15-fold increase. The main destination was Australia. However, the factory closed in October 2017. The closure of the factory caused a sharp decrease in exports from US$20.12 million in 2016 to US$9.52 million in 2017. Since then, the major export commodity has been fishery production, and in 2018, fishery products were exported mainly to American Samoa, which is located in the southeast of Samoa. The total amount of exports has decreased from 2005, with exports to Australia decreasing.

Samoa also promotes inbound tourism, and now it has become a famous tourist destination, next only to Fiji, among the South Pacific Island Countries.

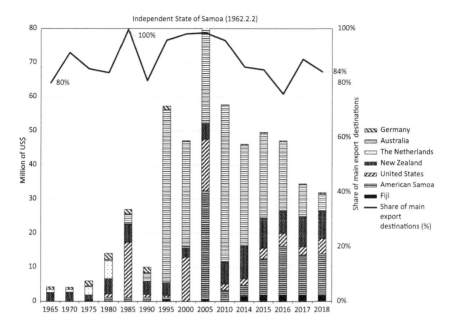

Figure 10.8 Export destination share in Samoa
Source: Based on Direction of Trade Statistics database (IMF).

10.3.2.7 Export destination analysis of the Solomon Islands

The Solomon Islands were colonized by the UK in the 1880s, then occupied by Japan and the US during and after World War II. Among the nine Pacific Island Countries outlined in this chapter, the per capita GDP of the Solomon Islands is the lowest with US$1,920 in 2017 since the principal economic activity is subsistence. This economic situation does not mean that people in the Solomon Islands are poor. Non-monetary business is dominant in the country so that this subsistence is not counted in the economic statistics. However, there is also no mention of income disparity.

The independence of the Solomon Islands occurred on July 7, 1978. Their export commodities in 1975 were copra, wood, and tuna, and the major destinations were Japan, the UK, Australia, the US, and New Zealand worth US$40.65 million. Around 2003, the export share of China, namely, wood exports, increased rapidly. This caused an economic boom in the Solomon Islands. Wood exports to China now occupy 61 percent of total exports and totaled US$564.7 million, which is 14 times larger, in 2018 (Figure 10.9).

On the other hand, the destruction of forests is now a serious issue. Also, the economic slowdown of China is affecting its imports from the Solomon islands. Moreover, the quality of exported woods is poor, so that the economy

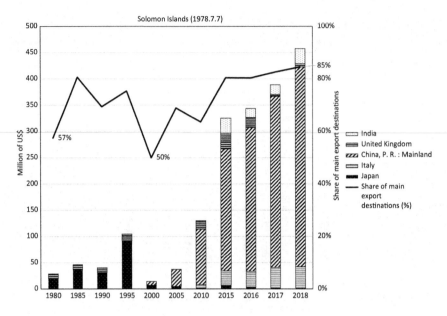

Figure 10.9 Export destination share in the Solomon Islands
Source: Based on Direction of Trade Statistics database (IMF).

of the Solomon Islands might slow down within a couple of years. Anyway, the Solomon Islands also have a limited manufacturing sector; fisheries and tourism are promising industries.

10.3.2.8 Export destination analysis of Tonga

Tonga is the only kingdom among the nine island countries, and it has a strong relationship with the UK. In 1975, Tonga exported copra which made up 67.4 percent of the total exports. In the 1980s, the major export destinations of Tonga were Australia and New Zealand.

After that, pumpkins were exported to Japan, and fishery products were exported to the US in 2000. Recently, the export share of China has increased to 29 percent, which is the top of all destinations in 2018. The other export destinations were Australia (13.6 percent), the US (13.5 percent), New Zealand (13.2 percent), Japan (9.4 percent), and Italy (5.5 percent) (Figure 10.10). Major export commodities were vegetables, roots, and tubers (pumpkins) with 39 percent and fishery products with 26 percent. Pumpkins were mainly exported to Japan, but recently they have been exported to Korea and New Zealand. The second major export commodity is fishery products, which are exported mostly to the US.

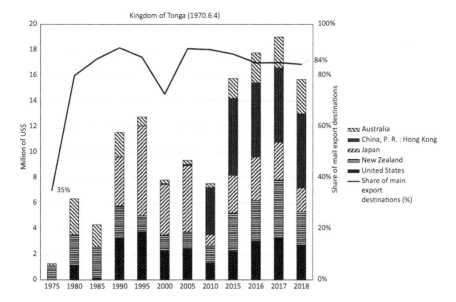

Figure 10.10 Export destination share in Tonga
Source: Based on Direction of Trade Statistics database (IMF).

The merchandise exports of Tonga are minimal, at around 7 percent of its GDP. The most crucial foreign exchange source is workers' remittance, so that this foreign exchange enables Tonga to import large quantities of goods, but it creates a significant trade deficit. To fulfill these deficits, the Tongan government also promotes inbound tourism as a source of foreign exchange.

10.3.2.9 Export destination analysis of Vanuatu

The UK and France shared joint sovereignty of Vanuatu in 1906 and it became independent on July 30, 1980. Before independence, the major export destinations were France, and the US. In 1980, these shares were the US (33.6 percent), France (23.4 percent) and Japan (3.5 percent) with mainly fish exports and export commodities still the same (Figure 10.11). In 2018, the export share were Australia (13.0 percent), the Philippines (12.0 percent), and the US (10.7 percent).

Flag-of-convenience ships have been exported to Turkey, in recent years. The average export growth rate was negative, at -0.2 percent from 2010 to 2017 because of political instability during the 2010s and limited industry. The GDP share of merchandise exports also decreased from 12 percent in 1995 to 6 percent in 2017.

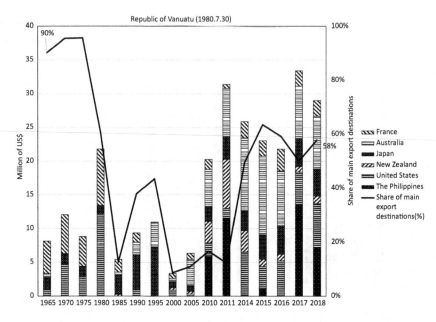

Figure 10.11 Export destination share in Vanuatu
Source: Based on Direction of Trade Statistics database (IMF).

There is also a limited manufacturing sector in Vanuatu since the subsistence economy is still dominant. The Vanuatu government, like other island countries, promotes inbound tourism to mitigate this problem.

10.4 The role of tourism in economic development in the Pacific Island Countries

International inbound tourism is perhaps the most promising sector for Pacific Island Countries. Tourism receipts account for service exports in the balance of payments (Figure 10.12). Foreign exchange earnings through inbound tourism enable these countries to import necessary goods. On the other hand, tourism has both pros and cons, which will be discussed later.

Fiji, known worldwide as a famous tourist destination, has the most significant tourism market and is a successful country in terms of tourism development. Fiji received 843,000 tourists in 2017. Most tourists come from Australia, New Zealand, the US, and Asian countries. Most of them come with their families and stay in the western division of Viti Levu island.

The second most prosperous tourism country is Samoa with 146,000 tourists. Tourists to Samoa come from New Zealand and Australia, and their shares are 40 percent and 20 percent respectively.

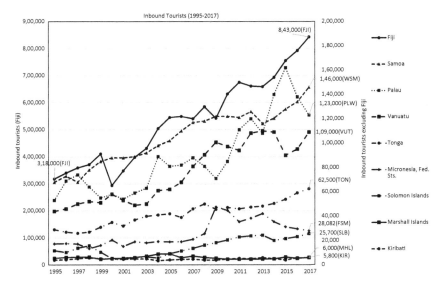

Figure 10.12 The trend of inbound tourism for all nine countries
Source: World Bank, World Development Indicator.

The third main tourist destination is Palau. Palau's economy relies entirely on tourism since there is no other major industry. Most tourists come from Taiwan, China, Korea, and Japan. The fourth main tourist destination is Vanuatu, which is a new tourism destination with an active volcano. Tonga is the next favorite destination and whale watching is the most popular tourist activity there. The Marshall Islands and Kiribati, which consist of atolls, have significant potential for tourism development, but poor transportation and tourism resources, such as hotels and activities, are obstacles.

Table 10.5 shows inbound tourism as an index with 100 in 1995. The total inbound tourism in all countries in 2017 was 2.45 times greater than in 1995. Fiji records the highest growth with a 2.65-fold increase, and its share of them is 62.5 percent. The second is Vanuatu (2.48-fold) and the third is Palau (2.32-fold). In terms of shares, Samoa and Vanuatu occupy 10.8 percent and 8.1 percent, respectively.

Table 10.6 shows the share of tourism receipts in GDP from 1995 to 2017. Palau recorded the highest, 50 percent, in 2017, which is potentially dangerous since tourism is easily affected by external factors such as natural disasters, the economic environment of the world, or political instability. Vanuatu (32 percent), Fiji (23 percent), and Samoa (20 percent), which are more than or equal to the average (20 percent) in 2017. However, Kiribati and the Marshall Islands recorded just 2 percent and 3 percent, respectively, which is a very small portion but there is still hope because their undeveloped nature can be a tourism resource.

Table 10.5 Numbers of inbound tourists and share in the Pacific Islands, 1995–2017

	1995	2000	2005	2010	2015	2017	Share in 2017 (%)
Fiji	100	92	171	199	237	265	62.5
Kiribati	100	123	105	121	100	149	0.4
Marshall Islands	100	95	167	84	115	109	0.4
Micronesia, Fed. States	100	118	109	257	179	161	2.1
Palau	100	109	153	160	306	232	9.1
Samoa	100	129	150	179	188	215	10.8
Solomon Islands	100	44	80	174	183	218	1.9
Tonga	100	121	145	162	186	216	4.6
Vanuatu	100	132	141	221	205	248	8.1
Total	100	103	159	192	227	245	100

Note: Index, 1995=100.
Source: World Bank, World Development Indicators, and author's calculation.

Table 10.6 Tourism receipt share of GDP (%)

	1995	2000	2005	2010	2015	2017
Fiji	19	17	24	26	24	23
Kiribati	4	4	3	3	1	2
Marshall Islands	2	3	3	2	3	3
Micronesia, Fed. States	6	7	8	8	8	8
Palau	N.A.	31	34	42	53	50
Samoa	16	15	16	19	18	20
Solomon Islands	3	1	2	7	5	6
Tonga	5	3	6	5	11	11
Vanuatu	19	25	26	35	34	32
Average	16	14	19	22	20	20

Source: World Bank, World Development Indicators.

Table 10.7 shows tourism receipts per tourists for individual countries. The average of tourism receipts per tourist increased from US$1,000 in 1995 to US$1,437 in 2017, which means, in general, Pacific Island Countries have benefitted from the expansion of international tourism.

In 2017, the Solomon Islands recorded the highest receipts with more than US$3,000 per tourist, and Vanuatu was the second, with US$2,514. Diving is a major tourist activity in these destinations, and tourists stay for relatively long stays so that tourism receipts per tourists are increasing. Fiji, Palau, and Samoa are well-established tourism destinations in the world, and good access by air makes it easy for tourists to visit these countries. Especially, Palau and Samoa effectively promote high-end tourism, and their tourism receipts keep increasing. Kiribati is the lowest tourist earner at US$483 because it has limited activities and accommodations. Tonga recorded US$776 per tourist in 2017, which is also

Table 10.7 International tourism receipts per tourist (USD)

	1995	2000	2005	2010	2015	2017
Fiji	1,160	990	1,325	1,305	1,375	1,409
Kiribati	513	563	756	915	462	483
Marshall Islands	455	577	401	804	810	857
Micronesia, Fed. States	830	829	1,105	537	801	961
Palau	1,038	776	778	894	963	1,179
Samoa	525	466	724	1,014	1,113	1,158
Solomon Islands	1,449	769	681	2,478	2,778	3,074
Tonga	345	200	357	367	862	776
Vanuatu	1,023	1,190	1,677	2,490	2,822	2,514
Average	1,000	844	1,158	1,292	1,381	1,437

Note: Units are nominal USD.

Source: World Bank, World Development Indicators.

relatively low. There are few top-class hotels in Tonga so that building a luxury hotel is necessary if the Tongan government wants to promote high-end tourism.

10.5 Industrial structure change in the Pacific Island Countries

Industrial structures are the focus of GDP percentages and its change. The Pacific Island Countries in this analysis can be classified into three regions, Micronesia (Kiribati, the Marshall Islands, Micronesia, and Palau), Melanesia (Fiji, the Solomon Islands, and Vanuatu), and Polynesia (Tonga and Samoa). Countries in the same region tend to have a similar background and socio-economic structure so that countries grouped into three regions are analyzed. Tables 10.8–10.16 present the four sectors, which are Agriculture, Industry, Manufacturing, and Services of these three regions.

10.5.1 The Micronesian region

In the Micronesian region, located above the equator, these islands were the battlefields in the Pacific War. Except for Kiribati, the countries gained independence from 1986 to 1994, which means they are relatively recently independent. Another common factor is that they were in compact treaties with the US, which means they have been heavily assisted financially by the US. This created a large government and large service sector. Their incomes are relatively high among developing countries, even though they are not heavily industrialized.

The manufacturing shares in 2016 was less than 4 percent, and the service sector takes more than 50 percent in all countries, and this tendency had continued.

Financial support for these countries by the US causes relatively high per capita income compared with the other Pacific Island Countries.

Table 10.8 Kiribati unit (% of GDP)

	1979	1980	1990	2000	2010	2016
Agriculture	18	20	18	21	23	25
Industry	47	9	7	11	11	14
Manufacturing	1	2	1	5	5	4
Services	33	69	73	63	60	58

Table 10.9 Marshall Islands unit (% of GDP)

	1970	1986	1990	2000	2010	2016
Agriculture	–	–	–	–	15	16
Industry	–	–	–	–	11	14
Manufacturing	–	–	–	–	2	2
Services	–	–	–	–	71	68

Table 10.10 Micronesia unit (% of GDP)

	1970	1988	1990	2000	2010	2016
Agriculture	–	–	–	24	27	27
Industry	–	–	–	8	8	6
Manufacturing	–	–	–	2	0	1
Services	–	–	–	66	65	66

Table 10.11 Palau unit (% of GDP)

	1970	1980	1990	2000	2010	2016
Agriculture	–	–	–	4	4	3
Industry	–	–	–	16	11	10
Manufacturing	–	–	–	3	1	1
Services	–	–	–	77	84	85

Source: World Bank, World Development Indicators. Asian Development Bank, Key Indicators.

Table 10.12 Fiji unit (% of GDP)

	1970	1980	1990	2000	2010	2016
Agriculture	25	20	18	15	10	12
Industry	21	20	21	20	18	16
Manufacturing	12	11	12	12	13	11
Services	42	50	49	53	60	61

Table 10.13 Solomon Islands unit (% of GDP)

	1978	1980	1990	2000	2010	2016
Agriculture	–	–	27	33	–	27.3
Industry	–	–	–	–	–	14.7
Manufacturing	–	–	–	–	–	–
Services	–	–	–	–	–	58.0

Table 10.14 Vanuatu unit (% of GDP)

	1970	1980	1990	2000	2010	2015
Agriculture	–	19	21	23	21	27
Industry	–	7	14	11	12	11
Manufacturing	–	4	5	5	5	4
Services	–	70	60	61	62	58

Source: World Bank, World Development Indicators, Asian Development Bank, Key Indicators.

Table 10.15 Samoa unit (% of GDP)

	1970	1980	1990	2000	2010	2016
Agriculture	–	–	–	16	10	10
Industry	–	–	–	25	26	24
Manufacturing	–	–	–	19	12	10
Services	–	–	–	40	52	57

Table 10.16 Tonga unit (% of GDP)

	1970	1980	1990	2000	2010	2016
Agriculture	–	33	30	20	16	17
Industry	–	13	12	19	18	17
Manufacturing	–	6	5	9	6	6
Services	–	48	53	52	60	59

Source: World Bank, World Development Indicators, Asian Development Bank, Key Indicators.

Per capita GDP in 2017, was US$3,843 in the Marshall Islands, US$3,188 in Micronesia, and US$13,338 in Palau. Kiribati is an exception with US$1,594. Because these countries do not have a potential manufacturing sector, they have found new foreign exchange-earners. The Marshall Islands has exported flag-of-convenience ships to Europe and the Asian countries. Palau promotes high-end international tourism from China, Taiwan, Korea, Japan, the US, and European countries. In Micronesia, the world heritage site, Nan Madol will enable a tourism-oriented economy.

10.5.2 The Melanesian region

In the Melanesian region, Fiji, Solomon, and Vanuatu are located in the South Pacific, and historically had strong ties with the European countries. Sugar cane plantations in Fiji still are part of its industrial structure, with 11 percent of the manufacturing sector. Also, Fiji introduced the Tax Free Factory/Tax-Free Zone scheme in 1987 to foster export-oriented industries to increase employment. Under this scheme, the garment industry has grown and contributed to the export of goods. Since 2000, the share of the services sector, which includes tourism, has been expanding.

Because of the enormous subsistence economy, the Solomon Islands and Vanuatu have relied on the public service sector of more than 50 percent of GDP. The share of agriculture was 27 percent for both countries in 2017, and it became the second-largest sector, which consists of forestry in the Solomon Islands, and fisheries in Vanuatu. As mentioned above, the tourism industry for both countries has been developing. Although the subsistence economy is dominant in these two countries, there is potential for economic development, if tourism is expanded.

10.5.3 The Polynesian region

Samoa and Tonga, similar to the other Pacific Island Countries, also rely more than 50 percent on the service sector. In Samoa, the decrease in the export of the wire harnesses, the manufacturing share decreased, and the share of the services sector increased.

Tonga also has a minimal manufacturing industry, and tourism is the second-largest industry. The numbers of inbound tourists to Samoa are sharply increasing and their per capita spending is relatively high. Samoa has a strong potential for tourism.

On the other hand, Tonga has heavily relied on the workers' remittances from abroad, tourism development seems to be stagnant, and the economy is facing difficulty in growth.

10.6 Panel analysis of economic growth in the Pacific Islands Countries

In this section, the MIRAB, TouRAB, and SITEs models, and the conventional export-oriented growth models are examined by panel analysis.

10.6.1 Specification of the estimation models

The panel analysis with a fixed-effect model is used to determine factors for economic growth in the Pacific Island Countries. All variables are transformed to the first difference of logged variables to avoid the unit root. The sample period is from 1995 to 2017, but if the model includes government expenditure, the sample period is from 2000 to 2017 because of data limitation. Nine countries are included: Fiji, Kiribati, the Marshall Islands, Micronesia, Palau, Samoa, the Solomon Islands, Tonga, and Vanuatu.

When examining the MIRAB model, two cases of estimation were conducted, without Fiji and Vanuatu, and with these countries, according to previous studies. The first estimated model is MIRAB, the second is TouRAB, and the third is SITEs. The fourth estimated model is an export-oriented model, which is an orthodox model of economic development.

The estimated formula is as follows:

$$GDP_{it} = \beta_0 + \beta_1 Remittance_{it} + \beta_2 Net\,ODA_{it} + \beta_3 Government\,expenditure_{it}$$
$$+ \beta_4 International\,tourism\,receipts_{it} + \beta_5 Export\,of\,goods_{it}$$
$$+ \beta_6 Dummy\,variable_{it} + \varepsilon_{it}$$

Where i is the Pacific island country, t is the time (year). The original unit of all variables except the dummy variable is in current US million dollars. These variables converted to the first difference of the natural logarithm form as below:

e.g. $GDP_t = \left(ln\left(GDP_{t+1}\right)\right) - \left(ln\left(GDP_t\right)\right)$

These variables and sources in the estimation formula are:

Remittance: Personal remittance, received (World Development Indicator 2019)

Net ODA: Net official development assistance received (World Development Indicator 2019)

Government expenditure: (ADB Key Indicator 2019)

International tourism receipts: (World Development Indicator 2019)

Export of goods: (BOP, ADB Key Indicator 2019)

Dummy variable

The dummy variable includes economic and political instability and natural disasters. When such an event happens, it takes a value of 1, otherwise 0. The details are:

1998 Asian Economic Crisis (all countries);

2007 the Global Financial Crisis (all countries);

2013 Tropical Cyclone Evan (Samoa only);

2000, 2001, 2004, 2010, 2011, political instability (the Solomon Islands only). World Development Indicator

The estimation formula for the MIRAB model is:

GDP = f (Remittance, Net ODA, Government expenditure,
        Dummy variables)

In this estimation, the variable of migration is not included because it has many definitions: "International migration," "Domestic migration," "Temporary migration," and "immigration." International migration means people migrate to other countries, and "domestic migration" means people migrate, for example, from rural to urban areas. "Temporary migration" basically means temporary overseas workers or students, and "immigration" means permanent migration. All these types of migrations are to help people who live in island countries survive. Since this chapter focuses on the economic aspects, "migration" means "overseas worker," then the impact on the Pacific Islands Countries would be financial flow by "personal remittance, received."

ODA consist of loans and grant aid. Loans should be repaid so that net ODA is used to avoid overvaluing.

The government expenditure is calculated in millions of US dollars, as GDP (WDI) multiply the share of government expenditure (ADB).

The estimation formula for the TouRAB model is:

GDP = f (International tourism receipts, Remittance, Net ODA, Government expenditure, Dummy variable)

The estimation formula for the SITEs model is:

GDP = f (International tourism receipts, Dummy variable)

The estimation formula for the export-oriented growth model is:

GDP = f (Export of goods, Tourism receipt, Government expenditure, Dummy variable) – (4)

10.6.2 Results of panel analysis

10.6.2.1 The MIRAB model

According to previous studies, seven countries, Kiribati, the Marshall Islands, Micronesia, Palau, Samoa, Solomon Islands, and Tonga, are included in the estimation (Table 10.17). The sample period is 17 years, from 2000 to 2017.

First of all, individual variables are included in the estimation (columns 1a–3a). The results showed that only government expenditure was significant (column 3a). Remittance and ODA were not significant. Then combinations of Remittance and Government expenditure, Remittance and ODA, Government expenditure and Dummy were estimated (columns 4a–6a). The results showed Remittance, ODA, and Dummy variables are insignificant (columns 4a, 5a, 6a), and the only Government expenditure is significant. This result was not expected. Remittance is vital for some island countries and ODA by European countries, the US and Japan obviously contributed to their economic development. This unexpected result needs to be further analyzed.

Table 10.18 shows the estimation results of the MIRAB model, including Fiji and Vanuatu. The estimation result seemed to be similar to Table 10.17 (without

Table 10.17 The MIRAB model without Fiji and Vanuatu dependent variable, GDP, 2000–2017

	(1a)	(2a)	(3a)	(4a)	(5a)	(6a)
Sample size	140	154	119	110	119	119
Constant	0.008	0.007	0.012	0.012	0.011	0.015
	(1.231)	(1.229)	(1.968)*	(1.931)*	(1.930)*	(2.345)**
Remittance	0.0004			−0.001		
	(0.035)			(−0.084)		
ODA		0.007			0.019	
		(0.507			(1.346)	
Government expenditure			0.178	0.182	0.180	0.164
			(4.599)***	(4.482)***	(4.672)***	(4.094)***
Dummy						−0.028
						(−1.352)
Adjusted R^2	−0.005	0.002	0.144	0.134	0.151	0.151

Notes: *,** and *** indicate significance at the 10%, 5% and 1% levels respectively.
t-statistics are in parentheses.

Table 10.18 The MIRAB model with Fiji and Vanuatu dependent variable, GDP, 2000–2017

	(1b)	(2b)	(3b)	(4b)	(5b)	(6b)
Sample size	184	198	153	144	153	153
Constant	0.0010	0.0093	0.014	0.015	0.014	0.021
	(1.708)*	(1.715)*	(2.645)***	(2.604)***	(2.581)**	(3.625)***
Remittance	0.0040			0.00023		
	(0.724)			(0.0022)		
ODA		0.010			0.017	
		(0.690)			(0.230)	
Government expenditure			0.209	0.213	0.210	0.181
			(5.474)***	(5.371)***	(5.514)***	(4.705)***
Dummy						−0.052
						(−2.904)***
Adjusted R^2	−0.009	−0.002	0.158	0.151	0.161	0.200

Notes: *,** and *** indicate significance at the 10%, 5% and 1% levels respectively.
t-statistics are in parentheses.
Fiji and Vanuatu are included, although these countries are excluded from the MIRAB model in the previous literature.

Fiji and Vanuatu). The combination of government expenditure and the dummy variable is significant, and coefficients are in the expected directions. The sign of government expenditure is positive, and the dummy variable is negative (column 6b). This result means government expenditure contributed to their economy, and obstructive external factors negatively affected the economy.

In this framework, the result does not fully support the MIRAB model, both with Fiji and Vanuatu, and without Fiji and Vanuatu. The reason is that this

Table 10.19 The TouRAB and SITEs model dependent variable, GDP, 1995–2017 or 2000–2017 (with Government expenditure)

	(7)	(8)	(9)	(10)	(11)	(12)
Sample size	198	184	198	153	184	153
Constant	0.007	0.008	0.007	0.010	0.008	0.017
	(1.436)	(1.451)	(1.440)	(1.928)*	(1.458)	(3.270)***
Tourism receipts	0.084	0.086	0.085	0.083	0.086	0.088
	(5.322)***	(5.195)***	(5.352)***	(5.721)***	(5.217)***	(6.257)***
Remittance		0.002			0.001	
		(0.152)			(0.089)	
ODA			0.013		0.012	
			(0.937)		(0.835)	
Government expenditure				0.240		0.209
				(6.869)***		(6.080)
Dummy						-0.060
						(-3.756)***
Adjusted R^2	0.127	0.123	0.126	0.311	0.121	0.369

Notes: *,** and *** indicate significance at the 10%, 5% and 1% levels respectively.
t-statistics are in parentheses.

estimated model includes large and small island countries. In terms of population, for example, it ranges from 53,000 in the Marshall Islands to 905,000 in Fiji in 2017, which is 17 times large, and this disparity affects the result.

10.6.2.2 The TOURAB and SITEs model

The TouRAB and SITEs model was examined for all nine countries. The sample period is from 1995 to 2017, if government expenditure is omitted from the estimation, the period is from 2000 to 2017 (Table 10.19). Three variables, "Tourism receipts," "Government expenditure," and the dummy variable were in the model.

The estimation (column 7) is for the SITEs model, and the others (columns 8–12) are for the TouRAB model. The result of the SITEs model shows tourism receipts are significant (7).

In terms of the TouRAB model, "Tourism receipt" and "Government expenditure" are significant predictors. The important finding is that "Tourism receipts," in any combination, are statistically significant and positive (columns 7–12).

Remittance and ODA are not significant in all cases. Factors examined for the MIRAB model showed that only government expenditure is significant, but factors examined with the TouRAB and the SITEs model showed tourism receipts, government expenditure, and their combinations, are significant.

The conclusion is that "Government expenditure" and "Tourism receipts" clearly and positively predict GDP in the Pacific Island Countries. However, the reason why remittance and ODA were insignificant should be examined.

Table 10.20 The orthodox export-oriented growth model dependent variable, GDP, 2000–2017

	(13)	(14)	(15)	(16)
Sample size	153	153	153	153
Constant	0.0186	0.015	0.009	0.016
	(3.233)***	(2.795)***	(1.867)*	(3.154)***
Export of goods	0.064	0.063	0.0551	0.049
	(2.596)**	(2.682)***	(2.708)***	(2.501)**
Tourism receipts		0.067	0.0825	0.087
		(4.143)***	(5.786)***	(6.297)***
Government expenditure			0.235	0.206
			(6.863)***	(6.107)***
Dummy				-0.056
				(-3.596)***
Adjusted R²	0.028	0.127	0.341	0.392

Notes: *,** and *** indicate significance at the 10%, 5% and 1% levels respectively.
t-statistics are in parentheses.

10.6.2.3 The export-oriented growth model

Finally, the orthodox export-oriented growth model was examined. Although the export competitiveness of these island countries was weak according to previous research, the Pacific Island Countries could export specific goods, mainly agricultural products, to other countries. The export destinations have mainly been Japan, the US, and European countries under preferential trade schemes such as the Rome agreement or as part of ODA.

Table 10.20 shows the estimation result. "Export of goods" is significant for all cases (columns 13–16). The estimation (column 16) including "Export of goods," "Tourism receipts," "Government expenditure," and the dummy variable is the best combination of all estimations, in terms of adjusted R square. From the estimation results of MIRAB, TouRAB, SITEs, and the Export-oriented models, the GDP of the Pacific Island Countries is likely affected by government expenditures, tourism receipts, and export of goods in a positive direction. The dummy variable, which includes political instability, global economic crises, and natural disasters, can be said to have negatively affected their economies.

The most important finding is that the "Tourism receipts" consistently and strongly affected GDP positively, followed by "Government expenditures" and "Export of goods" in the nine Pacific Island Countries.

10.7 Conclusion

This chapter has examined industrial development through the export of goods and their destinations for the nine Pacific Island Countries: Fiji, Kiribati, the Marshall Islands, Micronesia, Palau, Samoa, the Solomon Islands, Tonga, and Vanuatu, from post-World War II to recent years. To evaluate their development processes, their historical background, major export commodities, and export destinations were reviewed. Furthermore, the MIRAB, TouRAB, SITEs, and export-oriented growth models were examined by panel analysis.

The results are as follows.

1 Regarding export commodities in the 1970s and the 1980s, the variety of commodities was limited. Fiji mainly exported sugar, a remnant of its early plantations. In 1975, Kiribati exported phosphate, accounting for 96 percent of total exports, and Samoa, Solomon, Tonga, and Vanuatu mainly exported copra. In 1985, the main export commodities of Samoa and Tonga shifted from copra to coconut oil. This change means during these ten years, their industrial level improved because copra must be processed to make coconut oil. Kiribati, the Solomon Islands, and Vanuatu exported tuna and other fishery products. The Solomon Islands continuously exported wood. These commodities are still exported from these countries. Regarding the manufacturing sector, canning factories in the Solomon Islands and Fiji, and the wire harness factory in Samoa contributed to increasing their exports. Some of them are still in the exporting business, apart from the wire harness factory in Samoa.

   Recently, under globalization, several new export commodities from these countries were produced. "Fiji Water" is a typical case. The share of Fiji Water exports to the US was 24 percent of total exports in 2018. Noteworthy export activities are the flag-of-convenience ships exported from the Marshall Islands and Vanuatu. The Marshall Islands exported these ships to Korea, Cyprus, and 14 other countries, accounting for 76 percent of total exports in 2018. Vanuatu also exported ships to Turkey, Poland, and three other countries, accounting for 15 percent of total exports in 2018. This new type of export might contribute to economic improvement in these island countries.

2 After World War II, the colonial masters or developed countries that governed these countries, especially the European countries, did not import a lot from the Pacific Island Countries based on statistics. Recently, the US, Japan, and China have become important export destinations for these countries.

3 In most island countries, both inbound tourists and international tourism receipts have been increasing rapidly, except for Kiribati and the Marshall Islands. Comparing 1995 with 2017, the number of inbound tourists increased 2.7 times in Fiji, 2.5 times in Vanuatu, 2.3 times in Palau, 2.2 times in the Solomon Islands, Tonga, and Samoa, and 1.6 times in Micronesia. Tourism is an excellent opportunity for them to obtain foreign exchange, and all governments have changed their industrial policy to tourism promotion.

4 The result of panel analysis shows the MIRAB model was not well supported. Tourism and government expenditures in the TouRAB and SITEs models were well supported. Also, the export of goods was significant. Although European countries have not imported a lot from the Pacific Island Countries, Australia, New Zealand, Japan, the US, and China are the major export destinations, and these exports contribute to the economy of the island

countries. On the other hand, fragility due to political instability, global economic crises, and natural disasters has affected their economies negatively.

Since the Pacific Island Countries have experienced being colonized, occupied, or governed by influential developed countries, their development process and industrial structures have been affected.

Because these countries are located in a tropical area, tropical plants, fruits, and fish are for subsistence, domestic consumption, and export. Banana, copra, and coconut are traditional products. Coffee in Vanuatu and sugar in Fiji are traced back to the era of colonization. Since their domestic markets are tiny, and the location of the countries is far from big markets, the manufacturing sector has not developed. But ODA-related industries, such as canning factories in Solomon and Fiji, contribute to their economies and exports. The fisheries industry is also essential and demonstrates competitiveness. Fisheries resources, tuna, skipjack, or other fishery products have become staple export commodities. The export of fish and selling fishing rights are an essential revenue source for the island countries.

Currently, tourism receipts, which are a service export, are the most important economic driver for these countries, and all governments strongly promote inbound tourism. The only concern is that tourism is easily affected by external factors, such as the outbreak of infectious disease, so that over-dependence on tourism might be risky, and the governments should recognize this fact.

This chapter concludes that the industrial structure of the Pacific Islands Countries is shifting from the agriculture sector, including fisheries, to the services sector, mainly inbound tourism. As a result, the manufacturing industry could not support these countries. The concern is that Kiribati and the Marshall Islands will be left behind in the race for tourism development. However, the optimistic view is that all Pacific Island Countries have the potential not only for tourism development but also they have huge marine resources, so that they will be able to survive in the future.

Notes

1 See CIA (n.d.).
2 See PAFCO (n.d.).
3 Author's calculation based on UN COMTRADE database. The percentages by major export commodity of Fiji in 2018 are: fisheries products (20 percent), mineral water (15 percent).
4 Coconut oil and palm oil are different. Coconut oil is made from coconuts or copra and palm oil is made from oil palm.
5 Flag-of-convenience countries in 2019 are: Antigua and Barbuda, Bahamas, Barbados, Belize, Bermuda (UK), Bolivia, Cambodia, Cayman Islands, Comoros, Cyprus, Equatorial Guinea, Faroe Islands (FAS), French International Ship Register (FIS), German International Ship Register (GIS), Georgia, Gibraltar (UK), Honduras, Jamaica, Lebanon, Liberia, Malta, Madeira, Marshall Islands (USA), Mauritius, Moldova, Mongolia, Myanmar, Netherlands Antilles, North Korea, Panama, Sao Tome

and Príncipe, St Vincent, Sri Lanka, Tonga, Vanuatu (International Transport Workers' Federation, n.d.).

Bibliography

Baldacchino, G. (2006). Managing the hinterland beyond: Two ideal-type strategies of economic development for small island territories. *Asia Pacific Viewpoint, 47*(1), 45–60.

Baldacchino, G., & Bertram, G. (2009). The beak of the finch: Insights into the economic development of small economies. *The Round Table, 98*(401), 141–160.

Bertram, G. (1999). The MIRAB model twelve years on. *The Contemporary Pacific, 56*, 105–138.

Bertram, G. (2006). Introduction: The MIRAB model in the twenty-first century. *Asia Pacific Viewpoint, 47*(1), 1–13.

Bertram, G., & Watters, R. F. (1985). The MIRAB economy in South Pacific microstates. *Pacific Viewpoint, 26*(3), 497–519.

CIA. (n.d.). World factbook. Available at: www.cia.gov/library/publications/the-world-factbook/ (accessed January 17, 2020).

Guthunz, U., & Krosigk, F. (1996) Tourism development in small island states: From MIRAB to TouRAB? In L. Briguglio, B. Archer, J. Jafari, & G. Wall (Eds.), *Sustainable tourism in islands and small states: Issues and policies* (pp. 18–35). London: Pinter Publishers.

International Transport Workers' Federation. (n.d.). Flag of convenience. Available at: www.itfglobal.org/en/sector/).seafarers/flags-of-convenience (accessed January 17, 2020).

McElroy, J. L. (2006). Small island tourist economies across the life cycle. *Asia Pacific Viewpoint, 47*(1), 61–77.

Ministry of Foreign Affairs. (n.d.). Japan counties and regions. Available at: www.mofa.go.jp/region/index.html (accessed January 17, 2020).

Asia Pacific Press, *Pacific Economic Bulletin* (1986). Statistical annex. 1(1).

PAFCO, Fiji. (n.d.). Available at: www.pafcofiji.com/ (accessed January 17, 2020).

South Pacific Commission. (1985). Population 1983. *Statistical Bulletin of the South Pacific, 26*.

Statistical Bulletin of the South Pacific (18, 20, 23, 25, 27, 30, 32, 34, 36, 38, 40). Overseas trade. Nouméa, New Caledonia: South Pacific Commission.

UNCTAD. (n.d.). Fleet statistics database. Available at: https://unctadstat.unctad.org/wds/ReportFolders/reportFolders.aspx (accessed 8 September 2020).

Appendix

Table 10.A1 Chronological table of the history of the Pacific Island Countries

Year	FJI	KIR	MHL	FSM	PLW	WSM	SLB	TON	VUT
1800's	Colonized by UK (1874)		Dependence of DEU (1885)	Occupied by ESP and DEU(1899)	Occupied by DEU(1899)	Occupied by DEU (1899)	Colonized by UK (1893)		
1900's								Dependence of UK (1900)	Condominium by UK & FRA (1906)
1914	The outbreak of World War I								
1914–18		Colonized by UK	Occupied by JPN	Occupied by JPN	Occupied by JPN				
1918	End of World War I								
1919–20			UN Trust Territory by JPN	UN Trust Territory by JPN	UN Trust Territory by JPN	UN Trust Territory by NZL			
1939	The outbreak of World War II								
1939–1942		Occupied UK & USA					Occupied by JPN		
1945	End of World War II								
1945		Occupied by USA	Occupied by USA	Occupied by USA	Occupied by USA	UN Trust Territory	Occupied by USA		

(*continued*)

Table 10.A1 Cont.

Year	FJI	KIR	MHL	FSM	PLW	WSM	SLB	TON	VUT
1947			UN Trust Territory by USA	UN Trust Territory by USA	UN Trust Territory by USA				
1962	PAFCO (1963)					IDP 1962.1.1			
1970	IDP from UK 1970.10.10						Solomon Tiyo (1972)	IDP from UK 1970.6.4	
1976	The 1st Rome Treaty (1976.4–1980.2)								
1978							IDP from UK 1978.7.7		
1979		IDP 1979.7.12							
1980									IDP 1980.7.30
1981 1986	The 2nd Rome Treaty(1981.1–1982.5) / The 3rd Rome Treaty (1985–1990) / The 4th Rome Treaty (1990–1999)		COMPACT IDP 1986.10.21	COMPACT IDP 1986.11.3					
1987	Coup								

1993			COMPACT	Yazaki (1991)
1994			IDP 1994.10.1	
1997	Asian Financial Crisis (1997.7)			
2004	Revision COMPACT	Revision COMPACT		
2006	Coup			
2007	Global financial crisis (2007–2008)			

Note: COMPACT: The free association between USA and FSM, MHL, PLW, IDP=Independence, DEU: Germany, ESP: Spain, FRA: France, JPN: Japan, NZL: New Zealand, UK: United Kingdom.

Source: Ministry of Foreign Affairs Japan.

Table 10.A2 Export share of principal commodities in six South Pacific Island Countries, 1975 and 1985 (%)

1975	Fiji	Kiribati	Samoa	Solomon Islands	Tonga	Vanuatu
03 Tuna	0.1			20.8		32.7
05 Bananas	0.0		1.2		8.1	
05 Coconuts			1.9		7.5	
06 Sugar, honey, etc.	67.5					
07 Coffee						
07 Cocoa			26.0	0.9		5.0
08 Feedstuff for animals	0.4					
08 Copra		3	57.3	76.2	67.4	42.8
0842 Coconut oil	3.6					
0842 Palm oil						
24 Wood and manufactures thereof	1.1		3.3	26.9		0.2
28 Phosphate		96				
28 Metalliferous ores and scrap	0.1			0.2	0.0	8.6
29 Coral, shells, etc.	0.1			1.4	0.0	1.2
99 Gold	6.1					
Total	79	100	90	127	83	90
1985						
03 Tuna	4.3	16.8		27.3		0.0
05 Bananas	0.0		1.4		3.9	
05 Coconuts	0.0		7.8		8.0	0.0
06 Sugar, honey, etc.	41.2					
07 Coffee	0.0					0.6
07 Cocoa	0.2		6.5	4.8		4.1
08 Feedstuff for animals	0.5					
08 Copra		77.9	4.2	22.6	1.2	42.7
0842 Coconut oil	2.8		43.2		35.2	
0842 Palm oil			34.2			
24 Wood and manufactures thereof	1.1		2.3	23.8	0.0	4.3
28 Phosphate						
28 Metalliferous ores and scrap	0.1					
29 Coral, shells, etc.	0.2			0.8		0.7
99 Gold	8.0			0.8		
Total	59	95	100	80	48	52

Note: Original figures are in local currency. The total of Solomon Islands in 1975 might be a statistical error.

The numbers before the commodity name are the SITC code.

Source: *Statistical Bulletin of the South Pacific* various issues, South Pacific Commission.

Table 10.A3 Political status, independence, main export commodities and export destinations, 1975 and 2018

	Historical colonization or dependency status	In-dependence	Main export commodities in 1975	Main export partners in 1975	Main export commodities in 2018	Main export portents in 2018
Fiji	*UK	1970. 10.10	Sugar, honey, / Coconut oil / Wood / Coral / Gold	UK, AUS NZL	Beverages, spirits and vinegar, Meat, fish or crustaceans, molluscs and other aquatic invertebrates	USA, AUS, JPN, NZL
Kiribati	*UK **UK & USA→JPN	1979 .7.12	Copra / Phosphate	AUS NZL	Fish and crustaceans, molluscs and other aquatic invertebrates	USA, UK NZL
Marshall Islands	**U.N. Trust Territory (USA)	1986. 10.21			Ships, boats and floating structures	KOR CYP NLD
Micronesia	**U.N. Trust Territory (USA)	1988 .11.3			Fish and crustaceans, molluscs and other aquatic invertebrates	THA, GUM, CHN, JPN
Palau	**U.N. Trust Territory (USA)	1994. 10.1			Fish and crustaceans, molluscs and other aquatic invertebrates	JPN USA
Samoa	**U.N. Trust Territory (NZL)	1962. 1.1	Coconut / Cocoa / Copra / Wood	NZL USA AUS JPN	Vegetables and certain roots and tubers; edible	American Samoa, NZL, AUS, USA
Solomon Islands	*UK→ **USA	1978. 7.7	Tuna / Cocoa / Copra / Wood / Coral	JPN, UK AUS, USA, NZL	Wood and articles of wood; wood charcoal	CHN ITA IND

(continued)

Table 10.A3 Cont.

	Historical colonization or dependency status	In-dependence	Main export commodities in 1975	Main export partners in 1975	Main export commodities in 2018	Main export portents in 2018
Tonga	UK	1970.6.4	Banana / Copra	UK NZL AUS USA	Fish and crustaceans, molluscs and other aquatic invertebrates Vegetables and certain roots and tubers; edible	CHN AUS USA NZL
Vanuatu	***UK & ***FRA	1980.7.30	Copra / Wood / Coral	FRA USA JPN	Fish and crustaceans, molluscs and other aquatic invertebrates	AUS, PHL, USA, MYS

Notes: * denote colonial master. ** denote after World War II. *** denote condominium.

UK United Kingdom, JPN Japan, NZL New Zealand, FRA France, MLD the Netherland, KOR Korea, GUM Guam, CHN China, ITA Italy, IND India, PHL the Philippines, MYS Malaysia.

Main commodity export in 2018 is based on two digits levels of Harmonized System Code.

Source: "Countries & Regions," Ministry of Foreign Affairs, Japan. "OVERSEAS TRADE" Statistical Bulletin of the South Pacific, various issues, South Pacific Commission. UN-COMTRADE. The direction of Trade Statistics (IMF).

11 "Made in China 2025" and the recent industrial policy in China

Kucuk Ali Akkemik and Murat Yülek

11.1 Introduction

The effectiveness and need for industrial policies and government intervention for industrialization, in general, in developing economies have been discussed from various perspectives. While some studies (e.g., Akkemik, 2009; Amsden, 1989; Chang, 1993; Johnson, 1982; Wade, 1990; Yülek, 2018) have argued that the industrial policies specifically designed for certain industries are necessary for developing countries in East Asia (including Japan, Korea, Singapore, and Taiwan) and were instrumental in increasing national welfare in the postwar period until the 1990s, some others, such as Pack (2000), have argued that industrial policies were not really effective in stimulating reallocation of resources toward hi-tech industries in developing economies.

As Rodrik (2008) underlines, it is possible to find many examples of successes and failures of industrial policies from a number of countries. The existence of failed implementations of industrial policy does not necessarily reduce it only to a theoretical possibility. The successful example of East Asian industrial policies in the past has proved that industrial policy could stimulate structural changes and successful industrialization in the long run.

The recent case of Chinese industrial policy is especially important since not only is China the second largest economy in the world, but also government intervention in industrialization since the mid-1980s resembles the industrial policies in Japan, Korea, Singapore, and Taiwan in the past. Further, with the 13th Development Plan (2016–2020), China has concentrated on a new phase of value-added industrialization and technological development that would lead to sustained economic growth. Recently, the "Made in China 2025 Initiative" was launched with the objective of strengthening the position of China globally in high-tech industries (ISDP, 2018).

In this chapter, we elaborate on the process and patterns of industrialization and technology development in developing economies and discuss the theoretical underpinnings of industrial policies in East Asia in the past. We then discuss the evolution of industrial policies in China and evaluate them.

The rest of the chapter is organized as follows. In Section 11.2, we develop a framework to analyze the industrial policies in developing countries. Industrial policies in China are discussed at length in Section 11.3. The industrial policies of the Chinese government are then evaluated with respect to our theoretical framework in Section 11.4. Finally, Section 11.5 wraps up and concludes.

11.2 Industrial policy: Theoretical underpinnings

This section, drawing heavily on Yülek (2018) and Akkemik (2009), discusses the theoretical justifications of the industrial policies in East Asia. For brevity, we abstain from detailing these policies.

11.2.1 The process of industrialization

Industrialization has almost become synonymous with economic development for some time. While the manufacturing sector has been the engine of growth in many developing countries, enhanced productivity in manufacturing industries also stimulated productivity improvement at the aggregate economy level, as proposed by Kaldor and Verdoorn's laws.

The share of manufacturing has been in continuous decline in the advanced countries for the last four decades while the same share was on the rise at least until the late 1990s for most developing countries in East Asia, including China. However, recently, there is a visible and arguably premature decline in the share of manufacturing in GDP in the developing countries as well. Yülek (2018, pp. 128–130) emphasizes the inverse U-shaped share of manufacturing in GDP in developing countries and argues that it is the result of a Kaldorian mechanism as follows: With the advance of industrialization, labor productivity in manufacturing increases and pushes up GDP and average productivity, and stimulates further growth or birth of other sectors through technological spillovers. The resulting increase in output is far beyond the industrial output generated by the productivity in the manufacturing sector, thus leading to the declined percentage share of manufacturing.

On the other hand, it is also necessary to consider the possibility of the so-called "Baumol's cost disease." In an early study, Baumol (1967) classified economic activities into two sectors, namely, the technologically progressive sector (such as certain leading manufacturing industries) where technological improvement and innovation lead to increases in labor productivity, and a stagnant sector (mostly services), which lag behind in productivity increases. The progressive sectors are also characterized by an increasing share of capital as well as higher levels of technology. Baumol's unbalanced growth hypothesis states that the stagnant sector's prices would be higher due to slower productivity growth. During the course of economic growth, the share of the stagnant sector's output in total output (GDP) will be higher since its prices are higher and its output is also growing albeit at a slower rate than the progressive sector.[1] Yülek's (2018) observation of the declining share of manufacturing in the modern economic histories of the developing countries can be partially explained by Baumol's cost disease theory.

A popular and historical view of industrialization focuses on the evolution of industrial technologies (Yülek, 2018, pp. 175–176). The development of the textile manufacturing and the reorganization of production processes in the form of a factory as a result of new technologies based on water and steam power in the late eighteenth century mark the first industrial revolution (IR1). The second industrial revolution (IR2), at the end of the nineteenth century, introduced new technologies, based on electric power, and also made possible the invention of newer and faster means of communication and transportation as well as mass production in factories at unprecedented rates. The third industrial revolution (IR3) started in the late 1960s and it was based on the newly developing information technologies, which led to the development of computers and numerical control machines. Since the early 2010s, a new and fourth industrial revolution (IR4), starting in Germany, is thought to be under way. IR4 focuses on a new generation of high technologies including robots, machine learning, and artificial intelligence, which is thought to revolutionize not only manufacturing (smart manufacturing) but also various services, pharmaceuticals and medicine, in particular. Repetitive tasks, most of which are still done by humans, may soon be undertaken by machines and this is expected to bring about social changes as well.

The process of industrialization follows a pattern. In the early stages of industrialization, labor-intensive industries (e.g., textiles, clothing, food, etc.), which produce basic necessities, lead industrial development as the technology required for these industries can be adopted and mastered relatively easily. In the next stage, capital-intensive industries, i.e., heavy (e.g., machines, steel, etc.) and chemical industries, led industrial development. These are technologically more sophisticated industries with substantial scale economies and require massive investments. In the third stage of industrialization, the leading industries become knowledge-intensive industries, e.g., computers, electronic machines, sophisticated telecom equipment, software, robots, and automobiles, which produce higher value-added products. The transition from one stage to the next requires a substantial accumulation of industrial capital and know-how. While it is possible to acquire foreign technologies at the beginning of each stage, technology creation and innovation become essential throughout each stage, which requires a strong commitment and a large amount of investment. Progressing to the third stage, in particular, is necessary to avoid being stuck in the "middle income trap."

The industrialization pattern above is also related to industrial revolutions and accompanying technological changes. Another view of the stages of industrialization emphasizes technological sophistication in each stage (Yülek, 2018, pp. 176–181). According to this view, in the first stage, the technologies are related to IR1; production is mechanized through imports of machinery; and the output share of capital increases. Labor-intensive industries, such as textiles and clothing, are examples of such industries. In the second stage, technological sophistication and productivity increase as the country learns the technologies. It is common at this stage for developing countries to attract investments for assembly or parts production as well as production under licenses from advanced countries' firms due to lower production costs. At the end of this stage, capital intensity and productivity increase a great deal and the country learns and masters the technologies embedded in machines. In the third stage, highly sophisticated (hi-tech) products of the advanced countries are imitated and hi-tech industries such as automotive and electronics are established. These industries are also characterized by learning-by-doing, which enables upgrading of labor skills. National production capacity increases and the technology creation capacity of the country improves. In the fourth, and last, stage, innovation is the key and new industrial products need to be developed by intensive research and development. The country is competing at the technological frontier with advanced countries and total factor productivity growth becomes the most important source of long-run growth. Most of the economies in the middle-income trap still remain at the second stage while industrial policies have helped East Asian economies such as Korea, Singapore, and Taiwan to successfully progress to the third stage and subsequently to the fourth stage.

Economic histories of East Asian countries have shown that successful transformation of the industrial structure in the above-mentioned patterns of industrialization may be achieved through the use of the state power and deliberately designed industrial policies, if implemented successfully. In doing this, the state does not have to engage with industrialization as a producer but may oversee the activities of the public and private actors in the economy to achieve the long-run aim of industrialization. A number of countries in East Asia, which were subject to different initial conditions, were able to achieve rapid industrialization through systematic and transformative industrial policies and evolved from low-income countries to advanced countries within one or two generations. In the next section, we elaborate on the salient features of these policies.

11.2.2 Salient features of industrial policies in East Asia

Traditional industrial policies in East Asian economies have generally been justified on the grounds that markets fail to ensure effective resource allocation during the process of industrialization, "infant industries" need to be protected from foreign competition at least until they achieve dynamic comparative advantages warranting government intervention (Akkemik, 2009). The Big Push theory of industrialization argues that the government could play an important role by putting in place appropriate policies to exploit the complementarities across investments in related industries at the early stages of industrialization. Economies of scale and positive externalities across industries, heavy and chemical industries in particular, were seen as the sources of market failures. The government's involvement in infant industry protection is justified on the condition that average costs will decline in the future after achieving a minimum scale, i.e., there are "dynamic economies of scale," but the current high costs deter private firms from investing in the infant industry. Infant industry protection must be temporary in order to discourage unproductive rent-seeking activities, known as the Mill criterion, and the present value of future social returns of protection

Table 11.1 Instruments of traditional industrial policies in East Asia

Government intervention and public finance	*Policies for targeted firms*
• Allocation of foreign currency • R&D subsidies • Infrastructure improvement (health, education, etc.) • Bond finance • Deliberation councils • Tax incentives and accelerated depreciation • Autonomy in economic bureaucracy • Adjustment of exchange rate regime for competitiveness • Maintaining long-term price stability	• Financial support for investment under uncertainty • Protection via rigidity in entry and exit (e.g., setup costs, minimum capital requirements, etc.) • Allocation of cheap policy credits • Policies for domestic content and joint ventures with foreign firms • Incentives to enhance learning effect and innovation • Agglomeration of industries • Preferential investments in industrial infrastructure
Trade policies	*Human capital*
• Foreign aid at the beginning and FDI later • Import-substitute industrialisation, infant industry protection by import tariffs and quotas • Export-oriented industrialisation • Technology transfer through FDI	• Investments education and skills • Importance given to income distribution and inequality, alleviation of poverty • Policies and support schemes to foster productivity

Source: Adapted from Akkemik (2009).

(discounted at the social rate of discount) must be greater than current social costs of the protection of the infant industry, known as the Bastable criterion (Itoh et al., 1991, p. 43).

Industrial policy is generally understood as a set of policies ranging from those related to macroeconomic policies (fiscal and monetary) to those related to competition, trade, and the labor market, systematically designed for the development of either the entire manufacturing sector as a whole (general industrial policy) or targeted industries in particular (specific industrial policy). Table 11.1 briefly outlines these policies in the East Asian experience. These policies have been combined in various combinations by East Asian developmental states for rapid industrialization in the past.

The East Asian governments' response to market failures was to use the state apparatus to "discipline" private firms and bring them in line with the government's industrial policies. These governments were later dubbed "developmental states." While each country was subject to different political and economic conditions, a common feature is that the economic bureaucracy in the developmental state enjoyed a high level of autonomy, often free from political pressures. Table 11.2 outlines the specific features of the traditional industries in Japan, Korea, Singapore, and Taiwan.

Table 11.2 General characteristics of traditional industrial policies in East Asia

	Domestic firms	Foreign capital	Technology transfer	Competition policy
Japan (1940s–1980s)	Encouraged use of domestic resources for industrialization, promotion of large domestic firms in oligopolistic markets	Hostile attitude toward foreign capital, especially in strategic industries	Technology transfer during the 1960s and 1970s, license agreements and technology purchases, denial of dominant position by foreign firms	Nurturing of oligopolistic markets
Korea (1960s–1990s)	Nurturing of large conglomerates and oligopolistic markets	Permitted on condition of technology transfer and joint ventures, domestic content requirements	Massive R&D support public investments in technology infrastructure, strategic targeting	Nurturing of *chaebols* by government support, direction of *chaebols* to heavy industries
Singapore (1960s–1990s)	Local firms were ignored by the government, operated as subcontractors to MNCs, but promoted after 1985	Substantial support to MNCs; MNC dominance in industry	Technology transfer from MNCs to local firms (post-1985)	Government remained loyal to the free enterprise ideology
Taiwan (1950s–1990s)	Government support to increase domestic content, SMEs as the main pillar of industrial policies	EPZs and restricted competition with domestic firms	Effort to upgrade SMEs' technologies, public research institutes, public-private joint R&D projects	Generally directed to heavy industries by the government; some large firms were SOEs

Notes: MNCs: multinational corporations, SOEs: state-owned enterprises, SMEs: small and medium-sized enterprises, EPZs: export processing zones.

Source: Compiled from Akkemik (2009).

The developmental state and its industrial policies lost their importance in East Asia soon after these economies successfully industrialized and achieved mass production capacity in hi-tech industries. Firms, once operating under the guidance of the government, became large multinational corporations running large global value chains and national leaders of manufacturing and innovation. At the same time, complying with the rapid globalization of the world economy, the developmental states turned into neoliberal states and were integrated into the global commodity and financial markets and the previously powerful economies' bureaucracies lost their autonomy over economic decision-making.

11.2.3 Sequencing of policies for successful industrialization

Industrial policies have proved to accelerate industrialization and enhance economic welfare in the East Asian countries. However, industrial policies themselves have a limit in technological development and have to be augmented with science and technology policies at a certain level of industrial development, as evident from the East Asian experience. Yülek (2018, pp. 220–224) lays out the basic principles for the sequencing of policies in industrial development, which is portrayed in Figure 11.1.

At the earlier stages of industrial development, which also correspond to the first and second stages of technological development, emphasizing first the imports of machines and then adopting the embedded technologies, the accompanying industrial policies are of a general type. In other words, in the early stages, the acquisition of foreign technologies is important through capital deepening across the board. While still low-cost manufacturing bases, the developing countries at this stage are part of the global value chains due to their low costs, mainly by attracting foreign investments. In the third stage, building up national technological capabilities through imitation of foreign technologies is important and national technology policy becomes instrumentally important at this stage. In the previous two stages, technology policies are irrelevant and it is too early for them. Having built up a sufficient amount of capital stock is a necessary condition for technology policies. The accompanying industrial policies at this stage focus on specific industrial products (i.e., picking the winners) in the higher value-added section of the value chain, which, by their nature, are R&D-intensive. The winner industries are generally selected on the basis of the inherent

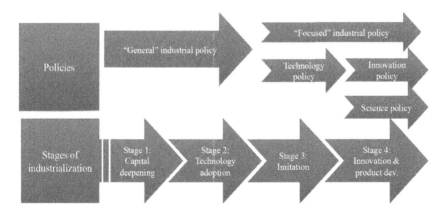

Figure 11.1 Sequencing of policies for industrialization
Source: Yülek (2018)

learning potential, their potential positive externalities, their strong linkages with other sectors, the potential for technological development, and the potential to earn foreign exchange. The successful industrial policies in Korea, Singapore, and Taiwan during the 1970s and 1980s are representative examples of such policies. Failure to move up to this stage and progress results in the "middle income trap." Finally, at the fourth stage of technological development, innovation-based smart manufacturing becomes important and this is accompanied by science and innovation policies. In this final stage, industrial policies transform into sector-specific science and technology policies. For instance, Akkemik (2015) argued that after the mid-1990s the traditional industrial policies in Japan evolved into "soft" science and technology policies where the government's role was narrowed down to a moderator across cooperating private firms for technology development and to make the market work more efficiently.

The sequence of the policies as depicted in Figure 11.1 is extremely important in industrial development. An interesting question would be whether it would be possible to implement all these policies simultaneously (Yülek, 2018, pp. 232–234). Certain aspects of industrial policy, science policy, and technology policy may well overlap with each other. In such a case, the borders between these policies may be thin. However, it is important to remember that each policy builds on the capacity built on the previous stages, e.g., without a strong industrial base, science and technology policies will be irrelevant or highly cost-inefficient. While it is possible to develop some high-level technologies even at the earlier stages of industrialization, for instance, due to individual effort, without sufficient manufacturing capacity and commercialization, science and technology policies will not yield the desired result. Therefore, science and technology policies are not appropriate policies at earlier stages.

11.3 Industrialization and industrial policies in China

It is generally accepted that China missed the first three industrial revolutions and remained in a catch up position with the advanced economies of the world. It became possible to devise policies aimed at industrialization only after political stability was achieved under the Communist Party rule after 1949. The Chinese Communist Party (CCP), under the leadership of Mao Zedong, reorganized the Chinese economy according to socialist principles and five-year plans, starting in 1953. During the Mao era (1949–1976), the market was replaced with a bureaucracy and all production was undertaken by state-owned enterprises (SOEs).

One of the important factors behind the extraordinary economic growth performance and rapid industrialization in China is the continuous structural changes toward new and higher value-added industries and technological upgrading (Lin, 2018, pp. 6–7). In the process of transition from plan to market economy after 1978, the stated structural change in the economy was realized by way of government intervention. Industrial policies became important, starting from the mid-1980s.

Like most other policies, industrial policies have to comply with the overarching five-year plans in China. On the other hand, it can be argued safely that industrial policies have become an integral component of national five-year plans in China starting from the Seventh Five-Year Plan (1986–1990). A major breakthrough happened in 2004 when the government ended its policy of picking the strategic industries (Li et al., 2010). Behind these changes, there have been ideological clashes among competing bureaucratic groups at the top echelons of the state (Heilmann & Shih, 2013). Therefore, it is necessary to consider the political economy of industrial policies in China as well.

In what follows, we descriptively analyze the industrial policies in China, over the last two decades in particular, in conjunction with the underlying political economy. We prefer to analyze industrial policies by periodizing the post-1978 period into four sub-periods: 1978–1989, 1989–2004, 2004–2015, and post-2015. Each period is characterized by a peculiar approach to industrial development.

11.3.1 Industrialization in China: Some stylized facts

In this section, we briefly discuss the structural changes in the Chinese industry after 1978. From 1978 to the early 1990s, the share of labor-intensive industries such as textiles and food led to industrialization and their share in manufacturing value-added increased.[2] According to the China Industrial Productivity Database of RIETI, the total share of food, beverages, textiles, and clothing industries in manufacturing value-added was as high as 35 percent in 1981 while that of metals, machinery, and transport vehicles industries was only 9.4 percent. Low labor costs in labor-intensive industries were important in this era during which the official development policy of the government was export-oriented industrialization. This era also witnessed market liberalization and continuous reforms. Increasing incomes and rapid reduction in poverty improved economic welfare and labor-intensive industrialization helped reduce unemployment.

A turning point in industrialization in China came in 1992. From 1989 to 1992, industrialization and economic growth slowed down as a result of political and macroeconomic instability. Starting in 1992, the government adopted a new policy of prioritizing the development of capital-intensive industries, including steel, machinery, and transport equipment. The share of these industries in industrial value-added increased rapidly. Total share of textiles and food in manufacturing dropped to 28 percent in 1992 and below 20 percent after 2004 while the total share of metal, steel, machinery, and transport equipment industries increased from 37.2 percent in 1992 to 43.6 percent in 2000 (further to 52 percent in 2010), leading to rapid capital deepening through massive investments in these industries. Government intervention was severe and most SOEs were restructured. Large inflows of foreign investment thanks to the government's Open Door policy helped the investment boom in the industry. Banks played a critical role in industrialization since the capital market was underdeveloped. State banks provided funds for industrial investments.

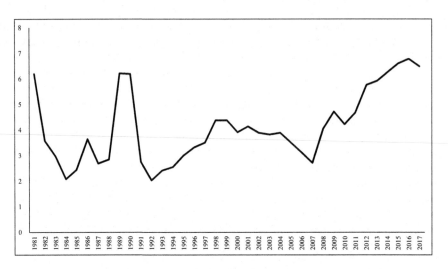

Figure 11.2 Incremental capital-output ratio in China, 1985–2017
Source: Computed using UN National Accounts data.

An important question here is whether investments were efficient. Figure 11.2 presents the incremental capital-output ratio (ICOR) in the long run, calculated as the ratio of the investment share in GDP to GDP growth rate. The higher the ICOR, the less the efficiency or productivity of capital, and vice versa. In the 1990s, the ICOR increased slightly, which is expected because rapid capital accumulation naturally leads to a decline in the efficiency of capital.

If we look at the sources of GDP growth by expenditure items, we see that private consumption was the main source of growth during the 1980s but investment gained importance under heavy industrialization starting in the early 1990s (Figure 11.3). During heavy industrialization, SOEs shared a large burden with foreign-invested enterprises. The share of the SOEs and other public firms, including township and village enterprises, in industrial value-added was as high as 72 percent in 1978 but it declined to 32 percent in 1998, it increased afterwards and reached 38 percent in 2010 (Lo & Wu, 2014). Most SOEs were large firms with high capital intensity.

Another critical turning point is 2001, the year China joined the World Trade Organization (WTO). The share of investments in GDP growth rose remarkably while ICOR declined until the global financial crisis in 2008. These imply efficiency improvement in capital and an investment-based growth model. There was a structural change after 2001 toward high-tech industries (electronic machinery, transport vehicles, and telecommunications equipment, in particular). The share of high-tech industries in total manufacturing value-added increased from 11.2 percent in 1992 to 13.5 percent in 2002 and reached 20 percent in 2010. The share of information technology products in Chinese merchandise exports reached 30 percent in 2004 and remained between 25–30 percent thereafter. These statistics imply the government's successful efforts to realize a structural

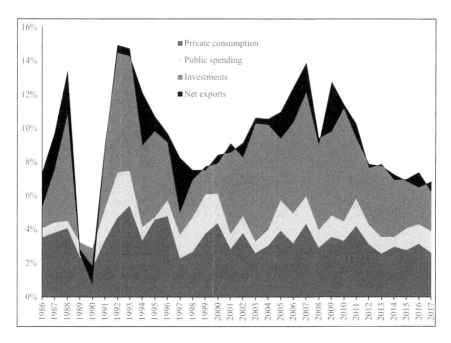

Figure 11.3 Sources of economic growth in China by expenditure items, 1986–2017
Source: Computed using UN National Accounts data.

change in the industry toward higher value-added activities after 2002. In fact, the government put in place various ambitious industrial policies after 2004 in order to promote innovative activities and technology development. Another important policy of the government was to reduce China's dependence on foreign firms and foreign technologies. Figure 11.4 shows that this policy yielded the desired results and the dependence of Chinese industries on imported inputs generally followed a declining trend after 2004.

On the other hand, excessive investments led to excess capacity and inefficiency of capital as evident from rising ICOR after 2007 (see Figure 11.2), which may be partially held responsible for the decline in economic growth rate. Starting in 2013, the government adopted a consumption-based growth strategy. Accordingly, the importance of investments has decreased since then (see Figure 11.3).

Behind the remarkable structural changes in the Chinese industry lie the government's industrial policies. Below we elaborate on these policies which exhibit peculiar characteristics in each period of industrialization.

11.3.2 An overview of industrial policies in China since 1978

In this section, we briefly discuss the industrial policies in China. We build our discussion in this section on Heilmann and Shih (2013), Lo and Wu (2014), Kenderdine (2017), Genç & Akkemik (2018), and Holz (2019).

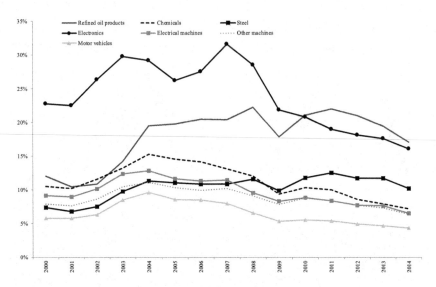

Figure 11.4 Dependence of Chinese industries on foreign inputs
Source: Computed using data from WIOD

11.3.2.1 Industrial policies, 1978–1992

With the opening up of the Chinese economy and the transformation from a strictly socialist to what will be later called a post-Mao "socialist market economy," the Chinese policymakers turned to Japan as a role model as early as 1979 due to its successful industrial policies, which were also praised by many economists in the western world at the time (Heilmann & Shih, 2013, pp. 5–8). Throughout the 1980s, Chinese economic bureaucrats studied the Japanese industrial experience and industrial policies and admitted that the Japanese practices fitted the Chinese institutional setup, which emphasized statism, since the Japanese industrial policies were based on administrative guidance and government intervention. This interaction had a long-lasting influence on Chinese policymaking.[3] Japanese industrial policies emphasized national policies and Chinese planning bureaucrats adopted this approach. Accordingly, national industrial policies rather than industry-specific policies were implemented during the 1980s.

Industrial policy was announced officially as part of the economic reform agenda first in the Seventh Five-Year Plan (1986–1990) in 1986. Economic reform bureaucrats dedicated to steering the transition toward a market economy smoothly deemed Japanese industrial policies a useful tool to allocate resources effectively. However, the strong position of SOEs and lack of competitive pressure resulted in the failure of these policies (Heilmann & Shih, 2013, p. 10; Lo & Wu, 2014, pp. 314–315).

11.3.2.2 Industrial policies, 1992–2004

Starting in 1989, Japanese-style national policies based on indirect interventions were gradually abandoned and industry-specific policies were adopted. The best-known cases of such industrial policies are those in the automobile industry, which started in 1987 and were revised in 1994, and the semiconductor industry, which started in 1986 and were revised in 1992 (Lo & Wu, 2014). In the case of the automobile industry, the industrial policy emphasized technology transfer through joint ventures between Chinese firms and foreign firms (including Chrysler, Citroën, Daihatsu, Honda, Peugeot, Toyota, and Volkswagen) while protecting the domestic market. A similar policy was also implemented in the semiconductor industry where the domestic firms were SOEs. These policies were highly successful as evident from the large increases in automobile and integrated circuit output after the mid-1990s.[4] According to the official statistics in the *China Statistical Yearbook*, annual motor vehicle (car, bus, and truck) production greatly increased from only 0.5 million vehicles in 1990 to 1.5 million in 1996, 2.3 million in 2001, rapidly increasing after 2001 to 5.1 million in 2004, 9.3 million in 2008, and further to 29.0 million in 2017. The output of integrated circuits (in billion pieces) increased from 0.1 in 1990 to 2.5 in 1997, 6.4 in 2001, 41.7 in 2008, and further to 156.5 in 2017.

The Chinese government was undertaking a large institutional change toward economic liberalization during this period and the Chinese economic system was officially labeled a "socialist market economy" in 1993. The restructuring of the enterprises continued in the second half of the 1990s, most notably through large-scale privatization of SOEs after 1997. Actually, the economic reforms of the 1990s introduced rapid market liberalization and a large reduction in import tariffs leading to trade liberalization, which eventually resulted in China's accession to the WTO in late 2001.

Industrial policies in the 1990s enlarged their focus by including technology and regional disparities (e.g., developing the relatively backward central and western provinces). The direct allocation of resources in the previous decade was replaced with indirect resource reallocation through tax and credit incentives (Heilmann & Shih, 2013, pp. 9–10). This helped increase the autonomy of enterprises in economic decision-making beyond that aimed by the reformers. In addition, firms became more exposed to competition from abroad and this helped improve efficiency.

11.3.2.3 Industrial policies, 2004–2015

Another breakthrough in industrial policies happened in 2004 when the government ended its policy of picking the strategic industries (Li et al., 2010). While there were a number of industrial policies specifically designed for individual industries from 1989 to 2004, the numbers of officially announced "national" industrial policies were limited but increased after 2004.[5] These national policies

Table 11.3 National industrial policies in China, 2004–2012

	Year(s)	Program	Agencies in charge
Cross-sectoral programs	2005	Adjustment of Industrial Structures	SC
	2007	Acceleration of Services Sector Development	SC
	2009	Industrial Technology Policy	MIIT
	2010	Acceleration of Strategic Emerging Industries' Development	SC
	2011	Promotion of Strategic Emerging Industries in 12th FYP	CC, NPC
	2011	Industrial Restructuring and Upgrading (2011–2015)	SC
Sectoral programs	2004	Automobile Industry	NDRC
	2006	Machine-building Industry	SC
	2009	Revitalization Programs for Nine Traditional Sectors	SC
	2009	Information Technology Industry	SC
	2009	Logistics Industry	SC
	2009	Culture Industry	SC
	2011	12th FYP, upgrading 9 traditional industries (2009 programs) and fostering 7 Strategic Emerging Industries	CC, SC, NPC
	2011	21 ministerial FYPs for sector-specific development	Ministries
Priority investment catalogs	2004 07-11	Catalog on Priority High-Technology Industries	NDRC
	2005-07	Catalog on Priority Industries for Foreign Investors	NDRC
	2005-11	Guidelines for Restructuring of Selected Industries	NDRC
	2007-09-11	Catalog on Priority Import Technologies and Products	NDRC
	2008	Guidelines for Overseas Investments	NDRC
Law	2007	Anti-Monopoly Law	NPC

Notes: CC: Communist Party of China Central Committee, FYP: Five-Year Plan, MIIT: Ministry of Industry and Information Technology, NDRC: National Development and Reform Commission, NPC: National People's Congress, SC: State Council.

Source: Heilmann & Shih (2013, p. 13).

are listed in Table 11.3. The new industrial policies emphasized indicative government intervention and broader national industrial policies, where firms had more freedom in business decisions the bureaucrats spent most of their energy on coordination across the newly designed national industrial and technology plans. The new objective of industrialization was not only enhancing industrial production capacity but also fostering the competitiveness of Chinese firms in the global economy.

Starting in 2004, the government adopted new investment regulations and controls on private sector investment were relaxed (Holz, 2019). The government issued guidance catalogs[6] from 2004 to 2011 to communicate the designated priority industries, to promote structural changes, foreign investments, technology transfer, and domestic technology creation capacity (see Table 11.3). There were special industrial policies for the automobile industries, high-speed railway, machinery, information technology, logistics, and creative industries as well.

The Eleventh Five-Year Plan (2006–2010) emphasized the importance of raising economic welfare as the ultimate long-run aim of the industrial policies. The Central Economic Committee in 2007 declared that priority should be given to quality in economic development (Li et al., 2010). However, the global financial crisis in 2008–2009 diverted the focus on industrial policies away from quality to quantity. The availability of large amounts of capital with the stimulus packages after the global crisis provided the necessary funds for the industrial policies, which were part of the economic revival agenda after the crisis. Expansion in industrial investments soon led to overinvestment and an excess capacity problem. On the other hand, industrial interest groups sought ways for this investment surge to continue. Economic bureaucracy, while still emphasizing industrial policies, aimed to dispose of the excess capacity. The famous "Belt and Road Policy" attempted to dispose of this excess capacity by creating external demand for the relevant industries (steel, machinery, etc.) in the form of large infrastructure projects abroad, which the Chinese government could also use as a diplomatic tool.

In 2010, the China State Council, the highest executive organ in China, announced that seven Strategic Emerging Industries (SEI) would receive special treatment and investments in these industries would be supported (Kenderdine, 2017), with the ultimate aim of increasing their share in GDP to 8 percent in 2015 and 15 percent in 2020, by encouraging private investments in these industries. The industries were biotechnology, energy-saving equipment, next-generation information technologies, new materials, new-energy vehicles, high-end advanced equipment manufacturing, high technology services, and digital creative industries. Digital innovation was added to this list in 2016. The SEI plan shows that the Chinese government shifted its attention to innovative new-generation high technologies, e.g., artificial intelligence, Big Data, the Cloud, the Internet of Things. The government further announced the Internet Plus Plan in 2015, which started in 2017 (Liu, 2018).

These policy actions after 2010, starting with the SEI, were part of a new strategy to catch up with the advanced economies and switch to science and technology policies. The Twelfth Five-Year Plan (2011–2015) included SEI as the main component of industrial policies and emphasized the need to promote smart manufacturing, also to promote the upgrading of technological proficiency in designated traditional industries (Holz, 2019), including equipment manufacturing, shipbuilding, automotive, iron and steel, metals, building materials, petrochemicals, and light industries (e.g., new batteries, high-tech fibers, and textile machinery).

11.2.3.4 Industrial policies after 2015

Chinese industrial policies after 2015 are characterized by the government's emphasis on technological development and technology policies. Previous industrial policies highlighted the importance of technological catch-up. The orientation of China's industrial policies toward innovation is evident from science and technology statistics. Total R&D expenditures and total patent applications have recently increased extensively. According to the World Bank's World Development Indicators Database, research and development expenditures as a percentage of GDP increased from only 0.6 percent in 1996 to 0.9 percent in 2001, 1.7 percent in 2009, and 2.1 percent in 2016. In 2016, this statistic was well below that of Korea (4.2 percent), Japan (3.1 percent), Germany (2.9 percent) and the US (2.7 percent). However, the rapid catch-up of China with these countries over the last quarter-century is remarkable (see Figure 11.5).[7]

In 2015, the government announced an ambitious plan to promote the Fourth Industrial Revolution in China, which was dubbed "Made in China 2025" (MIC 2025), with specific targets set for 2025. This plan designated 10 priority industries (Holz, 2019): information technology, numerical control tools and robotics, aerospace equipment, high-tech ships, railway equipment, energy-saving and new-energy vehicles, power equipment, new materials, medicines and medical devices, and agricultural machinery. The plan also designated strategic tasks to promote structural adjustment in industry, improve manufacturing innovation capacity, integrate information technology and industrialization, strengthen the industrial base, develop high-quality brands, internationalize manufacturing, and promote green manufacturing. Though ambitious, the plan did not specify investments by sector and did not select "winner" industries. With this feature,

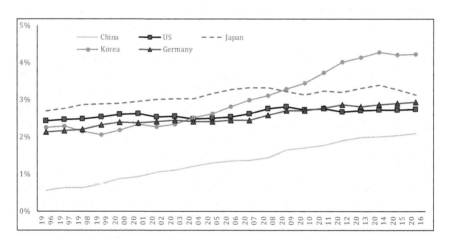

Figure 11.5 Research and development expenditures as percentage of GDP for selected countries, 1996–2016

Source: World Bank WDI Database

this plan is a representative example of the broad national industrial policies of the post-2004 period. In Section 11.3.3, we elaborate on this plan.

The Thirteenth Five-Year Plan (2016–2020), which was announced in 2016, described specific targets to promote the upgrading of the industrial structure (Holz, 2019). The plan envisaged accelerating the development of high-tech industries (digital information, biotechnologies, aerospace, new materials) and creative industries, to revitalize and promote innovation in advanced manufacturing (e.g., automotive and shipbuilding), to promote the development of new energies, to save energy and protect the environment, to promote light industries (e.g., high-quality textiles), and to promote new information technologies. The plan complements the MIC 2025 plan. The plan also specified targets such as raising the R&D expenditures to sales ratio in manufacturing to 1.26 by 2020 and 1.68 percent by 2025. Innovation, green manufacturing, and smart manufacturing were essential components of these plans. As to the results, according to the official statistics in the *China Statistical Yearbook*, R&D expenditures to sales revenue ratio for high-tech manufacturing industries were 1.06 percent in 2017, slightly below the 2020 target.

The excess capacity problem in coal and steel industries worsened during the 2010s and the government introduced some structural reforms in 2015 to eliminate this excess capacity by substantially reducing coal crude steel production through mergers and industrial restructuring (especially where firms with lower technologies are concerned). These measures were included in the Thirteenth Five-Year plan later.

11.3.3 Made in China 2025

At the beginning of the 2010s, there was awareness among Chinese policymakers that China needed to adapt to the Fourth Industrial Revolution (IR4), which is characterized by smart manufacturing, automation, digital technologies, and artificial intelligence (AI). The government admitted that sustained long-run economic growth in China depended on technological innovation and, for this purpose, it was necessary to raise the technological capability, and hence the competitiveness, of the Chinese economy by investing in IR4 industries and by promoting the absorption of these technologies across all sectors. China was lagging behind the major industrialized countries in automation. Wübbeke et al. (2016: 14) stressed that in 2015 the number of industrial robots per 10,000 industrial workers in China was only 19, compared with 531 in Korea, 308 in Japan, and 176 in the US.

In 2015, the government adopted a new industrial strategy called "Made in China 2025" (MIC 2025). This strategy was based on the principles regarding structural reforms in the Third Plenum of the 18th National Congress of the Communist Party in 2013.[8] Structural reforms implied a shift toward high-tech industries.

According to Wübbeke et al. (2016, p. 17), MIC 2025 is inspired by the Industry 4.0 strategy of the German government. In its final report submitted to the government in 2013, entitled *Manufacturing Superpower*, the Chinese Academy of Engineering (CAE) proposed to the central government specific and detailed policy actions to promote smart manufacturing technologies. These recommendations were later adopted by the Party Premier Xi Jinping and Prime Minister Le Keqiang in 2014. The Chinese government started to cooperate with the German government on Industry 4.0. Finally, in May 2015, the State Council declared the Made in China 2025 Plan, which is essentially built on the preceding recommendations of the CAE. Closing the technological gap between China and industrialized countries and reducing Chinese firms' dependence on foreign technology suppliers are the main drivers of this new grand strategy.

Backed by the political elites of the Chinese Communist Party, MIC 2025 is a top-down industrial policy and very little feedback from the business world was involved in its preparation. The Ministry of Industry and Information Technologies is in charge of the implementation of this industrial policy and the plan has officially announced specific targets to enhance innovative capacity and self-sufficiency in technology creation in specified areas, with interim targets for 2020 as well. The specified areas are as follows (Wübbeke et al., 2016, p. 19): new-generation information technology; high-end computerized machines and robots; space and aviation; maritime equipment and high-tech ships; advanced railway transportation equipment; new energy and energy-saving vehicles; energy equipment; agricultural machines; new materials; biopharma and high-tech medical devices. The plan also declared the official targets set out by the government regarding innovation, quality, the digitization of industry, and the environment for the year 2025 as shown in Table 11.4. As stated above, the plan envisaged China would increase the ratio of R&D expenditures to sales ratio of Chinese firms from 0.95 percent in 2015 to 1.68 percent in 2025. In addition,

Table 11.4 Selected targets in Made in China 2025

	2015	2020	2025
Innovation			
Ratio of R&D spending to corporate income (%)	0.95	1.26	1.68
Patents per 100 million RMB income	0.44	0.70	1.10
Quality			
Annual growth rate of industrial value-added (%)	5.9	7.9	9.9
Annual productivity growth rate (%)	6.6	7.5	6.5
Digitalization of industry			
Broadband internet penetration rate (%)	50	70	82
Rate of digital design tools use in R&D activities (%)	38	72	84
Environment			
Reduction in energy intensity in industry (compared to 2015, %)	–	–18	–34
Reduction in CO_2 emission (compared to 2015, %)	–	–22	–40
Reduction in water use (compared to 2015, %)	–	–23	–41
Reuse of solid industrial wastes (% of total waste)	65	73	79

Source: Wübbeke et al. (2016, p. 19).

patents per 100 million renminbi income is planned to increase from 0.44 to 1.10, and the broadband Internet penetration ratio is planned to increase from 50 percent to 82 percent. Besides these ambitious targets for innovation and digitization, the government also is devoted to a large improvement in environmental quality. Finally, the plan also states a long-term target for 2049, the centennial of the People's Republic of China, and foresees China achieving full competence in high technology areas and rising to the same rank as the technology superpowers in the world.[9]

The government is committed to devoting large amounts of resources to MIC 2025. Financial support comes mostly from specifically designed funds such as the Advanced Manufacturing Fund ($3 billion) and the National Integrated Circuit Fund ($21 billion). Funding from state banks is made available in the form of subsidies, low-interest credit, and bonds and local governments were also allocated large amounts of funds. The government also promotes Chinese firms' international operations, i.e., international brand awareness, firms' strategies to become more familiar with overseas cultures and markets, and investments in operation risk management (ISDP, 2018). In addition, between 2005 and 2016, Chinese firms invested $13.6 billion in Germany and $135 billion in the US for access to automation technologies and for joint ventures (ISDP, 2018).

Nine priorities in the plan were as follows (Morrison, 2019):

1. Development of manufacturing innovation;
2. Integration of technology and industry;
3. Strengthening of the industrial base;
4. Development of Chinese brands;
5. Development of green manufacturing;
6. Acceleration of the restructuring in the manufacturing sector;
7. Developing services and manufacturing-related services;
8. Internationalization of manufacturing;
9. Promotion of breakthrough in ten key sectors.

To promote the domestic technology creation capacity, MIC 2025 also aims to establish 40 innovation centers across China. Figure 11.6 presents some of these targets for 2025.

Due to its officially stated aim to increase the domestic content, MIC 2025 faced harsh criticism from advanced country governments as this means diversion of the suppliers of high-tech services from foreign firms to domestic firms. The recent US-China trade frictions are partially a result of China's MIC 2025 policy.[10] The Chinese government has clearly indicated in MIC 2025 that it plans to reduce its dependence of foreign technologies largely by 2025. Domestic content regulations also violate the WTO rules as they restrict competition to the disadvantage of foreign firms. In addition, global supply chains are so complex that a significant part of the production activities of the industrialized countries' firms in China belong to the global supply chains. Nurturing or promoting domestic firms implies the provision of large sums of subsidies and policy loans, which

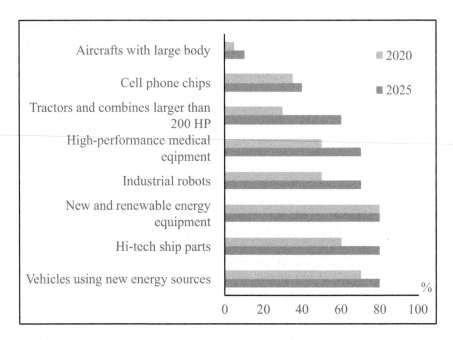

Figure 11.6 Some targets for self-sufficiency in Made in China 2025 (%)
Source: Wübbeke et al. (2016, p. 21)

foreign firms do not have access to. According to the plan, the share of domestic technology companies in computerized digital control machines sector would be raised to 80 percent, in industrial robot sector to 70 percent, in the Cloud and Big Data sector to 60 percent, and in industrial software sector to 50 percent by 2025 (Wübbeke et al., 2016, p. 38). Subsidies provided by the Chinese government in 2015 to domestic technology suppliers as a ratio of total operating revenues were as high as 10 percent for robot manufacturers and 35 percent for software development companies (Wübbeke et al., 2016, p. 39). According to the International Federation of Robotics (IFR), while China had the largest industrial robot demand in the world in 2017 with 137,900, 75 percent of this demand was met by foreign companies (IFR, 2018).[11] The share of domestic robot manufacturers increased from 24 percent in 2013 to 29 percent in 2015 and 31 percent in 2016. In 2017, this rate dropped to 25 percent.

Wübbeke et al. (2016) point out that MIC 2025 faces a major challenge. They argue that the major beneficiaries, i.e., the winners, of this plan will be a small number of large companies[12] that have already achieved advanced automation and digitalization levels. These firms are likely to be highly competitive multinational firms and lead further innovation in China. On the other hand, the remaining firms operating with lower technologies will benefit from MIC 2025 if they are eager to switch to smart manufacturing processes. Companies operating with backward technologies and not eager to switch to smart manufacturing will be the losers.

11.4 The political economy of industrial policies in China

Assessment of the role of the government in industrialization and industrial policy requires an analysis of the appropriateness of industrial policies for the institutional setup. While most researchers evaluate the economic policies in China over the plan or the market, Heilmann and Shih (2013, p. 28) show that there were actually four major rival "advocacy coalitions" in Chinese economic bureaucracy which have continuously interacted with each other. Following in the footsteps of Johnson (1982), who contributed to our understanding of industrial policies in Japan by paying attention to the political economy of industrial policymaking and bureaucracy at the Ministry of International Trade and Industry (MITI), we believe it is important to understand the political economy of industrial policies in China. In what follows, we elaborate on this subject by drawing on Heilmann and Shih (2013), Lo and Wu (2014), and Holz (2019).

11.4.1 Economic reforms, institutional changes, and bureaucratic competition

When the industrial policy was put on the policy agenda in the early 1980s, Chinese bureaucrats welcomed this concept they had adopted from Japan at the start of a process that aimed to reform a socialist economy by including market mechanisms. The relevant agencies to steer industrialization and implement the necessary policies were the State Planning Commission (SPC), which drafted plans, the State Economic Commission (SEC), which coordinated plans by controlling the public firms, and the Structural Reform Commission (SRC), which proposed reforms (Heilmann & Shih, 2013, p. 7).

These three agencies, while subscribing to the Japanese industrial policy paradigm, differed in their approaches (Heilmann & Shih, 2013, p. 8). SPC bureaucrats saw the industrial policy as a means to justify government intervention. For SRC bureaucrats, industrial policies were necessary for a period of transition and they argued that the dose of social planning should be reduced and the market mechanism should be reinforced. In the case of SEC bureaucrats, they had close ties with SOEs and retired SOE officials often served in this bureaucracy. Their main function was to establish and improve the relations between policymakers and the newly growing business world. These three agencies were each other's rivals and competed for dominance in economic policymaking.

Throughout the 1980s, the SRC bureaucrats, which Heilmann and Shih (2013) call "marketizers," followed the Japanese prescription of industrial policies (of the 1960s and the 1970s) and promoted administrative guidance and informal coordination across economic policymaking agencies. Their aim was to enlarge the market as much as possible with the extensive and direct allocation of resources and accompanying progress in gradual deregulation of the markets, well known as the dual-track system. Due to the resistance from the SOEs, which were essentially under the strong influence of the top political echelons, the SRC approach to industrialization in the 1980s largely failed to achieve the predetermined targets. Therefore, the ideological dominance of the proponents of market liberalization eroded by the end of the 1980s. Heilmann and Shih note that the marketizers never had the opportunity to possess a dominant position in policymaking.

Following a brief surge of socialist planning after the 1989 political events, the bureaucrats in SPC, which was restructured into the State Economic and Trade Commission (SETC) in 1993, became dominant in policymaking for industrial development and adopted industry-specific policies from 1989 onward. These bureaucrats diverted their attention from national industrial policy inspired by Japan and adopted a new reform agenda to restructure the economy via industry-specific policies and institutional reforms to break the institutional inertia, which was a barrier to industrial policies in the 1980s (Heilmann & Shih, 2013, pp. 11–12). Another important institutional change was the separation of the bureaucracy from SOEs, which granted more autonomy to firms. This was a large deviation from the administrative guidance of the 1980s. In short, the industrial policy bureaucracy was equipped with centralized policymaking and continued administrative guidance but without the strong influence of industrial interest groups. Lo and Wu (2014, p. 322) argue that after the late 1990s the government did not continue the cheap labor policy, on the contrary, it protected labor rights as evident from the large increase in unionization rate from 29 percent in 2000 to 36 percent in 2005 and 50 percent in 2010.

National industrial policies were brought back in 2004. There were institutional changes in 2003 with the change of leadership from Jiang Zemin to Hu Jintao. The SETC was abolished in 2003 and the newly established National Development and Reform Commission (NDRC) and the relevant industrial agencies in the Ministry of Industry and Information Technology, which was established later in 2008, were authorized with the making and implementation of industrial policies. NDRC was modeled on the MITI in Japan, which was the mastermind behind Japan's industrial policies from 1949 to its dismantling in 2001. The new economic administration aimed to avoid the potential flaws of sectoral policies, which were subject to rent-seeking from interest groups, SOEs in particular (Heilmann & Shih, 2013, p. 13). The abandoned indicative planning ideology of the former SPC during the 1980s, which was originally inspired by Japanese industrial policies, once again rose to dominance. Imperative planning emphasizing government intervention at the sectoral level was rejected and replaced with indicative planning emphasizing broader national industrial policies.[13] Firms were granted more autonomy in their daily business decision-making and the new national industrial policies emphasized coordination across various industrial and technology plans listed in Table 11.3.

The economic bureaucracy in the 2010s inherited the indicative planning culture and continued it. It seems that there is an informal consensus across the different bureaucratic groups discussed above regarding the appropriateness of indicative industrial policies for China. The centralized industrial policymaking and the renewed importance given to technological upgrading were instrumental in the implementation of the recent industrial policies such as Made in China

2025. Overall, government intervention in China is likely to endure, even during the current period where large private firms and SOEs from China have risen to the status of top global firms. One can see Chinese scholars emphasizing the need to liberalize markets in China more, however, the current stance of Chinese bureaucrats is that industrial policies of the East Asian type in the past are the right policies to ensure the swift transition toward an industrialized nation and to avoid the middle-income trap.

Industrial policymaking process in China involves participation by and coordination among various government agencies. Heilmann and Shih (2013, p. 16) argue that senior government officials, whom they call "policy brokers," are important in Chinese industrial policies. These officials act as intermediaries to ensure coordination among the different agencies and are connected with top political officials. The high level of autonomy enjoyed by the economic bureaucrats enables long-term planning. Nationalist sentiments are evident in Chinese economic planning bureaucracy as well. The rival groups with differing ideologies fought for dominance in bureaucracy over the years but this did not lead to a breakdown of the bureaucratic system nor did it fatally damage the national industrial policies.

11.4.2 Do Chinese industrial policies resemble East Asian industrial policies?

In this section, we evaluate the Chinese industrial policies since 2001 with reference to the theoretical framework in Section 11.2.

It is noted above that policy groups advocating more liberalization or more socialist planning compete with each other for dominance, but the industrial policies and technology policies are always on the policy agenda. Industrial policies in the 1980s emphasized capital deepening, FDI inflows, and technological catch-up and the industrial policies in the 1990s emphasized dynamic comparative advantages.[14] Industrial policies after 2004, MIC 2025 in particular, emphasized technology creation and science-technology policies. Below, we evaluate the evolution of the industrial policies in China from the 1980s onwards in conjunction with the framework regarding the appropriate sequence of policies set up in Section 11.2.

The industrial policies in the 1980s based on technological catchup and capital deepening are in line with stages 1 and 2. China mastered the embedded technologies in imported machinery and built capacity to improve the skills of the labor force. In addition, the traditional ("general," as described in Yülek, 2018) industrial policies learned from Japan were put in place. The third stage of the industrial and technological development in our setup, which corresponds to the 1990s in China, requires the launch of technology policies that emphasize imitation of advanced country technologies. Industrial and technology policies in China during the 1990s fit this framework well. China started to establish a national innovation system and significant technology transfer from foreign firms were realized, especially through joint ventures in high-tech industries. Lazonick (2004) argued that a national innovation system is needed even when the aim is the acquisition of transferred technologies from abroad. This is because learning and absorbing these technologies and building on them require a critical level of technological capacity. On the other hand, industrial policies designed narrowly for specific industries during the 1990s were not successful. Therefore, after 2004, Chinese policymakers turned to general industrial policies again.

The industrial policies in China after 2004 emphasize innovation and product development and the accompanying science and technology policies. Aware of the Flying Geese pattern of industrial development in East Asia leading to the emergence of low-cost rivals such as Vietnam, the Chinese government aimed to enhance the competitiveness of the Chinese firms by ensuring a transition from lower to a higher level of technological sophistication (ISDP, 2018). In other words, the Chinese government wants indigenous firms to compete with Japanese, Korean, American, and German firms rather than developing country firms. Chinese policymakers see MIC 2025 as an opportunity to integrate into the global value chains in smart manufacturing areas and create internationally competitive technology firms by heavily investing in innovative areas (ISDP, 2018).

Although the Japanese influence on industrial policies was reduced during the 1990s, the recent industrial policies after 2004, Made in China 2025, in particular, are reminiscent of Japanese and other East Asian industrial policies, which were characterized by heavy government intervention. While the current industrial policies of China resemble the traditional industrial policies in Japan during the 1960s and the 1970s, there are important differences as well. Japanese firms needed to look for cheap labor in search of profits and to remain competitive. However, Chinese industrial firms still enjoy significantly lower production costs vis-à-vis their international competitors and were able to expand their domestic investments (Kenderdine, 2017).

Japanese and other East Asian governments reduced government interventions and abolished the developmental states as industrialization progressed and they achieved the status of developed country status. The Chinese government, on the other hand, continues to intervene heavily in the market and controls entrepreneurial activity. In practice, the government reinforced the developmental state with Chinese characteristics (Genç & Akkemik, 2018). Looking at MIC 2025 and recent industrial policies, the Chinese government is likely to maintain interventions even if China attains high-income status. Global political and geostrategic reasons also seem to explain the behavior of the Chinese government.

Despite the government's financial support and massive investments by foreign firms, the achievements in domestic technology development are yet far from satisfactory. For instance, while China is a major manufacturer of computers and cell phones, it could not develop a domestic chip industry as 90 percent of the microchips used in computers and cell phones are imported (Hu, 2018). In addition, according to Global Competitiveness Index of the World Economic Forum (2018), China ranked 28th overall and 24th in innovative capacity, far below the advanced countries it competes within MIC 2025 plan, including Germany, the US, and Switzerland.

An empirical evaluation of industrial policies in China by Holz (2019) is noteworthy. Holz examined whether the industrial policies in China really caused a change in investment decisions. One possibility is that the investments followed the government's industrial policies, as in the case of Japan, Korea, Taiwan, and Singapore during the heyday of industrial policies in the past. In that case, the investment policies of both publicly and privately owned firms might have been affected. The other alternative is that the industrial policies may have followed the developments in the market. In other words, when productive resources flow to the profitable sectors, the industrial policies of the government just simply followed the trend ex-post. Holz found using the results from an econometric analysis for the period 2012–2015 that profitability, demand, and capital intensity strongly and positively influenced investments. Furthermore, he showed that the specific industrial policies did not have any statistically significant impact on investments except for the Made in China 2025 Plan, which has had a positive impact.

11.5 Conclusion

It is a matter of concern among researchers whether the recent industrial policies in China will achieve the predetermined targets. It is clear that the cooperation of the targeted firms is a necessary but sufficient condition for the success of Made in China 2025 Plan. Given the declining appetite of the industrial firms amidst excess capacity after a long period of rapid capital accumulation, this is a major challenge. The IMF and the World Bank are expecting the Chinese economy to grow by less than 5 percent in the short and medium term. With such low growth expectations, how the industrial firms would increase their investment spending is an important policy question as well.

The tension between the American and Chinese governments after 2017 urged the Chinese government to empower China with the capacity to produce high technologies at home and reduce dependence on foreign firms. These are reminiscent of the traditional industrial policies in Japan, Korea, Singapore, and Taiwan during the second half of the twentieth century.

Kenderdine (2017) argues that industrial policies in China will likely redefine the institutional framework and persist as a policy strategy to strengthen the national welfare and strength of the nation-state, an important nationalistic ideal of the Chinese state. This means that industrial policies constitute an institutional legacy. It is also important to bear in mind that the multipolar world economic system is likely to be maintained and China will be one of the leaders of the world economy as well as in East Asia. The institutional setting in the Chinese economy will surely affect the political economy in East Asia and may affect the economic development trajectories of the latecomers in the region. Therefore, the industrial policies and the Chinese developmental state will remain on the research agenda of development economics. It is too early to put the discussion on interventionist industrial policies on ice.

Notes

1 A natural extension of Baumol's cost disease is about the demand side of the economy. Increased labor productivity, due to technological improvements, in the progressive sector leads to an increase in wages and a decline in its price level due to the reduction in costs. On the other hand, the stagnant sector is affected negatively due to increased costs and this leads to increased wages relative to the progressive sector (low productivity growth but higher wages, hence a "disease"). The increase in wage conforms to the rising output share of the stagnant share as well. Such changes are counter-intuitive when one assumes that the sectors with higher technological levels are expected to experience an increase in their share in GDP in the long run.

2 Comprehensive analyses of China's industrialization are available elsewhere (e.g., Lau et al., 2000; Lin, 2018; World Bank, 2013; Zhu, 2012).

3 Examples of such interactions are the Chinese Japanese Exchange Forum on Economics and the Joint Conference of Chinese and Japanese Economists (Heilmann & Shih, 2013, p. 6).

4 On the other hand, Lo and Wu (2014, p. 320) also argue that the transfer of technology was limited to catchup technologies but not frontier technologies, as evident from very low automobile exports from the joint ventures. In other words, foreign firms may have been reluctant to transfer frontier technologies.

5 The number of industrial policies are as follows: 1989: 1, 1993: 1, 1994: 1, 1995: 1, 1997: 2, 1999: 1, 2000: 3, 2001: 1, 2002: 1, 2004: 2, 2005: 3, 2006: 1, 2007: 6, 2008: 2, 2009: 13, 2010: 1, 2011: 15 (Heilmann & Shih, 2013, p. 3).

6 Guidance catalog is a top-down policy transmission mechanism within the Chinese Communist political system and it has been used to coordinate economic policies in China (Kenderdine, 2017). Guidance catalogs specify details of industrial policies and their implementation. These catalogs are occasionally revised.

7 On the other hand, total patent applications (residents and nonresidents combined) in China was only 11 percent of that in the US in 1996. But this ratio increased to 54 percent in 2007 and from 2011 onward total patent applications in China have surpassed total applications in the US. In 2016, this figure was 2.3 times the number in the US, 4.3 times of that in Japan, and 9.9 times that of the European Union.

8 The Congress is important for policymaking in China because the policies set by the government and the bureaucracy turn into laws after they are accepted by the Congress.

9 As a case in point, China was able to develop its own satellite technologies that can compete with those produced and put in use by America and the European countries (Kenderdine, 2017). For instance, the Beidou Navigation Satellite System was developed as an alternative to the American Global Positioning System (GPS) and Europe's Global Navigation Satellite System (GALILEO).

10 Due to the large trade deficits of the US against China and claims of unfair trade practices of China, the US government implemented protectionist policies starting in early 2017. In March 2018, the US raised tariffs on Chinese steel by 25 percent and imposed a 10 percent ad valorem tariff on aluminum imports from China. China soon retaliated with counter-duties on imports from the US on more than 100 products. The tension has continued since then despite negotiations between two sides to relax the tension. The US government also banned exports of some high-tech products such as chips and mobile technologies to Chinese firms and blacklisted some Chinese technology firms, due to the Chinese government's control over these firms. The US government indirectly is forcing China to end the MIC 2025 policy. See USTR (2018)

on the US government's claims about China's unfair trade practices and CSC (2018) for the Chinese government's official response.

11 The demand for industrial robots in the US and Japan were 45,600 and 33,200, respectively.

12 These are firms supplying software, digital control machines, sensors, industrial robots, 3-D printers, etc.

13 Heilmann and Shih (2013, p. 15) point out that the core of the industrial policy bureaucracy in the 2000s was raised after the mid-1990s and these reform bureaucrats believed in market-oriented and non-imperative, i.e., indicative, industrial policies. They also show that these bureaucrats started their careers as academics or junior officials at the planning agency (SPC).

14 Lin and Chang (2009) have argued that China did not follow the standard comparative advantages theory but the dynamic comparative advantage theory starting in the 1990s. They called such policies "comparative advantage defying" policies. Chinese industrial policies resemble East Asian industrial policies in this respect. Industrial policies in the 1990s were a great success. Lo and Wu (2014, pp. 315–321) elaborate on the successful case studies in the automotive, semiconductor, and high-speed railway industries.

References

Akkemik, K. A. (2009). *Industrial development in East Asia: A comparative look at Japan, Korea, Taiwan, and Singapore.* Hackensack, NJ: World Scientific.

Akkemik, K. A. (2015). Recent industrial policies in Japan. In M. Yülek (Ed.), *National strategic planning and industrial policy in the globalizing economy: Revisiting concepts and experience* (pp. 181–206). Cham: Springer.

Amsden, A. (1989). *Asia's next giant: South Korea and late industrialization.* New York: Oxford University Press.

Baumol, W. J. (1967). Macroeconomics of unbalanced growth: The anatomy of urban crisis. *American Economic Review,* 57(3): 415–426.

Chang, H. J. (1993). The political economy of industrial policy in Korea. *Cambridge Journal of Economics,* 17(2): 131–157.

CSC (China State Council). (2018). The facts and China's position on China-US trade friction. 24 September.

Genç, H. O., & Akkemik, K. A. (2018). Developmental state, industrial policy and green growth in China. In M. Yülek (Ed.), *Industrial policy and sustainable development* (pp. 285–310). Singapore: Springer.

Heilmann, S., & Shih, L. (2013). The rise of industrial policy in China, 1978–2012. Harvard-Yenching Institute Working Paper.

Holz, C. A. (2019). Industrial policies and the changing patterns of investment in the Chinese economy. *The China Journal,* 81: 23–57.

Hu, F. (2018). The US is overly paranoid about China's tech rise. *New Perspectives Quarterly,* 35(4): 21–24.

ISDP (Institute for Security and Development Policy). (2018). Made in China 2025. Stockholm: ISDP.

IFR (International Federation of Robotics). (2018). *World robotics 2018: Industrial robots.* Frankfurt am Main, Germany: IFR.

Itoh, M., Kiyono, K., & Okuno-Fujiwara, M. (1991). *Economic analysis of industrial policy.* San Diego, CA: Academic Press.

Johnson, C. (1982). *MITI and the Japanese miracle: The growth of industrial policy 1925–75*. Stanford, CA: Stanford University Press.

Kenderdine, T. (2017). China's industrial policy, strategic emerging industries and space law. *Asia and the Pacific Policy Studies*, 4(2): 325–342.

Lau, L. J., Qian, Y., & Roland, G. (2000). Reform without losers: An interpretation of China's dual-track approach to transition. *Journal of Political Economy*, 108(1): 120–143.

Lazonick, W. (2004). Indigenous innovation and economic development: Lessons from China's leap into the information age. *Industry & Innovation*, 11(4): 273–298.

Li, W., Sui, F., & Zheng, L. (2010). *China's economy*. Beijing: China Intercontinental Press.

Lin, J. & Chang, H. J. (2009). Should industrial policy in developing countries conform to comparative advantage or defy it? A debate between Justin Lin and Ha-Joon Chang. *Development Policy Review*, 27(5): 483–502.

Lin, J. Y. (2018). China's growth miracle in the context of Asian transformation. United Nations University, WIDER Working Paper No. 2018/92.

Liu, K. (2018). Chinese manufacturing in the shadow of the China-US trade war. Institute of Economic Affairs Working Paper.

Lo, D., & Wu, M. (2014). The state and industrial policy in Chinese economic development. In J. M. Salazar-Xirinachs, I. Nübler, & R. Kozul-Wright (Eds.), *Transforming economies: Making industrial policy work for growth, jobs and development* (pp. 307–326). Geneva: International Labour Office.

Morrison, W. M. (2019). The Made in China 2025 initiative: Economic implications for the United States. *In Focus*. Congressional Research Service, 12 April.

Pack, H. (2000). Industrial policy: Growth elixir or poison. *World Bank Research Observer*, 15(1): 47–67.

Rodrik, D. (2008). Normalizing industrial policy. World Bank Commission on Growth and Development Working Paper No. 3.

USTR (United States Trade Representative). (2018). Findings of the investigation into China's acts, policies, and practices related to technology transfer, intellectual property, and innovation under Section 301 of the Trade Act of 1974', 22 March.

Wade, R. (1990). *Governing the market: Economic theory and the role of government in East Asian industrialization*. Princeton, NJ: Princeton University Press.

World Bank. (2013). *China 2030: Building a modern, harmonious, and creative society*. Washington, DC: World Bank and the Development Research Center of the State Council of China.

World Economic Forum. (2018). *Global competitiveness report 2018*. Davos, Switzerland: World Economic Forum.

Wübbeke, J., Meissner, M., Zenglein, M. J., Ives, J., & Conrad, B. (2016), Made in China 2025: The making of a high-tech superpower and consequences for industrial countries. Mercator Institute for China Studies (MERICS) Papers on China No. 2.

Yülek, M. (2018). *How nations succeed: Manufacturing, trade, industrial policy, and economic development*. Singapore: Palgrave Macmillan.

Zhu, X. (2012), Understanding China's growth: Past, present, and future. *Journal of Economic Perspectives*, 26(4), 103–124.

12 Promoting exports by the ASEAN SMEs

Impediments, drivers, and conducive policies

Utumporn Jitsutthiphakorn and
Shigeru Thomas Otsubo

12.1 Introduction

Looking back on the history of economic development among today's industrialized countries, one cannot overlook the important role that Small and Medium-Sized Enterprises (SMEs) have played in creating jobs and increasing gross domestic product (GDP). SMEs account for the majority of private enterprises and total employment, pointing to the importance of promoting SMEs to attain "inclusive" industrial development.

While the ongoing process of globalization in technology and innovation has made international trade more accessible, it has also led to a more competitive environment for new entrants and smaller businesses in developing countries. SMEs can enter the export market in order to grow and achieve economies of scale. As SMEs need to finance their investments in higher technology, internationalization (exporting activities, technology absorption from the outside) could enable them to meet their initial fixed costs more easily and effectively compared with operating only in domestic markets (Burgel, Fier, Licht, & Murray, 2000). Internationalization of business activities should be conducive to higher productivity growth and innovations that in turn enhance competitiveness and survivability.

The Association of Southeast Asian Nations (ASEAN) is one of the fastest-growing regional organizations in the world economy. SMEs have an important role in the ASEAN economy as they generate more than 60 percent of total employment (OECD/ERIA, 2018). However, the export shares of SMEs in ASEAN developing countries remain low compared to those in developed countries in East Asia. Therefore, this chapter aims to identify reasons for the relatively low levels of participation in exporting activities by the ASEAN SMEs in order for us to find ways to promote their internationalization.

As shown in Table 12.1, shares to total employment of SMEs in the ASEAN economies are more than 60 percent, while SME shares to GDP are more than 35 percent.

Comparing SMEs in East Asian countries (Japan, Korea, and China) to ASEAN SMEs, their contribution to total employment is not very different, but

Table 12.1 The important role of SMEs in the ASEAN economy (%)

Country	Share to total employment	Share to GDP	Year
Korea	87.9	51.2	2016
China	64.7	60.0	2013, 2011
Japan	70.2	50.0	2015
Thailand	82.2	42.4	2017
Malaysia	66.0	37.1	2017
the Philippines	62.9	35.7	2017
Indonesia	97.2	57.8	2018

Source: SME Corporation Malaysia, The Department of Trade and Industry Philippines, SME finance forum, Office of Small and Medium Enterprises Promotion, Thailand.

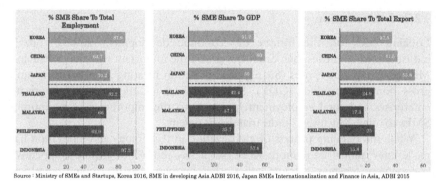

Source : Ministry of SMEs and Startups, Korea 2016, SME in developing Asia ADBI 2016, Japan SMEs Internationalization and Finance in Asia, ADBI 2015

Figure 12.1 SME share of total exports between East Asia and ASEAN

there are some differences in the shares of value-added in GDP. More importantly, as can be seen in Figure 12.1, ASEAN developing countries' SME exports to total exports are less than 25 percent, much lower than those of East Asian countries which range from 40–60 percent.

As seen in Table 12.1 and Figure 12.1, there is a mismatch in SME performance in the ASEAN economies. That is, while SMEs in ASEAN make significant contributions to ASEAN economies according to total employment and total value-added (GDP), SMEs' share of total exports remains subdued.

Therefore, this chapter will focus on the export activities of SMEs in ASEAN economies. In particular, the chapter aims to identify impediments and drivers of SMEs' engagement in export activities utilizing statistical analyses of the World Bank's Enterprise Survey Data and firm-level databases in the ASEAN economies. Findings from the analyses will shed light on a possible set of conducive policies for the internationalization of the ASEAN SMEs.

In this chapter, the following questions will be addressed.

Table 12.2 Definition of SMEs in the World Bank Enterprise Survey

Firm size	Small: 5–19 workers Medium: 20–99 workers Large: 100+ workers

1. What are the impediments to exports faced by the SMEs in ASEAN?
2. What are the internal and external factors that affect the export participation of SMEs?
3. What are the key drivers for SMEs' exporting activities in ASEAN?
4. What are the conducive policies to promote SMEs' export activities?

12.2 The World Bank Enterprise Survey Database

The current study utilizes World Bank Enterprise Surveys (WBESs) as the database for econometric analyses. Therefore, the study uses the definitions of SMEs given in the WBES, as shown in Table 12.2.

The study utilizes the WBESs of eight ASEAN developing countries: Cambodia (KHM), Indonesia (IDN), Lao PDR (LAO), Malaysia (MYS), Myanmar (MMR), the Philippines (PHL), Thailand (THA), and Vietnam (VNM).

The shares of exporting firms out of the total sample firms included in the WBESs are shown in Figure 12.2. The statistics are given for SMEs and larger firms, separately. Here, direct exporters are those who directly export their products, while indirect exporters are those who sell domestically to a third party that exports the products. This data sheds light on the underrepresentation of SMEs in foreign markets. SMEs in ASEAN have a lower percentage share of exporters compared to the larger firms. Shares of participants in export markets among SMEs, including both direct and indirect exporters, are generally less than 20 percent of the total number of SMEs, while those of larger firms make up 40 percent. Most SMEs in the ASEAN region export directly, rather than indirectly, as has also been observed among SMEs in OECD countries (WTO Secretariat, 2016). As more indirect exporters are found among larger firms, this again points to the widely observed phenomenon that it takes a certain size of operation for firms in developing countries to participate in global value chains (GVCs). The WBES databases also reveal that 80 percent of responding firms (to the surveys) in ASEAN developing countries are owned by domestic or local owners with a focus on local markets rather than foreign markets.

12.3 What are the impediments faced by SMEs in ASEAN?

This section investigates the impediments that ASEAN SMEs face in exporting their products. Examining the WBES databases in the eight developing ASEAN economies, the current study finds that obstacles faced by SMEs are somewhat different from those faced by larger enterprises. That is, SMEs may face more

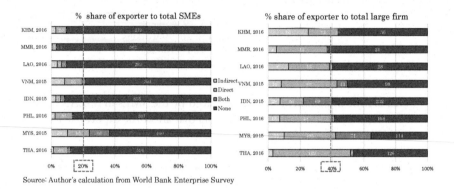

Source: Author's calculation from World Bank Enterprise Survey

Figure 12.2 Firm characteristics in the World Bank Enterprise Survey

difficulties in their efforts to export their products because of the small size of their operations. Identified impediments may also vary across sectors and countries in the region.

Table 12.3 summarizes the top five obstacles as reported by the exporting firms in the WBESs in the eight ASEAN developing countries, by firm size and industrial sector. Large firms and SMEs in ASEAN reported similar main obstacles. They were infrastructure (electricity and transportation), regulations (customs, trade regulations, and labor-market regulations), and educational attainment of the workforce. Access to finances and competition posed by firms in the informal sectors are relatively more important for SMEs. This survey also allows us to focus on SMEs in six key sectors that represent the top export products in ASEAN: electronic products, chemical products, rubber and plastic products, food and beverages, non-metallic mineral products, and textile and apparel. Transportation, customs and trade regulations, and educational attainment of labor are also major obstacles for the entire sample of SMEs. Still, it is interesting that access to finance does not appear as a top-five obstacle for the top export industries. To conclude, trade facilitation, regulations, and educational attainment of the workforce are widely perceived as major obstacles for exporters in developing countries in ASEAN.

12.4 What are the internal and external factors that affect the export participation of SMEs?

Concerning the low participation of SMEs in export markets, it is important to have a better understanding of the factors that promote the process of internationalization. This section explores the factors that affect SMEs' participation in the export markets. The OECD conducted SME surveys in 2014 and 2018, including reviews of policies for SME promotion (ERIA SME Research Working

Table 12.3 Top five obstacles facing exporting firms classified by size and sector

ASEAN

Large firm

1. Education of labor
2. Transportation
3. Custom and trade regulation
4. Labor regulation
5. Electricity

SMEs

1. Transportation
2. Custom and trade regulation
3. Competitor of the informal sector
4. Access to finance
5. Education of labor

Sector

Electronic products

1. Transportation
2. Custom and trade regulation
3. Tax rate
4. Electricity
5. Telecomunications

Rubber and plastic products

1. Transportation
2. Telecommunications
3. Political situation
4. Electricity
5. Corruption

Chemical products

1. Custom and trade regulation
2. Transportation
3. Competitor in the informal sector
4. Labor regulation
5. Education of labor

Non-metallic mineral products

1. Education of labor
2. Electricity
3. Transportation
4. Custom and trade regulation
5. Competition of informal sector

Food and beverages

1. Custom and trade regulation
2. Electricity
3. Telecommunications
4. Tax administration
5. Education of labor

Textiles and Apparel

1. Education of labor
2. Custom and trade regulation
3. Electricity
4. Transportation
5. Labor regulation

Source: Author's calculation from World Bank Enterprise Survey.

Group, 2014; OECD/ERIA, 2018). This study tries to map the database of the SME promotion policies collected by the OECD with the WBES data using the same dimensions of internal and external factors. Policies related to internal factors focus on access to finance, productivity, innovations, technology adoption, and entrepreneurial education. These are related to the management capacity of firms. Policies on external factors focus on legislation, regulations and taxes, and trade facilitation, including exposure to external markets.

OECD/ERIA (2018) reviewed ASEAN's SME promotion policies and found that the level of policy development and per capita income were correlated. As the SME policy formulation, implementation, and monitoring and evaluation (M&E) need budgetary support and human resources, the desired capacity for SME promotion policies naturally increases as the per capita income of a country rises. For instance, Laos, Myanmar, and Cambodia, as the younger members of ASEAN, have relatively limited budgets and human resources that can be mobilized for SME promotion. These limits are often visible in the areas of productivity enhancement and technology adoption.

Also, most external factors for the firms, in particular, legislation, regulations, and the tax system, in most ASEAN developing countries are still ranked relatively low in the Doing Business Indicators of the World Bank 2018. The respondents in the WBES assert that external factors such as the low quality of regulations and the lack of trade facilitation are the main obstacles of their business expansion to external markets.

Regarding policies to strengthen internal factors, labor productivity growth of Malaysia in the past 15 years has been less than that of its regional competitors, and this seems to have been the result of a declining share of skilled workers, insufficient technology diffusion, and a lack of innovation (OECD/ERIA, 2018). The WBES affirms this by showing that the education of the workforce is the major obstacle for both large firms and SMEs in Malaysia. In contrast, Vietnam has successfully facilitated firms' access to finances by broadening the scope of assets that can be used as collateral. This, in turn, has been reflected in the growing rank of Vietnam's indicator of ease in getting credit from banks (OECD/ERIA, 2018). It is also visible in the WBES for Vietnam, as access to finance was cited as one of the main obstacles in the 2009 survey but was dropped in the more recent 2015 survey.

Using the WBESs for ASEAN developing economies, Table 12.4 shows characteristics reported by exporting firms as compared to those reported by non-exporting firms. Regarding firm age (number of years in business), the ages of exporting firms are older than non-exporting firms. It confirms the finding in an earlier study by Wignaraja (2012). The older the firm is, the more experience in production and tacit knowledge is accumulated. This should facilitate their participation in the export markets.

Most survey samples are in manufacturing, and all the exporting firms in the WBES for ASEAN developing countries are in the manufacturing sectors. Although most of the SME employees are in the service sectors such as the wholesale and retails sectors, most exporting SMEs are in the manufacturing sectors (WTO Secretariat, 2016).

With regard to foreign ownership, Hiep and Nishijima (2009) and Wignaraja (2012) tested (partial) foreign ownership as a firm characteristic in ASEAN economies. Their studies find a positive effect on export intensity, explained by the advantage of foreign ownership in accessing marketing networks from parent companies and gaining know-how, better technology, and management experience; this makes the local firms more likely to participate in the export markets. However, Table 12.4 indicates that foreign ownership among exporting SMEs is generally low in ASEAN developing economies, except Malaysia and the Philippines.

Most of the large exporting firms use foreign content (imported content) in their products, but this is not the case for exporting SMEs that predominantly depend on domestic inputs. An OECD trading policy paper by Kowalski, Gonzalez, Ragoussis, and Ugarte (2015) finds that sourcing of foreign value-added products is associated with higher productivity and exporting more sophisticated products. Nevertheless, the WBES survey reveals that the SMEs in ASEAN developing countries still use foreign content only to serve their domestic markets. This is probably because these SMEs still have limited technology to integrate foreign content into their products, even if it may improve their productivity and competitiveness for them to enter export markets.

To investigate the mindset of managers, the WBES poses a question whether they have made any new or significant improvements in the methods of either manufacturing production or service offerings, or both, during the last three years. Survey results show that most of the exporting firms have made no improvement in this regard, except for the larger firms in Thailand, Malaysia, and Indonesia.

Using the WBES taken at two different time points, 2009 and 2015/16, Figure 12.3 shows the number of days required to clear customs procedures to export products for SME and large exporters separately. These statistics are considered to be good indicators of the extent of trade facilitation. It shows increases in the days required for customs clearing between 2009 and 2015/16, regardless of firm size. This indicates one emerging bottleneck for exporters in the ASEAN developing countries.

Figure 12.4 shows the number of firms that have not experienced product losses during export shipping. It shows that more and more firms are experiencing product losses during shipping. The losses could be incurred due to handling of products at customs or in freight service. In any event, as a policy to improve external factors, product safety in shipping should be enhanced, or improved access to trade insurance should be provided.

Concerning the export promotion policies in ASEAN developing countries, according to an ASEAN SME policy report (OECD/ERIA, 2018), export promotion policy in ASEAN developing countries has some gaps. Indonesia, Malaysia, the Philippines, Thailand, and Vietnam are at a more advanced stage. Meanwhile, Cambodia, Laos, and Myanmar are at the intermediate stage of policy development.

The levels of export promotion policies for SMEs in ASEAN developing countries serve as a good predictor of the stages of SMEs' engagement in the foreign markets. Abonyi and Kagami (2015) classified degrees of SME internationalization

Table 12.4 Characteristics of developing countries in ASEAN: comparison between exporting and non-exporting firms

Factors	Expected sign	ASEAN (2015, 2016)	THA 2016	MYS (2015)	PHL 2016
1. Age	+	Most exporters are older (exporter 20.8 yrs : non exporter 17.7 yrs)	Little older (Positive)	No difference	Younger (Negative)
2. Sector (Manu/ Non-Manu)		All exporters are in Manu	Manu	Manu	Manu
3. Foreign ownership L: Large firm	+	Most exporting large firms have foreign ownership but not exporting SMEs	L: Medium SME: Low	L: High SME: High	L: High SME: High
4. Foreign contents serve market F: Foreign market D: Domestic market L: Large firm	+	Most exporting large firms have foreign contents but not exporting SMEs	L: F SME: D	L: F SME: D	L: F&D SME: D
5. Manager's mindset L: Large firm	+	Only some of exporters have positive mindset to improve their production or services	L: Positive SME: No	L: Positive SME: No	L: No SME: No

Source: Author's illustration based on WBES

into three stages and stated that each stage needs a set of specific policies that effectively tackle their obstacles. Three stages of SME internationalization are the preparation stage, the active engagement stage, and the growth and expansion stage. After reviewing the ASEAN's SME Policy Report of 2018 (OECD/ ERIA, 2018), it can be said that Thailand, Malaysia, Indonesia, the Philippines, and Vietnam are in the growth and expansion stage of SMEs' engagement in foreign markets. The constraints at this stage, according to the study of Abonyi

IDN (2015)	VNM (2015)	LAO 2016	MMR 2016	KHM 2016
Older (Positive)	Mixed: SME older	A bit younger (Negative)	Much younger (Negative)	Mixed: Large younger (Negative)
Manu	Manu	Manu	Manu	Manu
L: High SME: Low	L: High SME: Low	L: High SME: Low	L: Medium SME: Low	L: High SME: Low
L: F SME: D	L: F SME: D	L: D SME: D	L: F SME: D	L: D SME: D
L: Positive SME: No	L: No SME: No	L: No SME: No	L: No SME: No	L: No SME: No

and Kagami (2015), are competitiveness and knowledge of the relevant range of international standards and certifications. Therefore, governments need to focus more on policies and facilitation in these areas. Meanwhile, Cambodia, Laos, and Myanmar, being at the intermediate stage, tend to face constraints in initiating contacts, getting to know foreign markets and foreign buyers through overseas trade offices and trade fairs, understanding, and using cross-border logistics, and knowing the rules and regulations for operating in foreign markets. The

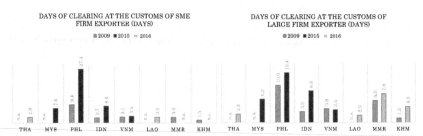

Source : Author's calculation from Enterprise Survey

Figure 12.3 Days to clear customs

Source : Author's calculation from enterprise survey

Figure 12.4 Number of firms without product loss during shipping

governments in these economies should focus more on policies and facilitation in these areas.

Moreover, it could be observed that there is a difference in SME export promotion policy between the advanced level and the intermediate level. At the advanced level, the policy on export promotion will be more targeted toward SMEs and more focused on the specific sectors which have good potential to get priority support from the government. For instance, Malaysia has selected export programs as one of its high impact programs under the country's SME Master Plan for 2012–2020 (OECD/ERIA, 2018). Compared to the intermediate level, SME policy on export promotion is not a specific policy and remains included in the universal national policy. Also, the ease of access for SMEs to get export promotion support still has limitations.

12.5 What are the drivers for SMEs' exporting activities in ASEAN?

In this section, the current study will investigate the significance of the internal and external factors, including policy facilitation, in explaining SMEs' exporting activities. The study augments the internal and external factors to be tested by drawing on the typical factors from previous studies and then applying regression analyses in order to identify the significance of those factors that potentially affect SMEs' participation in exporting activities. Logit models of participation in exporting activities (directly and/or indirectly) are estimated for the entire group of SMEs in the eight developing ASEAN economies, and separately by typical manufacturing sectors or industries.

12.5.1 Explanatory variables (drivers)

As presented in Table 12.5, this section will explain the expected sign of the relationship between the probability of firms' participation in exporting activities and each variable.

Following Leonidou (2004), factors that are the drivers for SMEs' exporting activity in ASEAN can be classified into internal factors and external factors. The internal factors are related to firm-level capability and resource constraints to internationalization; meanwhile, external factors are related to the business environment that affects internationalization, such as domestic governmental rules, regulations, and procedures associated with exporting, importing, and procurement.

12.5.1.1 Internal factors

1. Firm characteristics

    1.1 *Firm age*: Older firms that have more experience and networks with their customers have more propensity to join the international market. However, younger firms may also have more propensity to join in the international market as young firms leapfrog technology to access the export market, affirmed by the study of Van Dijk (2002). The study shows evidence that the younger firm is one of the export determinants in manufacturing firms in Indonesia.

    1.2 *Foreign ownership*: Firms with more (partial) foreign ownership have more probability of joining the export market. Since they have more advantages to learn technology, management systems, and networking from the parent company; therefore, they have more probability of joining in the export market, as has been confirmed in studies on the impact of foreign ownership on the export participation of ASEAN developing countries. A study by Hiep and Nishijima (2009) investigates a firm's impact on the export intensity, and the study finds that having foreign ownership leads to having a higher export intensity of firms in Vietnam. Also, a study by Ramstetter and Takii (2006) has found evidence that the higher the share of foreign ownership, the higher the export propensity in manufacturing firms in Indonesia.

2. Access to Information and Communication Technologies (ICT)

Table 12.5 Definitions of variables

Variables	Definition	Notes
Dependent variables		
Direct export	Denotes indicator variable of direct export participation	1 if participating in direct export, 0 otherwise
Direct export or indirect export	Denotes indicator variable of direct export or indirect export participation	1 if participating in direct export or indirect export, 0 otherwise
Internal factors		
Independent variables: 1. Firm characteristics		
Ln_age	Denotes years of formal operation of a firm	
% Foreign ownership	Denotes percentage of foreign ownership in a firm	Percentage of foreign ownership divided by 100
Independent variables: 2. Access to ICT		
Emails client and suppliers_ dummy	Denotes indicator variable of email communication	1 if using email to communicate with clients/suppliers, 0 otherwise
Have International Certification_dummy	Denotes indicator variable of international-recognized quality certification	1 if a firm obtains one(s), 0 otherwise
Independent variables: 3. Access to finance		
Have access to finance working capital_dummy	Denotes indicator variables of access to finance working capital	1 if firm obtains one(s), o otherwise
Have access to finance working capital from bank_dummy	Denotes indicator variable of access to working capital from banks	1 if a firm obtains one(s), 0 otherwise
Have access to finance working capital from supplier credits_dummy	Denotes indicator variable of access to working capital from supplier credits	1 if a firm obtains one(s), 0 otherwise
Have access to finance working capital from non-bank financial institutions_dummy	Denotes indicator variable of access to working capital from non-bank financial institutions	1 if a firm obtains one(s), 0 otherwise
Have access to finance working capital from informal sectors_dummy	Denotes indicator variable of access to working capital from informal sources	1 if a firm obtains one(s), 0 otherwise

(continued)

Table 12.5 Cont.

Variables	Definition	Notes
External factors		
Independent variable: 1.Trade facilitation		
% Product loss	Denotes the percentage of products shipped to supply domestic markets lost due to breakage or spoilage	Percentage of product lost divided by 100
Independent variables: 2. Macro variables		
SME policy in internal market expansion	Denotes indicator variable of SME policy index of ASEAN countries in international market expansion conducted in 2014 by OECD	
ln_REER	Denotes indicator variable of real effective exchange rate and source of data from UNCTAD	

ICT regarding the WBES indicators, the first indicator is email access to the suppliers and customers. Firms that can access ICT are more likely to access the export market because it could help SMEs to access the export market at a lower cost. Meanwhile, the second indicator is a qualified international certification, such as the International Organization for Standardization (ISO). SMEs who adhere to ISO rules will have more potential to meet international standards in the export market.

3. Access to finance

SMEs with access to finance working capital from banks, suppliers, non-bank financial institutions, and informal financiers are more likely to participate in export markets than other firms. Also, access to finance working capital could help support SMEs in both their expenditures and investments to improve their productivity and quality. As a result, it increases the probability of succeeding in the export market. The difficulties that most SMEs face in accessing formal bank finance are due to a lack of knowledge of accounting management and a lack of good collateral.

12.5.1.2 *External factors*

1. Trade facilitation

As Grainger (2008) has summarized, the coverage of trade facilitation according to the UN/CEFACT and UNCTAD (2002), trade facilitation covers trade procedures, customs, regulatory bodies, provisions of official control procedures that are applicable to import, export, and transit operations. Suitable trade facilitation measures are conducive to SMEs' engagement in international trade. In addition, Macasaquit Reyes (2009) studied the impact of trade facilitation on SMEs in the Philippines, the evidence shows that SMEs who are direct exporter types would get the benefit from trade facilitation measures since, in the Philippines, the cost of trade facilitation remains high and SMEs have smaller assets and operational capabilities compared to larger firms. Furthermore, trade procedures and costly requirements often prohibit SMEs from actively pursuing international trade.

2. SME policy (in the international market expansion)

This study uses the SME policy index compiled by the OECD in 2014 (ERIA SME Research Working Group, 2014). This index captures the dimension of export market expansion and enables us to see the significance of this set of SME policies on the export activities of SMEs. According to the SME Policy Report by the OECD (ERIA SME Research Working Group, 2014), a number of policies can support SMEs in entering export markets: These are export promotion programs in several activities such as the facilitation of SMEs' participation in international fairs, provision of business matching, and providing access to marketing information and product developments.

3. Real effective exchange rate (REER)

This study utilizes REER data provided by UNCTAD Stat (2019). According to the UNCTAD Secretariat (2019, p. 24):

> REER is a measure of the trade-weighted average exchange rate of a currency against a basket of currencies after adjusting for inflation differentials (consumer price index). It measures external competitiveness. In general, an appreciation in the REER results in a loss of competitiveness, while a decline in the REER indicates an increase in external competitiveness.

12.5.2 Model

The models and equations to be estimated in this study are based on Duval and Utoktham (2014). Binomial logit models are used in order to identify major drivers of SMEs' exporting activities. Our own set of internal as well as external factors presented in Table 12.5, are tested.

$$\text{logit}(P) = \alpha + \beta_1 X_1 + \beta_2 X_2 + \ldots \ldots + \beta_k X_k + \varepsilon \tag{12.1}$$

P = Probability of the event (Yes / No) Dichotomy / Binary.
β_i = Coefficient to explain the sign and size of the correlation of the variable X_i to the probability of the event.

Independent variables X_i can be classified into four groups:

Internal factors are: (1) firm characteristics; (2) access to ICT 3; and (3) access to finance. External factors are:(1) trade facilitation; and (2) macro variables which are (3) the SME policy index, and (4) Real effective exchange rate (REER).

12.5.3 Regression results

This study intends to consider the two types of exports that local SMEs could engage in: direct and indirect exports. According to Welch and Luostarinen (1993), the modalities of exports are (1) direct exports by exporting firms to the distributors/importers located in the target markets; (2) indirect exports where local firms sell their products domestically to the third party export intermediaries such as agents and brokers located in their own country, who in turn export them; (3) non-equity contractual agreements such as franchising, licensing; and (4) through foreign direct investment (FDI). However, due to data limitations, this study covers only the first two modalities of exporting. Indirect exports here also include the cases where parts or products produced by local firms are supplied to other domestic firms or foreign subsidiaries who export products that incorporate those local products.

Table 12.6 shows the top export industries of ASEAN and the numbers of firms in our enterprise survey database. It can confirm that the survey sample can be representative of the top exporting industries of ASEAN. The six selected industrial sectors for our regression analyses by sector are electronic products, non-metallic mineral products, rubber and plastic products, food and beverages, chemical products, and textiles and apparel.

Table 12.7 presents results from the logit-model regression analyses conducted on aggregate (all sectors) exports by SMEs of eight ASEAN developing countries

12.5.3.1 Internal factors

1. Firm characteristics
   1.1 *Firm age*: The regression results show the different marginal effects of the ages of the firms between direct exporters and other groups, including indirect exporters. Direct exporters tend to require more years in operation for them to participate in the export markets because it requires upfront costs, including sunk costs.

   Those sunk costs when directly selling abroad related to setting up distribution networks or investing in initial advertising campaigns whose costs cannot be recovered and are higher than that of the including indirect exporter (Brenton, Cadot & Pierola, 2012). There are more risks in being a direct exporter. Therefore, SMEs that are older are more likely to be able to take on these risks. It follows the hypothesis that the older the firm is, the greater the accumulation of tacit knowledge and experience in dealing with new marketing and searching for new customers. On the other hand, indirect exporters tend to face fewer risks

Table 12.6 Top export industries of ASEAN and share of firms from World Bank
Enterprise Survey

% Share to total export (2017)		Number of firms				Direct export	
Sector		SMEs	%	Large	%	SME	%
1. Electronic products	26.0	146.0	3.5	75.0	5.0	41.0	9.6
2. Mineral fuels and oils	10.6	166.0	4.0	79.0	5.3	16.0	3.7
3. Rubber and plastic products	6.0	241.0	5.8	138.0	9.2	21.0	4.9
4. Food and beverages	11.0	477.0	11.6	259.0	17.4	56.0	13.1
5. Chemicals	2.1	239.0	5.8	139.0	9.3	42.0	9.8
6. Textile, garments, apparel	4.0	110.0	2.7	124.0	8.3	15.0	3.5
Selected industries (from 1. to 6.)	59.6	1,379.0	33.4	814.0	54.6	191.0	44.6
Others	40.4	2,747.0	66.6	678.0	45.4	237.0	55.4
Manu		2,481.0	60.1	1,224.0	82.0	318.0	74.3
Non-Manu		1,645.0	39.9	268.0	18.0	110.0	25.7
Total	100.0	4,126.0	100.0	1,492.0	100.0	428.0	100.0

Source: ASEAN Secretariat and World Bank Enterprise Survey calculated by the author.

in entering export markets since these risks have already been taken and
diversified by export intermediaries such as agents and brokers.

1.2 *Foreign ownership*: Foreign ownership has a positive marginal effect on
the probability of SMEs in ASEAN developing countries to participate
in export markets both as direct and indirect exporters. It is estimated
to increase the probability of export participation by around 14–15 percent. As postulated earlier, foreign ownership enables SMEs to get an
advantage through access to superior marketing connections and know-
how of parent companies (Wignaraja, 2012).

2. Access to information and communication technology (ICT):

As a proxy of ICT access, this study uses an indicator of access to emails
in order to communicate with suppliers and customers, or both. The results
of logit-model analyses show positive marginal effects of ICT access on the
probability of SMEs' engagement in exporting activities, both for direct
exporters and the other group, including indirect exporters. It increases the
probability of export participation by about 5.6 percent and 3.6 percent,
respectively.

ISO certification: The results suggest that firms with internationally
recognized certifications, such as ISO certifications, tend to have a higher
probability of participating in export markets, again for both the direct and
the other group, including indirect exporters. It increases the exporting
probability by about 6 percent and 7 percent, respectively. ICT provides

		No direct export only indirect export				Direct or indirect export			
Large	%	SME	%	Large	%	SME	%	Large	%
47.0	7.7	19.0	10.6	14.0	11.5	60.0	9.9	61.0	8.3
24.0	3.9	5.0	2.8	5.0	4.1	21.0	3.5	29.0	4.0
59.0	9.7	1.0	0.6	5.0	4.1	22.0	3.6	64.0	8.8
98.0	16.1	27.0	15.1	15.0	12.3	83.0	13.7	113.0	15.5
75.0	12.3	9.0	5.0	14.0	11.5	51.0	8.4	89.0	12.2
51.0	8.4	43.0	24.0	38.0	31.1	58.0	9.6	89.0	12.2
354.0	58.1	104.0	58.1	91.0	74.6	295.0	48.6	445.0	60.9
255.0	41.9	75.0	41.9	31.0	25.4	312.0	51.4	286.0	39.1
562.0	92.3	122.0	68.2	105.0	86.1	440.0	72.5	667.0	91.2
47.0	7.7	57.0	31.8	17.0	13.9	167.0	27.5	64.0	8.8
609.0	100.0	179.0	100.0	122.0	100.0	607.0	100.0	731.0	100.0

SMEs with easier access to broader markets at lower costs. International certificates such as the ISO certificates, by augmenting the credibility of the firms, expand the chances for SMEs to qualify as potential suppliers.

3. Access to finance

This study tries to find answers to the two-tier questions by estimating logit models with different sets of dummies for access to various sources of finance. In the first model, the study tests whether SMEs' access to finance, regardless of the modalities of financing, has an impact on the probability of participating in exporting activities. The results suggest that SMEs that have access to finance will have higher probabilities of entering export markets. It increases the probability by about 5 percent and 5.6 percent for direct and the other group, including indirect exporters, respectively.

In the second model, the study investigates which modality or source of finance turns out to be more significant in increasing the probabilities of SMEs' participation in exporting: finance from formal banks, non-bank financial institutions, supplier and purchaser credits (purchases on credit from suppliers and advances from customers), or informal sector finance. The results show that for both direct and the other groups, including indirect exporters, financing from banks, non-banks, and informal sector financiers have a positive marginal effect on the likeliness of exporting activities. Finance from the non-bank financial institutions seem to increase the probability of exporting more substantially as compared to the impact of

Table 12.7 Logit model results: marginal effects on aggregate (all sectors) exports by SMEs of eight ASEAN developing countries

Marginal effects: ASEAN Variables	*SMEs*			
	Binary variable: 1 if direct export at least 1%, 0 otherwise		*Binary variable: 1 if direct export or indirect export at least 1%, 0 otherwise*	
	(1)	*(2)*	*(1)*	*(2)*
ln_age	0.0216**	0.0213**	0.0113	0.0108
	(0.00849)	(0.00840)	(0.00966)	(0.00960)
%product loss	−0.236*	−0.202	−0.210	−0.175
	(0.130)	(0.127)	(0.143)	(0.138)
%foreign ownership	0.152***	0.142***	0.153***	0.144***
	(0.0224)	(0.0219)	(0.0279)	(0.0276)
ICT_Email_dummy	0.0557***	0.0558***	0.0355***	0.0353***
	(0.0117)	(0.0117)	(0.0132)	(0.0132)
ICT_Certification_dummy	0.0672***	0.0641***	0.0792***	0.0754***
	(0.0124)	(0.0123)	(0.0157)	(0.0157)
Have access to finance working cap_dummy	0.0504***		0.0564***	
	(0.0107)		(0.0122)	
Have access to finance working cap from bank_dummy		0.0377***		0.0472***
		(0.0102)		(0.0119)
Have access to finance working cap from supplier_dummy		0.0219*		0.00888
		(0.0117)		(0.0140)
Have access to finance working cap from non-bank_dummy		0.0724***		0.0810***
		(0.0146)		(0.0185)
Have access to finance working cap from informal sectors_dummy		0.0492***		0.0449**
		(0.0154)		(0.0188)
ln_REER	0.122	0.173	−0.0980	−0.0575
	(0.303)	(0.289)	(0.426)	(0.414)
SME policy in international market expansion	0.0432	0.0516	−0.0207	−0.0132
	(0.0538)	(0.0515)	(0.0728)	(0.0709)
Fixed Country	Yes	Yes	Yes	Yes
Fixed Year	Yes	Yes	Yes	Yes
Fixed Sector	Yes	Yes	Yes	Yes
Observations	3,532	3,532	3,532	3,532

Notes: Standard errors in parentheses.
*** $p<0.01$, ** $p<0.05$, * $p<0.1$

Source: Author's calculations.

finance from banks and informal sector sources. This reflects the existing obstacles for SMEs in accessing formal bank finance in the context of the eight developing ASEAN economies. This difficulty of getting formal bank finance is also pointed out by the OECD (OECD/ERIA, 2018), as banks require higher levels of collateral. Meanwhile, purchasing on credit from suppliers, compared to other sources of financing of SMEs, has a small effect for direct exporters. Moreover, it does not show the significance for the indirect exporters, therefore comparing direct exporters and indirect exporters, it can imply that indirect exporters have lower bargaining power to purchase on credit since most of the indirect exporters are smaller firms with lower credit.

12.5.3.2 External factors

1. Trade facilitation product loss

   The reported percentages of product loss (breakage or spoilage) incurred during shipping are used in this study. Earlier, from this study on the impediments of SME exporters, the WBES data revealed that product losses representing trade facilitation were the top impediment for SMEs in engaging in exporting activities. The provision of countermeasures such as securing better and quicker handling of products in customs procedures and the provision of accessible trade insurance is an integral part of trade facilitation. Nevertheless, the results from logit-model estimations show that product losses tend to have small adverse effects on the probabilities of SMEs' exporting activities using direct exporters.

2. SME policy in international market expansion

   For the SME policy in international market expansion, the results do not show significant effects on the export probability either for direct or other groups including indirect exporters. As the study only takes into account the cross-country differences of the policy environment and as it is generally challenging to single out policy differences from other country fixed effects such as unaccounted differences in institutions, the impact of SME internationalization policies should also be tested in panel data analyses.

3. Real effective exchange rate (REER)

   It seems that REER has no statistically significant impact on the probability of participating in export markets, either for direct exporters and the other group, including indirect exporters. This result suggests that changes in the (real) exchange rates do not have significant effects on the probability of exporting among the eight ASEAN developing economies. It should also be noted that, as inflation rates are generally low and well under control among ASEAN economies, the variations in REERs are not significant in this region.

Table 12.8 presents results from the logit-model regression analyses conducted separately on each of the top six industrial sectors (as shown in Table 12.6). The

Table 12.8 Logit model results: marginal effects for the top six export industries of eight ASEAN developing countries

(a) Middle-to-high-tech industry

Marginal effects : ASEAN variables	Electronic products				Chemical products			
	Binary Variable: 1 if direct export at least 1%, 0 otherwise		Binary Variable: 1 if direct export or indirect export at least 1%, 0 otherwise		Binary Variable: 1 if direct export at least 1%, 0 otherwise		Binary Variable: 1 if direct export or indirect export at least 1%, 0 otherwise	
	(1)	*(2)*	*(1)*	*(2)*	*(1)*	*(2)*	*(1)*	*(2)*
ln_age	0.0353	0.0447	0.00657	0.00862	0.121***	0.115***	0.0977**	0.0879**
	(0.0730)	(0.0721)	(0.0730)	(0.0719)	(0.0429)	(0.0411)	(0.0449)	(0.0447)
% product loss	0.476	1.557*	0.894	1.251	−0.279	−0.200	0.466	0.332
	(0.781)	(0.826)	(0.818)	(0.855)	(0.451)	(0.393)	(0.476)	(0.457)
% foreign ownership	0.374**	0.291**	0.845***	0.731***	0.264***	0.243***	0.367***	0.346***
	(0.157)	(0.143)	(0.205)	(0.193)	(0.0872)	(0.0838)	(0.0839)	(0.0807)
ICT_Email_dummy	0.0504	0.0302	0.0514	0.00934	0.0553	0.0901*	0.0556	0.0717
	(0.0809)	(0.0821)	(0.0809)	(0.0832)	(0.0525)	(0.0542)	(0.0549)	(0.0561)
ICT_Certification_dummy	0.0405	−0.0172	0.142*	0.126	0.0982**	0.0758	0.0939*	0.0769
	(0.0823)	(0.0831)	(0.0827)	(0.0862)	(0.0494)	(0.0475)	(0.0553)	(0.0547)
Have access to finance working cap_dummy	0.142*		0.0855		0.122**		0.145***	
	(0.0776)		(0.0776)		(0.0514)		(0.0521)	
Have access to finance working cap from bank_dummy		0.207***		0.103		0.0277		0.0948*
		(0.0676)		(0.0711)		(0.0557)		(0.0562)
Have access to finance working cap from supplier_dummy		−0.0498		0.0604		0.124**		0.0908*
		(0.0848)		(0.0820)		(0.0500)		(0.0550)

Have access to finance working cap from non-bank_dummy		0.177* (0.0930)		0.169* (0.101)			0.0944 (0.0633)	0.0578 (0.0696)
Have access to finance working cap from informal sectors_ dummy		0.273*		0.124			0.0263	0.00130
		(0.157)		(0.171)			(0.0787)	(0.0848)
ln_REER	−4.329	−5.506	−5.422	−6.246	−0.362	−0.439	−0.225	−0.349
	(4.164)	(3.949)	(5.132)	(4.650)	(0.326)	(0.343)	(0.302)	(0.328)
SME policy in international market expansion	−2.411	−3.396	−2.741	−3.563	0.223**	0.229**	0.247**	0.232**
	(2.612)	(2.517)	(3.143)	(2.888)	(0.106)	(0.106)	(0.101)	(0.103)
Fixed Country	Yes	Yes	Yes	Yes	Yes	Yes	Yes	Yes
Fixed Year	Yes	Yes	Yes	Yes	Yes	Yes	Yes	Yes
Observations	194	194	194	194	206	206	206	206

Table 12.8 Cont.

Marginal effects : ASEAN Variables	Rubber and plastic products				Non-metallic and mineral products			
	Binary Variable: 1 if direct export at least 1 %, 0 otherwise		Binary Variable: 1 if direct export or indirect export at least 1 %, 0 otherwise		Binary Variable: 1 if direct export at least 1 %, 0 otherwise		Binary Variable: 1 if direct export or indirect export at least 1 %, 0 otherwise	
	(1)	(2)	(1)	(2)	(1)	(2)	(1)	(2)
ln_age	0.0892**	0.0946**	0.0989**	0.103**	0.0259	0.0212	0.0154	0.00853
	(0.0397)	(0.0439)	(0.0416)	(0.0450)	(0.0392)	(0.0390)	(0.0427)	(0.0419)
% product loss	−3.069	−3.237	−3.815	−3.194	−1.304	−1.158	−2.084	−1.815
	(5.914)	(6.936)	(6.310)	(6.933)	(1.805)	(1.842)	(2.052)	(2.070)
% foreign ownership	0.373**	0.405**	0.394**	0.437**	0.324**	0.368***	0.384**	0.437***
	(0.172)	(0.189)	(0.181)	(0.204)	(0.141)	(0.139)	(0.160)	(0.155)
ICT_Email_dummy	0.0510	0.0150	0.00904	−0.0285	0.0719	0.0847	0.105	0.107
	(0.0831)	(0.0909)	(0.0711)	(0.0783)	(0.0713)	(0.0729)	(0.0826)	(0.0813)
ICT_Certification_dummy	0.0554	0.0619	0.0551	0.0636	−0.0895	−0.110	−0.121	−0.141
	(0.0428)	(0.0467)	(0.0451)	(0.0488)	(0.102)	(0.104)	(0.117)	(0.118)
Have access to finance working cap_dummy	0.0920**		0.101**		0.0595		0.0438	
	(0.0396)		(0.0412)		(0.0530)		(0.0536)	
Have access to finance working cap from bank_dummy		0.0820*		0.0945**		0.0333		0.0107
		(0.0472)		(0.0473)		(0.0465)		(0.0498)
Have access to finance working cap from supplier_dummy		0.108		0.0954		0.0844		0.115**
		(0.0717)		(0.0714)		(0.0518)		(0.0573)

	(1)	(2)	(3)	(4)	(5)	(6)	(7)	(8)
Have access to finance working cap from non-bank_dummy		0.0588 (0.0899)		0.130* (0.0753)		0.0478 (0.0764)		0.0572 (0.0872)
Have access to finance working cap from informal sectors_dummy		—		—		0.0452 (0.0615)		0.0332 (0.0708)
ln_REER	−0.602 (0.782)	−0.534 (0.874)	−0.643 (0.817)	−0.634 (0.936)	0.237 (0.317)	0.356 (0.309)	0.394 (0.353)	0.565* (0.337)
SME policy in international market expansion	0.342*** (0.122)	0.480*** (0.167)	0.341*** (0.119)	0.461*** (0.157)	–	–	–	–
Fixed Country	Yes	Yes	Yes	Yes	Yes	Yes	Yes	Yes
Fixed Year	Yes	Yes	Yes	Yes	Yes	Yes	Yes	Yes
Observations	200	185	200	185	157	157	157	157

Table 12.8 Cont.

(b) Middle to low industry

Marginal effects : ASEAN variables	Food and beverages				Textiles and apparel			
	Binary Variable: 1 if direct export at least 1%, 0 otherwise		Binary Variable: 1 if direct export or indirect export at least 1%, 0 otherwise		Binary Variable: 1 if direct export at least 1%, 0 otherwise		Binary Variable: 1 if direct export or indirect export at least 1%, 0 otherwise	
	(1)	(2)	(1)	(2)	(1)	(2)	(1)	(2)
ln_age	-0.00560 (0.0264)	-0.00721 (0.0258)	0.00171 (0.0257)	-0.00247 (0.0262)	0.0380 (0.0240)	0.0307 (0.0238)	0.0291 (0.0306)	0.0217 (0.0305)
% product loss	-0.576 (0.422)	-0.876* (0.461)	0.157 (0.149)	0.218 (0.147)	-0.696 (0.515)	-0.540 (0.499)	0.122 (0.241)	0.166 (0.232)
% foreign ownership	0.0821 (0.143)	0.0958 (0.141)	0.222 (0.157)	0.240* (0.144)	0.652*** (0.160)	0.577*** (0.150)	1.596*** (0.490)	1.454*** (0.465)
ICT_Email_dummy	0.0964*** (0.0373)	0.121*** (0.0406)	0.111*** (0.0356)	0.118*** (0.0372)	0.0961*** (0.0303)	0.0881*** (0.0299)	0.132*** (0.0367)	0.127*** (0.0369)
ICT_Certification_ dummy	0.130*** (0.0356)	0.104*** (0.0356)	0.142*** (0.0394)	0.129*** (0.0403)	-0.00160 (0.0542)	0.00449 (0.0520)	0.00230 (0.0751)	0.0171 (0.0743)
Have access to finance working cap_dummy	0.112*** (0.0398)		0.159*** (0.0390)		0.0241 (0.0283)		0.0335 (0.0345)	
Have access to finance working cap from bank_dummy		0.0391 (0.0348)		0.0431 (0.0343)		0.0616** (0.0286)		0.0661* (0.0359)

Have access to finance working cap from supplier_dummy	0.0683* (0.0410)		0.128*** (0.0373)		-0.0331 (0.0318)			-0.0367 (0.0402)
Have access to finance working cap from non-bank_dummy	0.165*** (0.0431)		0.148*** (0.0487)		0.0865** (0.0375)			0.0832 (0.0530)
Have access to finance working cap from informal sectors_dummy	0.0503 (0.0587)		0.0401 (0.0586)		-0.0399 (0.0404)			-0.00315 (0.0473)
ln_age	-0.142 (0.335)	-0.0307 (0.339)	-15.27 (10.21)	-13.04 (10.64)	-0.0243 (0.246)	0.0364 (0.254)	0.361 (0.292)	0.275 (0.298)
SME policy in international market expansion	0.0526 (0.112)	0.0709 (0.111)	-4.946 (3.324)	-4.191 (3.468)	-0.233* (0.122)	-0.229* (0.130)	-0.236* (0.125)	-0.248** (0.125)
Fixed Country	Yes	Yes	Yes	Yes	Yes	Yes	Yes	Yes
Fixed Year	Yes	Yes	Yes	Yes	Yes	Yes	Yes	Yes
Observations	356	356	407	407	473	473	473	473

Notes: Standard errors in parentheses.
*** $p<0.01$, ** $p<0.05$, * $p<0.1$.

Source: Authors' calculations.

impact of internal and external factors on exports by SMEs of electronic products, non-metallic mineral products, rubber and plastic products, food and beverages, chemical products, and textiles and apparel sectors are estimated.

These top export industries can be grouped into two types of industries: middle-to-high-tech industries and middle- to low-tech industries. Electronic products, chemical products, rubber and plastic products, and non-metallic mineral products are grouped in the middle-to-high-tech industries. Food and beverages, and textile and apparel sectors are arranged in the middle- to low-tech industries.

Foreign ownership is a crucial export driver for SMEs in both middle-to-high-tech industries and middle- to low-tech industries. However, by looking into selected sectors, the results for food and beverages, which is a resource-based industry for SMEs in ASEAN developing countries, suggest that foreign ownership does not increase the probability of exporting.

Other internal factors in the firm characteristics category, such as age seem to have marginal effects on the export probabilities of chemical products, and rubber and plastic products. SMEs in these industrial sectors seem to need more years of operational experience to enter the export markets.

Access to ICT, another internal factor, does not seem to induce higher probabilities of exporting activities among SMEs in the middle-to-high-tech industries. As specialized technologies are often necessary for the firms in these high-tech industries, exporting probabilities also seem to depend more on technology endowments. Conversely, for the middle- to low-tech industries such as food and beverages, and the textile and apparel industries, the study finds significant marginal effects of ICT accessibility on exporting.

Food and beverages exports often require international certification for the proof of conforming to international food security standards. Regression results confirm this fact.

The study also finds that the access to finance factor has the highest marginal effect on export probabilities of SMEs in food and beverages as compared to the impact on other selected industries. SMEs in the food and beverages sector in the developing ASEAN economies are resource-based and predominantly owned by domestic private owners, not by foreign owners. Therefore, they are most likely in need of trade finance for them to participate in exporting activities. The demand for finance seems to be relatively lower for the other selected industries.

For the external factors such as trade facilitation, the indicator of product losses seems to have significant negative marginal effects only on the exporting activities of the SMEs in food and beverages, perhaps as they have a limited shelf life. In the same vein, the SME policy for international expansion seems to have no significant marginal effects on export participation except for the rubber and plastic products sector. Rubber and plastic products are globally traded commodities with relatively higher price elasticities of demand, and therefore, policy interventions tend to have some impact.

For the real effective exchange rate (REER), the results did not find significance for all six selected sectors. This lack of significance of REER in impacting the probabilities of exporting also found in the aggregate regressions in the previous subsection. The same explanation, the low and stable inflation in this region, should also apply here.

12.6 What policy approach helps to strengthen SME exporting?

As we have learned from statistical analyses of the World Bank's Enterprise Survey data, large firms and SMEs in ASEAN report similar main obstacles. They are infrastructure (electricity and transportation), regulations (customs, trade regulations, and labor-market regulations) and educational attainment of the workforce. By contrast, access to finance and competition posed by firms in informal sectors are relatively more important for SMEs.

By using the logit model to see the marginal effect of each factor that could induce SMEs to participate more in the export market, the marginal effects support the hypotheses regarding internal factors for the SMEs in ASEAN. Foreign ownership is the key driver for SMEs in ASEAN developing countries to participate in the export market, followed by access to ICT that is reflected in the indicator of access to emails with suppliers or customers and obtaining an internationally recognized certification. Meanwhile, the results suggest that SMEs that have access to finance will have higher probabilities of entering export markets, and the source of finance turns out to be more significant in increasing the probabilities of SMEs' participation in exporting. Both for direct exporters and the other groups, including indirect exporters, financing from banks, non-banks, and informal sector financiers has a positive marginal effect on the likelihood of participating in export activities. Finance from non-bank financial institutions seem to increase the probability of exporting more significantly as compared to the impact of finance from banks and informal sector sources. This reflects an existing obstacle for SMEs in accessing formal bank finance in the context of the eight developing ASEAN economies. The difficulty of getting formal bank finance is also pointed out by the OECD (OECD/ERIA, 2018), as the banks require higher levels of collateral.

Meanwhile, we must pay attention to external factors such as trade facilitation. Earlier, this study indicated that product losses were reported as the top obstacle for SMEs in engaging in exporting activities. Nevertheless, the results from the logit-model estimations show that product losses tend to have small adverse effects on the probabilities of SMEs' exporting activities using direct exporters.

Regarding SME policy in international market expansion and REER, the results do not show a significant impact on the export probability either for direct exporters or the other groups, including indirect exporters. The study only takes into account the cross-country differences of the policy environment, as it is generally challenging to single out policy differences from other country fixed effects such as unaccounted differences in institutions.

Meanwhile, REER has no statistically significant impact on the probability of participating in export markets, either in direct exporter or the other groups, including indirect exporters. This result suggests that changes in the (real) exchange rates do not have significant effects on the probability of exporting among the eight ASEAN developing economies. It should also be noted that as inflation rates are generally low and under control among ASEAN economics, variations in REERs are not significant factors in this region.

For testing purposes, the top six export industries can be grouped into two types of industries: middle-to-high-tech industries, and middle- to low-tech industries. Electronic products, chemical products, rubber and plastic products, and non-metallic mineral products are grouped as middle-to-high-tech industries. Food and beverages, and textiles and apparel sectors are grouped as middle- to low-tech industries.

The study finds that the crucial driver for exports is different between the two groups of industries. Foreign ownership is an essential export driver for SMEs in both middle-to-high-tech industries and middle- to low-tech industries. However, by looking into the specially selected sector, the results were different for the food and beverages sector, which is a resource-based industry for SMEs in ASEAN developing countries, suggesting that foreign ownership does not increase the probability of exporting.

Other internal factors in the firm characteristics category, such as age seem to have marginal effects on the export probabilities of chemical products, and rubber and plastic products. SMEs in these industrial sectors seem to need more years of operational experience to enter the export markets.

Access to ICT, another internal factor in middle-to-high-tech industries such as the electronic industry, is already required for high technology settlement. Therefore, it does not seem to induce higher probabilities for exporting activities. Moreover, another possibility is that those SMEs in middle-to high-tech industries in ASEAN developing countries are suppliers who directly export to the export-oriented domestic large firms or multinational companies (MNCs). Therefore, they already have pre-export qualified for the international standard. Conversely, for the middle- to low-tech industries such as food and beverages, and textiles and apparel industries, the study finds significant marginal effects of ICT accessibility on exporting.

The study affirms the importance of the targeted policy in each sector as we can see the different effects in a different type of industry. For example, food and beverages exports often require international certification for the proof of conforming to the set of international food security standards. Regression results confirm this fact.

Another important finding is that access to finance affects selected sectors but has a different marginal effect, such as in the food and beverages sector. The food and beverage industry is a resource based industry that mainly has domestic ownership.

Again, this finding confirms that the policy to promote SMEs' participation in the export market needs to be targeted to each potential sector, like the food and beverages sector, where that ASEAN developing countries have an advantage from the abundance of natural resources. Moreover, to reiterate, the access to finance factor has the highest marginal effect on export probabilities.

Conversely, external factors such as trade facilitation remain the top impediments for aggregated SMEs in ASEAN developing countries. However, by applying a logit model, trade facilitation has shown a small marginal effect to contribute to the export participation. However, only SMEs in food and beverages with a limited shelf life between continents are significantly impacted by trade facilitation. Moreover, the food and beverages sector is one of the significant exporting sectors of ASEAN developing countries. Therefore, streamlined trade facilitation could help to promote export participation, particularly in the food and beverage sector.

In the same vein, this study has tried to use the SME policy index of each country to test how SME policy in export promotion could support SMEs to participate in export markets. However, it is a challenge for this study to single out a policy for each sector to see the impact of SME policy on each selected sector. Most ASEAN developing countries still have an SME policy at the universal national level, not in a specific sector.

For the real effective exchange rate (REER) in ASEAN, developing countries are generally low and under control. The results do not find significance across any of the six selected sectors.

To encourage SMEs in ASEAN developing countries to have a higher probability of participating more in the export market, the policy recommendations are as follows:

1. Based on the World Bank Enterprise Survey results, the obstacles for the operations of the exporting for large firms and SME firms mostly are infrastructure and regulations that could facilitate increased participation in the export market. Therefore, the governments of ASEAN economy countries should streamline those infrastructure and regulations related to trade and customs to support large firms and SMEs. Notably, by looking into the food and beverages sector, which is one of the top exporting sectors of ASEAN developing countries, SMEs will get the most benefits from this policy.

2. By applying the logit model to test the impact of SME policy on export promotion, this study suggests that the SME policy on export promotion is still limited and does not show a statistically significant impact on export participation. This reflects the need to support SMEs' integration to enter the export market and also to be more pro-active to provide greater numbers of SMEs access to the policy.

3. Regarding the logit model, marginal effects show that using ICT, such as providing internet access and email support, could help a small company to reach the export market at a low cost. Also, to obtain a recognized international certification such as ISOs could induce SMEs to have a higher potential to meet the international standards in the export market. Moreover, it is important to support SMEs' access to finance, in particular, finance for working capital. Providing an export credit facility to serve working capital needs and insurance coverage to hedge the risk from foreign buyers'

non-payment both from the bank and non-bank institutions could strengthen SMEs in developing countries in ASEAN in the export market.

4. Regarding the result of the key drivers to export participation of SMEs in the top six selected industries, to have a more effective policy, it is not suggested that ASEAN economies should use a universal national SME export promotion policy. The policies need to differently target individual industries because the results reveal that potential factors have a marginal effect on each industry differently. For example, in the food and beverages industry, which is a resource-based industry of ASEAN, access to finance has the highest probability of driving export market participation compared to other sectors. Meanwhile, in the textiles and apparel industry, access to ICT is the priority for driving participation in export markets.

Acknowledgments

This chapter draws on the discussions and analyses in Chapters 2 and 3 of Utumporn Jitsutthiphakorn's PhD dissertation to be submitted to Nagoya University in 2021. The tentative title of the dissertation is "Promoting Exports by the ASEAN SMEs."

References

Abonyi, G., & Kagami, S. (Eds.) (2015). *Innovation, technology transfers, finance, and internationalization of SMEs' trade and investment* (pp. 37–96). Jakarta: The Economic Research Institute for ASEAN and East Asia.

Brenton, P., Cadot, O., & Pierola, M. D. (2012). *Pathways to African export sustainability*. Washington, DC: The World Bank.

Burgel, O., Fier, A., Licht, G., & Murray, G. C. (2000). Internationalisation of high-tech start-ups and fast growth-evidence for UK and Germany. ZEW Discussion Paper No. 00-35. Paris: The Organisation for Economic Co-operation and Development. http://dx.doi.org/10.2139/ssrn.373940.

Duval, Y., & Utoktham, C. (2014). Enabling participation of SMEs in international trade and production networks: Trade facilitation, trade finance and communication technology. The United Nations Economic and Social Commission for Asia and the Pacific, Artnet Working Paper Series No. 146.

ERIA SME Research Working Group. (2014). Policy Index 2014: Towards competitive and innovative ASEAN SMEs. *Eria Research Project Report. Jakarta, Indonesia: ERIA, 8.*

Grainger, A. (2008). Customs and trade facilitation: From concepts to implementation. *World Customs Journal, 2*(1), 17–30.

Kowalski, P., Gonzalez, J. L., Ragoussis, A., & Ugarte, C. (2015). Participation of developing countries in global value chains. OECD, Trade Policy Papers, No. 179.

Leonidou, L. C. (2004). An analysis of the barriers hindering small business export development. *Journal of Small Business Management, 42*(3), 279–302.

Macasaquit Reyes, M. (2009). Trade facilitation in the Philippines and the SME factor. Paper presented at Regional Policy Forum on Trade Facilitation and SMEs in Times of Crisis, 20–22 May 2009, Beijing, China.

Hiep, N., & Nishijima, S. (2009). Export intensity and impacts from firm characteristics, domestic competition and domestic constraints in Vietnam: A micro-data analysis. Kobe University Research Institute for Economics & Business Administration, Discussion Paper Series No. 238.

OECD/ERIA. (2018). SME Policy Index: ASEAN 2018: Boosting competitiveness and inclusive growth. Paris: OECD/Jakarta: Economic Research Institute for ASEAN and East Asia.

Ramstetter, E. D., & Takii, S. (2006). Exporting and foreign ownership in Indonesian manufacturing, 1990–2000. *Economics and Finance in Indonesia, 54*(3), 317–345.

UN/CEFACT & UNCTAD. (2002). Compendium of Trade Facilitation Recommendations. Geneva: UNCTAD.

UNCTAD Secretariat. (2019). Key statistics and trends in trade policy 2018. Geneva: UNCTAD.

UNCTAD Stat. (2019). UNCTADstat. [Data file]. Geneva: UNCTAD. Retrieved from https://unctadstat.unctad.org/EN/

Van Dijk, M. (2002). The determinants of export performance in developing countries: The case of Indonesian manufacturing. Eindhoven Centre for Innovation Studies, Working Paper No. 2-01.

Welch, L. S., & Luostarinen, R. K. (1993). Inward-outward connections in internationalization. *Journal of international Marketing, 1*(1), 44–56.

Wignaraja, G. (2012). Engaging small and medium enterprises in production networks: Firm-level analysis of five ASEAN economies. Asian Development Bank Working Paper No. 361.

WTO Secretariat. (2016). *World trade report 2016: Leveling the trading field for SMEs.* Geneva: The World Trade Organization.

Name index

Subject index

Printed in the United States
By Bookmasters